COUNTERCULTURE

COUNTERCULTURE

THE STORY
OF AMERICA
FROM BOHEMIA
TO HIP-HOP

ALEX ZAMALIN

BEACON PRESS, BOSTON

BEACON PRESS
Boston, Massachusetts
www.beacon.org

Beacon Press books
are published under the auspices of
the Unitarian Universalist Association of Congregations.

28 27 26 25   8 7 6 5 4 3 2 1

This book is printed on acid-free paper that meets the uncoated paper
ANSI/NISO specifications for permanence as revised in 1992.

Text design and composition by Kim Arney

*Library of Congress Cataloging-in-Publication
Data is available for this title.*

ISBN: 978-0-8070-4518-3; e-book: 978-0-8070-4519-0
audiobook: 978-0-8070-1813-2

CONTENTS

INTRODUCTION

I n 1855, a Brooklyn-based, thirty-six-year-old carpenter and journalist, Walt Whitman, publishes a book that scandalizes critics because it is infused with a spirit of radical democracy. It is called *Leaves of Grass*. Whitman is inspired by a group out of New England in the 1830s. They are abolitionists, feminists, and free thinkers who advance a gospel of iconoclastic individualism. This group calls itself the Transcendental Club. In the first decade of the twentieth century, an immigrant from imperial Russia named Emma Goldman champions direct action. She is a revolutionary anarchist. Goldman inspires a group of intellectuals who call themselves Village bohemians. They assault middle-class sensibilities and endorse left-wing politics. In the 1920s, a group of Black writers aim to change the meaning of race and American identity. This is known as the Harlem Renaissance. In the 1940s, a poet from Paterson, New Jersey, named Allen Ginsberg wants to transform the denigrated into the sublime, his downtrodden friends into angels. They are called the Beat Generation. In the 1960s, Ginsberg becomes a hero for the new student movements who are fed up with war and capitalism. They call themselves hippies. One of Ginsberg's friends from his time in Greenwich Village in the late 1950s is a Black playwright named Amiri Baraka. Baraka is less interested in personal liberation than in Black liberation. In the 1960s, Baraka is at the vanguard of a Black avant-garde that calls itself the Black Arts Movement. In the 1970s, a youth culture bearing witness to the destruction of racism, gentrification, and economic devastation in America is born in the South Bronx. It is known as the hip-hop generation.

American history is filled with these nonconformists. Outsiders who agitate against what's mainstream. Utopians who imagine unimaginable worlds. As these critics resist the world in which they live, they also advance new ways of feeling, of thinking, of acting. They do this through the art they make, through the words they utter, through the lives they live, and through the politics they make. This book tells their story. This is the story of the American counterculture.

Countercultural movements have been with us from the beginning. In attacking common sense about the meaning of justice, the ancient philosopher Socrates (470–399 BCE), moved around the Athenian city square and asked probing questions for which there were no answers. Jesus preached individual salvation among Jews who deferred to the law of scripture. Religious mystics—Sufis, Zen practitioners, and Kabbalists—were also countercultural in their time. So too were eighteenth-century Enlightenment philosophers—John Locke, Voltaire, Mary Wollstonecraft, and Jean-Jacques Rousseau—who argued for natural law, tolerance, and human dignity.

A counterculture is any cultural movement whose values counter the mainstream norms of their society. All countercultures exist insofar as they resist the culture of which they are part. At the same time, countercultures are movements driven by ideas about how to live differently. They have their own worldviews. Countercultures try to live according to their philosophy and create their own rules on what this might mean.

Central to any counterculture is freedom. Freedom is a well-known idea in the modern world. The twentieth-century political philosopher Isaiah Berlin categorized two distinct meanings of freedom. First, there is *negative freedom*. Negative freedom means an individual is free to do what they want as long as it doesn't harm others. They can be treated equally under the law. They can participate in the political process. Second, there is *positive freedom*. Positive freedom means that one can exercise their sense of the good in ways that are reasoned and deliberate. Negative freedom is freedom "from something," while positive freedom is freedom "to something." To have negative freedom, you need to be protected from encroachments by the state; to have positive freedom, the state ought to provide you basic socioeconomic resources to make good choices.[1]

The counterculture has, at various times, embraced both definitions of freedom. Yet, it is less interested in settling the debate about what freedom is. It is instead preoccupied with exercising a particular kind of freedom: *revolutionary freedom*. Revolutionary freedom means acting without regard for, and often in diametrical opposition to, social convention. Revolutionary freedom is about radical personal expression. It is about loving who you want, making what you need, and dreaming in whichever way you find necessary. When you have revolutionary freedom, you can explore your desires fully. Revolutionary freedom is never purely individualistic. It entails a social consciousnesses. When taken to its logical end, revolutionary freedom demands that one is actively committed to abolishing economic, political, and social systems of domination that contribute to human misery.

Revolutionary freedom can be realized in many ways. Through art, one's lifestyle, or philosophy. It can be seen in architecture, in political institutions, on canvases, in books, or in music. Revolutionary freedom can exist in the heart or in the mind, but it requires a community. To nourish your dreams and validate your behaviors, you must be surrounded by friends who provide you sustenance.

Community, in this way, insulates the counterculture from those who would like to tear it asunder. Because countercultures are, by definition, marginal, which is to say, they exist on the fringes, they are often under threat. This threat can come from the state, from the majority opinion, or from elites. Socrates, for instance, was executed by Athens for corrupting the youth. Religious mystics have always been persecuted wherever they've lived. Neither the church nor the monarchy was pleased with the seventeenth-century Enlightenment. Hippies were denounced both by antiwar activists and by upstanding middle-class suburbanites.

Critics have always tried to squash the counterculture, but one of the most effective ways they have tried to tame the rebellious energy of the counterculture is to make it their own. Think the Coca-Cola company using hippie images of peace and love to sell its bubbly soft drink. The clothing company GAP using photos of hipsters to sell denim. Corporate America using Zen mindfulness to improve workers' productivity. Hip-hop being used to sell luxury brands and fast cars. The list is far too long to enumerate here. But the point is clear: The counterculture can be profitable for the mainstream. It can be serviceable for the culture. Over time, it becomes *the* culture.

Threats to the counterculture don't only come from the mainstream. They emerge from within. Petty personal feuds between members can be as damaging as major philosophical debates about what a counterculture stands for. Tensions over whether the counterculture has sold out its principles can be as bad as falling too deep into, and getting lost in, the counterculture. "Turning on, tuning in, and dropping out" sounds nice. But it can get ugly. To alter your life, and change your mind, you might have to go all-in. This is why, throughout history, violence, excess, and abuse of power have been with the counterculture. So too have demagogues, false prophets, and hustlers.

Countercultures aren't static or ahistorical. They rise and fall. They change and disappear. But countercultures have always drawn people in. That is because every counterculture is something of a utopia: it offers its followers the prospect that, even if the world outside might be corrupt and misshapen, a new world can flourish here and now. This is a major reason why countercultures are often made up of young people (or, at least, those who identify with youth). Not surprisingly, the counterculture has always had special appeal for dreamers, for rebels, for dissenters, for iconoclasts. Everyone who is unsatisfied with what is and wants to prove that another world is possible. The counterculture makes the margins real. It makes authenticity matter. It makes the impossible tangible.

■   ■   ■

Every counterculture begins in a particular place and time, even if it doesn't always stay there. The focus of this book is the US counterculture. America was founded in the ideology—and I stress the term *ideology*, because it was never real to begin with—of a "New World," a fresh start, even if it was explicitly contradicted from the start (through the continued existence of slavery, racism, genocide, sexism, homophobia, classism, empire, war-making). For this reason, America has attracted more than its fair share of dissenters.

One might think there are many accounts of the US counterculture. There aren't. Most histories of the US counterculture are as narrow in their scope as they are tired in their claims. Part of this has to with how the term itself came to be defined. The word *counterculture* was first popularized by the historian Theodore Roszak in his seminal 1969 book, *The Making of a Counter Culture: Reflections on the Technocratic Society and Its Youthful Opposition.*[2]

Roszak took the youth movements of 1960s as the preeminent example of US counterculture. One hundred thousand hippies in tie-dye shirts dancing to the Grateful Dead and Jefferson Airplane in San Francisco's Haight-Ashbury neighborhood during the Summer of Love in 1967, saying things like "far out" and "groovy." College kids in coffee shops reading Jack Kerouac's *On the Road*. Hipsters tripping on LSD and reciting sections of William S. Burroughs's *Naked Lunch* with Bob Dylan blasting in the background. These kids partied hard. And died young. Eventually, they packed their bags up in the Haight-Ashbury. By the late 1970s, they sold out their radical lifestyles to become upstanding middle-class men and women. By the 1980s, they became stockbrokers, advertising executives, and corporate suits.

This story is far too simplistic. Yes, the hippies in the 1960s were a major counterculture in America, but they weren't the only one. Among the major US countercultures, there were also the New England transcendentalists, utopian socialists, and New York bohemians in the nineteenth century. There were the anarchists and Village bohemians of the 1910s; there was the Harlem Renaissance in the 1930s and the Beat Generation of the 1950s. There were also the Black Arts Movement in the 1970s and Black feminism and hip-hop in the 1980s.

Telling the story of US counterculture in this way, to encompass its breadth and scope, overturns a major misconception—that US counterculture has been white and middle-class. The counterculture has always been diverse, multicultural, and multiracial. And it's been a direct product of encounters between different groups. Without Village bohemians in the 1910s, you wouldn't have the Harlem Renaissance. Without the Harlem Renaissance, it's hard to speak of the Beats. Hip-hop makes no sense without nineteenth-century transcendentalism. The Black Arts Movement inspires graffiti culture. Once we appreciate the US counterculture in its complexity, we can better appreciate why it mattered, what it meant, and what lessons we might learn from it today.

■ ■ ■

This book is not an exhaustive study. Instead, through a survey of the major countercultural movements throughout US history, it explores the following questions: What did US counterculture stand for? What made someone want to participate in it? How did the US counterculture do so much with so little, and yet so profoundly change the world? Why did its bright flame quickly burn out? Was it destined to flare only in brief historic moments? What does it mean to take seriously the counterculture's injunction that life should be turned into art, and to politicize art?

Much of what we wear, how we walk, talk, argue, what's hip, and what's cool is only because of the counterculture. Now it may be mainstream, but there's a reason why it once wasn't. Why was the counterculture once radical—and what made it so unpalatable to the powerful?

From the beginning the counterculture wanted to change the world. For this reason, an overarching concern of this book is to assess the counterculture's politics. According to the classic definition of the political scientist Harold Lasswell, in his 1936 book of the same title, politics is about "who gets what, when, how."[3] Politics is thus about power—it is about the struggle over resources, who gets to have them and how they will get them. To examine the politics of the counterculture is to consider two things. First, how did the counterculture seek to affect political institutions? How did the counterculture shape congressional legislation, executive power, and US courts? Second, how did the counterculture seek to change core ideas in America? What image of freedom, peace, equality, or justice did it put forth? How did it challenge prevailing accounts of gender, race, and sexuality?

▪ ▪ ▪

American counterculture has always had a specific texture. A range of sights, smells, tastes, sounds, and feelings. The counterculture exists in specific places—in parks, cafés, university classrooms, community centers, schools, jazz clubs, dive bars, recording studios, and art galleries. It's true that the counterculture knows no geographic bounds. But major cities are part of the story—San Francisco, Los Angeles, Chicago, Philadelphia, Boston, Newark, Paris, London, Buenos Aires, Cape Town, Tokyo.

No city has arguably had as much of an impact on the development of the US counterculture as New York. In the nineteenth century, the cosmopolitan metropolis was on its way to becoming what it has now been for over two hundred years: an epicenter of youth rebellion.

The counterculture has been at the forefront of every major socioeconomic upheaval in American history: from early debates over slavery, which gave way to heated arguments about immigration from Europe and Black migration from the South to the North and Midwest, a consequence of the epidemic of lynching and Jim Crow; to unfettered capitalism caused by the Great Depression in the 1930s; to the hyper-segregation that led to urban uprisings in the 1960s. The counterculture was there to criticize Democrats in the 1980s, who had evolved into the party of civil rights but adopted a moderate position on socioeconomic equality. The counterculture denounced Republicans, who had become the party of big business and white grievance.

Good stories don't have happy endings. Neither do the stories told in this book. Few of the figures in the counterculture were heroes. Most of them failed to live up to their lofty ideals. Many of their ideals failed to materialize in the world, and even if they did, their materialization didn't look the way the counterculture had imagined. Some in the counterculture came to revolutionary freedom early, others late. Some expanded revolutionary freedom as fully as possible in their lives, their politics, and their art. Others, only briefly and haphazardly. Sometimes, their utopian aspirations were contradicted by, or coexisted alongside, inexcusable attitudes of racism, sexism, and homophobia. Sometimes, the counterculture's optimism transformed into cynicism. Sometimes the counterculture achieved astounding political changes in a short amount of time. Sometimes these changes led to its collapse.

Yet the US counterculture still matters. In a world that is marked by hopelessness and catastrophe—climate disaster, ecological collapse, the threat of global war, the rise of the far right, racial and gender domination, queer- and transphobia, and economic inequality—the counterculture offers something profound. It gives a powerful glimpse of how another world might be possible.

■ ■ ■

For many young people, the counterculture is their first encounter with politics. Before you know anything about political parties, or the history of social movements, you know something about counterculture. You may not know much about the intricacies of the legislative process or antidiscrimination law, but you've seen an abstract painting or listened to a hip-hop track, or read a poem from the Harlem Renaissance, or know something about Woodstock and the Summer of Love. When you first encounter the counterculture, it shocks you, because it gives you the raw emotional material and language to feel something intense about political injustice. You're outraged by the system and experience solidarity with everyone oppressed by it. Once you experience the counterculture, you think that something could change. That life needn't be the way it is.

This was my experience in the 1990s with counterculture when I was growing up in New York City. I was a newly arrived immigrant (I came to Brooklyn at the age of three, in 1989, as an asylum seeker and refugee with my parents, who were fleeing antisemitism in Ukraine, then a part of Soviet Russia). Subway graffiti on buildings gave me an early taste of youth rebellion, and hip-hop on the radio, a station called Hot 97, explained the legacy of white supremacy. Grunge and punk rock music playing on MTV registered opposition to the right-wing assault on reproductive rights and the bipartisan consensus on cutting welfare and slashing corporate taxes during the Bill Clinton and George W. Bush presidencies. When I first saw Jean-Michel Basquiat's paintings, it reminded me of the alienation I felt walking through defunded streets and playing in decrepit city parks. Langston Hughes and the Harlem Renaissance, and Harlem itself, taught me about the magic of style and the power of language to name love.

In the mid-2000s, I first saw Amiri Baraka in person. Sporting a black beret and white goatee, he was reading from his latest poetry collection at a sparsely populated gathering in the West Village. Baraka's poetry gave me the vocabulary to protest the US invasion of Iraq when I was a college student at Rutgers in New Brunswick, New Jersey. It was at Rutgers, the East Coast hub of the antiwar movement (Berkeley was the West Coast hub), where my professors introduced me to the Beats, Village bohemians, and anarchism.

The counterculture, at first, enabled me to better understand what was wrong; it was less effective at motivating me to act for what I thought was right. But something drew me to it. I couldn't help but feel emboldened by the audacity of these young people—many of them, like me, in their early twenties—doing remarkable things. They grooved to their own rhythms. They found poetry in the rubble. They felt hope in dark times, in the dark. This resonated with me. I didn't know why, how, or to what ends. Eventually, the counterculture opened me up to its real legacy: that of revolutionary freedom. The question now, as always, is what to do with it.

I CONTAIN MULTITUDES

During the spring of 1855—as the flowers began to bloom after a devastating cold winter in the Northeast—a modestly dressed, six-foot-tall, thirty-six-year-old carpenter who had once been a polished, cane-flouting and jacket vest–sporting Democratic journalist, ambled from a small house on 71 Prince Street in Brooklyn, where he was staying with his parents and siblings. He was on his way to a local redbrick printing shop, run by brothers James and Andrew Rome. It was there he would eagerly watch their printing press stream out the pages of his first book of poetry. It was called *Leaves of Grass*.[1] A total of eight hundred copies were printed of the volume. The author's goal was to suit different audiences at various price points. Some copies had a green cloth jacket and were stamped in gold leaf at a cost of two dollars. Some had promotional material and were affordably priced at one dollar. A few copies were draped in pink or light-green wrappers around a good deal of promotional material. These went for seventy-five cents. The author of the collection, a bombastic man with pale-blue eyes, short hair, and a close-cropped beard, was named Walt Whitman.

Up until then, Walt Whitman had never published a poetry volume. But he wasn't lacking in self-confidence as a critic of the American literary scene. "There is no great author," he once claimed, speaking of his fellow Americans. "Every one has demeaned himself to some etiquette or impotence. . . . Poets here . . . are to rest on organic different bases from other continents."[2] America already had respectable published poets like Edgar Allan Poe and Henry Wadsworth Longfellow, whose work was characterized by philosophical intensity and high-brow aesthetic formalism. Yet, according to Whitman, America needed poets like him—poets whose verse was epic in its breadth and megalomaniacal in its ambition; poets who, like him, said "Howdy" and "So long!," who wore simple, home-spun suits and bleached white linen-cotton shirts, who associated with horse-car conductors and railroad hands, who denounced conventional party politics, and who rallied against political elites. Above all, poets who venerated the common people.

Whitman's grand ambition was to inaugurate a new season of national reconciliation, not by glossing over difference, but by embracing the multitudes, everything from the peasant to the shipfitter, the runaway slave to the itinerant cigar-maker, from the industrial North to the agrarian South, the maritime culture of the eastern seaboard to the libertarianism of the western frontier. Whitman wanted to make a new culture. America wasn't interested. Economic inequality crushed that hope for many working Americans, who could barely pay their rent, let alone enjoy poetry. America had still not fully recovered from the financial panic of 1837, when a run on banks in major cities led to half of US banks collapsing, which led to unemployment skyrocketing. In New York City, the wealth gap was especially glaring. When he died in 1848, John Jacob Astor's real estate empire was worth over $20 million, while the average New York family who lived below Canal Street could barely afford their three-dollar-a-month rent for a two-bedroom tenement apartment with a window, in which one of the cramped rooms combined as a kitchen, living room, and dining room. A tenement apartment with a window was a luxury. Over 29,000 newly arrived Irish and German immigrants, out of a total city resident population of 515,000, lived in poorly ventilated basement cellars with no sunlight.

In the nineteenth century, thirty-five million people moved from Europe to the US. New York City was the epicenter of this multicultural migration. As the city's population increased, so too did its population density—from 94 persons per square acre in 1820 to 163 in 1850.[3] Waste management was nonexistent because the city's sewer system didn't cover the poorer areas. Smallpox, typhoid, tuberculosis, and cholera flowed freely through the garbage, which lay uncollected in the streets. Whereas rich New Yorkers would spend their afternoons visiting hairdressers and their evenings lounging at oyster cellars, child sex workers haunted afternoon corners and petty thieves stalked the alleyways. In the background, through it all, pigs rooted for food, cows roamed unattended, and stray dogs barked late into the night. This cacophony mixed with the turning wheels of vendor carts, the bells of white-and-gold omnibuses, and the whips of horse-drawn carriages.[4]

In the 1850s, America's two decades–long economic crisis was compounded by the crisis of white supremacy. On May 30, 1854, the Kansas-Nebraska Act became law, two months after the US Senate had passed it in a 37–14 vote at 5 a.m. in the morning. Charles Sumner, a Massachusetts antislavery senator who led the Radical Republicans, warned that the act, in repealing the long-standing Missouri Compromise of 1820 and allowing the newly created territories to enact popular sovereignty, would create "a dreary region of despotism, inhabited by masters and slaves."[5] The Kansas-Nebraska Act had compounded a problem that had been dire since the passage of the Fugitive Slave Act in 1850, which, by allowing bounty hunters to pursue escaped slaves north of the Mason–Dixon line and return them to their enslavers, nationalized slavery. Kansas was now known as "bleeding Kansas," having become a violent battleground between proslavery forces and abolitionists, known as Free Staters. Sickened by these developments, the usually reserved founder of the New England Anti-Slavery Society, William Lloyd Garrison, on a sweltering July 4, 1854, alongside hundreds assembled at Harmony Grove, sixteen miles outside of Boston, took out a match and burned a copy of the Fugitive Slave Act. Then Garrison took out a copy of the US Constitution and burned it as well, yelling, "So perish all compromises with tyranny!"[6]

Although *Leaves of Grass* was Walt Whitman's scream of protest into the wilderness, it wasn't accompanied by, or aimed to, burn the documents of state. To the contrary, it aimed to create a new language capable of uniting the nation. But Whitman's nation-building project was nothing short of perplexing. National unity, he thought, would only be achieved through a kind of personal disunion, a revolution of the self. If Americans unmoored themselves from everything they held dear—by maintaining radical openness toward everything, by dissolving boundaries, by making the sacred profane, the profane sacred—then they would finally feel united, in their mutual vulnerability, their nakedness. From the opening lines of the collection's first poem, "Song of Myself," where Whitman declares, "I celebrate myself," to where he says, "I am not an earth nor an adjunct of an earth, I am the mate and companion of people, all just as immortal and fathomless as myself; They do not know how immortal, but I know," Whitman is making a religion out of individualism.[7] The daring free verse, the orgiastic expression of love and orgasms of feeling, the unbridled love, the poetic speaker liberated from the masses, the masses glorified, builds toward Whitman's idea that the individual is free to be an iconoclast beyond social conventions. The message of *Leaves of Grass* is radical: only if Americans become countercultural could they finally be free.

After receiving a mailed copy of the book directly from Whitman himself, the esteemed essayist Ralph Waldo Emerson responded with an enthusiastic letter. "I find it the most extraordinary piece of wit and wisdom that America has yet contributed. . . . I greet you at the beginning of the career."[8] The wider reading public didn't share Emerson's glowing assessment. The first copies of *Leaves of Grass* appeared on Independence Day, July 4, 1855, at Swayne's bookstore in Brooklyn. Only a few copies sold. Within a week, many of them were removed from the store's shelves. Few people read the first edition of *Leaves*. And those who did felt compelled to respond negatively. "Ridicule, disgust, horror and anger," was what the book elicited from the critics who skimmed its pages. "Badly written, filthy, atheistical and utter reprehensible," was how it was described.[9]

■　■　■

The reason *Leaves of Grass* received such a harsh response from critics was because it put into poetic form the early nineteenth-century counterculture that assailed middle-class sensibilities—everything from marriage and love to decorum, community, sexuality, gender, and private property. Influenced by the insurrectionary spirit of the French Revolution of 1789, where popular power seemed within reach to the masses for the first time, and the earth-changing nature of the Industrial Revolution, the nineteenth century saw an unprecedented interest in utopianism.

Among the most famous examples was the commune known as New Harmony, Indiana, established in 1824. Its founder was the soft-spoken industrialist-turned-avid-socialist Robert Owen. "The members of any community may by degrees be trained to live without idleness, without poverty, without crime, and without punishment," emphatically declared Owen, the son of a farmer's daughter and fishmonger who was born poor in Newton, Wales, on May 14, 1771. "For each of these is the effect of error in the various systems prevalent throughout the world. They are all necessary consequences of ignorance. Train any population rationally, and they will be rational."[10]

New Harmony was an example of a world without class distinction and gender inequality. It had around nine hundred members. Children went to a small daycare. Every Tuesday, there was a jovial community dance in the Hall of New Harmony. New Harmonites read Shakespeare and Byron. One member—the anarchist Josiah Warren—led a brass orchestra every Thursday.[11] New Harmony residents called each other by their first names and walked around the gardens with arms interlocked. The "Constitution of the Community of Equality," which guaranteed everyone over the age of twenty-one equal right to the land, was ratified by everyone.

Not the only intentional community at the time, New Harmony helped inspire an interracial community in 1825 called Nashoba, started by a Scottish feminist named Frances Wright. Wright's 1825 manifesto was entitled *A Plan for the Gradual Abolition of Slavery in the United States, Without Danger or Loss to the Citizens of the South.* "Nashoba" was the Chickasaw name for the Wolf River that cut across the territory—640 acres near Memphis, Tennessee. Wright's plan was to buy enslaved Africans from Southern planters and to relocate them there. By educating Black children in the same schools with white ones, she aimed to prove that inequality was a societally produced phenomenon and wouldn't exist in a fair society.

Nineteenth-century utopia encompassed not only issues of class and race but love and marriage as well. The most well-known experiment of the time was the Oneida colony of New York started in 1848. Its founder was a shy, Vermont-born and Yale-trained preacher, John Humphrey Noyes, who had a strong messianic streak and whose philosophy was called *perfectionism.* "God has set me to cast up a highway across this chaos," he wrote in 1837, "and I am gathering out the stones and grading the track as fast as possible."[12] Oneida only had a population of three hundred at its peak, but it became well known across the nation for its system of "complex marriages." In these relationships, all men were husbands to all women, and all women were wives to all men. Sex was permitted if it was consensual, and, in a reversal of traditional gendered expectations, male sexual continence was encouraged.

Whether or not they could ever be a model for the entire nation, these nineteenth-century countercultural communities were attempts to radicalize Enlightenment liberalism beyond ideas of natural rights and representative democracy. They wanted to feel authentically. Realize their fantasies. Show the world that dreams could be real. They were looking for true believers. Walt Whitman was all-in.

■   ■   ■

Walt Whitman was born on May 31, 1819, in rural West Hills, Long Island. He was one of eight children of Walter Whitman Sr. and Louisa Van Velsor Whitman. The patriarch of the family, Walter Whitman, was a moody man with a mean streak and was prone to heavy drinking. A woodworker and occasional farmer, as well as an entrepreneur wanting to cash in on the growing real estate market, Walter Whitman moved his family from West Hills to Brooklyn in 1823. Disappointment set in immediately. Walter's business skills, it turned out, were no match for the cutthroat world of land speculation.

Walter Whitman had no financial acumen to share with his children, but he did pass on a fire for the era's populist ideas. A champion of democratic populism—the idea that ordinary people could rule themselves—he named one son Thomas Jefferson Whitman and another Andrew Jackson Whitman. A self-proclaimed free thinker, Walter revered the English son of a Quaker, Thomas Paine, who in *Common Sense* (1776) employed his caustic wit in the service of calling out smug elites whose nice manners were betrayed by abominable choices. Walt Whitman felt estranged from his father but looked back fondly on his early home schooling. "I may perhaps be the only one living today," he waxed poetically from his home in Camden, New Jersey, in 1888, "who can throw an authentic sidelight upon the radicalism of those post-Revolutionary decades."[13]

Walt Whitman adored his mother, a dutiful homemaker and elegantly dressed woman with a biting sense of humor. But the woman who made the biggest impact on him intellectually was someone he only knew from afar—Frances Wright. Whitman devoured her book *A Few Days in Athens* (1822) and avidly read her paper, *Free Inquirer*, to which his father was a religious subscriber. After hearing Wright lecture in New York, Whitman said she was "more than beautiful; she was grand."[14]

Though Whitman was a young romantic, the reality of working-class life made him settle for practical choices. Forced to leave school at the age of eleven in 1830 to support his family, suffering from financial difficulties, Whitman first worked as an office boy for two lawyers. Then he worked as an apprentice to Samuel E. Clements, the editor of the Democratic-leaning Long Island *Patriot*, and, after that, for Erastus Washington, a Brooklyn printer. Before long, Whitman discovered his wheelhouse was the written word.

By the 1840s, Whitman was making a career as a prolific journalist. He had written over twelve hundred pieces for the likes of the *New World, Aurora, The Tattler, New Mirror*, the *New York Sunday Times*, and the *Brooklyn Eagle*, where he addressed topics ranging from theater to immigration, feminism to parks, and tariffs to slavery. His best source material, however, would come from the streets. Between 1841 to 1845, among his favorite places to visit was Manhattan's Bowery District, a hub of working-class nightlife that was littered with smoky dancehalls, cheap theaters, and colorful billiard rooms. After enveloping himself in the lovely bel canto style of Italian composers Gaetano Donizetti or Giuseppe Verdi at the Park Theater or the Astor Place Opera House, Whitman, on his way home, would chat with streetwise shipbuilders, overworked butchers, and drunk firemen. Along the way, he would mingle with nineteenth-century hipsters called *b'hoys*, whose trademark style was short, cropped hair and a stovepipe hat, and the *b'ghals*, who flaunted delicate parasols and donned vibrantly colored dresses.[15] Some of these experiences made it into Whitman's work, which is why literary critics at the time like Charles Eliot Norton called him and *Leaves of Grass* a blend of "New England Transcendentalist and New York Rowdy."[16]

Ever since, this interpretation has become conventional wisdom. But Whitman came to transcendentalism late. It's true that, at the age of twenty-three, he was mesmerized by Emerson, America's best-known public intellectual, when he gave a series of six lectures in the first two weeks of March 1842, at the New York Society Library at Broadway and Leonard Street. Whitman would describe Emerson's essay "The Poet" as "one of the richest and most beautiful compositions, both for its matter and its style."[17] But Whitman only immersed himself in Emerson's work when he was living with his mother and working as a carpenter in Brooklyn in 1854. "I was simmering, simmering, simmering," he remembered. "Emerson brought me to a boil."[18]

Personality-wise, Emerson was the opposite of Whitman. A reserved man who always considered himself unworthy of his reputation no matter his towering achievements, Emerson was trained as a Unitarian minister.

It was only after the unexpected death of his nineteen-year-old wife from tuberculosis in 1831 that the twenty-eight-year-old Emerson experienced a revelation. Grieving so intensely, he couldn't return to his flock of parishioners at the Second Church of Boston. Like many young people, Emerson went abroad to find himself. In 1832 he traveled to Europe, where he met the great poets William Wordsworth and Samuel Coleridge. After Emerson returned in 1835, settled in Concord, Massachusetts, and remarried, he became what we known him as today—the prophet of self-reliance.

"Society everywhere is in conspiracy against the manhood of every one of its members," Emerson wrote in his 1841 essay entitled "Self-Reliance," which announced the philosophy of early American counterculture, "in which the members agree, for the better securing of his bread to each shareholder, to surrender the liberty and culture of the eater. The virtue in most request is conformity. Self-reliance is its aversion. It loves not realities and creators, but names and customs. Whoso would be a man must be a nonconformist."[19]

Self-reliance, in Emerson's view, has nothing to do with rugged individualism. It is about cultivating moral character. On this point Emerson and Whitman agree. Unafraid to traffic in Platonic ideals of justice, beauty, and truth, nonconformity is a virtue that creates its own moorings upon which to stand. The crowd is to be distrusted not because it demands equality, but because it aims only to invest in perpetuating itself.

Although he himself lived a conventional middle-class life, Emerson was the great apostle of apostasy. This contradiction is what gave his position weight. Emerson, who epitomized a comfortable, stuffy middle-class existence, argued that individual freedom cannot be achieved while injustice continued to spread its ugly tentacles across the nation. "We ought never to lose sight of the truth that national offences are private offences carried out and represented at full length," declared Emerson, because "every American is really responsible, in that proportion, to God and to men for the acts of government. . . . Let every man say then to himself—the cause of the Indian, it is mine; the cause of the slave, it is mine; the cause of the union, it is mine; the cause of public honesty, of education, of religion, they are mine."[20]

Emerson shared his countercultural philosophy of individualism among his friends in New England—among the most well known were Nathaniel Hawthorne, Henry David Thoreau, Amos Bronson Alcott, and Margaret Fuller. They called themselves the Transcendental Club. Transcendentalists were biting in their attacks. The three pillars of nineteenth-century American political development—the growth of racial enslavement, the expansion of industrial capitalism, and the plague of war for the acquisition of territory—were not a sign of progress, but subject to searing critique. The Enlightenment social contract, which was meant to create an informal agreement between the rulers and the ruled, was what sponsored a system of haves and have-nots. "Whilst the rights of all persons are equal," Emerson concluded in 1844, sounding more like his European contemporary Karl Marx than his countryman Thomas Jefferson, "their rights in property are very unequal. One man owns his clothes, and another owns a country. . . . Property demands a government framed on the ratio of owners and of owning."[21] "Actually, the laboring man has not leisure for a true integrity day by day," Thoreau proclaimed. "His labor would be depreciated in the market. He has no time to be anything but a machine. How can he remember well his ignorance—which his growth requires—who has so often to use his knowledge?"[22]

Given this withering critique of the status quo, it should come as no surprise that transcendentalists were among the nineteenth century's most outspoken abolitionists and proponents of women's rights, free love, anarchism, and popular democracy. What is less well known, however, is that, at one point, some of Emerson's truest believers sought to do what Emerson never explicitly endorsed, but what they believed was a logical outcome of his teaching: to make transcendentalism the basis for a new society.

Established in 1841, their communal experiment was called Brook Farm. It was modeled on the French socialist Charles Fourier's Associationist "phalanx"—a type of intentional community that thousands of people across the country lived in during in the nineteenth century. Hidden in the lush green countryside of West Roxbury, Massachusetts, Brook Farm was started by Emerson's friend, the Harvard-trained Unitarian minister George Ripley, and his wife, Sophia Ripley. Brook Farm would be "a reorganization of society itself, on those principles of love to God and love to men," according to the transcendentalist magazine *The Dial*.[23] It was established as a joint-stock company; the founding members brought $500 in shares, giving them lifelong membership and a 5 percent annual return. Those who didn't have the money for this large investment would have to augment their contribution through work. Yet, everyone under ten and over seventy received housing.[24] Boys worked in the fields and girls in the kitchen at a respectable hourly wage of ten cents. Children attended Brook Farm Academy, which was run by Sophia Ripley, who taught the *Divine Comedy* alongside language courses in Italian and German. Her pupils read the German philosophers Immanuel Kant and Friedrich Schiller, and the newly released Charles Dickens novel *Oliver Twist*.[25] The reclusive Emerson, sticking closely to the truism that he would never be part of a club that would have him as a member, only occasionally visited Brook Farm. The prickly Thoreau scoffed at it from afar, claiming, "I'd rather keep bachelor's hall in hell than go to board in heaven."[26]

Whitman never visited Brook Farm, but there were echoes of its spirit from 1858 to 1861, at a lager beer salon located at 647 Broadway, off Bleeker Street, where Whitman was a regular. The restaurant was called Pfaff's. Founded by the Swiss-German Charles Ignatius Pfaff (and mostly frequented by German immigrants, unemployed doctors, and the occasional stagecoach driver), the saloon consisted of a small, cigar-filled room with a few old chairs. But Pfaff's was the heart of a burgeoning scene of young pranksters, cynics, and critics. They called themselves *bohemians*.

The term *bohemian* was coined to describe Parisian artists who lived on the fringes of society. It had gained some cultural currency after French novelist Honoré de Balzac's *A Prince of Bohemia* (1841), and, later, after Henri Murger's much-discussed *Scènes de la vie de boheme* (1849), a collection of stories set in Paris's Latin Quarter in the 1840s (the stories would also inspire Giacomo Puccini's 1896 opera *La bohème*).[27] A century before *beatnik* and *hipster* became derogatory labels for the young people who espoused existentialism, wore skinny jeans, and smoked dope, the *New York Times* called the New York bohemians at Pfaff's in the late 1850s a "gipsy tribe" and referred to the venue as a nasty, dank cave, whose only redeeming quality was a remarkably long table.[28]

The physical structure of Pfaff's saloon aimed to echo the feeling of being in the underground and on the margins. Pfaff's was not for the claustrophobic. It had low ceilings, stone walls, and empty barrels stocked on top of one another. In spirit, Pfaff's wasn't for the easily scandalized. The most prominent figure to hold court there, called the "Prince of Bohemia," was the gray-bearded, Massachusetts-born son of merchants by the name of Henry Clapp Jr. Clapp had once been a Sunday school teacher, but by the 1850s, the only god Clapp deified was himself, or, perhaps, Charles Fourier, whose *The Social Destiny of Man* he had just translated in English from the original French. Born in 1814, Clapp at this time was in his late forties, twice the age of many of the regulars at Pfaff's: the actress Adah Isaacs Menken, the novelist Fitz-James O'Brien, and the poet N. G. Shepherd. What made critics describe Clapp as juvenile, and, well, annoying, was what made his followers mesmerized. Clapp was sarcastic, he liked to throw around puns indiscriminately, and he spoke over top of everyone.

The bohemian at Pfaff's was a contrarian for her own sake. She glorified the hobo and celebrated the vagabond as a symbol of nonconformity, even though society uniformly denigrated both figures as loafers. The bohemian read Charles Dickens as a proto-anti-capitalist and thought Edgar Allan Poe's stories foreboded a decline of Western civilization, a prospect which she embraced. "The Bohemian is a 'Cosmopolite,'" wrote another regular at Pfaff's, the essayist Ada Clare, "not, like the creature of society, a victim of rules and customs; he steps over them with an easy, graceful, joyous unconsciousnesses."[29]

The cultural organ of what we might call the bohemian persuasion (*worldview* is too strong a word, since there was no philosophical system of which to speak) was a literary magazine founded by Clapp in 1858. It was called the *Saturday Press*. "We want no reforms, no institutions, no parties," it announced. "We want a living principle as nature had, under which nothing can go wrong—this must be vital through the U.S."[30] Given such statements, it is apparent that bohemia's politics were anything but coherent. Bohemians opposed slavery but were against abolition; they were against thieving capitalists but romanticized violent New York street gangs like the Dead Rabbits and Bowery Boys. Bohemians liked to protest almost as much as they enjoyed the fruits of their protest—Fitz-James O'Brien would picket the offices of *Harper's* magazine after it refused to pay him a twenty-five-dollar advance for an article he had been commissioned to write. Then, after winning his battle, O'Brien would spend almost the whole sum on food and drink at an upscale New York restaurant called Delmonico's.[31]

"My own greatest pleasure at Pfaff's," Whitman remembered, "was to look on—to see, talk little, absorb."[32] But he wasn't a detached observer. Clapp's *Saturday Press* was crucial for his literary fame. That was where Whitman began to burnish his image as America's poet. For material appearing in the magazine that promoted the 1856 second edition of *Leaves of Grass*, Whitman had used Emerson's private endorsement of the book without his consent. (Emerson, for his part, was furious about being used in this way. Though the two men developed a cordial relationship, Emerson would often respond angrily whenever Whitman's name was mentioned in his presence.) Emerson had too many scruples to be a co-conspirator in Whitman's brazen marketing efforts; Henry Clapp had none. It was Clapp who introduced Whitman to his first major publisher, Thayer and Eldridge, an outfit out of Boston, which was looking to boost titles appealing to the expanding bohemian market. And it was with Clapp's enthusiastic assistance that Whitman wrote anonymous positive reviews of *Leaves* in the *Saturday Press* and would go so far as to respond to fictional critiques of *Leaves* that were themselves anonymously written by Clapp.

Despite their best efforts to make *Leaves* a smash hit, the third edition suffered the same fate as the first two—it was met with little fanfare. Who cared about poetry? The country was at a boiling point. War seemed inevitable—abolitionist John Brown's failed antislavery raid on Harpers Ferry, West Virginia, on October 16, 1859, his subsequent hanging on December 2, 1859, and the election of Republican Abraham Lincoln on November 6, 1860, all set the stage for Southern succession. The American reading public was uninterested in poetic experimentation. New York bohemians couldn't find an audience. Clapp shuttered the *Saturday Press* in 1860.

▪ ▪ ▪

Walt Whitman first saw the newly inaugurated Abraham Lincoln passing through New York on February 19, 1861—just months before Confederate troops fired on Fort Sumter on April 12, 1861. He was impressed by the sight of the lanky, awkward Midwestern man, former Whig state senator from Illinois, wearing a stovepipe hat and deftly managing a crowd of thirty thousand. A crowd, it should be noted, that wasn't entirely sympathetic to his politics. Lincoln won only 35 percent of the popular vote because many New Yorkers, like Whitman, were less interested in abolishing slavery than in maintaining a cordial economic relationship with the agrarian South.[33]

Like many Northerners, Whitman, for his part, opposed slavery. But no one would ever accuse him of being an abolitionist. An American patriot who prioritized stability above all else, he saw no point in abolitionist "ranting" or the movement's "abominable fanaticism," which he thought stood against "free thought" and "liberal sentiments."[34] But Whitman's art betrayed his own views. His affiliation with the Boston-based Thayer and Eldridge after the 1860 publication of the third edition of *Leaves* put him, in the public imagination, squarely on the side against the Confederacy and alongside abolition. "There is an unkempt, uncouth poet of New York, or rather of Brooklyn," wrote the *New Orleans Sunday Delta*, "whose name on earth, in common parlance, is Walt Whitman. The *Cincinnati Commercial* calls him the 'Yahoo of American literature.'"[35]

It was only when things got more personal for Whitman, however, that he became a booster of the Union cause during the Civil War—that is, after his brother, George, joined the Fifty-First New York Volunteers and started sending Walt reports from the front lines. (George was one of the few in his battalion to survive, though he couldn't shake the scars of battle, having traveled twenty thousand miles over four years across the human wreckage.) In January 1863, Whitman got directly involved too. He left his idyllic home in Brooklyn, his daily visits to Pfaff's, his part-time carpentry work, and moved to Washington, DC. There he worked as a copyist in the office of the army paymaster, while living in a small room at 394 L Street, just below his two friends, Nelly and William Douglas O'Connor. The gig was a way for Whitman to support his real passion—to work as a nurse at the Armory Square Hospital and visit wounded soldiers. In two years, Whitman made six hundred visits and tended to one hundred thousand men. (This number is staggering, but a small fraction of the war's toll. When the Civil War ended, it had claimed over six hundred thousand lives and four hundred thousand injuries.)

The Civil War ended on April 9, 1865, with General Robert E. Lee's surrender at Appomattox, Virginia. Whitman's initial elation was doused five days later on April 14, 1865, when Abraham Lincoln was assassinated by the well-known stage actor and Confederate sympathizer John Wilkes Booth, at Ford's Theatre, as the president was attending Laura Keene's performance of *Our American Cousin*. Whitman's friend (and, according to biographers, his longtime lover) Peter Doyle was in attendance. Doyle relayed the news of how the cocky Booth, son of Whitman's favorite actor, Junius Brutus Booth, walked behind Lincoln, seated in his private box, and fired a single shot from his .44-caliber derringer pistol. This, before rushing the stage and shouting, "Sic semper tyrranis! (Thus always to tyrants!)" Whitman was as stunned as he was devastated (he had come to support Lincoln and would tip his hat to the president whenever he saw him around Washington during the war years). At the same time, Whitman recognized that Lincoln's death was a springboard for the feeling of national unity that his own work had tried to, thus far unsuccessfully, occasion. "There is a cement to the whole people, subtler, more underlying, than anything in written constitution, or courts or armies," he wrote in response to news of the assassination.[36]

Sensing the national zeitgeist, Whitman contacted his old friend, Henry Clapp. Clapp, who hadn't published an issue of the *Saturday Press* since 1860, restarted it in 1865 for a few weeks to put out Whitman's elegy to Lincoln. The poem was called "O Captain!" And it would become Whitman's most famous poem. This is nothing short of ironic considering that "O Captain!" is missing both the irreverence and free-wheeling, unresolved tensions that so beautifully marked 1850s bohemia and *Leaves of Grass*. "O Captain!" is about deification, not irreverence; it abandons the perilous search for individual meaning for the certainty of its realization. It is history, rather than future; a conclusion of a successful journey, rather than a problematizing of the journey itself: "The ship is anchor'd safe and sound, its voyage closed and done, / From fearful trip the victor ship comes in with object won." Though largely forgotten, *Saturday Press* is now remembered for putting out Whitman's most patriotic poem, which aligned with the very bourgeois sensibilities Clapp and his circle stood against. As for Clapp? By 1865, he was no longer holding court at Pfaff's. He had a steady public-sector job as a clerk in a New York City office. When William O'Connor ran into him on the sidewalk in 1867, O'Connor gleefully relayed to Whitman that Clapp "was becoming a respectable citizen. When once a man enters upon the downward path . . . one can see as the guilty result of Bohemianism, a place on the Common Council or the Board of Aldermen."[37]

O'Connor's giddiness at Clapp's domestication was a touch too strong, for one could have said the same thing about him. Once a spirited abolitionist who tried to put his passion into an antislavery novel called *Harrington: A Story of True Love* (1860), O'Connor, the thin, bearded, blue-eyed husband and father, was now a clerk for the Lighthouse Board in the Treasury Department. Indeed, it was O'Connor who helped Whitman secure a well-paying government job as a clerk in the Interior Department of Indian Affairs at a salary of $1,200.[38]

Sustaining the counterculture, nineteenth century-citizens like Clapp, Whitman, and O'Connor found out, was much harder than envisioning it. Robert Owen, the utopian socialist who founded New Harmony, was more interested in expounding his utilitarian theorems to famous men than living them out himself. Upon arriving to the US in 1824 to promote his vision, he traveled to Washington, DC, to give two fiery speeches to the US Congress. Then he visited with presidential nominee Andrew Jackson and the ailing Thomas Jefferson, and he sent blueprints of New Harmony to Napoleon. Owen was most proud of the fact that a model replica of his ideal town was publicly displayed in President John Quincy Adams's White House after Adams won a contested election in 1824.

As far as New Harmony itself? Owen realized that, although he had spent $200,000 of his vast $250,000 personal fortune to keep it afloat, he still couldn't pay down the substantial mortgage remaining on the books. Offering to sell New Harmony to its residents for a reasonable sum of $126,000, to be paid over twelve years with minimal interest, New Harmony's residents politely refused.[39] They were utopians. Not fools.

Brook Farm, which began in 1841, only lasted for six years. It dissolved in 1847 after the Boston Brahmins, who liked the excellent schooling the commune provided for their children, showed no interest in the grueling task of its daily upkeep.

Oneida's sexual openness, it turned out, was less fulfilling than its adherents initially envisioned. The practice of "mutual criticism," in which community members blatantly called out bad behavior—impropriety, greed, lust, ambition—in group settings, was too emotionally taxing. More troubling is that its founder, Joseph Noyes, was a sexual predator who courted underage girls, and in 1878 he barely made it north of the US border to Ontario when his followers alerted him of his impending arrest for statutory rape. By the end of 1879, Oneida was no longer a commune. It was a silverware company.

■   ■   ■

Although Whitman had only started his administrative position copying reports at the Interior Department of Indian Affairs on January 24, 1866, on June 30, 1866, he was unceremoniously dismissed from his post. The new secretary of the interior under Democratic president Andrew Johnson, Senator James Harlan of Iowa, had embarked on a late-night unannounced visit to Whitman's office, where he found a marked-up copy of the 1860 edition of *Leaves of Grass*. Disturbed by the book's overt sexual promiscuity, Harlan determined Whitman was an unbefitting public servant. William O'Connor, who vouched for Whitman to get the job in the first place, cared more about saving Whitman's job than did Whitman himself. What is more, O'Connor saw a ripe opportunity for a fight about free expression.

O'Connor ran into the office of J. Hubley Ashton, the acting assistant attorney general, and demanded Whitman be reinstated. Ashton, embarrassed to have his authority challenged and focused on more pressing matters with the US federal government beginning to oversee Reconstruction, refused. In response, O'Connor wrote a pamphlet, entitled *The Good Gray Poet*, which criticized Harlan as a detached elite Republican prude (he was a Methodist minister and former president of Iowa Wesleyan College). In O'Connor's diatribe, Whitman was a misunderstand genius, in the company of figures like Rabelais and Shakespeare.[40] "The Good Gray Poet," the nickname affixed to Whitman for the rest of his life, was born.

As an increasingly public figure after the censorship affair, Whitman did what *Leaves of Grass* counseled against: he cozied up to the ruling class. After being transferred to the attorney general's office, where he worked from 1865 to 1872, part of his job entailed interviewing ex-Confederate soldiers seeking a pardon from the federal government. If Whitman did his work begrudgingly, that's one thing. But Whitman wasn't required to passionately defend the sitting president, an unrepentant white supremacist, Andrew Johnson. "Johnson was not a foul man," Whitman wrote to a friend after the president's impeachment by Republicans in the House of Representatives in 1868. "He had done nothing impeachable—had done his best, according to his integrity."[41] A curious statement, given that Andrew Johnson, a proud former slaveholder from Tennessee, in addition to issuing an astounding number of pardons to ex-Confederates (fourteen thousand), had done absolutely everything in his power to subvert the Republican Congress's newly created Freedmen's Bureau, which sought to provide government aid for newly emancipated Black citizens during Reconstruction.

The charitable interpretation of Whitman's words was that he was a flawed man brimming with empathy. The evidence, however, suggests there was a less pleasant reason Whitman was fond of Johnson: he was a garden-variety racist. In a 1980 essay, the Black feminist poet-critic June

Jordan wrote that it was through the "poems and the ideas of this particular white father that I have reached a tactical, if not strategic, understanding of the racist, sexist, and anti-American predicament that condemns most New World writing to peripheral."[42] Whitman glorified working people so long as they were white. He was an adherent of the Free Soil Party in the 1850s, which opposed the extension of slavery in the western territories only on the basis that it would depress the economic value of white men's labor. He supported the Fugitive Slave Law of 1850. Whitman, the direct descendant of Long Island slaveholding ancestors on both his father's and mother's sides, would sometimes reveal himself by parroting the prevailing discourse of white supremacy—"blacks" had as "much intellect and calibre (in the mass) as so many baboons."[43] After the 1868 election, they "looked like so many wild brutes let loose." Radical Republicans who actively pushed for a robust federal presence in the South, he believed, "have exploited the Negro too intensely."[44] Later in life, Whitman declared that "the blacks can never be to me what the whites are," because "the whites are my brothers and I love them."[45]

The era with which Whitman is associated and during which he came of age, "Jacksonian America," was named after the Democratic president Andrew Jackson, who came to power in 1828 on a platform of white nationalism. Whitman would never forget Jackson, the white-haired man who was affectionally called "Old Hickory," waving his white hat, parading through Brooklyn in 1833. Apparently, Whitman, the great poet of democracy, had no problem with the fact that Jackson, born to Scots-Irish settler parents, was once the most notorious land speculator in Tennessee in acquiring Choctaw and Chickasaw land, before becoming a favorite of President James Monroe because of his brutal wars against the Muscogee nation, and then against the Florida Seminoles during the First Seminole War (1817–18) to retake slaveholder plantations. By the time Whitman first saw him that afternoon in Brooklyn in 1833, Jackson had already made his name with the Indian Removal Act of 1830, which, over that decade, led to the genocide of over a hundred thousand Indigenous people.

In the twentieth century, the Black poet Langston Hughes would call *Leaves of Grass* an ode to racial egalitarianism, writing that Whitman's "all-embracing words lock arms with . . . Negroes and whites."[46] But Whitman, the man, never lived up to the artistic message of *Leaves*, because he shared a deleterious assumption with many in the nineteenth-century counterculture. They were philosophically opposed to bondage but assumed that liberation was reserved exclusively for whites.

Robert Owen's New Harmony had a racial covenant that excluded Black people from its founding charter. Ripley's Brook Farm had no Black members. Whitman's intellectual hero, Frances Wright, had always said that Nashoba was a beautiful beacon for racial equality, while ignoring that it was built on Indigenous land, which she bought for $320 with the direct help of Andrew Jackson. Moreover, not only was Wright a firm supporter of Black colonization abroad rather than immediate abolition to end slavery, but the reason American presidents like Andrew Jackson, Thomas Jefferson, and one of her greatest admirers, James Madison backed Wright was because she treated Nashoba's Black residents not as equals but as indentured servants. (Notably, all three men were, at times, vocal members of the American Colonization Society, a national organization that promoted mass-scale Black deportation to Africa as the solution for slavery.) Black Nashoba residents had to work in exchange for paying off their debt to Wright. To add insult to injury, they had no voting stake in the colony.

After Wright had a severe bout of malaria and left Nashoba in 1827, the commune was mismanaged by her disciple, James Richardson, whose diary also recorded instances of sexual violence in the colony that revealed Nashoba was like many places in the world—dangerous for women. Before long, Richardson's illicit love affair with a Black resident of Nashoba, Mam'selle Josephine, was discovered—which violated Nashoba's racist and puritan sensibilities. Once Nashoba fell apart, Wright paid to send its Black residents to Haiti and established a trust for Black advancement, though most of the money was spent on upkeep for schooling Nashoba's children.

■ ■ ■

In the last two decades of his life, Whitman was an elder statesman who still retained a bohemian aesthetic. One could see him in his gray felt sombrero and open-collared shirts among bowls of fragrant lilacs and roses, which adorned his home on Mickle Street in Camden, New Jersey, where he lived with his brother, George. Whitman had been in Camden since 1873—the same year his mother died, which was also the year he suffered the first of a series of debilitating strokes that left him partially paralyzed. It was in Camden where Whitman drank elderberry wine with

Oscar Wilde (even then, Whitman's "Calamus" poems in *Leaves*, which celebrate queer sexuality, made him a gay icon) and chatted over apple pies with British politician and reformer Richard Monckton Milnes.[47]

Although living less than a hundred miles from the Bleecker Street block where Pfaff's once stood, Whitman was now farther than ever from the bohemian margins of society he once occupied. Aggressively leveraging his fame as "America's" poet, he would only publish in outlets like *Harper's*, *New York Herald*, and the *Century Magazine*, and give poetry readings at venues like the Fortieth National Industrial Exposition, held in New York in 1871.[48] For his paid speaking commitments, Whitman would almost always talk about "O Captain!" These talks were so popular they came to be known as his "Lincoln Lectures."

But Whitman was still recycling his old tricks from his bohemian days. He continued to write anonymous reviews of his work to court controversy. In the January 16, 1876, issue of the *West Jersey Press*, a pro-business Republican paper, Whitman claimed that, for all his literary efforts, he was penniless and had only met "with a howl of criticism and the charge of obscenity."[49] This was hardly the case. But the article set off a heated debate in the pages of England's *London Daily News* and was soon at the center of debates in *Scribner's*, *Harper's*, and the *New York Tribune*. This brouhaha, entirely fabricated, was an astonishing success. It led to the publication of the centennial edition of *Leaves of Grass*, the fourth, in 1876, by his first major publisher, James R. Osgood and Company.

As Whitman finally made it big, his first order of business was to change the signature poem of "Poem of Walt Whitman, an American" to "Song of Myself." The iconic 1854 portrait of the first edition, which saw Whitman without suspenders, hat tilted to the side, right fist on his side, left hand in his pocket, looking with a sneer, was now pushed into the middle of the book. "The worst thing about this is," Whitman wrote, embarrassed of the photo of his bohemian days, was that it was "as if I was hurling bolts at somebody . . . full of mad oaths—saying defiantly, to hell with you!"[50]

No matter Whitman's repeated attempts to sanitize his image, *Leaves* would still garner controversy. On March 1, 1882, Boston district attorney Oliver Stevens, objecting to the sexually explicit imagery, sent Whitman's publisher, James R. Osgood, a letter to stop the book's publication. Osgood asked Whitman to make twenty-two deletions in a total of 150 lines. Whitman declined. The New England Free Love League on May 29 adopted a resolution condemning the decision as rank censorship. Whitman's old friend William O'Connor, who he had once split with over African American suffrage but with whom he had since reconciled, reprised his role as Whitman's publicity man, writing an article in the *Tribune* condemning the poster child of American puritanism and sexual repression: Anthony Comstock. Comstock had been well known since 1871, the year he founded the New York Society for the Suppression of Vice, and encouraged Congress to pass the Comstock Laws in 1873, which made it a federal crime to send obscene material through the mail. Rees Welsh, a Philadelphia publishing house, picked up *Leaves* and published it on July 18, 1882. Negative attention was still good attention. The thousand-copy printing of *Leaves* sold out in one day.

Widely anthologized over the last decade of his life, Whitman died of tuberculosis-induced pneumonia at the age of seventy-two on March 26, 1892, in Camden, New Jersey. Thousands lined the street on March 30, as the funeral procession carried his body to the Harleigh Cemetery, where it was placed in a $4,000 granite mausoleum, which weighed multiple tons. The mausoleum was twice the cost of the first house he bought on Mickle Street in Camden in 1884. Inscribed in the center of the triangular roof of this larger-than-life, ostentatious structure were two simple words, "Walt Whitman." The bard of the counterculture, who spent his life seeking an audience, was now, only in death, fully monumentalized into the American cultural canon.

Was Walt Whitman the greatest poet America ever produced, the greatest poet of democracy itself, or an ordinary white racist who couldn't see the obvious egalitarian message of his art?

Was Whitman a shameless self-promoter or a savvy marketer? Was Whitman only in the counterculture temporarily because he couldn't make it in the mainstream, and then happy to collude with the establishment once he made it? Does the countercultural message of *Leaves of Grass* exceed the parochial views of its author?

■　■　■

As the nineteenth century was drawing to a close, it became apparent that Whitman's legacy would reverberate into the future. In a letter dated July 13, 1888, a writer for the *Boston Herald* by the name of Sylvester Baxter wrote Whitman to share his enthusiasm about an exciting new book he had read: "I have lately been reading a beautiful and noble story by Edward Bellamy, 'Looking Backward.' It goes far in the direction pointed out by your prophetic [work]."[51] The book that Baxter praised had been published in January 1888. Its author, the thirty-eight-year-old Chicopee Falls, Massachusetts-born Edward Bellamy. The last person one would think to be a dreamer, Bellamy was the son of a solidly middle-class Baptist minister and doting mother. A self-described "homebody," Bellamy was a depressive who spent his entire life in the house in which he was born. He told his wife every afternoon to "pull down the curtains," so the neighbors wouldn't peek in. He would carve steak for family dinners, but he himself would only eat a single raw egg in a glass of milk.[52]

In his imagination, however, Edward Bellamy went farther than anyone before him in combining New England transcendentalism with European socialism. In so doing, Bellamy made utopia palpable for an American audience. Through a series of conversations between a nineteenth-century man named Julian West, awakening one hundred years into the future in the year 2000, in the home of a retired physician, Dr. Leete, Bellamy tells the story of a society in which state-run socialism supported by a conscripted workforce creates economic equality and prosperity for all men, women, and children. Crime is nonexistent. Class divisions are moot. An efficient bureaucracy manages the daily affairs of government. There are no bitter conflicts between warring political parties.[53]

Looking Backward was an unprecedented success. It inspired a new movement called Nationalism. On Sunday, April 7, 1889, a hundred people attended the first meeting of the Nationalist Club, held in the Everett House on Union Square in New York. The gathering was in response to a call by J. Edward Hall, who ran for New York governor as the Socialist Labor Party of America candidate in 1888. By 1890, 127 Nationalist clubs, from California to Boston, were formed. Two million copies of *Looking Backward* were sold in the US. Two hundred thousand copies in Great Britain. The novel was translated into fifteen different languages.

Nationalism's greatest cultural contribution wasn't to inspire Americans to begin communes like Brook Farm, New Harmony, or Nashoba; it was to contribute to the normalization of socialism in America. Membership in the Socialist Party exploded from 10,000 in 1902 to 118,000 in 1912. The year 1912 was the year that the socialist candidate for president, Eugene V. Debs, received almost one million votes, 6 percent of the national vote.

There were 1,200 Socialist officeholders nationwide—Milwaukee elected both a Socialist mayor and fire chief—and the first Socialist elected to Congress, Victor Berger of Wisconsin, took office in 1910. The socialist paper *New York Call* had twenty thousand daily subscribers.[54] In 1912, the socialist weekly, *Appeal to Reason*, out of Girard, Kansas, had a circulation of 761,747. The owner of *Metropolitan* magazine, Harry Payne Whitney, captured the national mood when he declared in 1910 that Americans had decided to "give Socialism a hearing."

As a political party, the Socialist Party was interested in legislative reform, serving as the alternative to reform-minded Progressives, racist Democrats, and industry-supporting Republicans. Socialists advocated an eight-hour workday, workers' compensation, a federal income tax, public control of local utilities, an end to Jim Crow, and full voting rights for women. Socialism, for this reason, was not a countercultural movement—not a sensibility, not a way of being.

The best attempt at fusing the radicalism of socialism with a new way of living, however, came from American youth, many of them children of immigrants from Europe, who were antiauthoritarian to the core. They, like the denizens of Pfaff's, hated institutions, political parties, and, well, organizations of any form. Like socialists, they despised capitalism. But unlike socialists, freedom of the individual was the only thing they held sacred. Whitman was their inspiration. They called themselves anarchists.

On May 25, 1882, Walt Whitman received a short letter from one of these youth, during the *Leaves of Grass* censorship fiasco. He was a twenty-eight-year-old man, born in New Bedford, Massachusetts, in 1854, the same year the first edition of *Leaves* was published. A partisan of free speech, the man was the editor of a little-known magazine called *Radical Review*. He wrote Whitman: "If I had the means, I would gladly, with your permission, put your book on the market advertised as the suppressed edition, and invite the authorities to dispute my right to do so . . . will become the responsible publisher, and go to prison if necessary. In case the verdict should be against me and I should be fined, I should decline to pay the fine."[55]

His name was Benjamin R. Tucker. In addition to *Radical Review*, Tucker was the publisher of a small journal called *Liberty*, founded in 1881. It was the first periodical to introduce anarchism, a political philosophy gaining interest in Europe, to an American audience.

Born to a New England Quaker family and a proud nephew of a well-respected abolitionist, Charles Almy, as a young boy Tucker attended lectures by abolitionist William Lloyd Garrison. Tucker would refer to Ralph Waldo Emerson as "King." Henry David Thoreau was one of Tucker's early heroes. And just like the sage of Walden Pond, Tucker, in 1876, was jailed for refusing to pay his Worcester poll tax. As an undergraduate student at the Massachusetts Institute of Technology in 1872, Tucker helped the mother of free love, Victoria Woodhull, arrange public speeches critical of marriage. The two soon became sexually involved, even though Woodhull was sixteen years his senior.

Benjamin Tucker was drawn to Walt Whitman for the same reasons he was drawn to Victoria Woodhull. Both Whitman and Woodhull endorsed liberated sexuality and were successful entrepreneurs. (Woodhull, along with her sister, Tennessee, was the first woman to open a speculative trading firm on Wall Street in 1870. On the first day, thousands of men lined up to place bets. Within six short weeks, the two sisters made a killing—$700,000.) Tucker, like Whitman, looked as fondly upon the small, free-market associations that the agrarian populist Thomas Jefferson championed, and treated with scorn the monopoly capitalism of industrialists like Cornelius Vanderbilt, Andrew Carnegie, and John Rockefeller.[56] Just as Whitman spent hours mingling with, and was the poet of, the b'hoy, b'ghal, the drifter, and the rowdy, Tucker, too, had a live-and-let-live attitude toward New York's many public shower takers, homeless street dwellers, and unruly alcoholics.

Tucker's admiration of Whitman, however, had its limits. If transcendentalist reformism was the religion of Tucker's parents, Whitman's romantic dreams of national reconciliation were the delusions of a naive old man. Tucker was a radical individualist. Reforming government was no cure for mass suffering. The very call for governmental reform assumed that government wasn't the root of all evil. Government, for Tucker, was *the* problem.

To spread the gospel of anarchism alongside his antigovernment views, it wasn't enough to just write books or edit journals. Tucker would need to open a bookstore. This is what he did in 1906. His store was called the Unique Book Shop, and it was located on 502 Sixth Avenue in New York City. Its shelves were stocked with a who's who of free thinkers—Friedrich Nietzsche, Fyodor Dostoevsky, Max Stirner, Henrik Ibsen, and Leo

Tolstoy. Visitors could peruse Tucker's own English translations of Pierre Proudhon and Victor Hugo (from the French) and Nikolay Chernyshevsky (from the Russian).

A frequent visitor to Tucker's bookstore was a charismatic woman who lived close by on the corner of 210 East Thirteenth Street. The two chatted regularly and became friends. Tucker is largely forgotten to history, though she would go on to become the greatest exponent of anarchism in America, the new counterculture of the early twentieth century. Her name was Emma Goldman.

CHAPTER 2

REBEL MISFITS

O n the sweltering summer morning of August 15, 1889, a twenty-three-year-old woman arrived by ferry to New York City on West Forty-Second Street. She came by way of the West Shore train, the cheapest she could afford, that had brought her to Weehawken, New Jersey, earlier in the day. She was short, with crystal-blue eyes and a charismatic smile. With nothing but five dollars in hand, a small handbag in tow, and a sewing machine, she began the long trek by foot downtown to the gritty Bowery neighborhood of the Lower East Side. That's where her aunt's photography gallery was located. It was among the tenement homes where a large percentage of her ancestors, 1.2 million Eastern European Jews, had come before her. They were newly arrived from Russia, escaping the anti-Semitic pogroms that had been unleashed upon Jews after Tsar Alexander II was assassinated in 1881.

Emma Goldman's reason for coming to New York City was an age-old one. She was fleeing a loveless marriage and a bad job. Her husband, Jacob Kershner, preferred cheap thrills. A compulsive gambler, Kershner's favorite pastime was to lose the vast sum of his fifteen-dollar weekly salary at the card table. At her grueling sewing job at a corset factory in Rochester, New York, Goldman had toiled for fifty hours a week for a meager fifty cents a day. Manhattan didn't appear any more inviting. "How confusing and endless a large city seems to the new-comer," she described the city as she walked downtown. "How cold and unfriendly!"[1] After she finally arrived at her aunt's photography studio, Goldman's head was throbbing. Her feet were swollen. Her aunt and uncle weren't sympathetic. Immediately, they began to ask her loaded questions: Had she left her husband for good? Did she intend to stay with them? For how long?

That feeling of dreams turning into nightmares was a feeling that Goldman knew well. In Russia, as a fifteen-year-old girl, she had met a twenty-year-old male clerk on her way home from the Hermitage Arcade corset factory where she worked. The daily flirtations and evening pastry-shop dates lifted her spirits at first. But things would soon take a dark turn, after the clerk sexually assaulted Goldman in a St. Petersburg hotel. Goldman tried to be tough. As he left the room, she didn't say anything; she just buttoned up her blouse and fixed up her corset. But privately, she felt "dazed, bruised in every nerve."[2]

As a young woman, Goldman read the great Russian novelists—Ivan Turgenev and Nikolai Gogol. This secret passion was discovered by her father, Abraham, a small-time businessman, a particular sort with no philosophical inclination. Abraham cared only about greener pastures and was always relocating his family in search of upward mobility. First, he brought them to the Jewish shtetl of Kovno, Lithuania, where Emma Goldman was born on June 27, 1869. Then it was Konigsberg and then St. Petersburg. Each time, the result was the same. Every one of his business ventures failed.

At home, Abraham was a petty authoritarian. He occasionally used a whip on Goldman when she disobeyed him. But when he discovered Goldman's interest in philosophical pursuits, he used the whip of his spiteful tongue: Jewish girls, Abraham screamed, only needed to know how to prepare gefilte fish for their husbands!

From early on, defiance was the quality that would make Goldman stand out. After the sexual assault in St. Petersburg, she felt "no shame" as she left the hotel.[3] After Abraham yelled at her, she resolved to leave Tsarist Russia. She and her sister departed in 1885. They arrived at Castle Garden—the New York point of entry would soon be replaced by Ellis Island—just before settling in Rochester, New York.

When Goldman arrived in New York City in 1889, the chilly response from her aunt and uncle didn't seem to faze her. She left her belongings at their photography studio and, on a whim, went in search of Hillel Solotaroff, a young anarchist. She had only once heard the man lecture in New Haven, Connecticut, where she lived for a short while. After many tries, Goldman didn't find Solotaroff. Finally, she found herself on Montgomery Street only because a janitor at Solotaroff's former apartment had directed her there. Goldman continued on even though she didn't know Solotaroff's building number. Then, by chance, she ran into him on the street. Goldman slogged up to the fifth-floor walk-up where Solotaroff shared his two-bedroom apartment with his parents and younger brother. It was a cramped tenement, she remembered, but it was "seething with humanity."

▪　▪　▪

Anarchism begins with a bang *and* a whimper. There are exciting moments and dazzling encounters. A meeting of spirits. But there's no premeditation, no secret plan. The self-possession and clear-sightedness that revolutionaries want you to embrace isn't there from the start. Anarchism is nothing if not haphazard. A product of fortuitous meetings, not pre-destined fates.

But anarchism was an improvised response to something specific: a cruel world that was unwelcoming to outsiders. Goldman, like many Eastern European Jewish immigrants, became a refugee from authoritarianism in Russia only to confront palpable anti-immigrant hostility in New York.

In 1882, the US Congress passed a fifty-cent tax on each arriving immigrant and excluded whole categories of people, so-called "lunatics, idiots, and paupers," those who might be a public charge. In 1891, Congress went further. It prohibited entry to those with infectious disease. Congress also shifted power away from individual states to the federal government by creating the Office of Superintendent of Immigration, which deputized immigration inspectors at points of entry throughout the country.

White Anglo-Americans could barely tolerate migrants from northern Europe—places like Scandinavia, England, Ireland, and Germany. But they were outraged to see those that they deemed racially inferior to northern Europeans—Italians and Jews—arriving in the 1880s. As a result, Congress passed the Foran Act in 1885, which made it illegal to import foreign laborers to break strikes. This wasn't just about union-busting. It particularly demonized Italians, who, now numbering around five hundred thousand, were known to contract work off the books and settle for little pay. The Democratic Party bosses of Tammany Hall, New York's old political dynasty, were, however, excited about the news. With the Foran Act, they could become political gatekeepers, recruiting new migrants for patronage city jobs, which, in return, would get them votes and considerable loyalty.[4]

Around this time, a growing array of New York reformers wanted to Americanize newcomers like Goldman. Charles Brace, of the Children's Aid Society, relocated a hundred thousand children to rural parts of the western United States. Those who stayed in New York weren't so lucky. In 1890, there were one million New Yorkers in 37,316 tenement homes. Plumbing renovations and sanitation updates had been nonexistent for decades.[5] Reformers established settlement houses to educate the poor. Neighborhood Guild, College Settlement, Henry Street House. Free textbooks arrived in 1877 and kindergarten came in 1885.

But what impact could education have upon economic inequality when New York factory workers like Goldman could barely pay rent, let alone have the comfort of a minimum wage or an eight-hour workday? By 1900, New York was the headquarters of sixty-nine of the largest one hundred corporations. A total of 25,399 factories produced an estimated $777 million in wealth. Its primary transportation system, however, was the horse carriage, used by fifty million passengers every year. Tuberculosis was soaring in the Lower East Side's population of sixty-four thousand, squeezed into just one square mile. Premature births in 1897 at Foundling Hospital had an astounding death rate of 97 percent.[6] It wasn't until 1893 that the 300 million gallons of potable water being delivered daily from upstate were finally treated with chlorine to kill harmful bacteria.[7] American anarchism emerged out of this historical context. With nowhere to turn, Goldman and her friends turned inward, becoming self-sufficient and creating their own rules.

■ ■ ■

Over an improvised dinner of his mother's traditional homemade cake and tea, Solotaroff told Goldman she could stay with him. He let her know that two friends of his—who were sisters—were looking for a third flatmate. As they sat at dinner, Solotaroff mesmerized Goldman with stories from the underground. There was a Yiddish anarchist scene, Solotaroff told her excitedly, where passionate debates about revolutionary strategy mattered more than where you got your next meal. Goldman was drawn to his generosity, while he was drawn to Goldman's dynamic personality. She was witty and a great conversationalist. She was tender without being self-deprecating, she had warmth and moral clarity.

Solotaroff then took Goldman to meet some of his friends at Sach's Café, on Suffolk Street. As they walked in the hot night air, a cool breeze offered them solace amid the stench of garbage piled on sidewalks. This was the setting for the frustrated aspirations of the immigrants cramped in apartments above—who, before their arrival, had no idea that this, the land of abundance, would be an inferno of the desolate and denigrated.

And yet, as Solotaroff and Goldman walked into Sach's Café, New York no longer seemed so dystopian. Like Pfaff's in the 1850s, Sach's was stuffy and dark. But it was bursting at the seams with poor students and aspiring writers gesticulating wildly. Their swinging arms matched the frenzied pace of the conversation, back and forth from broken Russian to broken Yiddish to broken English. Goldman felt at home. The "cruel reception from her kin" only two hours old was now a distant memory.[8]

Not far from where she was sitting, Goldman overheard a young man of about eighteen, with noticeably thick lips, a high forehead, and an intense gaze. He had the chest and neck of a giant, and yelled to a waiter in a booming voice, "Extra-Large Steak, Extra Cup of Coffee!" He gently approached the table where she was finishing her meal with Solotaroff. Like Goldman, he was new to the city and a Russian Jew from her hometown of Kovno. He had arrived in New York the year before in 1888. His name was Alexander Berkman. "Sasha," as he was known, would be Goldman's best friend, intellectual interlocutor, confidant, and one of the most in-famous representatives of the anarchist movement. At first Goldman was confused—how could Berkman afford such extravagance? But she soon realized that preserving the right of self-care was a must in a world governed by rules you couldn't control.[9]

Sasha Berkman wasn't supposed to be a radical. The youngest of four children, he was born in 1870 to a successful Jewish leather merchant, Osip, in Vilnius, Lithuania. Osip's business flourished to such an extent that in 1877 he moved the family to a fancy suburb of St. Petersburg and hired private tutors for his children. Before long, the anti-Semitic pogroms that came in the wake of Alexander II's assassination in 1881 made Jewish life outside the ghetto, the Pale of Settlement, untenable. Osip managed to escape to St. Petersburg with his family by selling his cherished business.

When Berkman was twelve, his father died, after which he moved to Kovno with his mother. Following the tragedy, Berkman became an avowed atheist and unruly student. As a teenager, he bribed a janitor to steal copies of a school exam, even though he was destined to earn high marks on it and finish at the top of the class anyway. The biggest influence on the young Berkman was an uncle he hardly knew, Maxim, who was exiled and sentenced to death in Siberia for partaking in an anti-Tsarist conspiracy. Maxim was part of the Nihilists, whom Berkman knew from his obsession with Nikolay Chernyshevsky's *What Is to Be Done?* Berkman, like his uncle, wanted to leave a mark. America, he thought, was the place to do it. It was a "land of noble achievements, a glorious free country."[10] Berkman hitched a ride to eastern Prussia with his brother, who was beginning medical school at the University of Leipzig, and then headed to Hamburg to set sail to New York in February 1888.

It soon became clear to Berkman that America was a purgatory of deferred dreams. When Goldman met Berkman at Sach's Café, she asked him who he worked for. A "slavedriver," was Berkman's response, in reference to the foreman of the factory where he had just quit his cigar-making job.[11] The America in which Goldman and Berkman found themselves wasn't made for them. Wealthy Americans, of which there were four thousand millionaires by 1890, made sure to keep them disempowered. Powerful fraternal organizations allowed the wealthy exclusive networking opportunities, to accumulate even greater wealth. Beta Theta Phi, a large college fraternity, had chapters in 16 cities in 1889. By 1912, it had chapters in 110 cities. Another fraternity, Delta Kappa Epsilon, had among its members six senators and forty congressmen, including Republican Henry Cabot Lodge and his close friend, the soon-to-be New York governor Theodore Roosevelt. In 1912, Delta Kappa Epsilon included eighteen New York bankers and three directors of Standard Oil.[12] One of the bankers at the club, J. P. Morgan, owned 100,000 miles of railroad and had three insurance companies with $1 billion in assets. Morgan made an $18 million profit from buying bonds from President Grover Cleveland's government in 1895, capitalizing on the recent depletion of the federal gold reserve. John D. Rockefeller's Standard Oil Company, a holding company, controlled $110 million in stock and turned $45 million in profits yearly. That was before the company expanded to stakes in copper and founded Chase Manhattan Bank. By 1900, John D. Rockefeller was worth $2 billion.[13]

Wealthy New Yorkers bought park side views in mansions along Fifth Avenue. They had private butlers. They dined at the newly opened Waldorf and Astoria luxury hotels, and shopped at R. H. Macy's department store, a dry-goods emporium that opened its flagship store, the world's largest, in 1902 on Thirty-Fourth Street.[14] New York was a playground for the rich, but also a fortress from which they could look down upon the immigrant working class from the hundreds of skyscrapers that dotted the skyline. One of the grandest was the twenty-five-floor Flatiron Building, replete with modern plumbing and elevator service and made of fortified steel rather than the traditional iron.

In response to such economic inequality, organized labor began organizing collective resistance. But the largest trade union at the time, the American Federation of Labor (AFL) wasn't interested in unskilled workers like Goldman. Founded in 1886, it represented the interests of skilled workers—masons, hatmakers, and cigarmakers—and it boasted hundreds of thousands of dues-paying members. AFL leader Samuel Gompers may have been the friendly London-born son of a Jewish cigar-maker, but his union was hostile to Eastern European Jews working in the needle and garment trade. In 1890s New York, this trade accounted for one in three workers. Hundreds of independent shops across Brooklyn and Manhattan placed bids upon precut fabric from large clothing suppliers. The lower the bid, the more likely they'd get the business. The cost borne by workers, however, was obscene: a sixteen-hour workday and unsanitary buildings. During the busy season, the lights stayed on late into the night.[15] Only 1 percent of Jewish married women worked, so most of the labor was performed by schoolgirls, many as young as sixteen.

Anarchism's promise was to do away with this life. Anarchism, as Goldman put it in her essay "Anarchism: What It Really Stands For" (1910), is "the philosophy of a new social order based on liberty unrestricted by man-made law; the theory that all forms of government rest on violence, and are therefore wrong and harmful, as well as unnecessary."[16] Capitalism impoverishes the worker, and it produces socioeconomic inequality. To the question, What happens after you abolish government?, the anarchist answers: *Things can't get worse, even if they may not get better.* If there are criminals now, there will be criminals later. But the key difference is that when a government is in place, it gets to make laws that define who is a criminal. It makes these laws to punish the powerless, while the powerless can never attain power.

Within months of meeting at Café Sachs, Goldman and Berkman decided to implement the principles of anarchism in their own lives. Along with Berkman's cousin, Modest "Fedya" Aronstam, a free-spirited figurative painter, and a mutual acquaintance, Helene Minkin, the four roommates established a small cooperative in a four-room apartment on Forty-Second Street. When they weren't arguing about "the cause," Berkman worked at a ladies' cloak factory and Minkin at a corset one. Goldman stitched shirtwaists and managed the household. Aronstam painted. Rent was expensive and these jobs were low paying, so the foursome tried their luck elsewhere, setting off to New Haven, Connecticut, where Goldman opened a dress shop as a seamstress. In New Haven, business was nonexistent, so in 1892, they headed to Worcester, Massachusetts, where they found a charming studio. By then, it was just Goldman, Berkman, and Aronstam—Minkin dropped out. Their neighbors were suspicious of the strange threesome, so Goldman and Berkman pretended to be married. Aronstam, they said, was Goldman's brother.[17]

Revolution is a full-time business. But one can't live on it alone. To eat, one needs to earn. And this threw a wrench into Goldman, Berkman, and Aronstam's desire to opt out. For all their anti-capitalist fervor, the Worcester threesome was moving from money-making scheme to money-making scheme. Aronstam sold his sketches to the *Worcester Commercial* newspaper, while Berkman and Goldman rented a horse and a wagon, which they valiantly dragged for hours around the local countryside to persuade farmers to procure Aronstam's artistic services to boost their small business (the farmers, despite appreciating Aronstam's talent, weren't interested). After impressing themselves with the delightful breakfasts of cheap herring they made on a kerosene stove, they opened a lunch restaurant at 86 Winter Street, three blocks from a popular grocery. It served homemade sandwiches, fresh coffee, fried pancakes, soft drinks, and ice cream to a loyal line of customers who could enjoy Aronstam's paintings hanging on the wall as they waited to be served.[18] (These get-rich-quick schemes would continue for many years after. As late as 1909, Goldman and Berkman planned to commission a bust of the Yiddish playwright Jacob Gordin, the replicas of which they would sell to his thousands of followers for profit.)[19]

At home in the Worcester apartment, however, things weren't so rosy. Goldman had struck up an affair with Johann Most, the well-known German anarchist and managing editor of *Die Freiheit*. A medium-height man with striking blue eyes and graying hair, along with a noticeable facial deformity—his jaw was dislocated to the left—Most was once christened by the Rochester, New York, press as the "personification of the devil."[20]

Twenty years older than Goldman, Most sought to educate the young woman in the finer things of life, wining and dining Goldman in expensive restaurants. However, he didn't like Emma's friends, calling them a bunch of "degenerates." Berkman became jealous of Most. Though he initially chalked up his feeling to "bourgeois values," which, he said, he inherited from his upbringing, Berkman became increasingly erratic. Things would get worse when Goldman drifted away from Most and fell in love with Berkman's cousin, the easygoing Fedya Aronstam. Most was an outsider, but Aronstam was family. His betrayal was too much. Berkman barely restrained himself from punching Aronstam after he had spent the Worcester commune's money on a blue and white striped silk jersey. Another time, Berkman berated Aronstam in public after finding out that he had spent twenty cents on a meal he could have eaten for two cents. Berkman, the man that Goldman remembered delighting in a large steak at Sach's Café, was now an unrecognizable miser.[21]

The Worcester commune was slowly deteriorating, but it abruptly collapsed in late 1892 when Berkman decided to go to battle during the Homestead Strike in Pennsylvania. Berkman followed the news of the eight hundred unionized workers at Homestead who went on strike and, after back-and-forth negotiations that extended for months, failed to reach a settlement. Henry Clay Frick, the chairman of the board of industrialist Andrew Carnegie's Amalgamated Steel in Pennsylvania, had recruited security forces to barricade the plant with barbed wire, within which loopholes were cut for the insertion of rifles. After this didn't deter the Homestead strikers, Frick brought in the Pinkerton private detective agency—paid mercenaries who were experts at crushing labor unrest. As Pinkertons arrived at the plant, they were met with fierce resistance by the strikers. A twelve-hour battle ensued overnight. By daybreak, seven strikers and three Pinkertons were killed.

Berkman was furious. Avenging the dead Homestead workers, he believed, would be the first shot of the revolution. His plan was to assassinate Henry Frick. To fund Berkman's deed, Goldman for one forgettable night moonlighted as a sex worker. Dressed in high heels and white silk stockings, she walked down Fourteenth Street in New York City, where she was picked up by an older man. The man, recognizing that this wasn't Goldman's regular line of work, told her he didn't want sex but gave her ten dollars anyway.[22]

On July 23, 1892, Berkman arrived at the second floor of the Carn-egie office at the Chronicle Telegraph Building in Pittsburgh. He had a sharp dagger in one hand and a .38-caliber revolver in another. Berkman walked in on Henry Clay Frick engaged in a lively conversation, after having arrived from his daily lunch break. The first bullet from Berkman's gun grazed Frick's left ear, the second hit the right side of his neck. Frick collapsed to the ground, like a wounded animal. Berkman stabbed Frick above the hipbone and in the back. Frick's assistants then came rushing into the office and tackled him. He was then taken into custody by police. (Remarkably, Frick survived Berkman's attack.)[23]

And yet, as Berkman began his fourteen-year sentence at Western Penitentiary in Pittsburgh, he discovered that revolutionary violence backfires for the same reason he thought it worked. Beyond the phys-ical harm it causes, revolutionary violence is self-aggrandizing, which people don't like. The few inmates who didn't view him as a repulsive pariah chuckled behind his back for his delusions of grandeur. What stung Berkman more than anything else, however, was his relationship with one prisoner—Jack Clifford—who had an active role in the Homestead strike. Berkman thought Clifford would sing his praises, but he did nothing of the sort. Himself a law-abiding citizen, Clifford lectured Berkman on the superiority of organized struggle with one's comrades, rather than lone wolf attacks that only enlivened one's enemies. The press response to Berkman's assassination attempt was even worse. The *New York Times*, with more than a hint of antisemitism, described Berkman as one of the many "hatched-faced, pimply, sallow cheeked, rat-eyed young men of the Russian Jewish colony."[24] To add insult to injury, Emma Goldman called Berkman's attempt a "failure."[25]

▪   ▪   ▪

Sasha Berkman could not shut out the criticism. He felt suicidal. Things turned for the better, however, in 1893, a year into his prison sentence, when an unexpected letter arrived in his cell. It was from a Michigan-born, Philadelphia-based anarchist named Voltairine "Voltai" de Cleyre. The letter gave Berkman, a tough guy, what nobody had given him in a long time: compassion. "It isn't my business to pass judgements on what you did," de Cleyre wrote, "but I know you did what you willed to do, and that appeals to me."[26]

Born to Midwestern Catholics in the Michigan flat farms of Leslie in 1866, de Cleyre was a precocious child who read newspapers at the age of four, spoke fluent French, wrote poetry inspired by Lord Byron at the age of six, and performed piano concertos for her parents. But de Cleyre never felt at ease with her gifts. She was a sickly child, and a persistent cough left her gasping for breath her whole life—a tragic prelude to her premature death in 1912 at the age of forty-six from meningitis. By the time de Cleyre had written Berkman prison, she, struggling with lifelong depression, had tried to kill herself not once but twice. Early on in their exchange of letters, de Cleyre agreed to smuggle poison into prison for Berkman so he could take his own life. But after getting to know him, she delayed it and, finally, decided against it, recognizing that, contrary to anarchist teachings, mutual vulnerability and not individual strength was a source of solidarity. "Touch hands across the gulf, Alex," de Cleyre wrote in one letter to Berkman, "we are not alone. There is comradeship in the depths. Let the lamps burn a while yet. To what indefinite end, let us not trouble. I salute you. And write soon again—write your soul out as gloomy as you feel it. I am listening and feeling."[27]

Voltai de Cleyre wasn't as fun as Emma Goldman. She was soft-spoken and wore plain white dresses. Her two long, thick plaits of brown hair, which rested just above her waist, stood in stark contrast to her icy-blue eyes. De Cleyre bristled at Goldman's propensity for upscale hotels. When asked to write an essay for the famed Russian anarchist Peter Kropotkin's seventieth birthday in 1912, de Cleyre snidely remarked, "I suppose that's what our dilettante have [sic] to have: birthdays, parties, concerts—anything lackadaisical and safe!"[28]

De Cleyre lived her politics among poor immigrant Jewish textile workers in Philadelphia. In addition to explaining to them her revolutionary politics, she helped with their broken English. In exchange for this, she learned how to read some Yiddish. Beyond being a sophisticated theorist of individualism, however, de Cleyre was an impressive interpreter of the way society degrades us. That was why she, of all people, was the greatest defender of the person who tried to murder her.

On the afternoon of December 19, 1902, as de Cleyre was getting onto a Philadelphia streetcar, one of her former students, a cigar-maker named Herman Helcher, tugged on de Cleyre's sleeve. She turned around, and he shot one bullet in her chest just above the heart, and two more in her torso. De Cleyre dragged her pierced body for one block and collapsed on a doorstep. Against all odds, she survived.[29] Helcher, as it turned out, was suffering from psychosis due to uric acid poisoning in his blood-stream. "I have no resentment towards the man," de Cleyre dictated to the Philadelphia-based journal *North American*, after she had recovered. "If society were so constituted as to allow every man, woman and child to lead a normal life there would be no violence in this world. It fills me with horror to think of the brutal acts done in the name of government. Every act of violence finds its echo in another act of violence. The policeman's club breeds criminals. Contrary to public understanding, Anarchism means 'Peace on earth, good will to men.'"[30]

A year earlier in 1901, Emma Goldman, like de Cleyre, also found herself defending a murderer—with higher political stakes. The man was a twenty-eight-year-old Polish American farmhand named Leon Czolgosz. He called himself an anarchist, but he was, in fact, a delirious misanthrope who railed against everything—voting, marriage, and taxes. After once hearing Goldman speak in Cleveland in 1901, the troubled young man, who had once been a steelworker at the Cleveland Rolling Mill, but lost his job during the economic crash of 1893, became obsessed with murdering the sitting president of the United States, Republican William McKinley. This is precisely what Czolgosz attempted to do on September 6, 1901, in Buffalo, New York, at four o'clock in the afternoon. Six months into his second term, McKinley, in top hat and long black overcoat, was meet-ing New York constituents at a public reception at a world's fair called the Pan-American Exposition, held at the Temple of Music. Czolgosz, holding a revolver covered with a white handkerchief, walked up to the president. McKinley, assuming the man wanted a greeting, reached out for a handshake. What he got instead was two bullets in his stomach. The sixty-year-old McKinley initially survived, but the gangrene infection caused by the bullet's exit wounds ensured his death eight days later.

Goldman only learned of Leon Czolgosz after the shooting, in the next morning's papers. That was when the front pages blamed "Red Emma" for inciting McKinley's attempted assassination. After seeing what hap-pened to Berkman after his failed attempt on Frick's life, Goldman had, by then, long soured on violence as a means for revolutionary struggle. But after Goldman was arrested by Buffalo police on September 10, 1901, she said that felt bad for "the boy in Buffalo." He is "a creature at bay," she said. "Millions of people are ready to spring on him and tear him limb from limb."[31] It wasn't just kind-heartedness, but political thinking that animated Goldman's defense of Czolgosz. Once government can control the narrative about its friends and enemies, foreign and domestic, it can exert more power upon all its citizens.

After two weeks of questioning, Goldman was released from police custody. But neither Goldman's innocence nor her empathy for Czolgosz could save him from the electric chair on October 29, 1901. It was only two years later when the true damage of McKinley's assassination became apparent: Congress passed the Immigration Act of 1903, which treated political dissidents like anarchists in the same category as sex traffickers, beggars, and epileptics—providing justification and discretion for immigration officials to restrict entry to migrants and deport those already here.

■　■　■

By 1901, Emma Goldman had acquired a reputation as the most famous anarchist in America since the Haymarket Martyrs, four of the eight anarchists executed by the state on what came to be known as Black Friday, November 11, 1887. This occurred after they were found guilty of detonating an explosive device in Chicago on May 4, 1886. Lucy Parsons, a widow of one of the Haymarket Martyrs, Albert Parsons, wasn't happy with Goldman's ascendance. A Black woman of mahogany complexion, Lucy Parsons was born to enslaved Africans in Virginia in 1851 and also claimed to have Mexican and Indigenous heritage. For her part, Parsons never explicitly took up the cause of Black people. (In Chicago, where she lived and organized from 1873, they made up only 1 percent of the population—four thousand out of four hundred thousand—in the 1880s.)[32] But anti-Black racism didn't ignore Parsons. Police patrol wagons known as "Black Marias," clanging their warning bells to announce their dominion over the German immigrant Chicago neighborhood where she worked as a seamstress, were quick to single her out as she strolled the horse excrement–filled roads and visited the polluted Chicago River to get relief on scorching August days.[33] Or when Parsons would walk the sidewalks as a traveling day-peddler, selling coffee, soap, and colorful spices from a rickety horse-drawn wagon.

Unlike Goldman, Lucy Parsons was a partisan of organizing—she liked trade unions and small cooperative groups. This position rankled many of her anarchist friends. But Parsons believed class solidarity couldn't be forged through organization alone. Working people, she believed, needed a taste of dignity. To do this, she arranged what came to be known as "monster picnics." A memorable one took place on June 16, 1878. This was the one-year anniversary of the commencement of the Great Railroad Strike of 1877, which cost thirty-five Chicago workers their lives. On the lawn of a Chicago park, people were eating popcorn, dancing, and riding the merry-go-round. Parsons's husband, Albert, tried to interrupt the festivities to give an impassioned political speech. Everyone was having so much fun, hardly anyone paid attention.[34]

Parsons didn't like Emma Goldman. One of the reasons was personal. She despised Goldman's longtime lover and booking agent for her speaking engagements, Ben Reitman. Reitman was known around Chicago for organizing Hobo College, a mutual aid society that provided migrant workers with free schooling and warm meals. Parsons would never forget what happened on January 17, 1908, at Chicago's Brand Hall. At a meeting of five hundred people, the crowd spontaneously began to chant her name, calling for her to discuss how the people should commemorate the third anniversary of "Bloody Sunday"—the day when hundreds of unarmed protesters were gunned down by the Russian Imperial guard as they were walking to present a petition to Tsar Nicholas in broad daylight. Heeding the crowd's call, Parsons ran up on the stage and declared that she was willing "to lead an army to city hall next Thursday afternoon." Reitman, overseeing the meeting, interrupted Parsons. "I am sorry to refuse the lady," he said, "but this is strictly a men's meeting, and we don't want women speakers."[35] A notorious womanizer who had "bedroom eyes"—he frequently scanned the room for a new tryst wherever he was—Reitman was an insufferable blowhard. The civil libertarian Roger Baldwin, known for his decorum, once described him as a "terrible man," with "no sense of humor," "vulgar."[36] Reitman wore a faded top hat, a cheap bowtie, and a well-worn three-piece suit. He wanted to appear like a tramp even though he was a highly educated Chicago gynecologist known for his experimental treatments of venereal disease.

Parsons herself was no deferential lady. She had no problem living unmarried to a much younger man, Martin Robert Lacher. She dressed like a rebel in a Berlin twill jacket, French heels, and a Gainsborough black hat with a half-dozen decorative feathers. Yet, Parsons would also sound like a run-of-the-mill first-wave feminist with statements such as,

"Family life, child life" are the "sweetest words."[37] "We love the names of father, home, and children too well for that," she explained. When it came to her personal life, Parsons didn't always live up to her ideals. She knew that Martin Lacher had abandoned his sick wife and two children to live with her. To make matters worse, Lacher was abusive. In 1891, after they argued at a party in their home, Lacher struck Parsons. After she locked him out of her apartment, Lacher came back with an axe, smashed the door, and wrecked all her furniture.

The heart of the dispute between Goldman and Parsons wasn't Reitman or Lacher. It was the question of love. In a lecture titled "Marriage and Love," which Goldman delivered regularly in 1910, with such emotional force that it made audience members weep openly, she asked, "Love, the strongest and deepest element in all life, the harbinger of hope, of joy, of ecstasy; love, the defier of all laws, of all conventions; love, the freest, the most powerful moulder of human destiny; how can such an all-compelling force be synonymous with that poor little State and Church-begotten weed, marriage?"[38]

Parsons abhorred Goldman's embrace of free love, which Parsons called a "damnable doctrine." Goldman, knowing that Reitman was unapologetically exploiting her tolerance of open relationships, was "bruised from all the wounds of the lack of stability."[39] Friends visited her, and she put on a happy face, but she wondered whether they could see how "the light has gone out of my life. . . . Can't they see my soul twitching in mortal agony?"[40] Yet Goldman championed free love in public. This was because, she believed, it would help to decriminalize sex work and criminalize capitalism. In a rebuke of social reformers who couldn't see the link between the hidden contracts of their own marriages and the contracts made by sex workers, Goldman wrote in "The Traffic of Women" (1910), "It is merely a question of degree whether she sells herself to one man, in or out of marriage, or to many men. Whether our reformers admit it or not, the economic and social inferiority of woman is responsible for prostitution."[41]

One woman moved by these words was a former sex worker from New Kensington, Pennsylvania, named Almeda Sperry, who gave sex education talks in her local school district. Goldman and Sperry became close friends. Eventually, Sperry fell in love with Goldman, though the feeling wasn't mutual. During one night of revelry at a New York party, Reitman interrupted a spirited debate Sperry was having about anarchism with the muckraking journalist Hutchins "Hutch" Hapgood. Reitman loudly fantasized about Hutch and him sexually assaulting her. Reitman turned to Sperry and coarsely asked her how many men she had "fucked."[42] Sperry wasn't against free love. What she *was* against was free love being used to cover up sexism. "Please ask him that, for the sake of the Cause . . . humanity's sake, for his own sake, and the woman's sake—not to begin 'fuck' talk," Sperry pleaded in a 1912 letter to Goldman. "Please ask him to remember that he stands by your side as representing anarchism."[43] Goldman didn't break it off with Reitman. The best she could do when Sperry next visited was to warn Reitman not to taunt her.

◼ ◼ ◼

As Emma Goldman was torturing herself into knots over Ben Reitman in 1912, her old friend, Sasha Berkman, released from prison six years earlier, was working as executive editor of the anarchist journal she founded, *Mother Earth*. (Initially, Goldman wanted to call the magazine *The Open Road*, based on a poem by her hero Walt Whitman, "A Song of the Open Road," from *Leaves of Grass*. But the threat of a copyright infringement lawsuit from Whitman's publisher quickly followed.) *Mother Earth*'s editorial office was Goldman's apartment. In the dining room, leftover plates of beefsteak sat next to reams of paper. In the sleeping quarters, books were piled up on bedsheets and messily stacked in bookcases. *Mother Earth* was as much a product of Goldman's sensibilities as it was of the new global print culture that was shaking up the world. By 1880, there were 186 million copies of newspapers issued every month—compared to 330,000 a century before.[44] If increasing electrification and the wireless telegraph made it possible to communicate messages within hours, the telephone had made it possible within minutes. News wasn't just local but national, if not international, in scope. The distance between Moscow and New York, Boston, and Berlin became negligible. Journalists could now rely on typewriters and make use of widely available train and steamship transport. In 1906, there were six thousand periodicals published in the US alone. The international avant-garde seized this opportunity. *Der Sturm*, a weekly out of Berlin from 1910 to 1914—together with another Berlin-based zine, *Die Aktion*—played a central role in bringing together abstract expressionists and surrealists to discuss craft and politics. Founded in 1913, *Lacerba*, the Italian futurist outfit, was known for the cutting-edge manifestos it shared with its weekly readership.

As the latest iteration in this wave, *Mother Earth* appeared on March 1, 1906. At sixty-four pages long, with a trim size of five by eight inches, it sold for an affordable ten cents. Its small print run of three thousand copies sold out in the first week. The cover of that first issue was an image of a naked Adam and Eve, broken chains laying at their feet, looking at the sunrise ahead. The thousands who subscribed to *Mother Earth* would find pieces on Fyodor Dostoyevsky's *The Brothers Karamazov*, commemorations of the Paris Commune in 1871, theories of the general strike, and profiles of Leon Trotsky at the beginning of the Russian Revolution in 1917. Among its best-known covers were two by the surrealist Emmanuel Radnitzky, otherwise known as Man Ray. One, at the start of the First World War in August 1914, depicts two monsters, "Capitalism" and "Government," fighting over and tearing apart a person, called "Humanity." The other cover, appearing in 1917, featured a flag, the face of which depicts a Civil War battle. Observing the flag are two imprisoned men behind bars—a protest against the hypocrisy of jailing conscientious objectors.

If *Mother Earth* was the written record of the anarchist counterculture, its institutionalization came through anarchist schools. "Ferrer Schools," named after the Spanish anarchist and progressive educator Francisco Ferrer, murdered by a firing squad at a Montjuich prison in Barcelona by the Spanish government on October 13, 1909, sprung up in Philadelphia, Detroit, New Jersey, Denver, and San Francisco, with classes taught in German, Italian, Yiddish, Czech, and Esperanto. The flagship anarchist school, called the Ferrer School, opened in New York, New Year's Day 1911, on 6 St. Mark's Place in the East Village. Save for the ten-day revolutionary experiment of the Paris Commune in 1871 and the three years of revolutionary Catalonia during the Spanish Civil War (1936–39), one could argue that anarchist schools such as the Ferrer School made the most tangible impact on people's lives.

The Ferrer School's adult education program didn't have an organized curriculum. Intellectual freedom was the entire point. Students paid a nominal weekly tuition rate of fifteen cents. Subjects under discussion in the small room were broad. The style was interdisciplinary. American literature—say, the work of Mark Twain's *The Gilded Age* or Henry David Thoreau's *Walden*—was a way into the mechanisms of government. Freudian psychoanalysis was the entry into discussions of surrealist art. Some nights, you could go to the school to watch an amateur musical. Other nights, you might find yourself browsing the stacks of its extensive library or enjoying an exciting book club discussion of one of Goldman's favorites, Henrik Ibsen's *A Doll House*.[45] On the occasional Sunday morning at the Ferrer School, you'd find the aging Sasha Berkman, bespectacled, on the other side of forty with a receding hair line, mustached, dressed in a light gray suit and Panama hat. Berkman would lecture about economics to a group of small children sitting in a circle, legs crossed, and excitedly asking him questions. One observer was thoroughly impressed to see Berkman patiently guiding his young pupils as a relaxed facilitator in discussion.

The *New York Times* warned its readers that the Ferrer School "is turning out, and is intended to turn out, graduates filled with a settled discontent with the present social system and a determination to end it."[46] The progressive Chicago reformer and founder of Hull House, Jane Addams, saw nothing of this sort when she arrived to observe a class. Addams, who was often invited to visit President Woodrow Wilson in Washington, DC, was no radical. Yet she was pleasantly surprised to find an "innocent affair." What she saw was a young male teacher in the back of a nondescript saloon cultivating the critical thinking skills of roughly two hundred kids. At no point was he indoctrinating them in atheism or violence.[47]

To be sure, the Ferrer School wasn't entirely innocent. The quiet Lithuanian janitor who worked at its newly expanded location on 104 East Twelfth Street in 1912 once decapitated a pesky cat in front of the kids to let them taste the hardships of life.[48] One could imagine better ways to get this point across. But this anecdote is illustrative of a larger point: anarchists thought children could handle uncomfortable situations. A dead cat wasn't the worst these students had seen. Many of them knew someone involved in, or at least had heard of, the deadliest workplace disaster in American history, which happened several blocks away from school in the Asch Building next to Washington Square Park.

On March 25, 1911, at 4:40 p.m. a fire broke out at the Triangle Shirtwaist Factory. One hundred and twenty-three women and twenty-three men burned to death. The reason they couldn't escape the flames was because they couldn't flee their workstations. The doors to the stairwell were bolted shut because management wanted to prevent cigarette breaks and what they perceived to be long lunches. Among the dead were several children: an eleven-year-old girl, two fourteen-year-olds, and three fifteen-year-olds. The fire itself came on the heels of a three-months-long strike by New York's garment workers in late 1909. In addition to higher wages and union representation, the workers wanted to abolish the cruel practice of locking doors from the outside. Management refused. Astonishingly, the Triangle Fire wasn't unique. In 1911, the US experienced six hundred thousand industrial accidents per year.[49]

Ferrer School students thus got what Triangle Shirtwaist managers denied their seamstresses: freedom. "Only in freedom," Goldman wrote in an essay, "can man grow to his full stature. Only in freedom will he learn to think and move, and give the very best in him. Only in freedom will he realize the true force of the social bonds which knit men together, and which are the true foundation of a normal social life."[50]

The Ferrer School's pedagogy was unlike anything school-aged children were accustomed to. New York public schools, at the time, required rote memorization from pupils to instill obedience and docility, the key traits on the garment line. Students were pitted against one another for the best marks. They were punished when they misbehaved. At the Ferrer School, however, students had freedom to come and go as they pleased from 9:30 a.m. to 3 p.m. They could sit where they wanted to when they arrived, play with whom they wished, and read whatever they found interesting. Once, a young girl decided to skip rope in the back of class while the head teacher of the lower school, Will Durant—who would later become internationally famous in the 1920s for selling millions of copies of *The Story of Philosophy*—was holding court on Darwinian evolution in the front of the class. On afternoons that students weren't immersed in work in the carpentry shop, Durant would take them to Stuyvesant Park on Second Avenue. To learn about pre-colonial, non-European cultures of the Global South, students took regular field trips to the Museum of Natural History. When discussing the Lawrence Textile Strike of 1912, students were asked to pull out a map, with pencil in hand, to trace the route from New York to Massachusetts.[51]

The Ferrer School's spirit of unbridled freedom, however, could not expunge the reactionary impulses of its teachers. Will Durant, drunk on Friedrich Nietzsche's philosophy of the superman, believed the Ferrer School crushed the masculine instinct he so admired in his young male pupils. "To ask the boy to repress his interest in war and battle is to ask him to be untrue to himself," he confessed. "It is to fly in the face of the libertarian principle; it is to confess at the outset that the libertarian principle is not sound. Let that wholesome barbarian instinct take its part in the molding of the child."[52] In May 1913, after eighteen months as director of the lower school, Durant quit his position to allow his barbarian instincts to roam free. At twenty-eight, Durant seduced a fifteen-year-old former Ferrer School student named Ariel. They were engaged to be married. As they were about to elope in City Hall on New Year's Eve 1913, Ariel arrived in roller skates, frazzled hair, and torn stockings (it was apparent to everyone she was just a child). As she stood with Durant before a New York City judge who was about to legalize their marriage, the judge wagged his finger and reminded Durant: "Remember, you're not to sleep with her until she's sixteen!"[53]

▪ ▪ ▪

Sasha Berkman's involvement in the New York Ferrer School may have softened him, though it did little to assuage his belief in revolutionary violence. "I am sick of the appeal to legality. It is high time to begin to fight Satan with his own hell fire," he fumed in *Mother Earth*, in response to yet another bloody event in American labor history, "An eye for an eye. A tooth for a tooth."[54] This was what Berkman wrote after the Ludlow Massacre.

In Ludlow, Colorado, on April 20, 1914, twenty-six men, women, and children were murdered by machine guns on the fields of Colorado Fuel and Iron Company, owned by robber baron titan of industry John D. Rockefeller. The shots came from a coalition of private and state forces of the Colorado National Guard, who were sent to break a monthslong coal miner strike. When the journalist John Reed went to Ludlow ten days after the massacre, reporting for the July 1914 edition of the *Metropolitan*, he was stunned. Stoves were filled with uneaten and rotting food. Ashen clothing was blending in with abandoned silverware. Children's toys, sprawled all over the place, were pierced with bullets. All that remained of the improvised tent colony set up by the coal miners was the smell of abandonment. A miner's wife recounted the horror to Reed: "When I come up again in the night, the tents burning and women and children burning alive, screaming, and I don't know what else. My husband is shot in the back when he is running away because he does not know the customs of this country; and why they should shoot at us, God knows."[55]

Ludlow reminded many of the Homestead Strike in 1892. Between June 22 and July 3, 1914, a group met at the Ferrer Center to plan their retaliation, settling on a plot to bomb Rockefeller's Pocantico Hills mansion in upstate New York. Although there was no evidence that tied Berkman to the planning and organizing of the attack, many of his associates would suspect that, even if he wasn't involved with making the bomb and organizing the plan, he certainly knew of it beforehand. Three of the conspirators, all young men, went to Tarrytown to scope out the location of Rockefeller's mansion. Rockefeller wasn't there. He had already left on a vacation trip to Maine. Looking to recalibrate, the trio came back to the New York apartment of another co-conspirator, Louise Berger. They stored the bomb there temporarily while they planned their next move.

The next morning, at 9:16 a.m., as Louise Berger walked to meet Berkman at the new headquarters of *Mother Earth* on 119th Street, not far from her apartment, the bomb exploded. Residents heard the sound from blocks away. The upper three floors of the six-story tenement where Berger lived were decimated. The fire escape was twisted, and bits of destroyed furniture were blown into the air. Four people died—all of them in Berger's apartment, all of them anarchists. Twenty more were injured. The horrific violence from Ludlow was, in fact, restaged in New York, but not how anarchists had imagined it. It wasn't against Rockefeller; it was against their own.

On the day of the bombing, Sasha Berkman was questioned by New York police. Cool and calm, he said he knew nothing about the plan. Upon release from the precinct, Berkman held a memorial to honor the dead at Union Square. Ten thousand people attended. "I hope that our comrades were manufacturing the bomb that caused their death and that they hoped to use it against our enemies," he said.[56] Berkman got the last word, but the Ferrer School was finished in New York. Police continued to spy on meetings, and an air of suspicion ensnared everything. It relocated across the river to Stelton, in central New Jersey.[57]

CHAPTER 3

PATRONS OF THE REVOLUTION

I n spring 1913, Emma Goldman was giving a mid-week lecture on the second floor of a large apartment on 23 Fifth Avenue in Greenwich Village. It was the home of a thirty-three-year-old socialite named Mabel Dodge. Dodge was holding her "Tuesday Evening" literary salon. In this sprawling home tailor-made for the best of old-world European aristocrats, the rooms were sparkling with light. Scotch was flowing generously. Waitstaff circulated freely, carrying plates of imported cheese. The conversation was, by turns, bombastic and combative. Street poets with no formal education mixed with physicians who were unwinding after seeing patients all day. Diplomats chatted up artists dappled in paint and streaked with grime, after hours of intensive focus at their makeshift studios.

At Mabel Dodge's Tuesday Evenings, the muckraking journalist Hutchins Hapgood would be in heated conversation with his mentor, Lincoln "Steff" Steffens, about the folly of US imperial desires in Latin America and the recent travails of the US labor movement. The art dealer of the 291 Gallery, a small fourth-floor space on Fifth Avenue, Alfred Stieglitz, would be feverishly discussing his newest acquisition—whether an Alvin Coburn photograph or a Francis Picabia painting. Stieglitz would be talking to a young man named Walter Lippmann, barely out of Harvard University, who liked art, but was more worried about the great danger of mass public opinion. The distinguished guests came from different walks of life, but they all shared Stieglitz's maxim that art was not for "art's sake—but for life's sake."[1] These were the Village bohemians.

Bohemians were great partiers. During all-night dress balls called "Pagan Routs," organized to support the Liberal Club in 1914, Goldman, on one theme night called the "Red Revel," would be dressed in black as a nun. She would be moving her legs back and forth on the dance floor doing what she called the "Anarchist's Slide." At another party, the poet Harry Kemp would appear as an ancient monarch. His royal crown was a rusty tin washbasin. A group of "New Pagans" held weekly sex parties by invitation only. The classically trained ballerina Isadora Duncan invited Villagers to join her in performing her rendition of modern dance. By this she meant they needed to be barefoot and dressed in a toga.[2] Goldman's onetime lover, Hippolyte Havel, once put it this way: "Greenwich Village is a state of mind, it has no boundaries."[3]

Bohemians called themselves "rebels" and "insurgents," and signed their letters, "Yours for revolution."[4] The men wore soft-flannel and corduroy shirts. Pastel green was a common color, orange ties were in vogue. Women were decked out in peasant dresses and sandals. Some of them preferred to wear their hair in the style of a bird's nest, while others liked to keep it shortly cropped.[5]

Bohemians would grab fifteen-cent lunches at Mother Bertolotti's (five cents for bread and soup, five more for a cheap glass of red wine, and another five for a tip to the servers). The more sophisticated among them would visit tea rooms like the Mad Hatter, where they would eat whole-grain bread. Most of them would get drunk at the Hell Hole. They were socially minded but unafraid of being sarcastic. A conversation snippet in a cartoon from a popular leftist magazine at the time captures this dichotomy: "Did you know that I am an Anarchist and a Free-lover?" went one conversation. "Oh, Indeed—I thought you were a Boy Scout."[6] Looking back on his Village bohemian life, Max Eastman recalled, "There was a sense of universal revolt and regeneration, of the just before dawn of a new day in American art and literature and living-of-life as well as politics."[7]

The bohemian ambition was to fuse the personal and political. What this meant was thinking psychoanalytically. Although the Austrian psychiatrist Sigmund Freud's *Interpretation of Dreams* (1900) received little attention in Europe when the book was first published, it became gospel in the Village after Freud delivered his 1909 lectures at Clark University in Massachusetts. Freud himself didn't like America. After he returned home to Europe, an ongoing joke of his was to describes his chronic intestinal disease as his "American indigestion." Max Eastman, who once visited

Freud on the second floor of his Vienna apartment at Bergstrasse 19, asked him what many were wondering at the time: Did he hate America? "I don't hate it. I regret it," Freud answered. "The prudery, hypocrisy, the national lack of independence, there is not independence in America."[8]

Yet, Eastman, who himself was undergoing psychoanalysis in New York by the Freudian analyst Beatrice M. Hinkle in 1915, explained the appeal of Freud among his friends. Psychoanalysis was a way to help "people of neurotic constitution," who have "never broken away, in the depths of their hearts, from the family situation . . . dominated by . . . repressed love, or a repressed hate."[9] (According to family lore, Hinkle helped none other than Franklin Delano Roosevelt gain confidence after he contracted polio in 1921, and was so friendly with his wife, Eleanor, that she later attended two White House award dinners.)[10] Freud's theory of free association was exciting for artists, who thought journeying to the recesses of their unconscious—with its cruel superego and unbridled id—would enrich their work. Freudianism became so fashionable, said playwright Susan Glaspell, "you could not go out to buy a bun [in the Village] without hearing of someone's complex."[11]

If Emma Goldman had been on the couch, she might have asked her analyst whether her interest in going to lavish parties like Mabel Dodge's was a product of her repressive childhood. What did it mean that Goldman, who lectured at dilapidated gymnasiums and modest banquet halls, was there at the ostentatious Dodge salon? Here, Goldman was surrounded by expensive white wallpaper, linen curtains, painted wood, a marble mantelpiece, a bearskin rug, delicate pastel antique chairs from Europe, velvet cushions, and blown glass on the mantel. Was Goldman selling out her radical credentials? Was she an opportunist? A savvy self-promoter?

The answer is far from clear, and subject to debate. What is clear was that Mabel Dodge, the only child of a wealthy Buffalo banking family, who would greet her guests outfitted in silk, wanted Goldman around. This was because Dodge was a romanticizer of revolution—Goldman's words, she said, "counted . . . had authority . . . rang true."[12] To escape the dreary domestic life of a housewife, Dodge, a short, gregarious women, would take afternoon joyrides in a privately chauffeured car with her trademark long robes and serpentine scarves into the slums of the Lower East Side. This, after enjoying prepared lunches in her stately mansion. Dodge wanted a taste—from a safe distance, of course—of how poor people lived.

Rich benefactors of bohemia like Dodge loved the idea of individual freedom but didn't want it to be connected to economic redistribution. That's why they embraced radical art. In what was seen as one of her greatest achievements, Dodge organized the landmark Sixty-Ninth Street Armory modernist show on the Upper East Side on February 17, 1913. It was attended by eighty-seven thousand over its four-week run. Its display of 1,368 works of European and American impressionists, cubists, surrealists, and Dadaists created a citywide scandal. Modernists like Kandinsky, Braque, Cezanne, Modigliani, Renoir, and Van Gogh, said the traditionalist critics enthralled with the High Renaissance masters, weren't suitable for New York.

Dodge was pleased with the Armory show for the very reason critics were enraged by, for instance, a piece like Marcel Duchamp's *Nude Descending a Staircase*, which they nicknamed "Rude Descending a Staircase." Critics said Duchamp's *Nude* was a panoply of abstract shapes, blocks, slabs, and rectangles, barely hanging together. Dodge disagreed. "Riot and revolution" is what it would create, Dodge wrote to her friend, the modernist poet Gertrude Stein, whom Dodge knew from her time in France and whose simple, concise poetic verse—"rose is a rose is a rose is a rose"—was, like Duchamp's cubism, a way to "induce new states of consciousness."[13]

■　■　■

Sometimes, however, the bohemians' philosophy of art for art's sake was betrayed by the way bohemian art itself reimagined life, which could become the springboard for political thinking. No one exemplified this contradiction more than Alfred Stieglitz, the father of American art photography.

Alfred Stieglitz was the son of assimilated German Jewish immigrants. His father was a successful dry-goods businessman who emigrated from Germany in 1849 and enlisted in the Union Army in 1861 during the US Civil War. Unlike his father, the young Alfred didn't love his homeland; he only loved himself. Self-absorbed, sure of himself, and witty to a fault, Stieglitz dreamed of standing out from his large extended family. (He had only four siblings but thirty-two first cousins.) For the teenage Stieglitz, rebellion meant wearing fashionable ties, keeping unkempt hair, and not caring about money.

Stieglitz harnessed his antiestablishment feelings after visiting Germany in the 1880s. That was where he discovered photography, as he said, "first as a toy, then as a passion, then as an obsession."[14] Above all else, photography offered Stieglitz the ability to distill life in its essence. Although the camera lens acted as a filter, it would still retain the subjective experience of the artist, who would find the composite elements of an image in the world. Photography, for Stieglitz, was the perfect way to capture stream of consciousness thought and the disarray of time, space, and human bodies in motion.

In 1903, after spending time with the New York Society of Amateur Photographers, whom he disparaged as unserious, Stieglitz started his own journal, *Camera Work*. The journal gave him the platform to spread his gospel of "straight" photography—no frills, no production studios, all feeling. Everything was to be spontaneous and ephemeral. Authentic experience, in the photograph, was to be elevated above all else. The price of such authenticity, ironically, was for the photographer to be immobile, to stage themselves outside the image. The photographer would need to be ready to receive the moment. Stieglitz would brag to friends that it would take him not days, but years, to be happy about the correct composition of a scene. He would stay for hours at one particular spot in search of the right image.

Thought Stieglitz was personally more interested in questions of aesthetics than questions of immigration policy, class, or nationalism, his photography nonetheless reimagined these political ideas. One of his earliest photos, *Winter, Fifth Avenue* (1893), taken on Thirty-Fifth Street and Fifth Avenue, depicts a coachman on a cab, pulled by two horses, heading straight toward the viewer through a pile of snow, which lies several inches deep. The haze of the image and the blurring of the subject is intentional. Stieglitz uses a long exposure to soften the image and highlight the motion. In so doing, he stresses the dignity of labor and laborers, as they anonymously cut through the streets of a merciless city.

Other street photographers during this time, like the Danish American Jacob Riis, used explosive flashes to stress the harsh grime and dirt on the clothing of poor immigrants—to emphasize their alienness. In his 1890 work of photojournalism, *How the Other Half Lives*, Riis chronicled the manure-filled streets that mixed with the pushcart food vendors in what he called "Jewtown," or, on Tenth Street, "Typhus Ward." This was a city, as Riis put it, not "fit" for Christian men and women.[15]

Stieglitz didn't share Riis's racism, and, unlike Riis, sought to make photography a means through which to highlight people's humanity. At times, however, Stieglitz, like many bohemians, sometimes romanticized poverty. At night, as Stieglitz left the fledgling printing business he owned in the 1890s and walked down to the East River, past the Tombs (the city's jail), he was "fascinated" by the streets. "Wherever I looked there was a picture that moved me," he explained, "the derelicts, the secondhand clothing shops, the rag pickers, the tattered and the torn."[16] But his voyeurism would not allow for a condescending view of his subjects. Consider his 1893 photo of New York's immigrant slum, *Five Points, New York*—the setting of which was three miles southeast of the setting for *Winter, Fifth Avenue*. Jacob Riis wanted Five Points razed by the city. (It was, ultimately, in 1897, when Mulberry Road was converted into a park.) But Stieglitz elevates it. There's a crowd of men in dark coats, standing on snow, their bodies lined up, away from the camera, blocking a narrow road. A young girl stands before them, to the side. Her back is facing us, as she's prancing through the street. Stieglitz isn't asking us to pity these newcomers—the photo was originally entitled *A New Importation*. He's connecting it to a larger study of everyday life, its ups and downs. Nothing to see here, the photo says, apart from a batch of people, just doing their thing. This is assimilation in the finest sense—where you, as the viewer, are assimilating your viewpoint to the humanity of the photographer's subject; they're not doing anything for you.

This idea is also the force behind Stieglitz's photograph *The Steerage* (1907). This image depicts immigrant passengers aboard the *Kaiser Wilhelm II* on two decks. Critics who first saw the photo thought that the image was of immigrants, in hats and suits, coming to America. But they're leaving America—part of a reverse migration of four million out of sixteen million immigrants who returned home, between 1890 and 1930.[17] The fact that coming and going, leaving and arriving are indistinguishable from each other in *The Steerage* cuts against the racist myth of the dirty, diseased, job-taking foreigner who is living off government handouts. *The Steerage* centers a cosmopolitan sensibility over a nationalist one. Perhaps there was more to Stieglitz's politics than he let on. After all, after having a "great talk" with Emma Goldman at a play in the Village in 1916, he lavished her with praise, calling her "a doer—a great women. It was interesting to compare notes."[18]

Although bohemian art often exalted marginalized citizens, sometimes the line between celebration and exoticism was blurred. Take the example of the photographer Gertrude Käsabier, whose work appeared in the first issue of *Camera Work*. The Pratt College–trained Käsabier was born in Iowa in 1852 and grew up in Leadville, Colorado, among silver miners. So moved was Käsabier by a "Wild West" parade marching below her New York apartment window that she felt transported to the Western frontier of her youth. This event prompted her to invite Native American performers to her New York studio so that she could stage one of her most famous photos, *The Red Man* (1900). Appearing on heavy tan paper, the image is a close-cropped portrait of an Indigenous man with a blanket partially covering his face. Stieglitz went outside to take pictures, but Käsabier only dug deep into the depths of her pockets to pay subjects, and then, into the recesses of her romanticized memory, as she recalled "the bands of roving red men, still free to come and go at will, never a thought of reservations."[19] If only she had bothered to go a few blocks from her apartment, on West Broadway, where she would meet small communities of Sioux and Iroquois, alive in the flesh. Perhaps then her photos might have been different.

A major goal of bohemian art was to decenter perception. Few devoted themselves more to this project than the Cubist artist Max Weber. Born to an Orthodox Jewish family in Białystok, Russia, in 1881, the twenty-eight-year-old painter arrived in New York in 1909 after spending three years in Paris, studying with Henri Matisse at Couvent des Oiseaux on the Rue de Sevres. Part of Stieglitz's inner circle, Weber was the first to recommend that Stieglitz buy a relatively unknown nude painting of a Spanish artist by the name of Pablo Picasso in 1909. Weber was particularly impressed by the Spaniard's decomposition of something as sanctified as the human body into squares and rectangles. (However, art buyers were less enthusiastic. In 1911, Picasso's American debut of eighty-three drawings was a dud—only one of his pieces was sold at Stieglitz's 291 Gallery.)

Abstraction was Weber's aesthetic preference; his work would take real places to unexpected dimensions. *The Chinese Restaurant* (1915) rearranges patterns from a Chinese restaurant in Manhattan—the red, gold, and black of a tablecloth—alongside cutouts of what appear to be drawings from newspapers. *Rush Hour, New York* (1915) overlays elevated and underground subways with shapes that recall New York skyscrapers, embodying the fast pace of city life. *Grand Central Terminal*, also painted in 1915, uses the frenzied juxtaposition of objects that look like buildings, pedestrians, and iron to tell the story of an American melting pot. The color pallet of *Grand Central Terminal* is dull, but the experience is anything but. Without hearing anything, you hear everything. Human figures are absent in Weber's work, but the viewer is enraptured by the delightful speed and sounds of things—a metaphor for the cacophony of modernity.

Weber's great achievement is to insist that, to humanize the world, you may not need realism—which is to say, representations of human beings doing human things. Art can humanize the world through shapes, things, and objects. The artist who showed this to be possible, through representations of flowers, was Stieglitz's wife, Georgia O'Keeffe.

The correspondence between Stieglitz and O'Keeffe first began in 1908, when Stieglitz was fifty-two and O'Keeffe was a twenty-eight-year-old art teacher in Texas. O'Keeffe admired the 291 Gallery from afar, but soon became enthralled by Stieglitz's open-mindedness—especially his view that women were central to the modernist avant-garde because, when they "throw off the male shackles," they imbue art with the "deepest feeling."[20] Stieglitz's 291 Gallery was a far distance from O'Keeffe's Midwestern roots on a small farm in Sun Prairie, Wisconsin, where she was born in 1887. But by the time she arrived in New York (her first show was at the 291 Gallery in 1917), she already had a unique feminist aesthetic. O'Keeffe liked to roll up her sleeves, with her short hair covered in a kerchief. Bowler hats and trench coats were staples in her extensive wardrobe. She scoffed at lace dresses. She liked to wear black not because it was chic, but because she didn't want to be bothered with choosing from different colors.

It wasn't long before O'Keeffe recognized that her painting was as political as her style. For one, O'Keeffe was intervening in a male-dominated space with a standpoint as a woman. "I decided I was a very stupid fool not at least to paint as I wanted to and say what I wanted to when I painted," O'Keeffe recalled.[21] At the time, women were expected to look nice, clean the house, and raise the kids. Not paint in general. Not paint abstractions. Not paint abstractions that looked like flowers, which resembled women's vulvas. In her work, O'Keeffe unapologetically asserts women's sexual desire. "I have no hesitancy in contending that my painting of a flower may be just as much a project of this age as a cartoon about the freedom of women—or the working class—or anything else."[22]

The working class was of central concern to bohemians, but few of them, like O'Keeffe, came directly from it. The closest many bohemians got to direct action to help the working class was through what came to be known as the "Paterson Strike Pageant." The idea emerged in April 1913, when "Big Bill" Haywood, cofounder of the Industrial Workers of the World (IWW) union, entered Dodge's salon with his large boots, massive body, partially blind right eye, and raspy voice, which had a Western twang. Haywood wasn't only looking to party that night; he was bringing news from the front line of the class war, just across the river in Paterson, New Jersey. It was in Paterson that the IWW, known as the "Wobblies," was aiding thousands of silk workers, who were striking for an eight-hour workday. The New Jersey silk workers were already two months into their work stoppage. The attendees at Dodge's salon were captivated by Haywood, who had firsthand experience of anarcho-syndicalism. A year earlier, he had been involved in the Lawrence Textile Strike in 1912. The Lawrence millowner, Haywood said, was explicit about how capitalism worked: "Any man who pays more for labor than the lowest sum he can get men for is robbing his stockholders. If he can secure $6 [per week] and pays more, he is stealing from the company."[23] In response, Haywood organized twenty thousand Italian, Canadian, Jewish, and Polish workers for a citywide strike that lasted for nine weeks and, when it concluded, won increased wages from management.[24]

After hearing Haywood hold court about his experiences that evening at Dodge's, a young exuberant poet named John Reed jumped up out of his chair. Up until then, Reed's claim to fame was that he was the Harvard University classmate of Walter Lippmann and T. S. Eliot. His father, a progressive Oregonian, was close friends with Lincoln Steffens. Since arriving to New York in 1910, Reed had felt adrift. He would spend days aimlessly wandering the streets, walking from the skyscrapers downtown all the way to the East River. Amid the clamor of pushcarts, he would hear drunken sailors talking to sex workers, who were standing next to drug dealers. Reed was pessimistic that socialism would ever arrive in America.

But things changed that April night at Mabel Dodge's. Reed had a brilliant idea. His green eyes were ablaze, his trademark short, brown curls were lifting in flight. Reed proclaimed that his friends ought to stage a pageant about the ongoing Paterson strike, as it was unfolding, a first of its kind in US history! The play, Reed explained, was to be performed by actual Paterson strikers, with the aim of providing financial support and media attention for their cause. New York City would be the setting, depicting the war between capital and labor. "Everything is to be found here," Reed said.

A month later, on May 19, 1913, Bill Haywood introduced Reed to the Paterson strikers, who shared with him their account of the first day of the strike. The morning, they told him, had begun in fear, but the day ended in defiant song. Perfect, thought Reed. This would be the opening act of the play, the first of six.

After a few weeks of rehearsal, the day before the play, 1,147 Paterson strikers took a train across the Hudson. They were led by a seventeen-year-old girl, a weaver named Hannah Silverman, in a march down Fifth Avenue. The next day, on June 7, 1913, at 8:30 p.m. at Madison Square Garden, large crowds lined up to watch the spectacle. Many were turned away, and only fifteen thousand were allowed to stay inside the packed auditorium free of charge. Three thousand of the audience members were Paterson strikers, of which one thousand stood on their feet. The audience witnessed the drama unfold in front of a two-hundred-foot-long backdrop of a large mill, painted by the illustrator John Sloan. The center aisle of Madison Square Garden became a Paterson city street.[25]

The show, by all accounts, was spectacular. But the revolution? It never materialized. In fact, the do-it-yourself production, whose costs become more exorbitant by the day and which was financed by a small pot of money from Paterson strikers and bohemians themselves, ran a sizable deficit of several thousand dollars. It was a good thing bohemians rejected the profit motive. There were no profits to be made. And even if there had been, the real Paterson strike across the river was crushed a few weeks later, in July 1913.

■   ■   ■

A woman named Margaret Sanger left the Paterson Pageant disappointed. She was a slight, soft-spoken nurse with gray eyes and auburn hair. It was in her New York uptown apartment where John Reed and the organizers of the Paterson Pageant met up on a weekly basis. Sanger's husband, William, an architect and painter, was a committed socialist who knew Eugene V. Debs. Margaret described Sasha Berkman as "the gentle anarchist," and Bill Haywood, "a bull about to plunge in the arena." The Sangers had just arrived in New York City from the suburban town of Hastings-on-Hudson with their two young children. Margaret was looking to exchange a life of perfume-filled dance parties and quiet evenings on the croquet court for a life of engagement with the IWW. Stuart, her eldest child, attended the Ferrer School. For Sanger, however, the Paterson Strike Pageant failed not only because it didn't accomplish its revolutionary goal but because of whose interests it left out:

> The pageant was a fitting conclusion to one period of my life. I was thoroughly despondent after the Paterson debacle, and had a sickening feeling that there was to be no end; it seemed to me the whole question of strikes for higher wages was based on man's economic need of supporting his family, and that this was a shallow principle upon which to found a new civilization. Furthermore, I was enough of a Feminist to resent the fact that woman and her requirements were not being taken into account in reconstructing this new world about which all were talking.[26]

Sanger experienced sexism acutely in ways her male comrades never did. Before she came to New York in 1910, she spent eight months in a Westchester sanatorium for a tubercular condition, which left her more despondent than when she arrived. "Existence there was depression," she confided to a friend.[27] In this state of confinement with her newborn infant daughter, Sanger, the sixth child of eleven, from Corning, New York, was haunted by memories of her doting mother, who was dead at forty-eight from tuberculosis. She remembered her father, who expected the young Margaret to do all the housework and forbade her to ever interact with boys her age, who had once violently slammed the house door in her face because she arrived home later than he allowed.

Margaret Sanger wouldn't be domesticated. She was part of a new social movement called the "New Woman." The New Woman let her hair down if she liked. She cut it short if she wanted. She read Nietzsche, Henri Bergson, Marx, and Wollstonecraft alongside romantic poets like Wordsworth and Keats. She was not afraid to read Marquis de Sade. The New Woman endorsed sexual liberation and reproductive freedom because she was unafraid of pleasure. She enjoyed her body—an idea advanced at that time by an influential Swedish psychologist, Ellen Key. The New Woman smoked and didn't wear a corset. She yelled in public and was argumentative without apology. She would say "fuck" among friends. The New Woman could have been a wife if she wanted to, but only if she wanted to. Children, for her, were just that, children. Not the primary purpose of her life. Sometimes, she might describe her children as mistakes.

The New Woman came from the ranks of either the 87 percent classified as "unoccupied," or the 13 percent, like Sanger, who worked for a living. The fifty-six thousand women who were enrolled at universities across the country. Birth rates were declining rapidly, and revolutions in technology—gas cookers, electric cookers, mechanized laundries, vacuum cleaners, and electric irons—offered for women the chance to be free from the drudgeries of unpaid domestic labor.[28]

Sanger was one of many New Women living in New York. There was the actress-poet Ida Rauh, a woman of impressive intellect and charisma. "She can move mountains," people said.[29] Rauh once rented a limousine and drove around the Village tossing out birth control pamphlets. The journalist Louise Bryant burned an effigy of President Woodrow Wilson right in front of the White House. The Stanford University–trained Cubist painter Marguerite Zorach would do odd things like throwing dead rats into parked cars, and do so while wearing a stunning silk turban with a red rose in the center.[30] Zorach's home on 123 West Tenth Street wasn't a play space for her two children. It was an invitation for stimulating the unconscious. The apartment was draped in white muslin, punctuated by red floors and yellow walls. Her hallway had a life-sized sculpture of Adam and Eve, standing next to a tree trunk enwrapped by a red and white serpent.

Eleanor Fitzgerald, from Madison, Wisconsin (she was Sasha Berkman's onetime romantic partner, and an assistant editor for *Mother Earth* and *Blast*), was as comfortable raising $15,000 for political prisoners as she was having her dog, a collie named Buff, psychoanalyzed.[31] The novelist Neith Boyce, whose father cofounded the *Los Angeles Times*, was the first woman reporter for the *Commercial Advertiser*. A pessimist without being a defeatist, she was married to but had an open relationship with Hutchins Hapgood. Eventually she realized romantic intimacy wasn't for her. "It was much better," she remarked, "to observe other people's love affairs and write about them."[32]

One of Neith Boyce's great achievements was to cofound the Provincetown Players theater company on 139 MacDougal Street, which from 1916 to 1922 produced one hundred plays by fifty writers. A third of the writers were women, and the most well regarded was Susan Glaspell. Glaspell's women protagonists are New Women—they are emotionally complex but trapped in a patriarchal society that denies their individuality and provokes their righteous rage, which is then, predictably, misinterpreted as madness. Take the amateur botanist Claire Archer in *The Verge* (1921). Claire is disappointed that a new species of plant she has bred, the Edge Vine, isn't "over the edge," as she had hoped but only looks like an ordinary weed. She wants it destroyed, and so, she throws it at her daughter, Elizabeth—a child from Claire's first marriage. Elizabeth wants nothing more than her mother's affection, but Claire is detached from her. Claire despises her sister, Adelaide, a mother of five, who thinks Claire's instincts are unbecoming of a mother and generally "unnatural."[33] Claire pities her husband, Harry, who thinks she's losing her mind and, as a result, invites a neurologist to dinner to have her examined, without her consent. In the concluding scene, Claire strangles her lover, Tom, because he has revealed his true colors by urging her to run away with him to India. He's just like all the other men Claire knows. He's too possessive and can't handle her independence.

A woman who could have easily been a heroine in a Glaspell play was Feminist Alliance founder Henrietta Rodman, a Columbia University-trained high school teacher known for wearing long, loose-fitting coats and making sarcastic remarks. The fifty members of the Feminist Alliance held their first meeting on April 4, 1914, at Rodman's apartment on 315 East Seventeenth Street. Among its aims were to organize opposition to the New York City school board's ban on married women teachers and to lobby President Woodrow Wilson to push for an amendment to the US Constitution that prohibited the denial of one's political or civil rights on the basis of sex.[34]

Rodman liked children. She adopted two while she was single, one of whom was an adult by this time and out as a lesbian. Later, when she was married, she adopted a third child. But Rodman, like Sanger, above all, cared about women's freedom. She designed a twelve-story cooperative, a "Female Apartment," where married women with children could learn professional skills and avoid domestic labor. "We want to see a condition where both men and women may work in their chosen professional life as equals," she explained.[35] The blueprint for the Female Apartment included designs for an in-house laundry, a dressmaking facility, a basement kitchen, a twenty-four-hour nursery, a Montessori school on the roof, a playground, a dumbwaiter that delivered ready-made food in a thermos, and a sick ward.[36] Rodman wanted all of the instructors at the nursery to be college educated, and the teacher/student ratio to be one to six for infants, and one to twenty for older children.

Enthusiasm for the Female Apartment was high. One hundred applications came in for 250 apartments. Rodman even hired an architect and found financial backers from prominent feminists. The Female Apartment, however, was never built because of exorbitant costs. Construction alone would cost over $400,000. A unionized staff to attend to each family would cost $400 per month, and a salaried dietician to prepare food for the residents would cost $3,000 yearly.

At the time, Rodman was a regular at another New Women's consciousness-raising meetup, founded in winter 1912. It was called the "Heterodoxy Club." A good friend of Mabel Dodge's, Marie Jenney Howe, organized a Sunday afternoon lunch at a small basement restaurant called Polly Holladay's, on MacDougal Street in the Village. Howe, who had studied at Unitarian Theological Seminary in Pennsylvania and become involved in pushing the Unitarian Church to include women ministers, had recently moved to New York in 1910 and been active in the suffragette movement. What Howe wanted was to find other like-minded women who shared her feminist sensibility and were interested in debating sexuality, gender, and reproductive rights. "We intend to be ourselves," Howe explained, "not just our little female selves, but our whole human selves."[37] The group was small—about twenty-five inaugural members. Among them were Crystal Eastman, Rose Pastor Stokes, and Zona Gale. Emma Goldman's niece, Stella Comen Ballantine, was also a member. At the beginning of each lunch, a Heterodoxy member would share a little bit of her background—where she came from, what her childhood was like, and what brought here there.

Margaret Sanger lectured at the Heterodoxy Club, but never joined the collective. The problem she had with reformist feminism was that it was preoccupied with middle-class concerns: "Unbelievable that they could be serious in occupying themselves with what I regarded as trivialities when mothers within a stone's throw of their meetings were dying shocking deaths. . . . Hundreds of thousands of laundresses, cloak makers, scrub women, servants, telephone girls, shop workers would have gladly changed places with the Feminists in return for the right to have leisure, to be lazy a little now and then."[38]

Sanger's understanding of gender domination was symbolized through an encounter she had with a Russian Jewish woman named Sadie Sachs. While working as a nurse on Grand Street in the Lower East Side, Sanger gave medical care to the twenty-eight-year-old Sachs, who lived in a cramped three-story tenement. Sachs had lost consciousness trying to induce a self-administered abortion. She already had three children and was terrified of having another. "Another baby will finish me, I suppose," she told Sanger. Turning to the male doctor next to her, Sachs asked him what she could do.

"Tell Jake [her truck-driver husband] to sleep on the roof," the doctor replied, as he picked up his hat and bag and departed.

Tears streamed down Sanger's face. Sachs lifted her pale hands and asked Sanger for help: "He can't understand. He's only a man. But you do, don't you? Please tell me the secret, and I'll never breathe it to a soul. *Please!*"[39]

Three months later, Sanger received a call to return to Sadie Sachs's home. Sachs, who had tried to perform yet another abortion, was in a coma by the time Sanger arrived. She died within ten minutes. That night, as Sanger was walking home, she thought about all the newborns wrapped in day-old newspapers being delivered by poor girls like Sadie Sachs, too young to be mothers and too old to be children themselves, crouching on stone floors. "The scenes piled one upon another on another. I could bear it no longer. . . . It was the dawn of a new day in my life also. . . . I was finished with palliatives and superficial cures; I was resolved to seek out the root of evil, to do something to change the destiny of mothers whose miseries were vast as the sky."[40]

Sanger's newsletter, *The Woman Rebel*, which she launched in 1914, was devoted to the "interests of working women" (employment, reproductive rights, marriage, and childcare). Its slogan was "No Gods, No Masters," lifted directly from IWW posters, which Sanger had distributed in Lawrence, Massachusetts, in 1912. *The Woman Rebel* only lasted eight issues, suffering the same fate as Whitman's *Leaves of Grass*: it was confiscated by the US Post Office under the Comstock Law of 1873, which prohibited the circulation of so-called obscene literature. As a result, Sanger fled to Canada, then to Europe, where she lived incognito under the name of "Bertha

Watson." While living abroad in 1915, she released a hundred thousand copies of a sixteen-page pamphlet that described six safe contraceptive methods, called *Family Limitation.* The pamphlet was distributed through IWW locals in America.

■ ■ ■

Mabel Dodge, at whose weekday salon Sanger was a regular, once described Sanger as a "Madonna type of a woman."[41] Dodge meant this as a compliment—Sanger's gentle demeanor, as one acquaintance put it, "hid her tremendous fighting spirit, the self-generating energy, and the relentless drive that lay beneath it."[42]

Above all, Sanger demanded public recognition for her crusading work. And this desire led her down the path of becoming a booster of eugenics. Panic was widespread among elites about declining birth rates of affluent Anglo-Saxons and increasing immigration of Southern and Eastern Europeans with bigger families. In 1902, the president of Harvard University, Charles W. Eliot, lamented that there were 28 percent fewer undergraduate enrollees than the year before. A later study reported that of the 75 percent of Harvard students who had graduated in the late nineteenth century and gone on to marry, 25 percent of couples were childless. A similar pattern existed at Yale University. Much to the chagrin of their parents, only half of Wellesley College women graduates were married at the turn of the century.[43]

In this climate, Sanger recognized an opportunity. She would align herself with those who called for decreasing the birthrate among populations deemed unfit for reproduction. "As long as civilized communities encourage unrestrained fecundity in the normal members of the population," Sanger declared, "and penalize every attempt to introduce the principle of discrimination and responsibility in parenthood, they will be faced with the ever-increasing problem of feeblemindedness, that fertile parent of degeneracy, crime, and pauperism."[44]

Margaret Sanger wasn't the only prominent New Woman to embrace eugenics. A Heterodoxy regular, the novelist Charlotte Perkins Gilman, was another. In her utopian novel *Herland* (1915), three men accidentally come upon an exceptional all-women community in which reproduction is done parthenogenetically. Herland is technologically advanced. There are electric cars used for transportation, and polluting factories are nowhere to be found. Children are raised collectively. Herland is also free of animal cruelty: feral cats are trained not to hunt birds, and dogs aren't kept as pets. Kitchen-less apartments are widespread.

Gilman wanted to topple masculine rule without dismantling the master's tools. To make Herland run smoothly according to a "mother instinct," "so painfully intense," elites, and only elites, are entrusted with the most precious task of childcare.[45] Everything, from the lush forest to the community's children, is naturally selected to be as "fit" as possible. Herlanders, we learn, have united in "power and wisdom to overcome the 'diseases of childhood'—of which there are none."[46] Eugenics, Gilman insists, will get rid of evil men—the rapists, sexists, misogynists—and breed the most virtuous women. Not only a supporter of eugenics, Gilman also subscribed to racism and xenophobia. In the sequel to *Herland*, *With Her in Ourland* (1916), New York is imagined as "the most ill-assorted and unassimilable mass of human material that ever was held together by artificial means."[47] Judaism, in the book, is described as "morally degrading."[48]

■   ■   ■

Such racism and anti-immigrant sentiment were sky-high by 1917. German Americans were accused of having secret allegiance to Germany during the First World War, and radicalism was associated with Jewish and Italian immigrants in New York. The national feeling of fear and distrust would turn for the worse when the US Congress passed the Espionage Act on June 15, 1917. The act deemed it illegal to agitate against the draft, which had been recently imposed by the Selective Service Act of 1917. The same afternoon, on June 15, 1917, an assistant US attorney, a US marshall, and members of the bomb squad and police department arrived at the *Mother Earth* headquarters. Alexander Berkman and Emma Goldman were arrested for organizing a No-Conscription League, which encouraged conscientious objection to the war.

On July 17, 1917, the postmaster general rendered the August issue of the socialist magazine *The Masses* "unmailable," because one piece, written by its editor, Max Eastman, called for raising funds to support the defense of Goldman and Berkman. Another piece in *The Masses* that inflamed censors was a cartoon by H. J. Glintenkamp, "Conscription," which depicts three naked bodies lying limp and dead. Upon the body of one is etched

"Labor," the other, "Youth," and the other, "Democracy." The three bodies are tied by rope to a cannon, which is stuck in mud. In front of them is a woman dressed in black, on her knees, screaming in grief to the heavens.

The cartoon fit *The Masses*' mission statement. From the time it was founded in 1911, the magazine's goal was to be in "bad taste," to be "arrogant," and "to conciliate nobody, not even our readers."[49] *The Masses*, like the bohemians who constituted its contributors and a large percentage of its subscribers, was as critical in its analysis of America as it was scandalizing in its tone. For this reason, George Bernard Shaw praised *The Masses* in the highest terms, as "a large, freely illustrated Socialist monthly . . . its equal, I should imagine, to any propagandist comic journal in the world. . . . The cruelties and squalors of civilization are not only their subject; social satire has a place. . . . It is a feat."[50] One story, "The Job," features two men who eat rats for a living. A 1915 illustration by Robert Minor, entitled "In Georgia: The Southern Gentleman Demonstrates His Superiority," shows a Jewish man crucified in between two Black men. In another image, "Benediction in Georgia," the artist George Bellows depicts a white minister presiding as a conductor over Black Southerners, who are imprisoned in a chain gang and whose tears are soaking the lithograph's paper.[51] In the Maurice Becker illustration "This Is a Gay World" (1914), an affluent woman, reclining on her lavish velvet couch, beside a doting husband looking lovingly at her, is reading the gossip page—about a yacht race—while the front-page headline reads "Bomb Kills."

As the government's case against *The Masses* moved through the district courts, its thirty-four-year-old editor, Max Eastman—a regular at Dodge's evenings and a friend of John Reed—embarked on the antiwar lecture circuit. Now, Eastman's hope was not, as with the magazine he edited, to scandalize, or to be in bad taste. He wanted to create a wide web of support for his cause.

Eastman was good at getting what he wanted. It wasn't because the six-foot-tall, handsome man was funny and a smooth talker, but because he adjusted his tactics. Eastman was a pragmatist. He had become intimately acquainted with the idea of pragmatism while at Columbia University completing his PhD in philosophy, under the supervision of pragmatism's greatest American philosopher: John Dewey. Dewey, a professor then in his forties, roamed Columbia's halls with torn clothing and disheveled hair. He pushed students to live their life to the fullest.

Eastman was Dewey's teaching assistant, for which he earned a meager stipend of $500 per year.

John Dewey didn't care about appearances, Max Eastman did. But what mattered for both men were results. The pragmatist endorses lived experimentation to find the best outcomes, rather than fixed absolute truths based in preconceived ideas. As Dewey wrote in *Art as Experience* (1934), "For life is no uniform uninterrupted march or flow. It is a thing of histories, each with its own plot, its own inception and movement toward its close, each having its own particular rhythmic movement; each with its own un-repeated quality pervading it throughout."[52]

Pragmatism, in this way, was what led Eastman to start the Men's League for Women's Suffrage of New York State in 1909. It was what made him undergo psychoanalytic treatment in 1916 with the cigar-smoking Freudian Dr. Smith Ely Jelliffe. The psychoanalyst bluntly told Eastman what he didn't want to hear: his socialism was a direct response to his minister father's repressiveness, and his failed marriage to his first wife, Ida Rauh, was a product of unresolved incestuous feelings toward Crystal, with whom he cohabited for a while. (Crystal was also a regular at the Heterodoxy Club and did graduate work in law and economics at Columbia University.)

In 1929, Max Eastman met Sigmund Freud in the master's Vienna apartment. Freud had invited him to discuss Eastman's recently published book on Lenin, psychoanalysis, and the Russian Revolution. Freud liked the book's methods but was dismissive of all political parties and leaders—"I could not have tolerated your great Lenin for ten minutes," he said. Eastman responded by saying that Bolshevism was informed by pragmatism, in that it was only "trying out of an [sic] hypothesis."[53] (Ironically, this thesis can also explain why in the 1950s Eastman, then an anti-Stalinist turned "radical conservative," rationalized Joseph McCarthy's anti-communist purges.)

From the moment Eastman was appointed editor of *The Masses* in 1912, pragmatism defined his tenure there. Monthly sales peaked at forty thousand, but high printing costs, at around $15,000 per year, made the periodical run at a perpetual deficit. As a result, Eastman became a prolific fundraiser, turning to costume balls and donations from the rich. Floyd Dell, its managing editor, called this unsavory reality the "skeleton in our proletarian revolutionary closet."[54]

To counteract the magazine's unsavory dependence upon funds from the bourgeoisie, Dell tried to convince Eastman to accept a democratic editorial process. For a while, pieces were chosen through monthly editorial meetings held on Thursday nights. Eastman and Dell read submitted manuscripts aloud, without letting anyone know the author's identity. Decisions on which jokes to include were subject to popular vote. Serious drawings were reconceived to be funnier—a process of "fitting a gag to a picture"—while satirical ones were made more serious.[55] The editors and staff would pause for refreshments, talk among themselves, and come back for the next round of deliberation. This process would last long into the night, burnishing the magazine's reputation. "It was an honor to get into its pages," Floyd Dell remembered, "an honor conferred by vote at the meetings."[56]

Not everyone was pleased with this editorial process. At one meeting, the anarchist Hippolyte Havel shot up from his chair and interrupted the conversation. "Bourgeois pigs!" he yelled. "Voting! Voting on Poetry! Poetry is something from the soul! You can't vote on poetry."[57] Havel was arguing against subjecting artistic expression to democratic procedure. However, if, for the anarchist, there is no divine truth, how could there be objective standards?

Eastman saw this paradox as an opportunity to solidify his status. He wanted more power to settle disagreements among staff, while the illustrator John Sloan wanted him to have less. In 1916, Sloan, speaking on behalf of several other illustrators, threatened a strike. His demand was for *The Masses* to do away with annual fundraisers, to eliminate the position of executive editor and to place all editorial decisions in separate art and literature boards, who would, in turn, give their final recommendations over to a "make-up committee." Eastman threatened to resign. Eventually, he forced a vote on Sloan's proposal, which was roundly defeated, 11–5. It was Sloan, not Eastman, who ultimately submitted his letter of resignation. Upon reading the letter, Eastman replied, "Dear Sloan: I shall regret the loss of your wit and artistic genius as much as I shall enjoy the absence of your cooperation."[58]

Eastman's confidence in front of a small group at his literary magazine, however, was betrayed by his fear of being arrested in front of a large crowd in public. In a lecture in Fargo, North Dakota, in 1917, Fargo police told Eastman they were planning a military drill with loaded rifles on the same block and at the same time that he was scheduled to give his antiwar speech. The manager of the hotel where Eastman was staying the night, The Gardner, threatened to hang him if he spoke out against the war. Emma Goldman had been used to these threats; she had been arrested a handful of times. Arrest was, in fact, the way to dramatize power disparities.

But Eastman liked being admired more so than making a scene. "How fun it is to travel with your expenses paid," he wrote to his lover, Florence Deshon, while expressing distress in "heart and body" that Deshon was, behind his back, seeing someone else back in New York while he was away.[59] On the night of the Fargo lecture, Eastman asked two men to drive him to the outskirts of town and spread word that the speaking venue had changed. Two hundred people showed up at the new venue, but so did Fargo police. Soldiers, Eastman was told by a Fargo local, were not far away. Eastman, terrified, hid behind a bush, clutching a revolver someone shoved into his unsuspecting hand. He remained hidden while waiting for his getaway car en route to his next stop in Minneapolis, Minnesota.[60] Eastman got away, though eventually was arrested for his role in the antiwar movement. But after two separate trails and two hung juries in 1917 and 1918, he was never convicted of seditious activity by the US government. As for *The Masses*? It never published another issue again.

■　■　■

If things looked bleak in the US, at least there was revolutionary Russia, which, in 1917 witnessed a series of unprecedented events when V. I. Lenin, Leon Trotsky, and the Bolsheviks stormed the royal palace and toppled the Russian monarchy, and eventually took over the government. It was sensational and unexpected. Awe-inspiring and chaotic. Everything, in other words, bohemians held dear. The Communist Revolution, which few observers thought would ever truly materialize, was now afoot.

John Reed was in Petrograd covering it. After he came back to America, Reed rented a Village apartment above a diner. It was there where, unshaven, greasy, and hyped up on cheap coffee and no sleep, Reed tried to explain to Americans the true meaning and impact of the Russian Revolution. When Max Eastman ran into Reed on Sheridan Square during this frantic ten-day period, he noticed Reed's half-crazed look. Reed's resulting book, *Ten Days That Shook the World* (1919), was praised by Lenin, who took precious time out away from fighting his domestic civil war against the Mensheviks to say he read the book "with the greatest interest and with never slackening attention."[61]

Reed had already covered one revolution—the Mexican Revolution. Decked out in a bright orange corduroy suit, he embedded as a freelance journalist for the *Metropolitan* covering the ongoing Mexican Revolution. Reed profiled the charismatic, mustached Pancho Villa, draped with ammunition around his chest and donning a wide-brimmed hat. Villa would be seen riding on white horseback leading La Tropa, his peasant army of several thousand soldiers, in its effort to topple the military coup of Victoriano Huerta. Reed traveled on the cowcatcher part of Villa's locomotive and sat atop its largest cannon, called "El Nino." At night, Reed was drinking multiple rounds of hard liquor, *sotol*, with Villa's men.

In Russia, as in Mexico, Reed's "sympathies were not neutral," and the story he told was a "slice of intensified history."[62] A true believer to the end, Reed was a founder of the US Communist Party in 1919. After he died of typhus in Moscow in 1920, he became one of only three Americans to be buried at the Kremlin Wall Necropolis, the highest honor reserved for Soviet war heroes. Bill Haywood, and C.E. Ruthenberg, were the two others.

Reed was there for only the very beginning. He never saw Joseph Stalin's volcanic rise, the mass starvation of millions of Kulaks in 1932–33, the antisemitic purges of the late 1940s, or the labor camps known as the Gulag, in which millions of imprisoned people died anonymously.

Emma Goldman, unlike Reed, did get a taste of the Soviet experiment. She wasn't pleased. In 1919, after serving two years in prison, she was released from a Missouri federal penitentiary. A twenty-four-year-old J. Edgar Hoover, at that time a special assistant to Attorney General A. Mitchell Palmer, called Goldman and Berkman "beyond doubt, two of the most dangerous anarchists in this country."[63] At 5 a.m. on the morning of December 1919, the two friends were put on a ship and deported to Russia.

Goldman's initial optimism faded. In Russia, she saw long bread queues, but even worse, the disintegration of the Soviet system, carried out by the ward leaders across the republic who operated in a consultive role with the Kremlin. Then there was the Kronstadt rebellion in 1921, when a joint sailor and civilian strike against the Bolshevik government was violently suppressed by none other than Leon Trotsky. Thousands were dead. Revolutionary Petrograd wasn't unlike America when Goldman arrived in 1885. Kronstadt, it seemed, was like the Homestead Strike of 1892, which both started Goldman's path to international fame and notoriety, and, as it turned out, was the beginning and the beginning of the end of anarchism as a revolutionary force.

Anarchists claimed to never care about political power, or about government. And no one would accuse them of changing the economic, religious, or military structure of American empire in the early twentieth century. If anything, anarchism did the exact opposite: it strengthened the state's hand. Through its sensational advocacy of the "propaganda of the deed," it created excellent propaganda for the US state to not only crush the anarchist movement in its infancy but also to intensify its tyrannical reach over the entire country, especially immigrants and dissenters. "Superstitions die hard," Goldman opined in *My Disillusionment in Russia* (1923). "The very efficient world propaganda of the Communist Party [has] kept the Bolshevik myth alive. . . . I did find the revolutionary faith of the people broken, the spirit of solidarity crushed, the meaning of comradeship and mutual helpfulness distorted."[64]

Goldman was talking about the communist myth in Russia. One can't help but wonder if Goldman, perhaps unconsciously, was also thinking about the anarchist myth in America. If we think about anarchism from the perspective of its tangible impact on structural inequality, the case is clear and closed. There was little to no impact. And yet, if we ask about what anarchism gave its adherents, then the picture is more complicated. Anarchism offered them a valuable source of community. It gave them an alternative way to be, to think, to learn, to dance, and to talk. It provided them hope to live amid despair. It made them feel alive. And all of this is no small thing.

CHAPTER 4

BELOVED COMMUNITIES

1901, a thirty-year-old classically trained Black guitarist named James Weldon Johnson arrived in New York from Florida to pursue a song-writing career full-time in the burgeoning musical theater scene. Joining him was his younger brother, J. Rosamond, who was a classically trained pianist. In 1890, New York's Black population was only twenty-four thousand people—just 2 percent of the city's entire population. But it was a thriving community. The Black women of Abyssinian Baptist ran a home for the elderly. A Colored Men's YMCA was established. Makeshift pool-halls, underground bars, gambling joints, poker clubs, and "policy shops" (lottery operations) dotted a forty-block stretch along Sixth Avenue—between West Twentieth and Sixtieth Streets—known as the "Tenderloin." Further downtown, comprising a couple of blocks of the southern border of Greenwich Village between Minetta Lane, Minetta Street, and Minetta Place, was a community known as "Little Africa." Amid the small brick houses, New York's Black population was practicing mutual aid, exchanging gossip, and caring for one another's children. Any given Sunday you would see Black New Yorkers at the Bethel AME Church. The men held canes and wore dark suits and long black overcoats, while the women wore bright dresses.

The Johnson brothers came to New York because they could no longer live in the racially authoritarian Jim Crow South. In 1896, the year that the Supreme Court had formalized racial segregation through *Plessy v. Ferguson*, James Weldon Johnson was sitting with a Cuban friend in a first-class cabin in a segregated train on his way to Clark Atlanta University when an aggressive white conductor told him to get to the back of the train. Fearing for his safety, Johnson responded in Spanish. The conductor apologized, assuming that he was a foreigner, not a Black Southerner. Even as Johnson moved up the social ranks, white supremacy was everywhere. After obtaining his law degree, he went before a panel of white lawyers to be admitted to the bar. Johnson earned high marks on his oral exam, yet one of the panelists stormed out in frustration, saying, "Well I can't forget he's a nigger; and I'll be damned if I'll stay here to see him admitted."[1]

The turning point for Johnson happened in May 1901. At the time, he was the principal of an all-Black grade school called Stanton School, in Jacksonville, Florida, when the Cleaveland Fibre Factory exploded. It burned for eight hours, creating an inferno that destroyed hundreds of frame houses spanning over 150 city blocks, leaving eight thousand Black people homeless. Johnson and his younger brother Rosamond rushed to Stanton School on their bicycles. The fire was about to engulf the school, but not one fireman was at the scene. The brothers grabbed all the relevant documents and rushed home, located in the white part of town. For two weeks, their home was a makeshift refuge—twenty-five friends, "our family," as the Johnsons called them, were given food, shelter, and clothing.

The Johnson home was a model of what an ideal community could be. Outside, it was a different story. After the fire, Jacksonville officials imposed martial law and the city was occupied by National Guardsmen to protect the city from the threat of vandalism and theft. White journalists—hunting for sensational images to affix to inflammatory headlines—found local Black teens to pose for pictures. These photos were then used to push the myth of Black looters on the loose.

One day, James Weldon Johnson found himself to be a target. He had been asked by a light-skinned Black woman journalist looking to interview people for an article about the fire's impact on the city's Black population. They were scheduled to meet on a hot summer afternoon at Riverside Park. Johnson, noticing the journalist strolling toward him, jumped off the train to warmly greet her. With barking bloodhounds in tow, white militia men, thinking that a forbidden interracial romance was afoot (the journalist, to them, appeared to be white), seized Johnson, tore his clothes, and beat him, screaming, "Kill that Black son of a bitch!"

Although Johnson managed to escape, this traumatizing near-lynching inspired one of the most famous scenes in his anonymously published novel, *The Autobiography of an Ex-Colored Man* (1912), in which, after witnessing a lynching, the light-skinned narrator of the novel decides to pass as white.

■　■　■

Unlike his unnamed protagonist, James Weldon Johnson's personal goal wasn't to pass as a white man; he left Jacksonville for New York with the hope that the multicultural capital would allow him to flourish as a Black man. The North, however, was no bastion for freedom. Seventy-five percent of Black New Yorkers received less than six dollars a week—three dollars less than the nine-dollar minimum wage recommended by New York's reformers.[2] In the 1880s, Black renters paid twenty dollars per month on a four-bedroom tenement house, while white families were charged fourteen. At the turn of the century, Black New Yorkers like Johnson were barred from the American Bar Association; and New York hospitals refused Black doctors' entry. There were only twenty-six Black lawyers and forty-two doctors serving a population of sixty thousand Black New Yorkers in 1900.[3] The mortality rate of Black New Yorkers was 35 percent higher than their white counterparts. Tuberculosis afflicted them twice as much.

The injustice went beyond racial inequality. The city that Johnson arrived to in 1901 had just been the site of a brutal spectacle of racial violence. On August 13, 1900, a twenty-two-year-old Black migrant from Virginia by the name of Arthur Harris got into a fistfight with a plainclothes New York policeman, Robert Thorpe, on the corner of Forty-First Street and Eight Avenue. This, after the white police officer mistook Harris's wife for a prostitute and tried to arrest her for solicitation. During their scuffle, Harris pulled out a knife and stabbed Thorpe, who would die of excessive bleeding. Recognizing the gravity of the situation, Harris fled to Washington, DC. Two days later, on August 15, a white mob of about a thousand men—with the aid of police, looking for vengeance—took out their rage indiscriminately on Black New Yorkers. They descended upon the Tenderloin, beating Black men and women at random. Many Black citizens were minding their business, others were at work, and still others were physically dragged out of moving streetcars. Even the Black American poet Paul Laurence Dunbar—by then a household name—wasn't immune from the terror. (In 1899, Dunbar was so well known that he was about to be introduced to New York governor Theodore Roosevelt in Albany, New York, before catching a bad bout of pneumonia. In 1901,

Dunbar was invited to the White House to attend Republican president William McKinley's inauguration parade.) Dunbar was enjoying a drink at the Hotel Wolcott at West Thirty-First when he saw the chaos unfold outside. He ran out of the bar and tried to reason with the mob. The next thing he knew Dunbar was waking up in an apartment he'd never before visited, with his diamond ring and watch gone. The forty dollars he had on him was missing from his pocket.[4]

■ ■ ■

When the Johnson brothers arrived in New York, they rented a room at a newly opened establishment, the Black-owned Marshall Hotel on 129 West Fifty-Third Street, between Sixth and Seventh Avenues. Located in the Tenderloin district, Marshall's had two adjoining four-story brownstones. One housed a restaurant where you could have intimate conversations, and the other had a boisterous nightclub for the Black intelligentsia. The food was excellent, the conversation was lively, cigarette smoke saturated the air, ragtime piano blasted in the background, and everyone, men and women, was well-dressed. You would have to book a table well in advance for a Sunday evening dinner, where you could hear a four-piece ensemble. "Sunday evenings the crowd became a crush; and to be sure of service one had to book a table in advance," Johnson remembered. "This new center also brought about a revolutionary change in Negro artistic life."[5]

Another Black-owned club, Ike Hines's, opened its doors the same year as Marshall's, in 1901. Although it had no liquor license and banned gambling, Hines was an elegant three-story walk-up, with a chop-suey restaurant in its basement. Visitors were surrounded by decorative lace curtains and exquisitely carpeted floors. They wore tailored clothing. Three-piece suits, top hats, overcoats, and ascots. As they entered through the iron gate and stepped past the red lantern illuminating the entrance, they had the option of sitting in chairs in the adjacent piano room, which encircled the main wooden stage where live singers performed nightly shows and, eventually, everyone joined in the revelry. Photographs and lithographs of Black performers lined the walls, and there was a large buffet station in the back room. Hines was a favorite meeting ground for interracial couples, who could flirt in private with total abandon. Marshall's and Hines's were the center of Black Bohemia. "We went into the main room and I was little prepared for what I saw," says the narrator of

The Autobiography of an Ex-Colored Man, referring to the fictional "The Club." "The brilliancy of the place, the display of diamond rings, scarf-pins, ear-rings, and breast-pins, the big rolls of money that were brought into evidence when drinks were paid for, and the air of gaiety that pervaded the place, all completely dazzled and dazed me."[6] (This is what made Black Bohemia such a target. As part of the temperance movement, crusading social reformer agencies, like the Committee of Fourteen, partook in undercover raids of New York's clubs to shut down Marshall's and Hines's.)

Blaring in the background of Johnson's fictional club was ragtime, the soundtrack of Black Bohemia. "It was music that demanded physical response," says the unnamed narrator in *The Autobiography*, "patting of the feet, drumming of the fingers, or nodding of the head in time with the beat. The barbaric harmonies, the audacious resolutions, often consisting of an abrupt jump from one key to another, the intricate rhythms in which the accents fell in the most unexpected places, but in which the beat was never lost, produced a most curious effect."[7] Black elites—doctors, lawyers, businessmen—preferred for their children to study classical music in the vein of Dvořák, Mozart, Handel, Haydn, and Beethoven. But their children wanted excitement.

Ragtime was just that. Characterized by syncopation—with a strong and steady bass rhythm, mixing with dynamic, quick interruptions of sound from everything, sometimes violins and clarinets—ragtime was a blending of high and low, mixing up orchestral music and slave spirituals. Many of ragtime's major performers—like the conductor James Reese Europe, pianist Eubie Blake, and violinist Will Marion Cook, a student of Antonin Dvořák—were classically trained. But they were also reared in the Black Church and, in New York's restaurants and on its street corners, they'd hear recently arrived Eastern European musicians adding their lively texture to string and piano compositions. Walking along New York's theater district at the time—between Twenty-Third and Forty-Second Streets—Black youth would revel in the electric lights, large buildings, soft-roofed cars alongside handsome cabs, stunning glass window displays, twenty-foot billboards, and lithograph-screened color posters. Dazzling color was everywhere they looked. Red bricks and clay shingles surrounded them. This was the pinnacle of modernity.

Ragtime was like New York itself, improvised and multicultural. Bohemians were drawn to ragtime for these reasons, and also because it epitomized a radical idea of freedom. To make ragtime, you didn't need to read music or be professionally trained (though many were), and even if you were, what was more important in ragtime was a willingness to collaborate, and adjust the chords, tempo, key, and pitch accordingly. Ragtime wasn't about assimilating into white culture or being respectable. Disorientation was okay. So, too, was the thrill of sexuality—that was what the pulsation and unexpected time signatures condoned. Ragtime wasn't church music, where you paid homage to God. In ragtime, you became your own God.

This is what made ragtime, like anarchism, so frightening to the mainstream. (Emma Goldman's favorite dance music was ragtime, to which she did the "Anarchist's Slide.") The Black ragtime composer, Will Marion Cook, sitting with Paul Laurence Dunbar in a humid basement in his brother's Washington, DC, apartment, composed the storyline for what would become his hit piece, *Clorindy*. The two men spent a night writing and jamming over dozens of beers, a raw porterhouse steak, and a quart of whiskey. As Cook was playing one of the title songs on the parlor piano the next morning, "Who Dat Say Chicken in Dis Crowd," his mother ran into the room. Tears in her eyes, she yelled, "Oh Will! Will! I've sent you all over the world to study and become a great musician [studying with Antonin Dvořák], and you return such a nigger!"[8] The problem, for Cook's mother, wasn't the minstrelsy, which she knew was being reimagined by Black performers like her son, who added their own touch to the racist farce, seizing it from whites in blackface who knew nothing about Black life. The issue, instead, was the groove, which was unbecoming of middle-class youth like her son.

New York's Black countercultural scene wasn't for everyone. Dunbar, for his part, was both drawn to and repulsed by bohemia. Heavy drinking, excessive touching, loud laughter, and boisterous sexual energy was, for Dunbar, not a joyful release, but a serious moral problem. This was the message of *The Sport of the Gods* (1902), Dunbar's novel about a middle-class Black family, the Hamiltons, who migrates from the South to New York. Throughout the narrative, there's remarkably little discussion of systemic racism. There are, however, many family quarrels, ill-fated romances, and failed showmen and confused showgirls. Much of the action takes place in the underbelly of the Banner Club—modeled on Marshall's Club—where Joe Hamilton, the novel's tragic protagonist, works. Dunbar describes Joe's arrival in New York, foreboding the spiral of despair to come, in which he will become an alcoholic and murder his girlfriend in a fit of rage, resulting in his incarceration: "The lights in the busy streets will bewilder and entice him. He will feel shy and helpless amid the hurrying crowds. A new emotion will take his heart as the people hasten by him—a feeling of loneliness, almost of grief, that with all of these souls about him he knows not one and not one of them cares for him."[9]

▪ ▪ ▪

In the 1850s, white bohemians like Henry Clapp at Pfaff's lager beer salon had a laissez-faire attitude toward racism. Black bohemians at the turn of the century did not. In 1900, the Johnson brothers, still in Jacksonville, had written "Lift Every Voice and Sing," in honor of Abraham Lincoln's birthday. Though the song was dedicated to the founder of Tuskegee University, the preacher of self-reliance Booker T. Washington, its lyrics were critical of American exceptionalism. The song would be known as the "Black National Anthem" and, unlike the US national anthem—which was originally an 1814 poem by Francis Scott Key—the lyrics speak of hope forged in the crucible of catastrophe: "Sing a song full of the faith that the dark past has taught us / Sing a song full of the hope that the present has brought us / Facing the rising sun of our new day begun / Let us march on till victory is won."[10]

After arriving to New York, the Johnson brothers linked up with a Black performer named Bob Cole, who was staging his own revolt on Broadway. Cognizant of the need for Black solidarity amid white racism, Cole had formed the All-Star Stock Company for Black actors on Sixth Avenue and Thirteenth Street in 1894. In 1896, Cole had worked as a performer with Black Patti's Troubadours, a company started up by the Black opera singer Sissieretta Jones. Cole's time with Black Patti's Troubadours, however, was short-lived. The troupe's white manager, Rudolph Voelckel, wrongly accused Cole of making a false claim to authorship of a song that Cole had written. Voelckel had Cole arrested on stage during a performance. The judge offered Cole leniency if he recanted his claim to have written the song but Cole didn't back down, saying "It's mine," and "I won't give it up."[11] For his defiance, he was jailed. Upon release, he was blacklisted from Black Patti's. In response, Cole wrote the "Colored Actor's Declaration of Independence," in which he said, "We are going to have our own shows. . . . We are going to write them ourselves, we are going to have our own stage manager, our own orchestra leader and our own manager out front to count up. No divided houses—our race must be seated from the boxes back."[12]

Cole's decision to form a production trio with the Johnson brothers was for the sake of, as Cole put it, "a conscious effort to raise the level of Negro songs, especially the level of the words, which at that time was pretty low."[13] Their company wrote hundreds of songs and performed socially conscious musicals. At the time, this was novel. In terms of their content, Broadway musicals were racist to the bone. Despicable representations of Black men as sexual predators and Black women as doting matriarchs eating porkchops, watermelon, and fried chicken came to dominate the minstrel genre of "coon songs," which were printed as sheet music in Sunday editions of *New York Journal* and the *New York World*. These racist portrayals were part of a general revisionism suffusing Broadway depictions of the country's recent past. For example, Civil War hero William Tecumseh Sherman, the Union general originally from Ohio but now living in retirement on Fifth Avenue, attended the 250th Broadway performance of Bronson Howard's smash hit, *Shenandoah* (1889), which was a love story between a young woman and a dashing Confederate soldier. Sherman commended the play's "historical accuracy," which painted the Old South in a decidedly sympathetic way.

In terms of the performances themselves, Broadway was still segregated by race—white patrons got front-row seats and Black patrons had to sit in the balcony. In 1900, only 329 Black New Yorkers were employed as professionals in Black nightclubs. An additional 268 were musicians or music teachers.[14] The minstrel tradition of blackface—white performers portraying African Americans as jolly simpletons—still sold tickets to a primarily white audience.

Cole and the Johnson brothers sought to change Broadway from the inside. Take their musical *The Shoo-Fly Regiment* (1906). Set during the Spanish-American War of 1898, the play, on its surface, is a romantic satire. It is the story of a Black man, Ned Jackson, who joins the US army to fight in the Spanish-American War in the Philippines. He does this after his sweetheart's father refuses the request for the hand in marriage of his daughter, Rose Maxwell. By presenting Black Americans as heroes and humanizing Filipinos, Cole and the Johnson brothers subverted stereotypes about Black passivity at a moment when they were being widely propagated. Reflecting on why the show wasn't picked up by major producers like Oscar Hammerstein, James Weldon Johnson remembered in his 1931 farewell speech to the NAACP (since 1920, he had been the organization's executive chair) that it was deemed "unpatriotic. The Spanish-American War had closed, and the opera . . . attempted to satirize the new American imperialism."[15]

Another musical the trio wrote was *The Red Moon* (1908), the story of Minnehaha—part African American, part Native American—who lives in Virginia but is kidnapped by her estranged Native father and brought to a reservation out West. Minnehaha is then rescued by a Black lawyer and brought home to her family. The comedy thus reimagines Black-Native solidarity and overturn myths of Black deviance. The characters in the play are genuinely funny, not caricatures. The reconciliation between Minnehaha and her family at the end is meant to restore the Black family, rather than use it as a prop for white laughter. Precisely because it challenged myths of Native savagery as well, the play earned high marks from Canada's Indigenous community. When *The Red Moon* was staged in Montreal in March 1909, several of the play's Black actors visited the Iroquois tribe on the Caughnawaga Reservation, located south of the city, as guests of Chief Mitchal Dial Bount.[16] In 1921, J. Rosamond Johnson himself was inducted into the tribe as a "sub-chief" in Quebec.

▪   ▪   ▪

At the same time that Black bohemians like the Johnson brothers and Bob Cole were creating a politically conscious theater, Black novelists were expanding the idea of utopia and unmooring it from its racist history.

One novel that accomplished this was Frances E. W. Harper's *Iola Leroy* (1892). The book is the story of a woman who is raised as a white Southern aristocrat but, just before the Civil War, learns that she's of mixed race. She's briefly sold into slavery, before being rescued by the Union Army and later reunited with her family. The narrative then segues into the concluding utopian section of the book, which features a vibrant Black public sphere of doctors, clergy, and academics—cosmopolitan men and feminist women—debating racial uplift inside gorgeous parlors. Iola Leroy isn't a degraded domestic worker in this setting, subject to the threat of sexual violence and racial discrimination, but a schoolteacher and church helper, living among Black people. Leroy plans "meetings for the especial benefit of mothers and children. . . . She has no carpets too fine for the tread of their little feet. . . . In lowly homes and windowless cabins her visits are always welcome. Little children love her. Old age turns to her for comfort, young girls for guidance, and mothers for counsel. Her life is full of blessedness."[17] Iola Leroy's friend, the Black doctor Latimer, is "more than a successful doctor; he is a true patriot and a good citizen. Honest, just, and discriminating, he endeavors by precept and example to instill into the minds of others sentiments of good citizenship. He is a leader in every reform movement for the benefit of the community; but his patriotism is not confined to race lines."[18]

Iola Leroy was Harper's first major novel, published at the age of sixty-seven, but by then she was already a major poet. Her second collection of poetry, *Poems on Miscellaneous Subjects* (1854), was published the same year as Whitman's *Leaves of Grass*. Yet Harper's book did what Whitman's book didn't: it immediately became successful. The collection went through seventeen printings and sold ten thousand copies. This made Harper a rarity: a financially independent Black women.[19] And yet, if Whitman's success only made him more convinced of his retrograde ideas, Harper used her success as a springboard for Black freedom. In 1859, she consoled John Brown's wife, Mary Ann Day Brown, on the eve of his execution. Harper spoke alongside Frederick Douglass and was close friends with Harriet Tubman. After the Civil War ended, Harper embraced women's suffrage and Black voting rights. She denounced the rise of white supremacist organizations like the Ku Klux Klan, the Night Riders, and the Redeemers that were spreading like wildfire. (These organizations were part of a reign of terror that included the imposition of poll taxes and literacy tests, resulting in Black political participation plunging from a high of 95 percent in 1865 after the Civil War to 3 percent by the early 1900s.)

A figure who could have been part of Harper's utopian society in *Iola Leroy* was a Black feminist novelist named Pauline Elizabeth Hopkins. Born in Portland, Maine, in 1859, Hopkins was a brilliant student, a dazzling soprano vocalist, a playwright of musical theater, and a prolific public performer. Among her most well-known performances was a recounting of Haitian revolutionary Toussaint Louverture's anti-colonial revolt against the French Empire, which she performed at Boston's Tremont Temple, the headquarters of the New England Women's Club and a onetime hub for abolitionist organizing.

Throughout her life, Hopkins tried to revive the transcendentalist tradition of radical politics. Her first novel, *Contending Forces*, was published by the Colored Co-operative Publishing Company out of Boston, started by four Black men under the age of thirty from Virginia. That same year, the Co-operative would publish the *Colored American Magazine* in 1900. Imagined as a cooperative in the spirit of Brook Farm, the magazine's readers and contributors were invited to buy certificates of deposit, which were then pooled to compensate contributors. The goal of the journal was to strengthen the "bonds of that racial brotherhood, which alone can enable a people, to assert their racial rights as men, and demand their privileges as citizens."[20] By 1901, its first-year anniversary, the magazine claimed one hundred thousand readers, with a monthly circulation of twenty thousand. It maintained branches throughout the US, as well as in the West Indies and Liberia. Hopkins was the magazine's most well-known writer, contributing nonfiction essays on Ida B. Wells, Mary Church Terrell, Frances Harper, and Harriet Tubman.

It was in the *Colored American Magazine* that Hopkins serialized her second novel, *Of One Blood* (1902–3). The book is an account of Black utopia. The plot follows a Black Harvard medical student, named Reuel Briggs, who discovers an ancient forgotten Black matrilineal society ruled by a queen and twenty-five sages in an Ethiopian kingdom, called "Telassar." In depictions that would have made Fourier and Owen proud, there's a sacred temple for the seating of up to twelve thousand, and the inner city features a court with gardens, schools, baths, and hospitals, in which the Black population assembles. In Telassar, gold is plentiful; the social fabric is strong, education and the arts are held in high esteem, and women are in political power. Throughout the novel, Hopkins idealizes Black beauty—most vividly in the image of the queen, who serves as a representation of uplifted Blackness: "Yes, she was a Venus, a superb statue of bronze, moulded by a great sculptor."[21]

Another classic text of Black utopianism during this period was *Imperium in Imperio* (1899) by Sutton E. Griggs. Born in Chatfield, Texas, in 1872, Griggs followed in the footsteps of his minister father, an ex-slave from Georgia, to become a well-respected National Baptist Convention preacher in Nashville, Tennessee, where he moved with his wife in 1899.

A conciliatory man by nature who never compromised his religious faith, Griggs personally believed in the philosophy of Christian brotherhood. But upon learning of the lynching in 1898 of a Black US postmaster, Frazier B. Baker—along with his wife and child—in Lake City, Utah, he was aghast. White supremacy, Griggs thought, would never go calmly into the night; it would need to be vanquished through Black power.

What would Black power look like? How would it be organized? *Imperium in Imperio* attempts an answer to these questions. Through chronicling the activities of a secret, all-Black government—the Imperium, in Waco, Texas, which plots to overthrow the state of Texas—Griggs charts competing visions of Black politics, represented through two childhood friends from Richmond, Virginia. A dark-skinned man who comes from a one-room home and intense poverty, Belton Piedmont is subject to daily beatings by his racist schoolteacher. Given the brutality he has faced, Piedmont has every reason to reject America; but he is a patriot. Piedmont is the opposite of his childhood friend, Bernard Belgrave, a Black nationalist who wants Black liberation by any means necessary, even if he is the beneficiary of an elite education from Harvard University, and his biological father is a white US senator.

The conclusion of *Imperium* is tragic: Piedmont is executed by Belgrave for threatening to reveal the Imperium's existence. But the book is, as much as anything else, an argument for a utopian form of Black self-determination. The Imperium council is depicted as operating as a constitutional republic, where elected leaders express their reasoned judgments before an audience of their peers. Their disagreements reflect the power of Black citizens to write their own destiny outside the boundaries of the standard political culture. "If we enter a place where a sign tells us that the public is served," Belgrave declares, during Jim Crow, "we do not know whether we are to be waited upon or driven out like dogs."[22] So, he concludes, "let us . . . strike a blow for freedom. . . . If contending for our rights, given unto us by God, causes us to be slain, let us perish on the field of battle, singing as we pass out of the world, 'Sweet Freedom's song,' though every word of this soul-inspiring hymn must come forth wrapped in our hearts' warm blood."[23]

Five years after *Imperium* was published, Edward A. Johnson took Black utopia in a socialist direction. A distinguished professor of law at Shaw University who never lost a case he argued before the North Carolina

Supreme Court, Johnson was one of only two Black men in Raleigh to make enough money to pay the state's income tax. And yet, the Wilmington race massacre of 1898—in which a white mob of two thousand perpetrated a coup that burned down the prospering Black town and crushed its Fusionist local government—shook Johnson to the core. What good was Black inclusion into a racist society, Johnson wondered, that would use violence to maintain its stranglehold on power?

Only a revolution in values, Johnson believed, could overturn this dynamic. His novel *Light Ahead for the Negro* (1904) paints a picture of what this might look like. It is the story of a protagonist, Gilbert Twitchell, who travels one hundred years into the future. Twitchell finds Jim Crow destroyed, direct democracy realized, popular referendum the mode of policymaking, interracial class solidarity to be a fact of life, women now equal with men, and neither the president nor Congress leading the nation. "Individuality gives room for thought," says the narrator, echoing Whitman's creed, "out of which is born invention and progress."[24] *Light Ahead* didn't receive much critical attention. But Johnson didn't care. Unlike Whitman, Johnson turned away from marketing his work and toward making a concrete impact in his community. He opened a law office in Harlem in 1907 and funded youth services. In 1917, he was elected as a Republican to the New York State legislature.

Coming at the end of the Black utopian golden age was the release of W. E. B. Du Bois's utopian short story, "The Comet" (1920), published in his collection *Darkwater*. "The Comet" details several hours of intimacy between a working Black man, Jim, and an affluent white woman, Julia. They're the two lone survivors of a postapocalyptic New York, decimated by a comet that has struck the city. What if, Du Bois wonders, genuine interracial intimacy is possible? Jim and Julia, alone in the world, disregard race, gender, and class, and feel hopeful that the uncertain future can be confronted. They listen to one another, collaborate in search of survivors, and give each other reciprocal emotional support. This is, we might say, for Du Bois what an anarchist society, without law and order, would look like. "The rich and the poor are met together. . . . How foolish our human distinctions seem—now," says Julia.[25] In the end, however, the reality principle intercedes. It turns out that Julia's white husband, Fred, and her father are alive. And, as they approach the utopian interracial couple, Fred, assuming Jim to be a rapist, threatens to lynch him. A gathering crowd of surviving New Yorkers arrive on the scene and they agree with Fred. Julia, however, intervenes on Jim's behalf. Jim is a good, decent man, she says. As a token of what Fred thinks is generous reparation, he tells Jim that he can get him a job downtown. Jim politely declines, and then sees his Black wife from a distance—she's alive, but their child is dead, lying limp in her arms. Jim runs toward them, with a mixture of relief and sadness.

Disaster is avoided, but so, too, is a romantic conception of utopia. Black utopians were aware of the zigs and zags of history, the fantasy of total progress, and the recurrence of racial violence. Democracy, or interracial solidarity, or justice could be dashed as quickly as it could be summoned. Black utopia wasn't easily achievable. It was messy and complicated. Iola Leroy is re-enslaved. Reuel Briggs has to leave his home to find a new one. Belton Piedmont is executed by his best friend, Bernard Belgrave. Gilbert Twitchell is in a daze when he witnesses the future. The reader, like him, isn't sure whether what she sees is fact or fiction. Yet Black utopia, like Black Bohemia, and like the gatherings at Marshall's and Hines's, is full of life. It's ready to improvise and change key, to adjust on a whim, like the artists of the Harlem Renaissance who, taking over from ragtime performers, will in short order wow their readers with dazzling turns of phrase and unexpected encounters.

CHAPTER 5

LOST AND FOUND

In the early morning hours of September 5, 1921, a twenty-year-old Black poet from Kansas walked off a vessel that originated from Mexico. Stepping onto Manhattan Island, he was thrilled to see the gleaming towers, which looked like mountains above the green water. He was astounded to see the glorious Brooklyn Bridge at dusk, and the faint glowing lights all over the downtown skyline. He didn't know the exact directions to Harlem, or where to stay. So, along with two men he met on the voyage to New York—one, a senior visiting his son's family in New Jersey; another, a young auto mechanic—he spent his first night at a cheap hotel in Times Square, between Broadway and Sixth Avenue. For nine dollars the trio rented a personal suite, and each man had a large single bed to sleep in. When the poet named Langston Hughes awoke the following morning refreshed after a long journey, he took the subway to Harlem, eagerly awaiting his stop. The noise and speed of the train took his breath away.

When Hughes set out from the Bronx Park Subway platform with his two bags, he took in the scenery and proceeded to walk in the beautiful sunny September morning. His destination was the Harlem YMCA on 181 West 135th Street. It was there, where, for seven dollars, Hughes would spend the next week. Harlem was miles away from the Hughes's childhood home, a modest two-bedroom house in a quiet Midwestern neighborhood in Lawrence, Kansas. The Black utopias that Frances Harper, Edward Johnson, and Pauline Hopkins imagined in their turn-of-the-century fiction seemed to have settled in Harlem, what James Weldon Johnson called the "Negro Metropolis."[1] Harlem in the 1920s was the center of both the Black world and another world in which a new future felt within reach.

By 1921, out of a total Black New York population of three hundred thousand, over one-third lived in a two-square-mile section of Harlem situated between 113th and 145th Streets and between Fifth and Eighth Avenues. Harlem migrants came from as far as Barbados, Trinidad, and Jamaica. They came from the shores of Tampa, the Mississippi plantations, and the steels mills of Alabama. Part of the reason they were drawn to Harlem was its modern housing. The apartments were sunny and airy. It also helped that the housing was relatively affordable. With Jim Crow segregation entrenched in the South and racial violence alarmingly on the rise, it made sense why the North provided the hope of starting anew. The prospect of securing a job also appeared more likely in Harlem. Periodicals like the *Chicago Defender*, read by 1.3 million Black Americans across the country, spread the news that domestic workers earned over three dollars per day, and steelworkers up to four-fifty.[2]

If you walked through Harlem in the 1920s, you would experience a feast for your senses. On the intersection of 125th Street and Seventh Avenue, along the well-paved and well-lit streets, you would see residents in their best clothes going to the Lincoln and Crescent Theatre. On Sundays, they would be leaving the 160 churches in the neighborhood, among which Mother AME Zion Church was the most notable. There would be parade processions, teeming with auto horns and sirens. Marchers would be doing the cakewalk with their batons swirling and white plumes flitting in the air. On one corner, there might be a mourning procession for a funeral. Across the street, an impromptu religious sermon. You would see devotees of Black nationalist Marcus Garvey's Universal Negro Improvement Association (UNIA) heading into its headquarters at Liberty Hall. The 135th Street Branch of the New York Public Library in Harlem was not only a grand container of the written word; it was a marvelous stage for public lectures. The topics included the political philosophy of Karl Marx and antislavery activism before the Civil War. The YMCA and YWCA organized debates between Democrats and Republicans there as well. On the same street, the well-known socialist Hubert Harrison set up the Institute for Social Study, where he spoke on Darwin, Lenin, empire, and Third World solidarity.

In New York, the city that never slept, the underground was wide awake at night in Harlem. Number runners, who handled tens of millions of dollars every year, would be standing alongside hustlers. Jazz musicians would jam their saxophones right next to the easels of painters, who would sit quietly beside the trolleys, while motor cars sped by them both. At a time when electrification wasn't widespread, ice dealers, on summer nights, would be jockeying for commercial real estate beside the shoe shiners and bootleggers, who were running the speakeasys during the era of Prohibition. Through the half-open apartment windows, you would smell oxtail stew and sweet potatoes being prepared for rent parties or "buffet flats."

Harlem was the center of Black cultural production in New York and, increasingly, the US. But Harlem was no utopia. It was, after all, a part of America, where racism was lurking beneath the shadows. The all-white Property Owners Protective Association of Harlem policed the neighborhood's relatively small housing market. White conductors operated public buses. Private automobiles owned by whites made up the bulk of traffic on Lenox Avenue. The tallest building in Harlem, the thirteen-floor Hotel Theresa, remained segregated until 1940. The first Black firefighter in the New York Fire Department joined in 1919; the first Black New York City police officer was sworn in in 1911. White police officers made up most of the city's police force. And their behavior was characterized by a mixture of aggression and apathy toward Black Harlemites. Some cops wouldn't think twice about breaking bones and bruising flesh, while others were happy to turn a blind eye toward the gambling, the flow of cheap liquor, and the accessibility of sex work—all of which, not surprisingly, was disproportionately patronized by whites who came to Harlem in search of a good time. Traffic accidents were not only common in Harlem. They were also emblematic of the neighborhood's racialized economic inequality. White cabbies in garish limousines, like the ones who took white patrons to the all-white Cotton Club for a night on the town, would injure Black deliverymen, barbers, and domestic workers on their way to work. In the 1920s, almost ten people per day suffered car-related injuries in Harlem.

A 1929 survey suggested that of the over ten thousand businesses in Harlem, 80 percent were owned by whites.[3] From 1919 to 1927, the mean average monthly rent doubled from twenty-one dollars to forty-two dollars.[4] In 1925, New York's population density was 223 people per acre—in Harlem it was 336 per acre. Two streets in Harlem were the most densely populated in the whole world.[5] A recurrent problem Harlem residents faced was the unwillingness of landlords to address broken pipes, broken ceilings, roaches, and vermin, especially rats. Between 1923 and 1927,

Harlem's death rate was 42 percent higher than the city as a whole, and its infant mortality was twice as high.[6]

Harlem in the 1920s was ripe for rebellion, though it didn't materialize (that would come a decade later, on March 19, 1935, in what would be called one of the first "race riots"). Aspiring artists like Langston Hughes who came to Harlem in the 1920s, but weren't born in and didn't grow up there, were less concerned with the realities of the daily grind, and more interested in using Harlem as a launching pad for a new Black counterculture.

■　■　■

Langston Hughes arrived in Harlem out of necessity, rather than idealism. If he wanted to be a poet, Hughes needed money, of which he had none to speak. His father, a domineering lawyer named James Nathaniel Hughes, had the means to support him, but James had been absent from his son's life. He had left his wife, Carrie, and a two-year-old Langston in 1903, moving to Mexico to work for the Pullman Company. James wasn't a great father, and he was neither approachable nor warm, but "only interested in making money."[7] Which, in some sense, was good for Langston. It meant his father could support him to study engineering at Columbia University.

Soon after Hughes enrolled at Columbia, the school seemed "too big" and it was "no fun. You didn't get to know anybody, hardly," Hughes lamented. "The buildings looked like factories." Worse, Columbia lectures were dreary. Math was like Chinese to Hughes. Physics was too abstract. French felt like hurtling along in an express train. Nobody asked Hughes to join a fraternity, and when he tried to get involved in the school newspaper, *The Spectator*, the editors asked him to only report on social gossip—"an assignment impossible," he recalled, "for a colored boy to fill, they knew."[8]

Hughes, like the Johnson brothers before him, found himself drifting from a formal education toward an improvised one. Columbia, in Hughes's estimate, couldn't compare to the stimulating lectures at the Rand School by socialists Ludwig Lewisohn and Heywood Broun. It paled in comparison to the dazzling performances of Black stage actors Florence Mills and Caterina Jarboro, the stars of *Shuffle Along*, which Hughes would watch for fifty cents at the 63rd Street Theater. Even death mattered more than good grades to Langston: he once skipped an important test during the spring semester of 1922 to go to the funeral of famous Black vaudeville actor Bert Williams.

Before his first year at Columbia concluded, Hughes decided to drop out of college. (Given his lack of attendance and subpar grades, one wonders whether he would have been expelled anyway.) On his way out of the university, Hughes made sure to do the one thing he wanted to do most of all: irritate his father. James Hughes didn't like people who didn't fit his image of respectability—he condescended to his estranged wife and berated his sensitive son with the same intensity in which he denigrated Black people and poor people in general. "My father hated Negroes. I think he hated himself, too, for being a Negro," Langston remembered. "My father had a great contempt for all poor people."⁹ Langston wrote James to say he was leaving school and wouldn't pay back his stipend. James got the message: he never responded, and never sent Langston any more money.

Hughes didn't mind confrontation, but he preferred to express his rebellion in words. In 1914, when he entered the seventh grade at Central School, a racially integrated middle school in Lawrence, Kansas, a white teacher forced the Black children in his class to sit apart from the white ones. Infuriated, Hughes wrote out several cards with the words "JIM CROW ROW" and placed them on his and his Black classmates' desks. He then ran out of the classroom and escaped the clutches of a school administrator in the hallway. After he was finally apprehended outside, Hughes was swiftly expelled. It was only after the few Black parents of Central School mobilized on his behalf that he was reinstated. (Hughes never meant to cause a huge stir, but thanks to his outburst, segregated seating arrangements were eliminated from Central School.) Five years after this incident, when Hughes reluctantly arrived in Mexico as a seventeen-year-old to live with his father, he, much like all brooding teenagers, wasn't interested in reconciling with the man he had hardly known. What Hughes wanted was an outlet for his rage, so he spent many hot afternoons watching gory bullfights, intoxicated by the "dust and tobacco and animals and leather, sweat and blood and the scent of death."¹⁰

A major reason Langston Hughes had the confidence to leave Columbia is that he never suffered from crippling self-doubt. He grew up in a supportive family. As a boy, Hughes lived with his seventy-year-old stoic grandmother, Mary Langston, who would nurture her precocious grandson. An Oberlin College graduate, Mary prayed quietly at night, didn't like to watch movies, and thought novels were "cheap." But she had a long history of political resistance through her involvement in the antislavery movement with her husband. At bedtime, she would tell Langston that his grandfather, Charles Hughes, was on the front lines resisting the Fugitive Slave Act of 1850 through what came to be known as the Oberlin-Wellington Rescue of 1858. In Oberlin, Ohio, Charles and thirty-six others tried to help a runaway slave, John Price, from Kentucky. For his efforts, Charles was sentenced by a federal jury for inciting a riot. John Brown attended the trial. Brown was so impressed by Charles that he asked him to join his assault on Harpers Ferry, West Virginia, to liberate enslaved people, but Charles refused. Many historians consider Brown's assault on October 16, 1859, was the opening shot for the Civil War.[11]

Hughes didn't see much of his mother, Carrie Langston, whose work demanded her to spend extended time on the road. As a teen, Carrie was known around Lawrence for beautifully reciting her own poetry and for holding the inaugural position of cultural critic at her local church. Though she didn't enroll at Kansas State University, she took a German language course there. Carrie was disappointed that she never became an artist, but her disappointment didn't trickle down to her son. On weekends, she took Langston to see Goethe's *Faust* and encouraged him to sing alongside Jewish cantors at Saturday synagogue services.

Quick to recognize the power of social connections with well-connected people, after he dropped out of Columbia in 1922, Langston Hughes formed an adopted family in New York. He met his boyhood idol, W. E. B. Du Bois, whose work gave Hughes the "earliest memories of written words."[12] Du Bois was known for his gruff and detached affect, but the elder statesman took an immediate liking to Hughes's sophisticated and easygoing nature.[13] Jessie Redmon Fauset, the literary editor of Du Bois's *The Crisis* and the first Black woman to matriculate at Cornell University, had known of Hughes's work—*The Crisis* had published Hughes's first poem "The Negro Speaks of Rivers," which he claimed to have composed in ten minutes on a train from Mississippi to Mexico in 1919. But when Fauset met Hughes in person, she found his personality even more charming than his poetry.

Hughes respected his elders, but he found a comrade in arms in the twenty-year-old Black poet Countee Cullen. It was Cullen who introduced Hughes to a Harvard-educated philosopher and Howard University classics professor named Alain Locke. Hughes wanted a father figure, but Locke had other plans: he wanted a protégé and a lover. "Countee already means so much to me," Locke wrote to Hughes, "but he generously insists on deeding over a certain part of me to you."[14]

Hughes wanted to stay in Harlem but had no money. Worse than that, he didn't have the raw experience he craved for his poetry. So Hughes found a low-paying job as a farmhand on 2289 Richmond Avenue in Staten Island, working on a forty-three-acre vegetable farm run by two Greek brothers, where—along with room and board—he was paid fifty dollars a month. Hughes awoke at 5 a.m., drank a cup of bitter black coffee, ate a breakfast of cheese and olives, and then hoed, spread manure, and harvested beets, carrots, lettuce, and onions. This didn't last long and inaugurated several years of wandering around the world. By 1923, Hughes was a dishwasher on a ship to Dakar, Senegal, which eventually sailed the entire African continent for four months. The next year, he was a doorman at a nightclub in France.

By 1925, Hughes was in Washington, DC, living with his mother (who had settled in with her wealthy Mercer relatives in the LeDroit Park section of town). Through Carrie, Hughes found work as a personal assistant for the famed Black historian Carter G. Woodson, founder of the *Journal of Negro History* in 1916—whose Negro History Week (established in 1926), chronicling Black achievement, eventually became the basis for Black History Month. The pay was fine, but the tedious work—dusting furniture, sorting mail, and mailing books—"hurt" Hughes's eyes.

▪ ▪ ▪

It was while working as a hotel busboy in the Wardman Park Hotel in DC that Langston Hughes learned that his first book of poetry, *The Weary Blues* (1926), would be published by Alfred A. Knopf upon the recommendation of a friend of Gertrude Stein, Carl Van Vechten. The Iowa-born, University of Chicago–trained Van Vechten, who wrote the introduction to *The Weary Blues*, was a man of eclectic tastes. He was a music critic for the *New York Times* (opera was his specialty) who also enjoyed writing about Isadora Duncan's contributions to modern dance and had a peculiar interest in the cultural history of cats. More than anything else, however, Van Vechten was known for his interest in Black culture. Critics accused the tall, lanky white man with a heavy jaw and thinning, slicked-back white hair of exoticizing his Black friends. This accusation rang true for those who read his novel about Harlem, controversially titled *Nigger Heaven* (1926).

"Racist" might be the best way to describe Van Vechten, as his novel was quick to identify Black life with a sense of primitiveness—of sex, partying, and alcohol. (Zora Neale Hurston, however, saw Van Vechten differently. She called him an honorary "Niggeratus"—a term of endearment.) In his introduction to *The Weary Blues*, Van Vechten applauded Hughes of crafting verse that was of a "sensitive and subtly illusive nature, seeking always to break through the veil that obscures for him . . . the ultimate needs of that nature."[15]

The Weary Blues accomplished what Van Vechten never did in his own writing: it evoked the complexity of Black life; the pain and the resilience, the anger and the joy. Hughes's poems were meant to be accompanied to the music of the blues and its ethereal vocals, elongated piano notes, and melancholic brass sounds. The title poem begins with "Droning a drowsy syncopated tune, / Rocking back and forth to a mellow croon, I heard a Negro play," and ends with, "The singer stopped playing and went to bed / While the Weary Blues echoed through his head. / He slept like a rock or a man that's dead."[16] This poem is defined by the depth of loss but says nothing directly about racism. Another poem in the collection, "I, Too," puts racism front and center. "I, too, sing America," says the "darker brother." They send him to eat in the kitchen when company comes, "But I laugh, / And eat well, / And grow strong," and tomorrow "Nobody'll dare" say to him, 'Eat in the kitchen.'"[17]

If we're talking strictly about politics (whether on matters of seizing the state or acquiring the means of production, for instance), there's nothing revolutionary in either of these poems, or in the blues itself. But the way the blues and *The Weary Blues* reimagine American freedom is, in fact, revolutionary. Consider that most Americans are raised on stories of progress, and on naive individualism—the belief that, if we just try hard enough, everything will work out. They are unaccustomed to hearing what they hear in the blues, the idea that freedom isn't immune from the weight of constraint but isn't crushed by it either. Hughes locates a productive feeling of alienation; he finds tragedy without the romance, and notices quiet acts of rebellion. "The Blues are *city* songs rising from the crowded streets of big towns or beating against the lonely walls of hall bed-rooms where you can't sleep at night," Hughes later commented, drawing a contrast he saw between Black spirituals and the blues. While the spirituals are "escape songs," the blues are "*today* songs, here and now."[18]

Not long after *The Weary Blues* was published, Hughes got an opportunity to test his theory of the genre with the "Empress of the Blues" herself. After a performance in Baltimore, Hughes met Bessie Smith, whose first record, *Downhearted Blues* (1923), for Columbia Records, had just sold an astonishing 750,000 copies. Hughes, starstruck, tried to play it cool. He turned to small talk. Did she know his friend, Carl Van Vechten? Yes, Smith said, but the two weren't close. Did Smith spend much time in New York? Not really, she replied. Recognizing that the conversation was at a standstill, Hughes abandoned niceties and blurted out: How would Smith interpret the blues? The blues paid her bills, Smith said, bought her a nice house, and she liked to sing them.[19]

Smith sniffed out Hughes's insecurity as a burgeoning intellectual who wanted to make an impression on the thirty-two-year-old best-selling musician. Smith's own life was a testament to a blues-infused freedom Hughes identified in *Weary Blues*.

Bessie Smith was born in 1894 to a part-time Baptist minister father and a mother who was a laundress. Smith was one of seven children. Her father died when she was just a preschooler, and her mother and one of her older brothers died when she turned eleven. Living with their aunt in crushing poverty, the remaining Smith children managed to scrape by, though no one knew how. Yet everyone recognized that Bessie could sing. As a twelve-year-old, she mesmerized with her contralto voice, singing for spare change on Chattanooga, Tennessee, on Ninth Street—the center of the downtown music scene—as her brother, Andrew, stood beside her and strummed his guitar.

Bessie was fourteen when she got her big break. This came after she was noticed by the twenty-two-year-old Gertrude "Ma" Rainey. Already established in vaudeville circles, the Columbus, Georgia–born Rainey was a blues singer whose baritone voice was as deep and rich as her style was flamboyant. Rainey liked ostrich plumes and fur boas, and she had gold-capped teeth that glistened when she sang. Rainey, eight years older than Smith, was a world-class performer, but to Bessie she became a mentor. (Like Smith, Rainey was bisexual, and they were allegedly lovers.) Rainey took Bessie under her wing. Traveling in music circuits as a teenager herself, Rainey, nicknamed "the Mother of the Blues," did for Bessie what nobody did for her. She taught her how to dress, how to perform, how to sing from her viewpoint, and, crucially, how to avoid the two main pitfalls for a Black woman in the music industry: corrupt promoters and racist hotel managers.

Hard times didn't escape Smith's music but, from Ma Rainey, she learned they didn't need to fully envelop her music either. In a song like "Jailhouse Blues" (1923), Smith stares disaster straight in the face and gives it a warm greeting. "Good mornin', blues, blues, how do you do, how do you do / Good mornin', blues, blues, how do you do / Say, I just come here to have a few words with you."[20] Most of Smith's 160 recordings offer some variation on this theme, and they are about everyday life. But Smith will sometimes tell a personal story to criticize the American nation in which she was born and lived. A decade after World War I witnessed Black veterans fight for democracy abroad, only to return to Jim Crow at home, Smith proclaims in her ballad "Poor Man's Blues" (1928), "Poor man fought all the battles, poor man would fight again today / He would do anything you ask him in the name of the U.S.A. / Now the war is over, poor man must live the same as you / If it wasn't for the poor man, mister rich man, what would you do?"[21]

■　■　■

The blues assume we know *who* is on the run. Resilient sisters, jealous partners, and forlorn lovers. But what if you want to put your identity on the run, to remake who you are? This was the lifelong preoccupation of a man whom Hughes met at a 1925 Harlem evening lecture. The handsome, fair-skinned, and straight-haired Black man was discussing the eccentric ideas of the Russian mystic, George Gurdjieff. The man's charisma was undeniable as he stood there and fervently preached Gurdjieff's gospel of daydreaming, free association, and worldly asceticism as a way toward self-discovery. "He had an evolved soul," Hughes recalled, "[as if] nothing mattered, not even writing."[22]

Up until he was a young adult, Jean Toomer was known around Washington, DC, where he grew up, as the grandson of the distinguished Black statesman P. B. S. Pinchback. In *Black Reconstruction* (1935), W. E. B. Du Bois remarked that, for all intents and purposes, Pinchback lived as a white man who passed as a Black man for electoral gain.[23] In 1872, during Reconstruction, Pinchback was the Republican governor of Louisiana for forty-three days. Some said that when Pinchback was mistaken for the steel magnate Andrew Carnegie, he was so proud of this misrecognition that he left the error stand uncorrected.[24]

Pinchback was attuned to the profitability of appearances. So it made sense that he was skeptical of the man who would become Jean Toomer's father. Nathan Toomer was a multiracial ex-slave and farmer who had inherited a fortune from his second wife after she passed away. He had exquisite taste and was impeccably dressed. Twice the age of Pinchback's daughter, Nina, when they met (Nathan was fifty-four, Nina was twenty-eight), Nathan had, as Nina recalled, a "way with people."[25] To win over his father-in-law, Nathan paid cash for a small home on Twelfth Street in a delightful neighborhood in DC. But not long after Nathan's son, Jean, was born in 1894, Nathan vanished without a trace.

Jean Toomer, like his father and grandfather, cared about appearances. But he was more philosophical about them than either of them. As a high schooler, in between weightlifting, wrestling, and riding his motorcycle—which he bought from the money he saved as a paperboy for the *Saturday Evening Post*—Toomer began to ask the question that would preoccupy his life: Should he pass as white or identify as Black? Although he wasn't sure, this question would be briefly set aside when he found a new identity as a student at the University of Chicago: devoted Marxist. Marxism introduced Toomer to concepts such as class struggle and class consciousness, which brought him to socialism. So eager was Toomer to align with like-minded people that he left the Midwest and came to the center of left activity in the US: New York. In 1917, as a twenty-three-year-old, Toomer enrolled at New York's City College and lived in a small room on Ninth Street in the West Village.

Socialism was appealing to Toomer because it offered "a sort of whole into which everything fit, or seemed to fit, a body of ideas which held a consistent view of life and which enabled me to see and understand as one does when he sees a map."[26] Eager to test out his new theory of life, Toomer found work as a shipfitter in the Elizabeth, New Jersey, shipyards. It was there where, at the end of a bitterly cold December week in 1919, he was toiling in a cramped cabin in subzero temperatures for a meager twenty-two dollars a week. Toomer was on the lookout for loyal comrades. But what he found instead was false consciousness. "The men who worked in those yards—and they were realistic workmen," he reflected in retrospect, "had two main interests: playing craps and sleeping with women. Socialism? . . . a pipe dream."[27] Toomer lasted for ten days on the shipyards.

The brief experience of working at the Jersey docks left a bitter taste for Toomer, but after seeing the "wretched character of the worker and his life," it also reinforced his conviction in "the *need* for socialism, the *need* of a radical change of the conditions of human society."[28] America wasn't ready. Toomer's last day of work was also the first day of the infamous Palmer Raids on January 2, 1920, led by a zealously anti-communist twenty-four-year-old, J. Edgar Hoover, which deported thousands of radicals. Emma Goldman was among them.

Toomer, now twenty-six and out of work, dreaded the humiliating prospect of moving back to Washington, DC, where his grandfather promised him a five-dollar weekly allowance to take care of him and his aging wife. With no good options, Toomer agreed. He stayed in DC through the summer of 1921 until he found a new caretake role—this one as principal of Sparta Agricultural and Industrial Institute in Sparta, Georgia.

Toomer arrived in Sparta as the fall leaves were turning in September 1921. This was his first extended stay in Georgia and in the South generally. (Georgia was his father's longtime home, though Nathaniel Toomer had died in 1906.) Georgia was the land of lush green fields and idyllic flowing rivers. From 1877 to 1950, it was also the US state with the second-most lynchings on record: 589 plundered bodies.[29] On a muggy August day in 1921, a few weeks before Toomer arrived, Walter Smalley, a Black chauffeur, was falsely accused of stripping the lugs and bolts from his white employer's car. Smalley was shot to death by a white mob. Later that night, his lifeless body was taken from the town's morgue and burned along a country road.

This sadistic murder of Smalley was Toomer's introduction to Sparta. And it raised a difficult question for which Toomer, the socialist, had no easy answer. White workers' economic resentment couldn't explain this religious destruction of the Black body—this perverse "wake," as the white mob called it. Class consciousness alone couldn't dampen these violent racist fantasies. Confronted with these unsettling conclusions, Toomer attempted an experimental response through his modernist collage, *Cane* (1923).

Cane stands as a triumph of the Black counterculture. An assortment of fiction, poetry, stream of consciousness, and literary prose, *Cane* is defined by vignettes and images: Black reapers sharpening a blood-stained scythe, disembodied brown eyes love without fear, faces are ripe with worms, cotton bales look like bare feet, a plum becomes an everlasting song. There's Becky, a white woman who is estranged from her family after giving birth to two Black sons. Carma, whose husband is sent to a chain gang. There's a white woman named Bona, who struggles with her attraction to a Black man, Paul.

But this melancholic strain in *Cane* is balanced by a spirit of generosity. There is Old David Georgia, who supports Becky. David Georgia "grinding cane and boiling syrup, never went her way without some sugar sap." There's John, brother of the manager of the Howard Theater, who is transfixed by the dancing Dorris. "She forgets her tricks. She dances. Glorious songs are the muscles of her limbs. And her singing is of canebrake loves and mangrove feastings. . . . The scene is Dorris. She dances. Dorris dances. Glorious Dorris. Dorris whirls, whirls, dances . . . "[30]

Cane isn't a political book, but it couldn't avoid the politics of the country in which it was published in 1923. That year, Ku Klux Klan membership reached an astounding three million. The Klan, seemingly on the wane at the beginning of the twentieth century, had been emboldened to reascend in public, and to do so publicly. One of the biggest reasons was filmmaker D. W. Griffith's *Birth of a Nation* (1915), which depicted Klansmen during the period of Reconstruction (1865–1877) as saviors. To make matters worse, the sitting Democratic president of the time, Woodrow Wilson, declared that *The Birth of a Nation* wasn't fiction (it was) but was "like writing history with lightning." Lynching was such a national epidemic in the US at the time that, in 1918, Leonidas C. Dyer, a white Republican representative from St. Louis, Missouri, introduced a bill to make lynching a federal crime, with a $5,000 fine and accompanying five-year jail term. Passed in the US House of Representatives in 1922, the antilynching bill was filibustered to death by the racist block of Southern Democrats, called "Dixiecrats," in the Senate.

If you read *Cane* with this racial climate in mind, you can see its subtle political intervention. *Cane* doesn't advocate any party politics. It instead recenters how we see the world. *Cane*'s kaleidoscopic apparitions cut against the certainty racists desire. The more we know about the lives of others, the more we hear their intimate thoughts, their unfiltered desires, their sorrow, the less likely we are to dehumanize them. *Cane* accomplishes this shift not through sociological analysis, but through surrealism—dreams, half-images, and stream of consciousness.

But what if *Cane*'s strength, its surrealism, is also its weakness? Confronting racism requires one to think in terms of clear identities—Black or white. It requires one to make a commitment. Are you a racist or an anti-racist?

Jean Toomer didn't like binary choices. Bristling at the suggestion by his publisher, Horace Liveright, that *Cane* be marketed as written by a Black man, Toomer threatened to cancel publication. "My racial composition and my position in the world are realities which I alone may determine," he wrote. "I do not expect to be told what I should consider myself to be."[31] Toomer felt sick when his longtime champion and friend, the white novelist Waldo Frank, in *Cane*'s preface, described Toomer as a "Negro."

Toomer wanted to be post-racial not only because he wanted to be class-conscious. It was because he wanted to be more spiritually enlightened. Precisely as his literary star rose and the opportunity for making a direct contribution to radical politics became greater than ever, he turned inward and went abroad. Toomer found what he was seeking in George Gurdjieff's Institute for the Harmonious Development of Man on two hundred acres of land, just outside Fontainebleau, France. Little is known about George Gurdjieff, the bald, mustached mystic with the intense gaze. What we do know is that he was born in 1866 in Alexandropol, Armenia, and was, like Toomer, a wanderer looking for meaning in a world in crisis. He left his Moscow home in revolutionary Russia in 1917, crossing through the wreckage of civil war between the Bolsheviks and Menshevik armies, to Tiblisi, Georgia. Gurdjieff, like his disciples, was mysterious. This only added to his aura. When he and his students arrived in New York in 1924, they did so unannounced. They would spontaneously perform their mystical dances, according to some strict geometric formula, which no one could understand. They did this in unnamed locations, to a selected group of invitees. Gurdjieff and his circle performed "concentration tests" and, allegedly, engaged in mind-bending acts of thought transference.

Closer inspection reveals that Gurdjieff wasn't some saint who could live on prayer alone. Back in Moscow and St. Petersburg, Gurdjieff, always short on money, sold Asian carpets and billed himself as a homeopath who, for a small free, could hypnotize patients out of the scourge of drug addiction.[32] Like Toomer, he was a shapeshifter. This explains his puzzling belief in the divine power of plastics. If one mastered them, Gurdjieff argued, they could change their appearance, or disappear altogether. When the British short-story writer Katherine Mansfield arrived at Gurdjieff's institute at Fontainebleau in 1922, shortly after it opened, with a serious case of tuberculosis, Gurdjieff told her to drink milk, soak up the sunshine, and sleep in the barn in order to inhale the breath of cows. Mansfield died shortly thereafter arriving. Perhaps she didn't master plastics, but the result would have been the same even if she had.

As someone in the market for spiritual meaning, Jean Toomer didn't notice any signs that Gurdjieff could be a false prophet. In April 1926, after a mystical vision on the subway platform of New York's Sixty-Sixth Street L station at ten in the morning, Toomer described discovering that "my being was in vital contact with the vast universe." He drifted toward those whose lives were malleable like plastic, "conscious and dynamic," "involving an extension of experience and the uncovering of new materials."[33] Gurdjieff was, at the time, in France, so the next closest thing in New York was the bohemians. Toomer befriended photographer Alfred Stieglitz and painter Georgia O'Keeffe, as well as Mabel Dodge, whose famous Tuesday Salons were once the center of it all.

Bohemians loved Toomer. By all accounts, he was an attractive man who liked to flirt. Toomer garnered many women suitors, many of whom were married. He had a three-year-long affair with his onetime champion Waldo Frank's wife, the psychologist Margaret Naumburg, which began immediately after he came back to New York from Sparta in 1923. A decade later, Toomer had a short-lived affair around Christmas of 1933 with O'Keeffe in Lake George, New York, while her husband, Stieglitz, was visiting Manhattan. In 1926, Toomer's next romantic tryst was with Mabel Dodge (at the time, Dodge was still married to Tony Luhan). After hearing one of his lectures, Dodge was enamored by Toomer's capacity to "transmute" her to a "more lofty region . . . where every cell is filled with light and no more weight remains in matter."[34]

As a result, Dodge would go on to lend Toomer a large amount of money—$14,000—to set up a new branch of Gurdjieff's institute in Taos, New Mexico. But Dodge's pull was less powerful than Gurdjieff's. Under Gurdjieff's direct orders, Toomer funneled Dodge's loan back to Fontainebleau. The Taos center was never built, and, despite placating letters from Dodge to return the money, Toomer never paid her back.

Langston Hughes, who called Toomer "one of the most talented of all the writers," accused him of escaping from his Blackness because he believed whiteness was more profitable. "Toomer shortly left his Harlem group and went downtown to drop the seeds of Gurdjieff in less dark and poverty-stricken fields. . . . Certainly nobody in Harlem could afford to pay for Gurdjieff," Hughes quipped. "And very few there have evolved souls."[35] Toomer's onetime friend, Waldo Frank, was more charitable, though less diplomatic than Hughes. Gurdjieff filled a meaningful need for Toomer, but "in his need to forget he was a Negro, he joined the transcendental . . . cult of Gurdjieff, whose psychological techniques aimed at obliterating . . . the condition of being a man."[36]

■ ■ ■

Shortly before *Cane* was published by Liveright, in December 1921, Jean Toomer had sent some selections of the novel in progress to *The Liberator,* the magazine that Max Eastman and Crystal Eastman founded after *The Masses* shuttered. The coeditor at the time rejected them. Toomer's writing had a "bright local coloring and individual poetic power," but the editor wasn't impressed with its ambiguity. It didn't seem to "carry clear through from beginning to end," the editor said.[37] If Toomer ran away from both Blackness and from revolution, then the editor who wrote these words, named Claude McKay, barreled toward both.

This wasn't initially the plan for the young man from the rustic Jamaican countryside born in 1890 to a solidly middle-class family of respectable Black farmers. McKay's mother, a religious and caring woman, wanted McKay to be a good Christian. His father, a stern patriarch, was more concerned about him continuing the family business and being a practical head of household. As a boy, McKay wanted neither of these things. He wanted to read books and to play outside. Realizing that his education was limited in the small village of Sunny Ville where he was born, McKay went to live with his brother, a schoolteacher outside of Montego Bay named U'Theo. It was there that McKay was able to formulate his spontaneous sense of play into the science of words. His brother's extensive library introduced McKay to the sentimental fiction of Charles Dickens and the epic tragedies of William Shakespeare, and Darwinian evolution through Thomas Huxley. The year, 1912, that McKay published his first book of poems, *Songs of Jamaica,* was also the year he decided to mark a new phase in his life—to study agronomy at Booker T. Washington's crown jewel, Tuskegee University, in Alabama.

Upon arriving to US shores, McKay had an open mind. Maybe upward mobility was possible in America? But the fantasy came crashing down after McKay found Tuskegee's "semi-military, machine-like existence" suffocating. Also, Alabama racism was horrific beyond McKay's wildest imagination. "I heard of prejudice in America," he recalled, "but never dreamed of it being so intensely bitter."[38]

McKay's big break as a writer came in 1919. He was living in Harlem and working as a waiter on the Pennsylvania Railroad while trying to unsuccessfully send out poems to *The Liberator*. After yet another rejection, the magazine's cofounder, Crystal Eastman, invited him to her office. The two immediately hit it off. Was it hard for McKay to work and at the same time write? How did he find the time? His answer came through an anecdote. One day, while he was serving food to customers in a railcar he heard an intense buzzing. Feeling nauseous, he ran to the bathroom and locked the door. Instead of vomiting, McKay took out a scrap of paper and wrote a poem. "Got rid of your birth pains," Eastman quipped. McKay and Eastman both laughed.[39]

Eastman was perhaps more intrigued by McKay's charming personality than his verse. Before leaving for a scheduled appointment, Crystal gave him her brother Max Eastman's home address. McKay walked out of *The Liberator*'s office, exchanged pleasantries with Floyd Dell, who was writing literary essays for the magazine at the time, and walked to Max's West Village apartment at St. Luke's Place. McKay headed for a backroom study, where he saw a tall figure with white hair and a bright orange tie against a brown-gray suit. Eastman was sitting lazily on a couch. McKay showed Eastman the poem that had "exploded" out of him that day on the Pennsylvania Railroad. After Eastman published the poem called "If We Must Die" (1919), McKay exploded onto the literary scene. After first reading "If We Must Die," Langston Hughes eagerly awaited each issue of *The Liberator* to know the "revolutionary attitude toward Negroes."[40]

Revolutionary art comes from a specific historical moment, and from a concrete place. On the Pennsylvania Railroad dining car that summer of 1919, where McKay was a waiter for weeklong stretches, shuttling between New York, Baltimore, and Washington, DC, he breathlessly read aloud "If We Must Die" to his Black coworkers. They understood the poem immediately. In the newspapers each day, all of them learned of the gruesome events of June and July of 1919, in what came to be known as the "Red Summer." That summer, over twenty race riots, sparked by white vigilantes descending upon Black neighborhoods, dramatized the fire of white racial violence spreading throughout the country.

In Chicago, a spate of rioting led to twenty-three dead and one thousand homeless. After a July 27, 1919, incident at an unofficially segregated Chicago beach in which a Black seventeen-year-old drowned after being hit with rocks thrown by white kids, Black Chicagoans, protesting the fact that no one was held accountable, were met with bricks and guns. Two hundred Black people were killed in Elaine, Arkansas, in a massacre that began on September 30, 1919. This, after a white mob presumed that the efforts of a Black sharecropper, Robert Hill, to unionize farmworkers had signaled a Black insurrection was afoot. Dozens more were dead in Washington, DC, after a mob of white sailors, soldiers, and marines on July 19, 1919, spread the lie that a white sailor's wife had been assaulted by a Black man. No wonder McKay and his coworkers were nervous. They came to work bearing concealed pistols. "We stayed in our quarters all through the dreary ominous nights," McKay recalled, "for we never knew what was going to happen."[41]

McKay's "If We Must Die" concludes with, "What though before us lies the open grave?" "Like men we'll face the murderous cowardly pack, / Pressed to the wall, dying, but fighting back!"[42] Like Whitman before him, McKay isn't interested in subtly expressing a point. He does so directly, though not with overflowing love, but with a sense of prophetic rage.

Taking a side, and fighting for it, is crucial for politics, even if it isn't always for art. McKay liked to do all these things at once. And unlike Jean Toomer, McKay insisted on having multiple sources of self. McKay was Black, but he was also a worker. In 1919, the same year as the "Red Summer," with inflation running at 30 percent and wages falling rapidly, four million workers—20 percent of the workforce—went on strike. To support Pan-African decolonization, working-class revolution, and the fight against white terror, McKay, along with fellow Afro-Caribbean intellectual Cyril V. Briggs, founded the African Blood Brotherhood. Though it was short-lived, at its height, the organization boasted three thousand members. McKay was now targeted by government authorities. When he landed on the Justice Department's watchlist, he sailed to London in 1921, where he began to contribute to the socialist daily *Workers' Dreadnought* and was an active member of England's International Club.

If forced to choose between art and revolution, McKay would have probably chosen revolutionary art. Upon learning of McKay's return to New York from the UK in February 1922, Crystal and Max Eastman invited him to their summer cottage in Croton-on-Hudson. They made him associate editor of *The Liberator*. Because McKay was a meticulous editor who cared about style, his views didn't square with members of the staff who saw *The Liberator* as a vehicle for waging class war. Tensions would come to a head when Max Eastman, exhausted by heading up yet another money-losing magazine, resigned as editor. McKay now had to share editorial duties with Michael Gold.

Michael Gold was his pen name, though he was born Irwin Granich in 1893, a child of working-class Romanian Jews from the tenements of the Lower East Side. Despite being an exceptional student (Gold attended City College and spent a year at Harvard), Gold promoted his street cred. He wore dirty Stetson hats and stained shirts. He smoked cheap cigars and spat on the floor, for exaggerated effect.[43] He bragged that he was an amateur boxer and, to prove it, once challenged McKay to a fistfight at John's Italian Restaurant. It was only after McKay was able to talk Gold down that the two men had some red wine and a good laugh. Gold still harbored his suspicions about McKay. Most bothersome for him was McKay's racial position. Given that Black Americans made up 10 percent of the population, McKay thought it prudent to have *The Liberator* devote a similar percentage to Black authors, or, at the very least, to issues of race. Gold, a Jewish American who was convinced that he had transcended race and thought Marxism would overcome antisemitism, was enraged. After McKay's proposal was put to a vote, it was vetoed by *The Liberator* staff. McKay both loved and hated what *The Liberator* stood for. For a casual reader, that was okay. But for an editor, it was impossible. McKay resigned his position as editor in July 1922.

The American left, it seemed, was done with McKay. But Claude McKay wasn't done with the international left. In 1920, the then-ailing John Reed had personally sent McKay an invitation to the Second Congress of the Communist International. At the time, Vladimir Lenin was eager to show the difference between the universal brotherhood of Soviet Communism and the racism of US democracy. McKay didn't go in 1920. When, however, he did finally arrive to Russia in 1923, he was treated like a celebrity everywhere on the streets. (The locals weren't accustomed to seeing Black men in their midst.)

But things were different for McKay in the halls of power. He got only the cold shoulder from the Communist elite in Russia. That changed only when McKay tapped his old connections. A Japanese Communist held in high esteem by the Soviets, Sen Katayama, vouched for McKay because he enjoyed their long conversations about Global South solidarity over dinner at Asian restaurants in New York when McKay was with *The Liberator*. Now McKay was invited to official party gatherings.

But McKay's Russian comrades abroad, it turned out, weren't better than his American frenemies. At the inaugural session of the Fourth Congress of the Comintern in a cold November 1922, as McKay entered the Bolshoi Theatre, he was stunned to be aggressively forced on stage by ushers. This was done at the request of the chairman of the Comintern, Grigory Zinoviev. Zinoviev wanted McKay to speak about the "Negro problem" in America. Flustered, McKay stood there and for a while said nothing. When he did speak, he said that he was a "writer, not an agitator." McKay was being honest. But the reason he was so adored by the Soviets was because his "If We Must Die" appeared to the Soviets as political art, or what they called "socialist realism." By denying that all art was inherently political, McKay agitated his Soviet audience even more.[44]

Three days later, McKay sauntered toward the Throne Room of the Kremlin, as an invited speaker. He was wearing a sport jacket and a button-down shirt. His hands in his pockets, McKay approached the cloth-draped podium. Although he was no expert on the matter, McKay confessed, he knew race couldn't be divorced from class, that fighting economic oligarchy and white supremacy go hand in hand. "I have found demonstrations of prejudice," he told the party leaders, "on the various occasions when the White and Black comrades had to get together: and this is the greatest difficulty that the Communists of America have to overcome—the fact that they first have got to emancipate themselves from the ideas they entertain toward Negroes before they can be able to reach the Negroes with any kind of radical propaganda."[45]

This wasn't what the Soviet party faithful expected to hear. But V. I. Lenin, seriously ill though in attendance, and Trotsky, whom McKay had a nice rapport with, were persuaded. At least enough to issue a formal statement. By the end of the session, the Fourth Congress had adopted an official platform that outlined how Africans and African Americans could be part of the international class struggle.

McKay spent another six months in the Soviet Union. He was commissioned to write essays for local papers—which were later collected as *The Negroes in America* (1923). And Leon Trotsky sent him on a tour of Bolshevik military and naval installations. As a distinguished guest, McKay arrived at the Kronstadt airfield by car to find sailors waiting on the tarmac in the cold for him. The Soviets couldn't tokenize McKay, but, it turns out, McKay tokenized Russia: "The famine had ended and the NEP [Russia's New Economic Policy] was flourishing, the people were simply happy. I was the first Negro to arrive in Russia since the Revolution. . . . I was like a black ikon."[46]

McKay was, we can say in retrospect, mistaken about the Soviet Union, but what was unmistakable was that, above all else, he wanted to write literature, rather than be involved in Communist politics. Things came to a head in the summer of 1923. McKay was badly shaken after the physical stress of having a tooth pulled in Petrograd caused him to have a temporary paralytic stroke (it was a result of his chronic hypertension).[47] After the extravagant May Day celebration of 1923, where he stayed at the royal palace of Grand Duke Alexander, McKay made his choice to depart Russia. He sailed to Berlin, then to Paris, and then to Marseilles. It was in France where McKay learned of Lenin's death in 1924, and that Joseph Stalin had won the power struggle over Trotsky to succeed Lenin as leader in 1925. From correspondence with his friend, Max Eastman, who had sources inside the Kremlin, McKay learned that Stalin was a power-hungry realist. McKay's visit to Russia would be his first and his last. Never would he again step foot on Russian soil.

CHAPTER 6

FRUITS OF SPLENDOR

A s Claude McKay was in France working on drafts of his first novel, later to be published as *Home to Harlem* in 1928, he learned about a March 1925 special edition of a magazine called *Survey Graphic*. This issue had omitted one of the poems he submitted for inclusion, "Mulatto," and it included another whose title was changed from "The White House" "to "White Houses." McKay didn't like that "Mulatto" wouldn't appear in the issue, but he was even more troubled by the fact that the editor took it upon himself to change the title of "The White House." The poem's original title, like the poem's first lines, made plain McKay's critique of American power: "Your door is shut against my tightened face, And I am sharp as steel with discontent / To hold me to the letter of your law! Oh, I must keep my heart inviolate / Against the potent poison of your hate." Furious, McKay wrote to the editor: "Your attitude is that of Booker T. Washington's in social reform. . . . Principles mean something to my life."[1]

The editor, a man by the name of Alain Locke, scoffed at McKay's overzealous tone. The poem, Locke insisted, would be seen as an attack on the US presidency and might even prevent McKay from traveling from France back to the US. Pluralizing the title to "White Houses," Locke thought, might be beneficially read as a plea for Black inclusion into middle-class life. White houses were, after all, symbols of the American dream. As Locke wrote in the introduction to the special issue of *Survey Graphic*, in which Jean Toomer and Langston Hughes were also featured, "To all of this the New Negro is keenly responsive as an augury of a new democracy in American culture. He is contributing his share to the new social understanding."[2] The issue sold forty-two thousand copies through two printings. What we now call the "Harlem Renaissance" was born.

Locke's idea for putting the "New Negro" on the map was hatched on March 21, 1924, at a dinner at New York City's Civic Club on West Twelfth Street, off Fifth Avenue. The celebration, conceived by Charles S. Johnson, editor of *Opportunity* magazine, was initially meant to be small. On its surface, it was a literary coming-out party for Jessie Redmon Fauset and her forthcoming novel, *There Is Confusion*, the story of Joanna Marshall, a talented Black singer and dancer whose efforts to forge a career are blocked by her husband's desire that she remain a housewife and nothing more. But when Locke was asked by Johnson to be master of ceremonies that evening, he recognized the opportunity to introduce a group of Black artists before an influential group of white tastemakers. An intimate dinner of twenty had now turned into a lavish ceremony for one hundred. Publishers such as Frederick Allen of Harper's Brothers, Walter Bartlett of Scribner's, and Carl Van Doren, editor of *The Century*, attended. Playwright Eugene O'Neill and essayist H. L. Mencken were there. Carl Van Doren cleared his throat to address the gathering: "What American literature decidedly needs at this moment is color, music, gusto, the free expression of gay or desperate moods. If the Negroes are not in a position to contribute these items, I do not know what Americans are."[3] By then Locke had to have known the evening was a smashing success.

Making Black artists mainstream wasn't always Alain Locke's ambition. As the first Black Rhodes Scholar at Oxford University and then a philosophy student at University of Berlin (1907–11), Locke was more concerned about Western imperialism and economic colonization. World War I, he wrote at the time, was a "race war" for "the utopia of empire and the dream of an unlimited and permanent overlordship."[4] But now, as a distinguished member of what W. E. B. Du Bois called the "talented tenth," making him an elite gatekeeper of the race, Locke worried about respectability. To have a platform to say anything in a racist society, he believed, the Black artist must work from within the boundaries of what's mainstream. Sure, they could push the margins gently, but not explode them. Locke came to this conclusion not out of ideological conviction, but pragmatic calculation. It wasn't his fault that white racism circumscribed Black creative possibility. In a *Crisis* review, Locke could, on the one hand, glowingly describe Fauset's *There Is Confusion* as the "novel the Negro intelligentsia have been waiting for." But at the same time, he could ignore the fact that when Horace Liveright, a white man and Jessie Fauset's publisher, spoke at the Civic Club dinner in 1924, he did so not to applaud Fauset's gifts as a talented writer but to complain about the low sales of another book he had just recently published: Jean Toomer's *Cane*.

Claude McKay disagreed with Locke's pragmatism. The Black artist, McKay thought, needed to say what she wanted to say no matter the pushback. This ambition was apparent with McKay's first novel, *Home to Harlem* (1928). The novel chronicles Black veteran Jake Brown, a World War I deserter. Jake's quest—through dive bars, cabarets, brothels, night-clubs—is in search of a Black cabaret singer, Felice, a sex worker whom he meets on his first night back home to Harlem.

Upon publication, *Home to Harlem* became an instant bestseller. The writer F. Scott Fitzgerald, who coined the term "Jazz Age," told McKay that the book reminded him of the French naturalist Émile Zola. Langston Hughes wrote McKay saying it was "the finest thing 'we've done yet.'"[5] Not everyone was pleased. The reason white people flocked to buy the book, Du Bois wrote in a scathing review, was because McKay's image of Harlem played to their racist fantasies of Black criminality and hypersexuality. "It nauseates me," Du Bois complained, "and after the dirtiest parts of its filth I feel distinctly like taking a bath."[6] McKay was pained but shot back: "Deep-sunk in depravity though he may be, the author of *Home to Harlem* prefers to remain unrepentant and unregenerate and he 'distinctly' is not grateful for any free baptism of grace in the cleansing pages of the *Crisis*."[7]

The public feud between McKay and Du Bois was in no small part so ferocious because of what neither man could say out loud in magazines like *The Liberator*, *The Crisis*, or *Survey Graphic*. *Home to Harlem* was, at its core, an account of the queer Harlem counterculture. At a Harlem cabaret called the Congo, for instance, Jake witnesses "dark dandies loving up their pansies. Feet tickling under the tables. . . . Everybody was teased up to high point of excitement."[8] Later, Jake sees "gleaming-skinned black boys bearing goblets of wine and obedient eunuchs."[9]

Home to Harlem wasn't purely a work of McKay's imagination. As a gay Black man himself, McKay knew the scene. Queer Black men and women were denied access to segregated downtown speakeasies. They flocked to Harlem, where most of the clubs stayed open past midnight, and some only opened around then.[10] Harlem's queer community could be seen at a cabaret saloon or a tenement party. They rubbed shoulders with, danced with, gossiped with, and chain-smoked with everyone else who was there. But many queer men and women were also fixtures aboveground as well. Drag queens, wearing silk stockings and luxurious furs, were regulars at Cyril's Café and would be seen walking Lenox Avenue by day. After several queens were arrested and sentenced to sixty days in the workhouse at the 123rd Street police station, they shouted to the cops, "Goodbye, dearie," as they were being escorted out of the courthouse.[11]

The most glamorous representation of Black Bohemia was the Hamilton Lodge Ball at the Rockland Palace Casino. It was a masquerade ball, at the corner of 280 West 155th Street and Frederick Douglass Avenue. Founded in 1869 by the Black activist and drag queen William Dorsey Swann, the ball drew hundreds of gay men from all over the country. They donned wigs, dresses, frocks, and cheap jewelry, while performing among thousands of spectators—many of them straight. The blues singer Ethel Waters once bragged about lending her dress to a prize-winning contestant, while the vaudeville performer Taylor Gordon phoned a group of his friends to share the news that he had been asked to judge a contest.[12] Harlem's leading newspaper, *Amsterdam News*, regularly posted illustrations of the prize-winning costumes. At the Hamilton Lodge Ball, attendees would strut, sing, and wear long dresses. What they were doing was facilitating new images of freedom.

This was why the cabaret, according to Black socialist Chandler Owen, cofounder in 1917 with A. Philip Randolph of the magazine *The Messenger*, was the "most democratic institution." Owen, a North Carolina–born atheist, almost cared as much about radical politics as he did about the club—he supported Black Pullman workers in their effort at unionization, and even, unsuccessfully, ran for the New York State Assembly. The cabaret was a sacred place where you could be yourself. It was where, said Owen, you could be in the moment. Nothing else mattered. And when your guard is down, as it was at the cabaret, ideas change and small-scale transformations of the self can occur. It's where the "prison bars of prejudice are temporarily at least torn down, and people act . . . kind, cordial, friendly, gentle."[13]

For the very reason that Owen found cabarets so appealing, the Hamilton Lodge Ball drew the ire of the puritanical Committee of Fourteen, founded by New York's Anti-Saloon League. At one point, the Committee of Fourteen released a report detailing 130 infractions against the lodge. It wasn't just citizens hell-bent on instituting Prohibition. Queer Harlem was also seen by many self-described liberals as a threat to the civil rights struggle because it contradicted middle-class respectability. The influential Black reverend Adam Clayton Powell Sr., head of the Abyssinian Baptist Church, waged a homophobic crusade against gay men in 1929, singling out cabarets and rent parties as sites of "perversion." Business manager of *The Crisis*, Augustus Granville Dill, was dismissed by W. E. B. Du Bois himself in 1928 after Dill was arrested for engaging in a consensual sexual encounter with a male hairdresser in a New York subway station.

From the perspective of queer Harlem, however, the interracial composition of the audience and the ornate costumes signified another world in the making. Hughes attended the Hamilton Lodge Ball, and fondly recalled it as a brilliant "spectacle in colour."[14] The ball was itself an extension of a cosmopolitan attitude that marked the Black counterculture. Hughes freely mingled with European aristocrats, communists, publishers, and hobo poets at the British aristocrat Nancy Cunard's home. With her trademark silver turban covering her hair, Cunard pontificated about modernist culture, swinging her twelve bracelets, while the crooner Gus Simons sang alongside African drums.[15] At the apartment of Black painter Aaron Douglas and his wife Alta, Hughes pooled his money—along with everyone else's—to find the nearest bootlegger, who could procure a sampling of cheap scotch, bourbon, or rye.[16] Downtown at Carl Van Vechten's house, Hughes listened to an intimate performance of Bessie Smith, while Van Vechten, along with his wife, the actress Fania Marinoff, would swerve around the room, overfilling everyone's glass with expensive champagne. Another night at the Van Vechtens' home, Hughes attended what came to be known as a "Vechten gossip party." Everyone there was forced to share the most embarrassing stories they heard about the person sitting right across from them.[17]

■   ■   ■

After a party in 1925—this one not in Harlem but in Washington, DC, at the LeDroit Park home of the Black poet Georgia Douglas Johnson— Langston Hughes met a nineteen-year-old gadfly, Bruce Nugent. Hughes was dressed in his trademark shabby mackinaw plaid jacket, whereas

Nugent, a bohemian, was the master of keeping up a disheveled appearance. Standing at six feet tall, Nugent didn't wear socks—this was his trademark. The two men hit it off. They left Georgia Johnson's home and, entranced by the depth of their conversation and the strength of their connection, they began walking down S Street to Thirteenth. They first arrived at Nugent's grandmother's apartment. But they weren't done talking, so they went back to Hughes's mother's home, where he was staying. They did this back-and-forth stroll for hours into the early morning.

It's not clear if Hughes and Nugent ever had a sexual relationship, though Nugent, who was openly gay at the time, summarized the Black bohemian ethic like this: "You did what you wanted do. . . . Nobody was in the closet. There was no closet."[18] True, sexuality wasn't policed by Black Bohemia. Yet there was an ethics by which Hughes and his circle lived. No one was scandalized, for example, when the Utah-born Black writer, Wallace Thurman, was arrested for having sex with a male hairdresser in the 135th Street Subway bathroom, days after he arrived in Harlem in 1925. They were, however, disappointed to learn that Thurman's marriage to another one of their friends, Louise Thompson, only lasted a brief six months. Everybody in Black Bohemia knew Alain Locke was gay, but they didn't like how he acted like a petty, mercurial dictator in elevating his favorite literary styles over others.

Hughes, for his part, was courted by Locke and enjoyed the company of men. Still, no one cared about the exact nature of Hughes's sexuality—was he gay or straight, both, or neither? What mattered to Black Bohemia was that Hughes didn't lead on Locke, or any other man, who was attracted to him. This is the message Countee Cullen shared directly with Langston. And after chatting with Hughes, Cullen reassured Locke that "no more skeins have been tangled. . . . I am doing my utmost to unravel those which are twisted."[19] Cullen, it should be noted, didn't always take his own advice. He was briefly married to W. E. B. Du Bois's daughter, Yolande Du Bois, while secretly pursuing romantic affairs with several men.

No place in the 1920s encapsulated the aspirations of Black Bohemia as the three-story walk-up town house on 267 West 136th Street—which they, tongue and cheek, called "Niggerati Manor." Wallace Thurman, along with Bruce Nugent, moved into the home in the summer of 1926. At the "Manor," the rent was cheap, if ever collected. A makeshift artistic colony at 267 West 136th had an open-door policy. Artists were coming and going, listening to the blues, smoking cigarettes, and drinking excessively. Hughes lived there briefly. The walls of the Manor were painted red and black, and dotted with murals of brightly painted phalluses, encapsulating a boisterous and homoerotic spirit.

Black bohemians wanted to make their lives the stuff of fiction. The magazine in which they did this was provocatively called *Fire!!* It only published one issue, in November 1926. Far from being respectable like Locke's *Survey Graphic*, *Fire!!* was, like *The Masses* and *Mother Earth* before it, biting in its tone and avant-garde in its approach in addressing taboo topics like gay love, liberated women, and clandestine interracial affairs. The magazine's ethos was captured by the double meaning of its declarative title, referring both to the command to shoot (as in, "Ready, aim, fire!") and the scream someone makes when they see something burning.

Fire!! was a fuller version of what Claude McKay once hoped he might find a little bit of in *The Liberator*. As its subtitle announced, "Devoted to Younger Negro Artists," *Fire!!* was preoccupied with the margins of experience of Black youth living on the margins. Giving voice to what was unsayable about young Black men and women in the racist world outside made it revolutionary.

Fire!!'s cover page, designed in reddish-pink and block font, was drawn by a talented Black painter from Topeka, Kansas, Aaron Douglas. What you see on the cover is an Egyptian sphinx laying down with an African mask. But if you look closely, you realize that the sphinx is, in fact, an extension of an earring belonging to a silhouette of a Black person looking to the left. In a letter to Hughes, Douglas said he wanted make art that is "transcendentally material, mystically objected. Earthy. Spiritually earthy. Dynamic."[20]

Fire!!'s contributors succeeded in achieving these goals. Zora Neale Hurston's award-winning play, *Color Struck*, depicts the meaning of Black love within a colorist society that sees beauty in terms of white and black hues. John, a light-skinned Black man, is attracted to a lighter-skinned woman, Effie, much to the anger of his friend, a dark-skinned Black woman called Emmaline. Bruce Nugent's "Smoke, Lilies and Jade," a stream-of-consciousness story reminiscent of Toomer's *Cane*, captures queer desire in a heterosexual relationship: Alex, the bohemian protagonist, Nugent writes, "liked the sound of the approaching man's footsteps . . . he walked music also . . . he knew the beauty of the narrow blue . . . Alex knew that by the way their echoes mingled . . .”[21] Wallace Thurman's "Cordelia the Crude" is the story of a sixteen-year-old sex worker who doesn't go to school and can't hold a job. Cordelia accepts her choices, and Thurman doesn't criticize them. And Hughes's poem "Elevator Boy" details the inner life of an elevator boy at the "Dennison Hotel in Jersey," who fantasizes about quitting his job and finding a woman to sleep with.

An overview of this works reveals that *Fire!!* was committed to a do-it-yourself ethic, which cut against the demands of American capitalism. At the time of its publication, a sophisticated advertising industry, drawing on Freudian concepts of lust and repression, was pushing to sell durable goods. Refrigerators to keep food ice-cold, washing machines to clean your Sunday best, and radiators to keep you warm during the winter months. *Fire!!*, which had no advertisements in its pages (60 percent of newspaper content at the time was devoted to advertisements), had as its message spiritual liberation, not conspicuous consumption. *Fire!!* sought to realize the vision Hughes put forward in his June 1926 piece for *The Nation* magazine:

> Let the blare of Negro jazz bands and the bellowing voice of Bessie Smith singing the Blues penetrate the closed ears of the colored near-intellectuals until they listen and perhaps understand. Let Paul Robeson singing "Water Boy" . . . and Jean Toomer holding the heart of Georgia in his hands, and Aaron Douglas drawing strange black fantasies cause the smug Negro middle class to turn from their white, respectable, ordinary books and papers to catch a glimmer of their own beauty. We younger Negro artists who create now intend to express our individual dark-skinned selves without fear or shame. . . . We know we are beautiful. And ugly, too. . . . We build our temples for tomorrow, strong as we know how, and we stand on top of the mountain, free within ourselves.[22]

Given these words, it should come as no surprise that *Fire!!* was met with hostility from critics. Alain Locke condemned its "sex radicalism," whereas the vast majority of white critics ignored it altogether. But what the young artists weren't prepared for—though perhaps it was obvious given the history of the counterculture—was that the dazzling free-spirited energy that animated *Fire!!* is also what sank it.

Each of the eight writer-editors was supposed to voluntarily contribute fifty dollars to the collective venture. Only three of them followed through (Hughes, it should be noted, held up his end of the bargain). Wallace Thurman, the magazine's editor, whom Hughes described as a "brilliant Black boy," was a perfectionist. Thurman could read eleven lines at once, but he could also find a million things wrong with everything he laid his eyes on. To make *Fire!!* worthy of his exacting editorial standards, he borrowed three hundred dollars from the local Harlem Community Church and the Mutual League. But on his way home, he was mugged at a subway station. Both the three-hundred-dollar loan and the clothes on Thurman's back were stolen. To cut down on distributing costs, Bruce Nugent, who didn't even bother to read proofs of his short story, sold individual copies of the initial print run of *Fire!!* by going to local bookstores on foot. But this didn't work in the way he had hoped. On his way walking around town, Nugent, hungry and tired, spent most of the money he earned on cheap sandwiches and drinks. In an ironic, even if appropriate twist, hundreds of unbought copies of *Fire!!* burned in an actual house fire in a printer's basement, where they were being stored.

▪   ▪   ▪

Among the contributors to *Fire!!*, and also a regular visitor to the "Manor," was a fiery Barnard College student. She wanted to be an anthropologist after studying with renowned scholar Franz Boas, whom she called "Papa Franz." Her play, *Color Struck*, won second-place prize for best drama script at *Opportunity* magazine's 1925 literary awards dinner. At that ceremony, after her name was announced as a winner, she walked toward the stage with a long, multicolored scarf around her neck and roared, "Color Struck!" Everyone stopped what they were doing. They chatted in hushed whispers among themselves. Langston Hughes was intrigued. "Zora Neale Hurston is a clever girl, isn't she?" he wrote a friend. "I would like to know her."[23]

Hughes's response was a common one for Zora Neale Hurston. In Eatonville, Florida, an all-Black town, where she was raised, Hurston never felt the need to stand out because she saw Black achievement, in all its complexity, everywhere. Zora's father, John, nicknamed "God's Battle Axe," was a well-respected Baptist preacher whose moral zeal would vanish as soon as he stepped away from the pulpit. He took up many extramarital affairs. Zora's mother, Lucy, was an excellent seamstress and part-time Sunday school teacher. Lucy would confront her husband about his infidelities but also loved to watch him be adored by his parishioners. Although Zora Neale Hurston had her father's charisma, she needed her mother's encouragement. Lucy would tell all eight Hurston children, and especially Zora, the baby, to "jump at de sun. . . . We might not land on the sun, but at least we would get off the ground."[24] To get closer to the sun, Hurston read voraciously—everything from stories about Hercules, her hero, to the Grimms' fairy tales. "My soul was with the gods and my body in the village," she remembered. This meant that Hurston suffered no mortal fools. She was "impudent and given to talking back."[25]

At age thirteen, not long after her mother died, Hurston enrolled at the Florida Baptist Academy in Jacksonville. Strikingly, it was 135 miles away from Eatonville, in the larger, predominantly white city of Jacksonville—where Hurston had to sit in segregated streetcars and drink at segregated water fountains—that she first felt "colored." Yet Hurston would not be defined by others' choices. When her father lapsed on her tuition and room and board payments, for instance, Hurston paid her tuition for the academic year by scrubbing the school's floors and helping in the school's kitchen.[26] After cycling through some temporary odd jobs, she landed work in 1915 as a maid to "Mrs. M.," the lead singer of a Gilbert and Sullivan traveling theater troupe of about thirty. For eight months, Hurston traveled the East Coast, going between Pennsylvania, Connecticut, and Virginia.

Then, Hurston settled in Baltimore, where she began waiting tables. At that point, she decided to take her story into her own hands by changing it. Hurston was, in fact, twenty-six, but she lied and said she was sixteen so she could attend high school in Baltimore. After graduating in 1918, she enrolled at Howard University and worked at the Cosmos Club as a waitress, where Teddy Roosevelt and Rudyard Kipling played pool and ordered drinks from its cherrywood bar.[27] Howard, however, wasn't going well. Hurston received a D in geology and an F in Spanish. Her social prospects were a different matter. In that area, she was exceeding her expectations. After joining the Howard literary magazine, *The Stylus*, whose faculty adviser was Alain Locke (Hurston called him a "genius"), she became a regular at Georgia Douglas's Saturday salons on S Street, where she'd mingle with Black Washingtonians like Bruce Nugent and Jean Toomer.

Only after the semi-autobiographical short story about her girlhood in Eatonville, "Drenched in Light," was published in a 1924 issue of *Opportunity* did Hurston try her hand at being a writer full-time. She moved from DC to New York the first week of January 1925, with one dollar and fifty cents. As she later recalled, she had "no job, no friends, and a lot of hope."[28] But within months, Hurston, in her own genius act of marketing, would be noticed everywhere she went. She mixed Norwegian ski wear with a multicolored scarf draped around her neck. Her witticisms possessed a wonderful sense of self-assuredness. "Sometimes, I feel discriminated against, but it does not make me angry. It merely astonishes me. How can any deny themselves the pleasure of my company? It's beyond me."[29] And yet, Hurston's jokes would often have rich layers of social criticism. One day, as she was walking along Lenox Avenue toward the subway heading downtown, a blind beggar stopped her, held out his cup, and pled: "Please help the blind! Help the blind! A nickel for the blind!" Hurston took five cents from *his* cup, and said, "I need money worse than you today. . . . Lend me this! Next time, I'll give it back."[30]

Hurston was the life of the party because, in a sexist and racist society, if she didn't seize space, her voice would remain unknown. That's why she once stormed into a Harlem rent-party dressed in her trademark pearls, bright white gloves, and one of her dazzling collection of hats. She said things like, "I love myself when I am laughing," and "when I am looking mean and impressive."[31] Hurston bewildered her friends and drew the ire of her critics when, as she controversially put it in a 1928 essay, she was "not tragically colored," and said that slavery "fails to register depression with me. Slavery is sixty years past."[32] Hurston developed these arguments in her 1937 book, *Their Eyes Were Watching God*, the story of a Black woman, Janie Crawford, who, at various times in her life escapes awful situations—an absent mother, sexual violence, an unhappy marriage—to make a life for herself.

Philosophically, Hurston was race-conscious but not race-centric. When she was a student at Barnard College, among a thousand white faces, she admitted that she felt like a "dark rock, surged upon."[33] But when Hurston was at a club listening to jazz, she knew she was part of a beautiful Black history of struggle. The memory of her enslaved ancestors—making a resonant sound, dreaming of utopia—made her move with reckless abandon. She captures this experience in her 1928 essay "How It Feels to Be Colored Me": "I dance wildly inside myself; I yell within, I whoop; I shake my assegai above my head, I hurl it true to the mark *yeeeeooww*! . . . My pulse is throbbing like a war drum. I want to slaughter something—give pain, give death to what, I do not know."[34] Hurston's experience was incomparable to that of her white male friend, who, sitting beside her, quietly drummed the table with his fingertips, and automatically, as if scripted and on cue, said when the performance was over: "Good music they have here."[35]

It is precisely this militant individualism that made Hurston's politics deeply unorthodox. For example, Hurston opposed the public school desegregation mandate in *Brown v. Board of Education* because she thought the 1954 Supreme Court decision was an example of judicial overreach: "While it is being frantic over the segregation ruling, it had better keep its eyes on more important things. . . . Govt by fiat has been rammed down its throat. . . . The stubborn South . . . kept this nation from being dragged farther left than it was ruing the New Deal."[36] Sounding like a classical liberal that would have agreed more with Thomas Jefferson than with Martin Luther King Jr., Hurston asserted that once "you turn an executive loose to go outside the law in your favor on Monday . . . you have also given him the power to go outside the law on Thursday against you. No country is safe from tyranny unless the chief executive is kept within the bounds of law made and provided."[37]

Hurston reserved special praise for Ohio Republican senator Robert A. Taft—who she believed had "some strange passion for justice"—during his 1952 campaign for president. (Taft would lose the presidential nomination to Dwight D. Eisenhower.)[38] She urged Black voters to see past Taft's party label because she agreed with the senator's position to eliminate poll taxes, support public housing, and fight racial discrimination in the federal government. These were not far-right positions. But Taft, it should be remembered, was a staunch critic of Franklin Delano Roosevelt's New Deal. And he was the instrumental figure in crafting the Taft-Hartley Act in 1947, which aggressively targeted labor's ability to go on the picket line and engage in wildcat strikes. The Taft-Hartley Act was the opening for ultra-conservative right-to-work laws, which sprung up in Jim Crow states like Georgia, South Carolina, Texas, Virginia, and Alabama, prohibiting unions from requiring dues from their members.

Hurston professed "deep love for my country," but hated communism more than she loved America. She thought the average Black voter would feel the same way as her because communism created a herd instinct and was un-American. Hurston didn't like to be governed, and for precisely this reason, she was anti-colonial. She attacked the Soviets who wanted to carry out their "Czarist Russian plans to be masters of Asia," and she questioned America's key international alliance because, "so long as we support France and England in their colonial policies in Asia, so long shall our young men die over there."[39]

Hurston was a complicated person with eclectic political views. But, in her unapologetic defense of everything she did, she could have been a character in the fiction of another Black woman writer who hung around in her bohemian social circles. Nella Larsen differed from Hurston in that she didn't write essays about colonialism, civil rights, or US party politics. But she did share with Hurston a deep concern about power in interpersonal relationships.

Nella Larsen was born the same year as Hurston, 1891 (though, like Hurston, she, too, would misrepresent her birthdate, saying it was 1893), to a white Danish mother and an Afro-Caribbean father in the working-class neighborhood of Chicago's South Side. Yet Larsen never felt at home in either world. She completed her nursing degree in New York in 1915, and for a brief stint was the head nurse at Tuskegee University. It was in New York where she met and, at the age of twenty-eight, married a Black physicist eight years older than her, Elmer S. Imes, who held a PhD from the University of Michigan.

The image of middle-class femininity was there for Larsen's taking. She wasn't interested. Larsen casually chain-smoked and wore short dresses. She was an atheist who liked to sew. She was a fine cook and played a decent game of bridge—only when she wasn't writing. For a brief spell in 1925, Larsen joined Jean Toomer's Gurdjieff circle in Harlem, when she was a librarian at the local branch of the New York Public Library, not far from her five-room walk-up apartment on 236 West 135th Street. Larsen befriended Carl Van Vechten, with whom she shared social banter. "DuBois is about to celebrate his sixtieth birthday," she wrote to Van Vechten. "Some committee is sending around letters asking people to subscribe $50 and $100 towards a purse of $2500 as a gift. Some nerve I say."[40] It was Van Vechten, like he did for Hughes two years earlier, who helped Larsen publish her first semi-autobiographical novel, *Quicksand* (1928), with Knopf. In the book, written in only six weeks, the mixed-race protagonist, Helga Crane, struggles with a similar kind of angst about her identity as Larsen.

Larsen's second novel, *Passing* (1929), arrived the following year. Lauded by Du Bois as "one of the finest novels of the year," it is structured around the relationship between two light-skinned Black women, Clare Kendry and Irene Redfield.[41] Clare, who passes as white, is married to and has two children with an unsuspecting white racist, a man named Jack Bellew. Irene proudly embraces her Black skin and identity and is married to a Black man. The final scene of *Passing*, which gives the novel its status as a great melodrama, is also the one that sticks with most readers. Clare jumps to her death when Jack Bellew finds out her secret that she has been passing as white.

Passing is more than an account of white racism; it is also an homage to a new image of Black womanhood. Irene is appalled by Clare's behavior, whereas Clare is unapologetic in her choices. But if Irene is critical of Clare's choices, she still appreciates her decisiveness. Clare, she says, is "catlike. . . . There was about her an amazing soft malice. . . . Driven to anger, she would fight with a ferocity and impetuousness that disregarded or forgot any danger; superior strength, numbers, or other unfavorable circumstances."[42] Irene's description of Clare could have applied to Nella Larsen herself. In 1930, Larsen was briefly embroiled in a plagiarism scandal for a short story she wrote, "Sanctuary," about a woman who hides a man—on the run from the police after shooting someone—in her apartment, only to find that the person he has killed and robbed is her son. The story was identical in plot to that of British writer Sheila Kaye-Smith's "Mrs. Adis," written eight years earlier than "Sanctuary." Larson denied the allegations, but her reputation never recovered. Rather than remain in New York, after winning the prestigious Guggenheim Fellowship award the summer of 1930, she sailed to Europe, where she visited Lisbon and Majorca. Larsen rode horses and socialized with the novelist Somerset Maugham. She had a short-lived, though passionate, affair with an unnamed Scotsman. "But it didn't last," Larsen writes in *Quicksand*, "this happiness of Helga Crane."[43] The same could be said of Larsen.

When Larsen's husband, Elmer, visited her when she was vacationing in Paris, it was only to admonish her for being wasteful with their money. Not long after she returned to New York in 1932, Larsen, like Mrs. Adis, experienced a cruel twist in her life. She learned that her husband had been having an affair with a white staff member at Fisk University in Nashville, where he had moved in 1930, without Larsen, to chair the physics department. Upon learning of this unforgiveable betrayal, Larsen filed for divorce. According to court documents from 1933, Elmer would ship whatever household furniture Larsen wanted from Nashville to New York and pay her a monthly alimony of $150.

Then, just like that, Nella Larsen, like Clare Kendry in *Passing*, disappeared. It wasn't for the sake of attaining upward mobility, but for maintaining her sanity. Larsen changed addresses and encouraged rumors that she had left New York for good, even if this wasn't true. To earn a living and escape the socializing that had marked her married life in New York, Larsen stepped out of the limelight, and worked as a nurse at Gouverneur Hospital. She never wrote another novel.

■ ■ ■

Nella Larsen's stories scandalized contemporaries who were brought up on Victorian images of prim femininity and racist images of Black women's deference. Yet no Black bohemian made it his goal to scandalize everyone he could like the office manager for Chandler Owen's and A. Philip Randolph's socialist magazine, *The Messenger*. His name was George Schuyler. Langston Hughes described Schuyler, who first joined *The Messenger* in 1922, as its most "interesting" contributor. Hughes made this observation not because he thought Schuyler was always right, but because he was always offending everyone.

Born in Providence, Rhode Island, in 1895, Schuyler seemed like he was on his way to a career in public service. He enlisted in the military at seventeen, and was promoted to lieutenant, eventually serving in the Twenty-Fifth US infantry during the First World War. But in 1918, not long after his promotion, Schuyler deserted his post after experiencing a racist incident in Des Moines, Iowa: a shoe shiner, an immigrant from Greece, had refused to shine his shoes. As a result, Schuyler served nine months in a Chicago prison. When he arrived in New York upon release, he lived in church basements on the Bowery (although he wasn't religious). Schuyler proudly called himself a "Hobohemian," even though he thought hobos needed to get jobs and bohemians needed to stop living off their parents.

Schuyler's first novel, *Black No More* (1931), was also his most well known. It imagines what might happen if Black people could undergo a magical procedure to permanently bleach their skin, through a painful procedure called Black No More. The last name of Black No More's inventor, Junius Crookman, tells the reader everything they need to know about what Schuyler thinks about him. Schuyler describes Dr. Agamemnon Beard, modeled on W. E. B. Du Bois, as someone who worries that Black No More will put him out of business, for he's "never so happy and excited as when a Negro was barred from a theater or fried to a crisp."[44] Another character, Santorp Licorice, modeled on the Black nationalist Marcus Garvey, is "vigorously attacking all of the Negro organizations and at the same time preaching racial solidarity and cooperation in his weekly newspaper."[45]

Beyond such satire, *Black No More* asks a serious question: Is postracialism possible? Even if race were dead, Americans, Schuyler insists, would reinvent it. That is because racism is a political weapon that pays rich dividends for its abusers. For his first order of business, Max Disher, a Black man who undergoes the Black No More procedure, becomes a white supremacist. Disher isn't an anti-Black racist, but the lucrative speaking fees on the white supremacist circuit are irresistible. Moreover, once race "disappears" in the novel, white people begin to panic that some among them are formerly "Black." As a result, very pale skin becomes fashionable, and a new antidiscrimination league is formed to protest injustices directed against the "New Caucasians."

In the novel's penultimate scene, two notable white supremacist leaders, Samuel Buggerie, a eugenicist, and Arthur Snobbcraft, Democratic nominee for vice president—who spend the novel defending the truth of white genetic purity—find out, they, like everyone else in America, have some Black ancestry. As the two men try to escape the ensuing public outrage, they board a small plane that during flight, runs out of gas and crashes in a small town. To avoid recognition from the town's residents, the two men smear themselves with black shoe polish to hide their faces (and thus appear to be Black men, even though they are, actually, white men in blackface). Little do they know that the town in which they find land, Happy Hill, Mississippi, is filled with white supremacists who, assuming them to be the last two Black men in the US, lynch them.

By the time *Black No More* was published in 1931, Black Bohemia's bright light was reduced to a flicker. White publishers like Knopf and Liveright stopped supporting Black writers. Were they ever truly committed to the art? Or were they just opportunistic, sensing a new cultural market to be briefly exploited? Whatever the case, white publishers had a ready-made excuse to jump ship after the Great Crash of October 1929. The ensuing Depression wreaked havoc on all Americans, but New York was especially hit hard. By 1932, a third of the city's manufacturing plants were closed. A quarter of New Yorkers were out of work. The city's unsurmountable mountain of debt was $1.9 billion. Its budget deficit stood at $30 million, and approximately 142,000 families were on relief.

Black bohemians now had a smaller audience, fewer opportunities to generate a steady income, and little incentive to experiment creatively. Frayed relationships, like they always do in the counterculture, also played a major role in dwindling artistic production. Wallace Thurman died tragically of alcohol-exacerbated tuberculosis in 1934, at the age of thirty-two. But his last published novel, a literary satire of the "Niggerati Manor" entitled *Infants of the Spring*, was marked not by a sense of fun, but by a feeling of bitterness toward Black Bohemia. Critics called it a "pretty inept book," prone to "ponderous philosophizing."[46] Zora Neale Hurston and Langston Hughes cowrote a play, *Mule Bone*, in 1930, which made use of Black vernacular traditions to tell the story of Jim and Dave, who quarrel over a love interest, Daisy. Jim is arrested after he hits Dave over the head with a bone from a mule, and in the ensuing trial, Jim is found guilty. But after Hughes insisted that the play's stenographer and Thurman's ex-wife, the Black communist Louise Thompson, be given equal billing as a third co-writer, Hurston—who not only got the Southern source material for the play but acted out all the roles during its rehearsal—was incredulous. The play was never released during their lives. The friendship between Hughes and Hurston never recovered.

Jean Toomer turned even more inward than before. In 1931, he organized a Gurdjieff-inspired commune in an isolated cottage, with six other people and his then partner, Margery Latimer, on the outskirts of Portage, Wisconsin. Toomer believed spiritual awakening was within reach, but gossip circulated around town that the Portage commune was a communist-nudist colony. Margery Latimer, whom Toomer eventually married, died during childbirth a year later in 1932. Toomer, struggling with unimaginable grief over this unexpected loss, gave his newborn daughter up to his friends, a childless Chicago couple. In 1934, he remarried forty-year-old Marjorie Content, with Georgia O'Keeffe serving as witness at the wedding. (Marjorie's second husband, Harold Loeb, was founder of the magazine *Broom*, which had once published Toomer's early work.) With the help of Marjorie's father, a wealthy Wall Street stockbroker, Toomer purchased a property in Doylestown, Pennsylvania. The couple moved in 1935 to the stately country home. They called it Mill House.

Friends who visited Mill House were not impressed. Gorham Munson, who occasionally dragged himself out to rural Pennsylvania from New York on the weekend, described a typical evening in the following way: "Jean imitated Gurdjieff, and these imitations were embarrassing. . . . Jean would actually go into broken English too, you know, and he would tear loaves of bread apart. He would use bad, vulgar language at times. He would try to shock people by going into these seemingly rambling discourses."[47] For all his bombast, Toomer wasn't oblivious to Munson's negative reaction. With a bottle of scotch at his bedside, Toomer relied on sleeping pills to get through most nights. Suffering from debilitating bouts of depression, he was suicidal.

Other Black bohemians embraced the political right. Beneath the veneer of George Schuyler's jokes was a thinly veiled conservatism, which became apparent over the 1930s in his editorials for the *Pittsburgh Courier*. The clearest expression of these views was in his work of speculative fiction serialized in that weekly newspaper from 1936 to 1937—later published as *Black Empire* (1938). The book imagines a Black-led totalitarian movement that celebrates eugenics and practices repression. Its leader, Henry Belsidus, makes a catastrophic biological weapon to trigger civil war between all white people. Schuyler was unrecognizable. Gone was the man who was satirizing white liberalism in *Black No More*—now his target was Black liberation.

Five years after publishing his memoir, *Long Way from Home* (1937), McKay himself was, like Schuyler, a long way from the Black bohemian underground he was part of throughout the 1920s. McKay, who had come back from Europe to the US in 1932, was on death's door in 1942. A lethal mixture of the flu, heart disease, and high blood pressure made him homebound. A writer friend of McKay's, a devout Catholic by the name of Ellen Tarry, found McKay in his small basement apartment. With the help of the Catholic organization with which Tarry was associated, Friendship House, McKay was brought back to health. McKay wasn't just grateful; he was politically transformed. Not only an anti-communist like Zora Neale Hurston, McKay also found religion as a conservative Catholic.[48]

■ ■ ■

Langston Hughes was jaded with American politics. He had lived through a miserable decade of pro-business, union-busting, and deregulation-happy Republicans controlling both chambers of Congress, and a US Supreme Court that unleashed an unprecedented assault against Progressive-era laws meant to protect workers through the minimum wage, child labor protections, and antitrust laws. Led by Republican president Calvin Coolidge and his head of the Commerce Department, Herbert Hoover, who said, "The chief business of the American people is business," the 1920s was, indeed, a roaring decade. But only for the rich. Disposable income for the 1 percent rose 75 percent, while 99 percent of the population saw growth at less than 10 percent.

A decade into his career, Hughes was right back to where he started when he arrived in 1921. He had little money. But at the same time, few Black artists had as commanding a voice as Langston Hughes. Still fewer—least of all Hughes—could have anticipated that the lithe, soft-spoken, mustached bohemian of the 1920s would be one of the most well-known spokespersons for the political left. This happened slowly, then all at once.

On March 25, 1931, two policemen and an armed mob of white men took nine Black teens—ages twelve to nineteen—off a train going from Chattanooga to Memphis in Paint Rock, Alabama. The mob brought the boys to the nearest prison cell in the neighboring town of Scottsboro. Two white women, playing on a post-Reconstruction racist trope of Black hypersexuality, maliciously accused the nine boys of brutally raping them. Within a week, the Scottsboro Boys were on trial. On the first day of the proceedings against them, April 6, ten thousand visitors descended upon the two-thousand-person town. On April 8, eight of the nine boys were convicted and sentenced to death by electric chair. An exception was made for one of the defendants, a fourteen-year-old child named Roy Wright. Seven of the nine members of the all-white Scottsboro jury wanted death, but the Alabama prosecutors wanted leniency for Wright. Imagining themselves humane, they only asked for a life sentence.

Hughes was in Florida as the Scottsboro trial unfolded. Days after learning of the guilty verdict, he heard that a lawyer named Samuel Leibowitz, representing the Communist Party–sponsored International Labor

Defense, had visited with the Scottsboro Boys and their parents in Kilby Prison, launching the "Free the Scottsboro Boys" movement. Scottsboro cemented Hughes's turn to the left. His poem "Scottsboro," which asks, "8 black boys and one white lie. Is it too much to die?," was a dress rehearsal for his one-act stage play, *Scottsboro Limited* (1932). In the play, eight Black boys, surrounded by an electric chair, express their innocence to a white man, before being urged to smash the chair and fight the man in solidarity with the eight white workers standing beside them. Another poem written that year, "Good Morning, Revolution" (1932), begins, "You're the very best friend." Hughes's "White Man" (1936) goes further in its critique, locating the economic interests of white racism: "You're a White Man / I'm a Negro / You take all the best jobs / And leave us the garbage cans to empty and / The halls to clean. . . . Is your name spelled C-A-P-I-T-A-L-I-S-T?"[49]

Going to the political left was no cakewalk for Hughes. His old friend, Carl Van Vechten, insisted his new poems were "lacking in any of the elementary requisites of a work of art."[50] These comments stung Hughes, but less charitable were the locals in Carmel-by-the-Sea, California, where in 1932 Hughes was living at the summer home of his friend Noel Sullivan. Carmel was a conservative town that had overwhelmingly voted for Herbert Hoover, but also had a vibrant local chapter of the John Reed Club, which was founded by *New Masses* and affiliated with the Communist Party. The onetime goateed Village bohemian Lincoln Steffens was a regular at Carmel's John Reed Club gatherings. As for Hughes? He was usually the only Black person there. This unpleasant reality would take a sinister turn in 1932 after a citywide strike of longshoremen in nearby San Francisco turned violent, killing two and wounding hundreds.

The John Reed Club of Carmel called a public meeting to discuss the matter, and Carmel residents took sides. Hughes was, by turns, accused of being a shill for the Soviets, fraternizing with white women in public, and radicalizing Carmel's minuscule Black population. Carmelites knew Hughes had just arrived there from Soviet Union, where he was recruited by the Soviet film company Meschrabprom to collaborate on a script for a Russian film about the Black American experience entitled *Black and White*. (Within months of Hughes's arrival via the *SS Europa*, the project was abruptly canceled and the film never made, in part due to creative differences between Hughes and the film's writers.) "Carmel bubbled with a kind of hysteria," Hughes recalled, as he overheard rumors of an imminent attack on him. "I *was* in physical danger."[51]

Hughes wasn't the only Black artist to be moved by Scottsboro, or to be entranced by communism, or to be the target of red-baiting. Born in 1898 in Princeton, New Jersey, to an escaped slave Presbyterian minister father and Quaker schoolteacher mother, the towering six-foot-three, 230-pound Paul Robeson was a man of many talents. He spoke twenty languages. He read Marx in the original Russian. He was an angelic singer. First a star college athlete at Rutgers University and then a world-class professional football player (he was a defensive end), Robeson was also a Columbia University–trained lawyer.

While Robeson was passionate like his father, he directed his energies to the stage, not the pulpit. And in contrast to his mother, the stage, not the schoolhouse, was where he would educate the public. The place to do this when Robeson was coming up in the 1920s as a young actor was the Village. Long into the night, Robeson and playwright Eugene O'Neill would drink and discuss the state of politics, the state of the world, and the state of the theater. During the day, Robeson would sit in the nude for hours in a walk-up studio overlooking Washington Square Park, as the sculptor Antonio Salemme meticulously sculpted his likeness into bronze. This was appointment viewing for many Villagers, who walked up to the apartment just to watch Salemme complete his piece, which he entitled *Negro Spiritual*.

Robeson's big break came in 1925. After the Black Broadway actor Charles Gilpin gave up his star role in O'Neill's *Emperor Jones* (regarding the script, he thought no Black man in real life would so frequently utter "nigger" so many times, while O'Neill was adamant that he would), the twenty-seven-year-old Robeson took over as the title character, Brutus Jones. Brutus Jones is a Black American Pullman porter who, after killing a man, escapes to a Caribbean island, of which he crowns himself emperor. Robeson tells Jones's story in monologue to the audience as he's being pursued in the jungle by former subjects, who are waging an armed rebellion against his corrupt rule. In addition to the play's gratuitously racist language, one could see how *Emperor Jones* would also confirm time-worn racist stereotypes of Black people as conniving and politically inept. Robeson knew this and didn't like it, but he agreed to play the role because he personally liked O'Neill and needed the work. One amateur critic who marveled at Robeson's performance more so than at O'Neill's script was Emma Goldman. After she first saw Robeson as Brutus Jones in London in 1925, Goldman was blown away by Robeson's capacity for infusing dark comedy with moral seriousness: "I wish with all my heart that Paul's interpretation of *The Emperor* . . . should make the cold-blooded Englishman realize his greatness."[52] Having spent some time with Robeson and his wife, Essie Robeson, and remembering how graciously Robeson enjoyed her coffee and cooking, Goldman described him as a "lovable personality, entirely free from the self-importance of the star."[53]

Goldman wasn't the only one who held Robeson in high regard. *Time* magazine didn't exaggerate when, in 1943, it called Robeson "probably the most famous living Negro."[54] What many Americans didn't know, however, was that Robeson was immersed in socialist intellectual circles, and that his art was increasingly taking up radical themes. In 1928, Langston Hughes asked Robeson to star in a play he had been working on, entitled *Emperor of Haiti*, which told the story of Jean-Jacques Dessalines, the first ruler of an independent Haiti. Robeson politely declined Hughes's offer. Less than a decade later, however, in 1936, Robeson authoritatively took the stage at the 730-seat Westminster Theatre in London's West End to perform Trinidadian Marxist-philosopher C. L. R James's play, entitled *Toussaint Louverture*. The play was not about Dessalines, but another eighteenth-century Black Haitian revolutionary, Toussaint Louverture, who leads the anti-colonial revolt against Napoleon's French empire. Robeson recited Louverture's last words before being executed by the French: "You have got rid of one leader. But there are two thousand other leaders to be got rid of as well, and two thousand more when those are killed."[55]

The opening-night performance of *Toussaint Louverture*, on March 15, 1935, was the first time a Black actor starred in a play in the UK written by a Black playwright. Robeson's performance was met with a standing ovation and roaring applause. For good reason. *Toussaint Louverture* was no *Emperor Jones*. It wasn't written by a white bohemian like Eugene O'Neill. Based partly on the research for the book that would make him an internationally known man of the left, *The Black Jacobins* (1938), James's *Toussaint Louverture* is unabashedly anti-racist, an account of a rebellion by the enslaved from the perspective of the oppressed.

Over the next years, Robeson intensified his commitment to anti-racism. In 1937, he lent his sonorous voice to a thirty-three-minute documentary, *My Song Goes Forth*, an early instance of opposition to South African apartheid. The same year, Robeson organized the Council on African Affairs, whose mission was to liberate Black people of the African continent, who, in turn, could then join with Black Americans in a Pan-African working-class revolution. In 1938, after soliciting funds for the Spanish rebel Republicans fighting against fascist Nationalists, led by Francisco Franco, Robeson traveled to Spain for a week, where he sang over loudspeakers on the front lines for wounded Republican rebels. Back home in London shortly thereafter, Robeson proclaimed the maxim that had long been a core tenet for many in the counterculture, but which Robeson now embraced publicly: "Every artist . . . must decide NOW where he stands. He has no alternative. . . . The artist must take sides. He must elect to fight for freedom or slavery. I have made my choice. I had no alternative."[56]

In 1937, Langston Hughes, too, traveled to Spain to support the Republicans. There was, Hughes believed, an undeniable parallel between Francisco Franco and the Grand Wizard of the Klan in America. "Give Franco a hood," Hughes wrote from the front lines, "and he would be a member of the Ku Klux Klan."[57] In the Mexican countryside two decades before, a young Hughes had romanticized violence as he watched bullfights. Now, as he saw the horror of war, he could no longer take up such a romantic view. In Barcelona, where Hughes was staying, he would run to the air-raid shelter upon hearing the sirens alert him to the possibility of an imminent attack. When bombs finally exploded close to the hotel where he was sleeping, the force of the blast lifted him out of his bed. In Madrid, a sniper's bullet grazed Hughes's elbow as he was walking in broad daylight.

After Hughes returned from Spain to Harlem in 1937, he, like Robeson, was reinvigorated to "take sides." With the aid of his old friend, Louise Thompson, he enlisted in his endeavor the Communist Party–affiliated IWO (International Workers Order), which had 145,000 members, and the New Theatre League. Hughes's goal was to make a revolutionary people's theater. Called the Harlem Suitcase Theatre, it would be located on the second floor of 317 West 125th Street. Hughes would be its first director.

Trouble came immediately. For one, financial support for the theater was nonexistent. When Hughes wanted to build an additional platform for the set, he had to use his own money, of which he had little to speak.

Worse than that, he was stretched thin emotionally and creatively. His mother, Carrie Langston, was on her deathbed. And Hughes was preparing to head to Paris to show his solidarity with Theodore Dreiser's Congress for Peace Action and Against Bombing of Open Cities. In addition to managing his directorial duties, Hughes was also working on a script he had promised to the Gilpin Players at Karamu Theatre in Cleveland, Ohio.

For all these reasons, it's not surprising that the Harlem Suitcase Theatre lasted for only two seasons. But its short stint left an indelible impact on the 3,500 people, three-quarters of them Black, who had paid seventy-five cents per show to attend a total of thirty-eight performances. For a moment, it seemed like the Suitcase Theatre could realize the boldest ambitions of both bohemians and radicals, that it could fuse the personal and the political, that it could be both experimental and educative. This was because the Suitcase Theatre attempted to blend all genres (surrealism, tragedy, comedy) across different mediums (poetry, rhetoric, prose) to deal with pressing topics of the time (class struggle, slavery, individualism).

The Suitcase Theater's aesthetic involved minimal lightening; there was neither a curtain nor a fully developed set. It was just performers reading scripts, with blues tunes and spiritual hymns in the background punctuating the rhythms. The flagship play, written by Hughes himself, *Don't You Want to Be Free?*, captured these grand ambitions in its wordy subtitle: *From Slavery Through the Blues to Now—and Then Some! With Singing, Music, and Dancing.* The play didn't have a traditional cast of characters, or a plot. It was a series of vignettes and montages, dreamlike, which aimed to evoke the conflicting meanings of race in America. The play opens with an unnamed young man, with only a lynch rope behind him, addressing the audience, "This is your show, as well as ours. Now I'll tell you what this show is about. It's about me, except that it's not just about me now standing here talking to you—but it's about me yesterday, and about me tomorrow. I'm colored!"[58] The action then moves to Jamestown in 1619, with the first enslaved Africans arriving to the US, then to Frederick Douglass, William Lloyd Garrison, and John Brown and the antislavery rebellion. From there, we move to monologues about lynching and race riots, before concluding on a note of interracial class solidarity: "But when they do learn, and black and white really get together," says a young man on stage, "what power in the world can stop us from getting what we want?"[59]

Were the montages, politics, the blending of genres, the lack of narrative—the stuff that made it experimental—the very things that doomed the Suitcase Theatre? Would the Suitcase Theatre have inspired more work had it lasted longer? We'll never know. What we do know, however, is that when Black bohemian ideas of the 1920s went mainstream in 1940, they did so in a way no one could have anticipated.

■   ■   ■

A young Chicago South Side Writers Group member, a card-carrying Communist and writer for the Depression-era Federal Writers' Project (a program of the Works Progress Administration, or WPA) named Richard Wright, wanted to take Dorothy West's *Challenge* magazine further left than she ever wanted. West, unlike Wright, was an aesthete. She accompanied Langston Hughes to Russia in 1932 for the *Black and White* film project and described her time there as "the most carefree year of her life."[60] As a Black woman who couldn't move freely in her own country, West was entranced by the white sandy beaches in the summer resort of Odessa, Ukraine, and by the charm of the great Soviet director, Sergei Eisenstein, who once asked her to dance after they watched a ballet performance at the Bolshoi Theatre.

With a budget of $300, funded by what West received for her work for *Black and White*, West returned to the US and, along with Marian Minus, created a magazine to realize her vision. It was called *Challenge*. The magazine was supposed to recreate the youthful energy of *Fire!!*, but West's tastes were conservative. "We care a lot about style," she wrote in a moment of candor. "And we think a message is doubly effective when written effectively without bombast or bad spelling."[61] Most of the six issues that were published before *Challenge* folded in 1937 were filled with the work of West's old friends—Hughes, Countee Cullen, James Johnson, and Claude McKay.

West shuttered *Challenge* not long after she invited an up-and-coming writer, Richard Wright, to be a guest editor for an issue. He then became associate editor for the magazine that emerged, called *New Challenge*. That publication's only issue featured Wright's "Blueprint for Negro Writing," in which he wrote that he wanted Black literature to move away from the "humble novels" and "prim and decorous ambassadors" of the race. Wright cared less about style than about visceral emotional impact. In 1935, he had briefly worked in Chicago as a publicity agent for the WPA-funded Federal Negro Theatre. There, he encouraged a group of Black actors to do a play about the chain gang. Wright was disappointed when the Black actors wanted to do a vaudeville play instead. Lashing out about their decision, using words that could have been uttered by a white racist, he declared "perhaps the whites were right, that Negroes were children and would never grow up."[62]

Wright was a practical man. In 1937, to support himself after he moved from Chicago to New York in search of a literary career, he took the best-paying job available. At eighty dollars a month, it was as the Harlem editor for the Communist newspaper *Daily Worker*, published by New York's most well-known Black Communist, the Harvard-educated lawyer Ben Davis Jr. When Langston Hughes, a fan of Wright's early poetry published in *New Masses*, first met the twenty-seven-year-old Wright on a trip to Chicago in winter 1935, at a house party, Hughes noticed that the shy and serious Wright stood in the corner and alone. When one of Hughes's friends, Arna Bontemps, ran into Wright on a Chicago sidewalk waiting for a Cottage Grove streetcar, Wright, two cents short of covering his uptown fare, asked Bontemps if he had spare change. Not thinking about it twice, Bontemps gave Wright a nickel, and told the young man not to worry about paying him back. Wright did worry. He promised to return Bontemps the spare change. The next Friday evening, after a two-mile trek by foot, Wright showed up to the Bontemps' Chicago home unannounced. In his outstretched hand were two pennies.[63]

Richard Wright believed in dichotomies. He saw things in black and white. The main function of art, he believed, was to clarify the real world. His first short-story collection, *Uncle Tom's Children* (1938), attempted to fictionalize his childhood, growing up in gut-wrenching poverty in rural Mississippi. It was his novel *Native Son* (1940) that fully operationalized his "Blueprint for Negro Writing." *Native Son* is the story of a twenty-year-old Black man, Bigger Thomas, whose economic position—crumbling home in public housing, lack of job prospects, limited education—leads him to a fate of being tried and convicted of sexually assaulting and murdering a white woman named Mary Dalton. The crime, the reader knows, is done accidentally. What Wright wants the reader to see, however, is the malice of the racist-capitalist system. He accidentally suffocates Mary to death only because he wants to keep her from speaking and revealing his presence to her mother. At the end of the book, despite the appeals and provocations of his lawyer to show leniency toward him, Bigger is executed.

Wright hoped to have the book read like a sociological study, but *Native Son* would have been impossible without Black Bohemia. There are frank depictions of sex and violence, there is interracial intimacy, and there is rebellion. But Bigger is no bohemian. *Native Son* does not have the sex positivism of *Fire!!*, nor the blues ethos of Hughes's poetry. If *Native Son* does have the hard-edged tone of McKay's "If We Must Die," it's missing the playfulness of *Home to Harlem*. *Native Son* has none of *Cane's* surrealism, only stifling realism. Nothing is lighthearted about *Native Son*; its aim is to bring a hard-boiled style from which no one can turn away.

Few American readers turned away from *Native Son*. It went mainstream beyond anyone's wildest dreams. A smashing success, it sold 250,000 copies within a few weeks, after it was selected to the Book-of-the-Month Club in January 1940. The press release for the novel featured a headshot of Wright in a respectable gray suit, white-collared shirt, and black tie. Overnight, Richard Wright became the best-selling Black American writer in American literary history.

Cognizant of the need to help young Black authors, Langston Hughes supported *Native Son* in public, calling it a "tremendous performance" and "ballyhooing the book at all my lectures." But Hughes had reservations in private.[64] Was Wright's depiction of Black rage representative of Black life? Was it, even according to Wright's own calculus, politically useful? Onetime nemesis of Claude McKay and coeditor of *The Liberator*, Mike Gold, was smitten with *Native Son*. "It is a rare and special thing that Wright has done, as no American writer before him," he wrote in the *Sunday Worker*. "He has written a story without sentimentalizing it. . . . The story of *Native Son* is one that will burn itself on the imagination of this country."[65]

But did Americans read the book and join the socialist struggle? No. At the time of *Native Son's* publication, the Second World War had started, patriotism was everywhere, and anti-communist sentiment was stronger than ever. Many white readers felt some combination of guilt and pity for Bigger Thomas. "That a Negro should be bitter about his treatment in America shocks white Americans to their moral depth," wrote the Black sociologist Horace Cayton. "To be confronted with the fact that a group of people hate, even though these people have been outraged, creates a feeling of guilt."[66]

What did such a response mean for the prospects of achieving racial justice? One queer Harlem-born Black bohemian, James Baldwin, who had spent time in the Village in the 1940s, came to see *Native Son* as both an artistic and political failure. It was thanks to Wright, whom a twenty-year-old Baldwin first met in 1944, that he obtained a prestigious fellowship to complete his first novel, *Go Tell It on the Mountain* (1953). It was also because of Wright that Baldwin moved to Paris in 1948. (Wright had moved there in 1947, with his white wife, to escape American racism and to socialize with his existentialist friends, Jean-Paul Sartre and Simone de Beauvoir.) But in a 1950 essay entitled "Many Thousands Gone," Baldwin went after Wright with a vengeance. He argued that *Native Son*, in an obsessive effort to depict Black rage, made it impossible to see how Black people, like Baldwin, were beautifully creating the world they wanted to inhabit, not the world in which white people wanted them to live trapped within. "What the novel reflects . . . is the isolation of the Negro within his own group and the resulting fury of impatient scorn. It is this which creates its climate of anarchy and unmotivated and unapprehend disaster," and it is this which makes us believe that "in Negro life there exists no tradition."[67] After Baldwin's view of Bigger Thomas became public, Wright and Baldwin had a loud shouting match on the streets of Paris. Their friendship collapsed. Up until the day he died in 1987, Baldwin never rescinded this interpretation of *Native Son*.

■ ■ ■

The image of resistance inscribed by Black Bohemia didn't die with *Native Son*. It was quietly percolating underground at a New York nightclub in 1939. A twenty-four-year-old Black jazz singer, Eleanora Fagan, was making political art. Filled with trepidation and unease, a small spotlight settled on her face, she began to recite a harrowing song. The lyrics were drawn from a poem written by a Jewish American Bronx schoolteacher, Abel Meeropol (his pseudonym was Lewis Allan), and published in *New Masses* in 1937. (Founded by Mike Gold in 1926, *New Masses* had succeeded *The Liberator* as the premier magazine for the cultural left.) Meeropol wrote the poem after he was haunted by a disturbing photograph of two Black men who were lynched on August 7, 1930, in Marion, Indiana.

As the jazz singer recited Meeropol's poem in the basement venue with a white gardenia pinned to her hair, her voice cracked, each breath moving with an escalating urgency. She didn't move; her arms sat eerily still at her side. She was conjuring and mourning the brutal image she brought forward in her audience's mind at Café Society in the Village's Sheridan Square that cold night in 1939. "Southern trees bear a strange fruit / Blood on the leaves and blood at the root / Black bodies swinging in the Southern breeze / Strange fruit," she quietly sang. As the lights dimmed and the cigarette smoke settled once the performance ended, Fagan, now performing under her stage name Billie Holiday, slowly walked off. She recalled that the song would remind her of her deceased father, Clarence Holiday. A travelling jazz guitarist on tour, he had died two years before in 1937 because racist doctors in Dallas, Texas, had denied him treatment for a fatal lung disease, induced by the mustard gas he had swallowed while serving in the US Army in World War I.

The venue where Holiday sang "Strange Fruit," Café Society, was no Cotton Club. The Cotton Club featured Black artists, jungle decoration, and fake palm trees, and, though located in Harlem, it only admitted white customers who paid exorbitant prices for cheap glasses of scotch. (It was said that Duke Ellington, who performed at the Cotton Club, couldn't invite his mother to watch him play.) Café Society, in contrast, was the first integrated club outside Harlem when it opened its doors in December 1938. From the outset, it was meant to be an experiment in interracial collaboration, even though it tried not to take itself too seriously. Café Society's slogan, painted as a mural on its wall, had a light touch: "The Right Place for the Wrong People." Its founder, a shoe salesman by trade, was Barney Josephson, a Trenton, New Jersey–born white child of immigrant Latvian Jewish garment workers, whose brother worked in the anti-Nazi underground in Europe. "I wanted a club," he explained, "where blacks and whites worked together behind the footlights and sat together out front."[68]

When Billie Holiday was approached by Josephson to not only sing "Strange Fruit" but to close every set with it, she was afraid the audience would mercilessly boo her off-stage. Holiday eventually agreed to the request. Josephson had specific instructions for her. No encores, just finish singing and walk off without saying anything—so that audience members "get their insides burned with ['Strange Fruit']."[69]

Holiday didn't just accept the gig. She was fanatical about perfecting her performance: "I worked like the devil on it . . . because I was never sure I . . . could get across to a plush nightclub audience the things that it meant to me."[70] Though she called "Strange Fruit" her "personal protest," Holiday wasn't a revolutionary like Robeson. She wasn't well-versed in Marx like Hughes or the Red Summer like Toomer or McKay. Holiday liked comic books. She had no formal education past the fifth grade.

But Billie Holiday was familiar with Black protest music. Her favorite singer was Bessie Smith. Growing up in Baltimore, Holiday also knew about life on the streets. Why its myriad injustices would make the masses revolt. One night her mother, Sadie, came home on Christmas Eve 1926 to find Billie, then eleven years old, being sexually assaulted by a neighbor, a man called Wilbur Rich. As the State of Maryland was waging its criminal case against Rich, Holiday was placed in the custody of a Catholic social organization. Later that year, she dropped out of school. After she was released from the Catholic organization at the age of twelve, Holiday began to run errands for a local brothel. At the age of thirteen, she went to join her mother, Sadie, now a sex worker, in Harlem on West 140th Street. Within days of her arrival to New York, Holiday was trafficked herself. In 1929, both mother and daughter were incarcerated for one hundred days at the Blackwell's Island workhouse, after they were arrested on the charge of "vagrancy." Holiday's singing was a commemoration of the nameless people whose stories hadn't been told—stories she knew intimately: "There was nothing about living on the sidewalks that I didn't know," she recalled, "the corner hoodlum, the streetwalker, the laborer, the numbers runner, the rooming-house ladies and landlords, the people who existed off the twenty-five and thirty-dollars-a-week salaries they were paying in those days."[71]

Langston Hughes's favorite song was a Billie Holiday standard—"God Bless the Child," (1941). On many occasions, Hughes would listen to the vinyl spin late into the night in his Harlem apartment. Holiday claimed "God Bless the Child" was written after a fight with her mother—Holiday had asked her for a loan, but her mother refused. It makes sense why Hughes loved this song—it reminded him of his own life. The song is about children who can't rely on their parents and must make their own way in the world. But Holiday was herself Hughes's spiritual child, which is to say a child of Black Bohemia. Here was Billie Holiday speaking to Black people's blues-like experience in America. Here was her harrowing voice describing surreal images, which provided a new way to see the Black body. Here she was in a venue, Café Society, that was a model for inciting new solidarities between Black and white people.

One cannot say for sure whether this was how the audience responded to "Strange Fruit" when they first heard it. Upon hearing Holiday's raspy voice and listening to images of "Black bodies swinging," some white members of the audience, perversely, thought Holiday was reciting a love ballad, or a song about sex. They failed to see it as it was: a song about death and anti-Black violence. And yet, even if the audience was sometimes confused about the song's meaning, the US government wasn't. After a performance in 1939, Holiday received a warning from the commissioner of the Federal Bureau of Narcotics, Harry Anslinger, to never again sing "Strange Fruit." Anslinger, an unabashed racist, believed that jazz, when fused with anti-racist messaging sung by a formerly incarcerated Black sex worker like Holiday, could irreparably damage US interests at home and abroad. No longer merely a jazz singer, Billie Holiday was now a domestic enemy. Holiday didn't give in to Anslinger's demand. For singing "Stanger Fruit" night in and night out, she paid a heavy price. Holiday's yearslong struggle with heroin addiction was a perfect entry point for Anslinger to surveil her every move and recruit a string of informants to build a federal case against her. On May 16, 1947, Anslinger finally succeeded. Holiday was arrested in her New York apartment on a federal drug charge and sentenced to the all-women's Alderson Federal Prison Camp in West Virginia. As a result, Holiday lost her license to perform in cabaret theaters.

Eleven days after her release from prison, Holiday performed a sold-out evening on March 27, 1948. She stood before a crowd of twenty-seven hundred at New York's esteemed Carnegie Hall in Midtown Manhattan. Holiday's seven-song setlist concluded with "Strange Fruit." She would go on to perform "Strange Fruit" for the next decade until she died in 1959. Holiday's records went on to sell hundreds of thousands of copies. To this day, she is remembered as one of the most important singers in American history.

In 1947, an unknown twenty-one-year-old English major, originally from Paterson, New Jersey, who had been listening to Billie Holiday in his college dorm room at Columbia University, was moved by her voice. As he jotted down in his journal, Holiday expressed "her resignation and suffering joy at the prospect of a repetition of the old pleasure-pain of an unhappy love-affair."[72] Two decades later, in 1966, now a well-known leader of the student-led counterculture, the poet from Paterson would invoke Holiday's name as he sat before the US Senate subcommittee investigating drugs. "The mortal sufferings of [one of] our most celebrated heroic Negro musicians . . . [like] Billie Holiday . . . at the hands of police over the drug issue are well-known. Such sadistic persecutions have outraged the heart of America for decades."[73] The poet was using Holiday's memory to critique the US government's war on those who disobeyed its rules and challenged its authority. His name was Allen Ginsberg.

CHAPTER 7

PROPHETS OF THE
LIVING AND THE DEAD

O n Thursday evening, October 13, 1955, a twenty-nine-year-old poet from Paterson, New Jersey, stepped up to a podium after a brief inter-mission at the Six Gallery, an experimental art venue in San Francisco. On any given night, the Six Gallery seated a few dozen for small intimate events. But on this particular Thursday, the gallery, a former auto shop, was packed. The audience members—some seated in chairs, though most of them were standing, pressed along the walls—were prepared for a fes-tive atmosphere to listen to six poets. Around North Beach bars in San Francisco, they had seen a small handbill that promised wine, music, and dancing girls. A "charming event," it said. The poet, who personally made the handbill and had spent weeks advertising the event, was nervous be-cause he was fourth up. He already had a bit too much red wine. Behind his thick-framed black glasses was a sensitive intellectual who had, for years, been struggling with self-doubt. But as the lights slowly dimmed and the audience listened intently, he began to recite the first words of his poem: "I saw the best minds of my generation destroyed by madness."[1]

Allen Ginsberg felt emboldened. After he furiously finished each verse, the audience chanted "GO!" They must have thought Ginsberg was a sea-soned professional, but he, in truth, had no idea what to expect. This was, by far, his biggest crowd. He had worked on numerous drafts of this poem, called "Howl"—and, only after feedback from a fifty-year-old anarchist poet from the Bay Area, Kenneth Rexroth, made it sound freer and more relaxed. He was capturing the language of drug pushers, addicts, hipsters, con artists, sidewalk musicians, gamblers, and thieves he was familiar with on the streets in back alleys, dilapidated warehouses, and grimy dive bars in New York and San Francisco. For many in the audience, "Howl" must have sounded like something of an ode, as one line put it, to those, "who poverty and tatters and hollow-eyed and high sat up smoking in the supernatural darkness of cold-water flats floating across the tops of cities contemplating jazz." The publisher and owner of the City Lights bookstore in San Francisco, Lawrence Ferlinghetti, was so impressed by Ginsberg's reading he sent him a note. In a clear parallel of what Ralph Waldo Emerson wrote to Walt Whitman upon reading *Leaves of Grass* (1855), Ferlinghetti said: "I greet you at the beginning of a great career." Ironically, as Ginsberg later confessed, *Howl* was forged not from a place of hope, but from the dark shadows of "worldly defeat."[2]

▪ ▪ ▪

It wasn't a message of worldly defeat that Allen Ginsberg heard from his mentors in 1943 when, at the age of seventeen, he left North Jersey and arrived in the Upper West Side to Columbia University, thanks to a generous scholarship from the Young Men's Hebrew Association of New Jersey. Initially, Ginsberg's goal was to be a labor lawyer, but the naive, clean-shaved young man—who wore ties and crisp suits—switched to pursue an English major. Not only because Ginsberg had little patience for studying esoteric legal codes, but because he was mesmerized by one of his charismatic professors, Lionel Trilling. The first Jewish scholar to be awarded tenure at Columbia's English department in 1939, Trilling was an idealist for whom liberalism was more than a political philosophy—it was a sensibility and injunction for one to be cosmopolitan, and just. If Trilling was the role model to which Ginsberg aspired to be one day, Trilling's senior colleague in the English department, Mark Van Doren, the Pulitzer Prize–winning poet and critic for *The Nation*, embodied the meaning of high-brow intellectualism. A onetime chair of the department, Van Doren was a proponent of a liberal education, exemplified by the fact that he taught the Great Books course, Humanities A, for seventeen consecutive years at Columbia. (Van Doren's brother, Carl Van Doren, was one of the main speakers at the famous Civic Club dinner in 1924 that ushered in the Harlem Renaissance.)[3]

Trilling and Van Doren were versions of what Ginsberg's own father, Louis Ginsberg, had dreamed of becoming. As the father of two children

(Allen and his older brother, Eugene) and husband to Naomi Ginsberg, who suffered from paranoid schizophrenia, Louis Ginsberg eked out a middle-class existence as an English high school teacher in Paterson. Only in his spare time did Louis write poetry. His claim to fame was having a piece anthologized in *Modern American Poetry* (1925). That was one year before Allen was born, on June 3, 1926, in Newark, New Jersey.

Louis Ginsberg, Lionel Trilling, and Carl Van Doren came from a generation of intellectuals who believed in providing grand narratives about the human condition, whether it was about the battle between the working class and the capitalists, the birth and death of empire, the rise of the bureaucratic state, or the invention of modern society. Such narratives, they insisted, were necessary to buoy the world during a period of great upheaval, when fascism was ascendant and the Great Depression had plunged the masses into a state of despair. Louis Ginsberg, a socialist, had published a 1930 poem entitled "Slaves" in *New Masses*, whereas Trilling, a man of the anti-Stalinist left, in his 1950 essay collection *Liberal Imagination*, wrote, "It is the wide sense of the word [politics] that is nowadays forced upon us, for clearly it is no longer possible to think of politics except as the politics of culture, the organization of human life toward some end or other, toward the modification of sentiments, which is to say the quality of life."[4] The social responsibility of the artist, according to Trilling and Louis Ginsberg, isn't to make political propaganda (they were socialists, but not communists), but something much more subtle. To elevate the world around them, skillfully, with the written word, as if it were a sharp scalpel through which one could uncover hidden gems, layered beneath mounds of dirt that obscured sparkling truths. From this vantage point, literature contested relations of power, which meant that, fundamentally, it was a political act.

Unlike these men, Allen Ginsberg had little energy to elevate the world because he was too disheartened by politics. The Second World War had murdered millions of ordinary innocents who worked for a living, citizens for whom the fate of the parliamentary system of government, or the legacy of the Enlightenment, meant very little. Besides, even if ordinary people cared about these grand questions, the limitations of liberalism were apparent to everyone. Adolf Hitler accomplished a coup of the German parliamentary system that put his Nazi Party into power. And after V. I. Lenin's death, Joseph Stalin assumed power on the platform of national unity, only to set up the prison system of the Gulag to incarcerate his enemies—real and imagined. "I think I am growing cynical. Our stupidity has reaped its harvest and we have a bumper crop, since we sowed the world's biggest blunder," wrote the fifteen-year-old Ginsberg in 1941. "The death toll in this war has been at least four million. . . . There is no preventable catastrophe in recorded history paralleling this. That is a grim joke on ourselves, four million dead as the result of mental impotence and political infirmity on the part of a handful of U.S. Congressmen."[5]

Forget about utopia. Not even *progress* was an accurate term to define Ginsberg's adolescence. His mother was a proud Communist, but rather than, say, establish a John Reed Club in Paterson, Naomi was in and out of psychiatric institutions for paranoid schizophrenia. Allen was aware of his attraction to boys by the time he was seven, but his father, like many Americans, was homophobic. Society treated homosexuality as a moral deficiency, and medical professionals, through the *DSM* (*Diagnostic and Statistical Manual of Mental Disorders*) up until 1973, thought of it as a mental illness in need of serious psychological treatment.

Ginsberg would have to resort to clandestine acts to experience sexual desire. Sometimes, he would stand on the porch of his Paterson home for hours and expose himself to passing vehicles. On one occasion, he watched voyeuristically as a group at school pulled down the pants of a classmate.[6] Although Ginsberg had decided to attend Columbia because of a crush—a male Paterson high school classmate of his had also enrolled there—when he arrived on campus, the young man ignored him. Unfulfilled desires for sexual intimacy left Ginsberg in a dark place. "I want to unburden my soul to a loved one," he confessed in a journal, "and yet, if people knew me, I should have to commit suicide."[7]

It's tempting to say that Ginsberg gravitated toward a circle of young men at Columbia because he, like they, were great artists in search of community. But this isn't accurate. The two Columbia classmates that Allen became close to in 1944 were two to whom he was sexually attracted, and the first to give him a sense of emotional safety. Both men symbolized the competing emotional impulses to which Allen was always drawn. The first was a shy former jock who had the aura of spiritual transcendence. He talked slowly and gave the impression that the only thing that mattered was in the moment, right in front of him. His name was Jack Kerouac. A Columbia University football player on scholarship, Kerouac was the youngest of four from a working-class Roman Catholic family in Lowell,

Massachusetts. When Ginsberg first met him at the apartment of Kerouac's then girlfriend Edie Parker, on West 118th Street at 11 a.m., Kerouac was sitting hunched on an armchair eating a late breakfast. His first question to Ginsberg wasn't what books he read, but if Ginsberg wanted a cold beer from the fridge. Kerouac claimed to have written a million words before he was eighteen, though he had only taken up writing full-time recently while recovering from a hairline fracture in his right tibia that he sustained returning a punt in the first (and what would be the last) game of his college football career.

The second young man to which Ginsberg was drawn was Lucien Carr. Carr's boyish demeaner—with his almond-shaped eyes and golden hair—was belied by his flair for violent provocation. "He had to be genius or nothing," Ginsberg wrote in his journal. "And since he couldn't be creative he turned to bohemianism, eccentricity, social versatility, conquests."[8] The St. Louis–born Carr, unlike Kerouac, wasn't much of a writer, but he wasn't subtle about playing the role of a tortured poet in public. Observers would be shocked to see that among Carr's favorite pastimes were to chew on shards of glass, fling full plates of food on the floor, drunkenly quote lines of verse from the nineteenth-century French poet Baudelaire, and tell everyone his passion for Verlaine and Rimbaud. "Know these words," Ginsberg recalled, "and you speak the Carr language: fruit, phallus . . . feces, feotus, womb, Rimbaud."[9]

Carr had no qualms being playful with Ginsberg in the streets around Columbia's campus. It was Kerouac, however, who was tender with Ginsberg in private. Kerouac claimed to be mostly attracted to women, but knew Ginsberg was infatuated with him. Ginsberg, who was still a virgin, was desperate for his first sexual encounter. "Beat me up—do anything you like—anything!" he once wrote in a letter to Kerouac.[10] When Ginsberg's fantasy became real—the two of them engaged in mutual masturbation, in between parked trucks and cars in an abandoned parking lot near the waterfront—the event was unromantic. Even more, Ginsberg's first moment of intimacy, tragically, was a reproduction of his own unsatisfying childhood fantasies—secretive and furtive.

Kerouac preferred to keep his sexuality private. When a Columbia University football coach, Luigi Piccirilli, whom Kerouac knew from his playing days on the team, walked into Ginsberg's dorm room one morning to find Kerouac and Ginsberg lying together on his bed, Kerouac swiftly ran out of the room. Though they were fully clothed, the school policy didn't allow for overnight visitors, and the two had been out until 3 a.m. the night before at a local pub. Kerouac hid under the covers of a bed in an adjoining room, leaving Ginsberg, alone, to answer for himself. As a fumbling Ginsberg tried to explain the situation—it wasn't what the coach thought it was, he said—it didn't help that, the day before, he had smeared in grime on his dorm window two explicit messages. One said "Fuck the Jews," and another, in reference to Columbia University president Nicholas Murray Butler, declared "Butler has no balls."[11]

Less a wry commentary on Columbia's latent antisemitism or a critique of President Butler's leadership, Ginsberg's off-the-cuff scrawls were passive-aggressive jokes meant for the university cleaner to wipe off. Ginsberg wasn't making a searing public critique; he was annoyed that his window hadn't been cleaned for weeks. Once the cleaner saw Ginsberg's messages, however, she interpreted them as something he never meant them to be: political statements. Frightened, and assuming she was in the room of a neo-Nazi, the cleaner didn't wipe off the crude words but instead immediately ran to the Columbia administration.

Ginsberg meant nothing by the scribbles, but school administrators were happy to use his words as a pretext to push the university's exclusionary campus housing policy (which was meant to keep out poor kids), and conveniently avoid its own systemic homophobia. Columbia, not Ginsberg, got the last laugh. He was expelled.

A major reason Ginsberg was treated so harshly by Columbia administrators was he had already achieved notoriety though his association with Lucien Carr. On the night of August 13, 1944, the nineteen-year-old Carr was out drinking with friends at a West End bar, where he was approached by a thirty-one-year-old David Kammerer. Kammerer, a tall man with red hair and a high-pitched voice, had been obsessed with Carr for years, ever since Kammerer was Carr's teacher at a summer camp for boys in St. Louis. Kammerer had obtained a PhD from and taught literature courses at Washington University in St. Louis, though in New York, he had worked as a janitor in a building where he lived. Kammerer was infatuated with Carr in a way that was unhealthy for both—he followed him everywhere he went, first to Andover Academy in Massachusetts, then to the University of Chicago and then Bowdoin College in Maine, before coming to New York, after Carr enrolled in Columbia.

As that night wore on, Kammerer and Carr drank into the early morning hours, and found themselves sitting on a bench in Riverside Park. Kammerer did what he had often done in these situations: he made drunken threats. If Carr didn't have sex with him, Kammerer would kill Carr's girlfriend, Celine; then he would kill Carr, and then commit suicide. This time, Carr got angry. Kammerer appeared less restrained than before. The two men struggled. At some point during this scuffle, Carr took out his Boy Scout knife, and stabbed Kammerer twice in the heart. Kammerer was dead.[12]

Frightened but also drunkenly disoriented, Carr tied Kammerer's hands with his shoelaces, ripped the man's shirt to shreds, and put Kammerer's lifeless body in the river, which he tried to weigh down with rocks. Carr ran to the apartment of a mutual friend of his and Kammerer's from St. Louis now living in New York, a man by the name of William S. Burroughs. Prudently, the thirty-one-year-old older man, Burroughs, advised Carr to get a lawyer and immediately turn himself in. Carr wasn't happy with this counsel. The next day, he sought the advice of someone closer in age and spirit. He showed up at Jack Kerouac's house. The two friends walked down to Riverside Park where they threw away the Boy Scout knife in the river, dumped Kammerer's glasses in a sewer, and then spent the rest of the day drinking. That is, before capping the day with a visit to the Museum of Modern Art in Midtown.[13]

Yet even Kerouac's mellowness and sympathy had a limit when death was at stake. He convinced Carr to confess to the killing, which he did. Burroughs and Kerouac were both arrested as material witnesses but, after questioning, were ultimately released. Indicted for second-degree murder, Carr struck a plea for first-degree manslaughter. He may have been remorseful, but on his way to serving his two-year prison sentence at the Elmira Correctional Facility in New York, he was more interested in elevating his cultivated image of the accursed poet: he took two books with him, William Butler Yeats's *A Vision* and Arthur Rimbaud's *A Season in Hell*.[14] While incarcerated, Carr wrote a letter to Ginsberg telling him he was enjoying Thomas Hardy's *Jude the Obscure* and becoming a "master" at crossword puzzles.[15] After he was released, he seemed to have a change of heart, as many bohemians before him. He stopped hanging out with Ginsberg and his friends. No longer citing Baudelaire, Carr joined a news agency and proudly called himself "petit bourgeois."[16]

Today, one might be struck at how Carr received such a relatively light prison sentence for such a heinous act. Back then, the reason would have been apparent. Carr played up the fact that Kammerer was an older gay man, while he was an innocent heterosexual student. According to a police report, Carr had claimed Kammerer "made improper advances to him, but that he had always rebuffed the older man." The *New York Daily News* called it an "honor slaying," while the *Daily Mirror* called it a "twisted sex murder."[17] None of this was true. Even the most casual observers who saw the two spend time together would remark that they appeared to be best friends, if not lovers.

On the face of it, the Kammerer killing represented an excellent opportunity for the Beats to take a principled stance to politicize American sexual attitudes, since they prided themselves on an antiauthoritarian ethos and had sexual experiences with men. In a journal entry, Ginsberg once wrote, "The argument of the idealist, the artist, and the anarchist is that he and others are oppressed and constricted by the injustice and mediocrity of the organized hypocrisy of the law."[18] Kammerer's infatuation with Carr (whom he had known for many years, and with whom he was comfortable to express his sexual desires) had, at least in part, to do with the tyrannical reach of American homophobia, which was embedded in and sustained through organized law.

Ginsberg did not make this argument publicly. Because he was aware of the reputational stakes involved, the most he would do at the time was to quietly praise Kammerer, in a short unpublished poem, as "quite brave / to shut his loving in his grave."[19] After Kammerer's death, Kerouac only doubled down on his heteronormative, hypermasculine presentation of self by marrying Edie Parker on August 22, 1944, in City Hall. Then, she and Kerouac moved to Grosse Pointe, Michigan, where he worked in a ball-bearing factory.[20] When a detective asked William Burroughs, "Did you know Kammerer was homosexual?," Burroughs replied, "I frequently remonstrated with him, but in vain."[21] This wasn't true. From an early age, Burroughs preferred men as sexual partners, but for years he had cultivated the image of a heterosexual intellectual. Burroughs wore business suits and snap-brim hats and spoke as if he were a nineteenth-century aristocrat.

"You shouldn't blame yourself at all," Burroughs later reassured Carr, "because [Kammerer] asked for it, he demanded it."[22] One can't help but wonder whether Burroughs's cruel statement came from the intensity of his own history of unrequited love. One of his earliest memories of love was at fifteen, a crush he had on a handsome and athletic boy named Kells Elvins, whose father was a former congressman. Schoolmates teased Burroughs mercilessly. "You're his slave," they said, as Burroughs walked with Elvins, his arm around his shoulder, though Elvins never reciprocated the affection. As a weak child with sinus trouble who was filled with anxiety, and surrounded by a cold and detached family, Burroughs turned to representations of virility to make him feel less vulnerable than how he felt.[23] He was obsessed with toy guns; he almost blew off his right hand after mixing chemicals for an improvised experiment. At the age of ten, he wrote his first short story, called "Autobiography of a Wolf," in which a wolf is shot by hunters, and her grieving mate is savagely destroyed by grizzly bears.

"The libertine circle is destroyed with the death of Kammerer," Ginsberg wrote, but this wasn't true.[24] To the contrary, Kammerer's death became useful source material for Beat writing. Ginsberg jotted down notes for a hard-boiled novella in which Kammerer tells Carr, "Choose to present me with your pecker or your knife," whereas Kerouac and Burroughs collaborated on a story whose working title was "I Wish I Were You" (which they thought was a witty allusion to Kammerer's desire to be Carr) but soon became "And the Hippos Were Boiled in Their Tanks." (They sent it to the publisher Simon & Schuster, who turned it down.)[25]

■　■　■

Ginsberg, Kerouac, and Burroughs all were similar in that they came from relatively privileged families. Crime wasn't their natural element. Enter Herbert Huncke. He and Burroughs were acquaintances, having met earlier in the 1940s. Huncke was a small-time hustler, Army veteran, and heroin addict. In other words, he was literature incarnate. Huncke was as much a person as he was a myth, known around Times Square as a jack-of-all-trades in the underworld. He was a one-stop shop for guns, drugs, sex, and stolen goods. Huncke and a group of thieves—an ex-convict called Little Jack Melody, and an ex-girlfriend of Kerouac's, Vicki Russell—began to use Ginsberg's Harlem apartment to stash stolen furniture and radios. Then they upped the ante by stealing $10,000 in jewelry from a Harlem detective's home.[26]

Huncke and his crew seemed like a safe ride to quality fiction, but soon the ride became the problem for Ginsberg. On April 22, 1949, Ginsberg wanted to visit his brother, Eugene, in Brooklyn. Huncke's gang offered to give him a lift (in a car they had stolen). Driving through Bayside, Queens, at 4 p.m., the crew found themselves on the wrong way of a major thoroughfare. The car jumped the curb, hit a telephone pole, and turned over. Nobody was fatally injured, but Ginsberg was badly shaken. His glasses were smashed. Bleeding, with blurry vision, he fled the scene. Breathless and exhausted, he finally got home to his Harlem apartment, but the police arrived shortly thereafter. Although Ginsberg was too traumatized to notice, the event was emblematic of something that would define the Beats for years: even bad publicity is good publicity. The artist's public image is as, if not more, important than their art. Ginsberg's name was on the front page of the following day's *Daily News* and the *New York Times*, which described him as a young writer looking for "realism" who had accidentally gotten mixed up with criminals.[27]

Ginsberg, who was held on $2,500 bail, which was paid by his father, would only play the role of a thief, while Huncke, who was denied bail, had no one to turn to. For all his talk of wanting an authentic taste of the hard life, when things got messy, Ginsberg fastidiously worked his elite connections to insulate himself from its unpleasant outcomes. Ginsberg contacted his old professor, Lionel Trilling, who introduced him to a Columbia University criminal law professor, who said the most pragmatic thing to do was to plead insanity. Harry Carman, Columbia University's dean, called the district attorney (a Columbia alumnus), and Mark Van Doren put in a good word. In lieu of prison time, Ginsberg was placed in the Columbia Presbyterian Institute, where he would spend eight months and receive world-class mental health treatment free of charge.[28]

At the Presbyterian Institute, Ginsberg had ample time to brush up on his French surrealism by way of a young writer also at the institute, Carl Solomon, who introduced him to the theater of cruelty by the playwright Antonin Artaud. Unlike Ginsberg, who went for treatment reluctantly, Solomon had voluntarily institutionalized himself and underwent electroconvulsive shock therapy. Solomon wasn't suffering from serious mental illness; he was suffering from a lack of experience, and thought being institutionalized would aid his art. It was during his time at the institute that Ginsberg, moved by Solomon's intensity and commitment, also became more spiritual. He was known to walk around the psychiatric facility clutching a copy of the Bhagavad Gita.[29]

Shortly after Ginsberg's release from Columbia Presbyterian, Jack Kerouac published his first novel, *The Town and the City*, and was the first of Ginsberg's circle to have literary success by fictionalizing their collective experiences. (Ginsberg, no doubt, rightly felt responsible for Kerouac's success—he had recommended Kerouac's novel to Mark Van Doren, who then handed it to his friend, the editor Robert Giroux, at Harcourt Brace.) Released on March 2, 1950, *The Town and the City* centers on the three Martin brothers, Joe (the all-American truck driver), Francis (the intellectual), and Peter (the poet), who move from the small fictional town of Galloway, Massachusetts, to the big city of New York in the 1930s and 1940s. Kerouac's novel was taken up by Giroux precisely because it was a conventional coming-of-age story, with some hard-boiled realism mixed in. Francis Martin could be a character in a Saul Bellow novel or an Arthur Miller play—he is described as a "musing, discontented, lonely . . . reader of books." Francis, influenced by T. S. Eliot and Auden, goes first to Harvard from Galloway (though he would have fit right in as a student in Trilling's classes at Columbia) and then to New York, where he has a wife, an apartment, and a steady job, and is able to afford all the luxuries of bourgeois life. What makes the book unique, however, is Peter, the bohemian. In contrast to Francis, Peter idolizes the romantic poet John Keats, hangs out in theaters and museums, drinks beers in dives, and goes to the Nickel-O in Times Square, where young hipsters are high on Benzedrine.[30]

Months after the book was published, Kerouac grew disenchanted with its traditional narrative structure. The turning point was in December 1950, after he received a rambling, stream-of-consciousness, sixteen-thousand-word letter from a mutual friend of his and Ginsberg's— the Denver, Colorado–raised Neal Cassady. Called the "Joan Anderson" letter by Kerouac, because it, among other things, described Cassady's relationship with a onetime girlfriend, Joan Anderson, the prose in Cassady's letter was unfiltered, fast, unedited, and threw out the conventions of punctuation and sentence structure: "Straight off her complection [sic] changed," Cassady writes, "pale lips quivered, then grimaced as tears sprung. From out incredulous eyes came stricken disbelief."[31]

Kerouac thought Cassady was a genius. It was the "greatest piece" of writing he had ever encountered.[32] Ginsberg wholeheartedly agreed with

Jack and tried to find a publisher to take it (no one did). Curiously, though not surprisingly, as neither Kerouac nor Ginsberg was interested in sociopolitical analysis or gender or feminism, and they promoted the myth of the heroic male individual, both young men conveniently overlooked, or took pleasure in, the fact that the letter was more than anything else a self-aggrandizing account of Neal Cassady. In the letter, Joan Anderson isn't a complicated person with feelings; she appears fragile and deranged, just one conquest among many for Cassady. Cassady's letter was like the man himself: rebellious in style but deeply problematic, if not repugnant, in content. Indeed, Kerouac and Ginsberg met Cassady in New York in 1946, just after he had finished a yearlong stint in prison for getting caught doing his favorite hobby: stealing cars. Moreover, the fast-talking, fast-driving, fast-reading twenty-year-old Cassady, brought up by an alcoholic father, bragged about his sexual exploits. (In *Howl*, Cassady is called the "secret hero of these poems, cocksman and Adonis of Denver.")[33] Cassady arrived in New York with his then sixteen-year-old wife, LuAnne Henderson, whom he abandoned shortly thereafter.

Kerouac described the "Joan Anderson" letter as a revelation; but another way to interpret it is, far more than influencing an emerging writing style of his based in what he called "spontaneous" prose, the letter gave both Kerouac and Ginsberg permission to see their own lives, in all their confusion, uncertainty, and questionable choices, as a form of art. By the time Kerouac received Cassady's letter, he himself had spent his days high on Benzedrine, drinking endless cups of coffee. He was not sleeping well.

As early as 1948, even before he was institutionalized at Columbia Presbyterian, Ginsberg experienced vivid hallucinations. Looking out the window of his Harlem apartment, he claimed to have seen a bright light saturate the sky and heard the baritone voice of poet William Blake reciting his 1794 poem "Ah! Sun-flower." The spiritual and emotional high of this experience was so great that Ginsberg attempted to recreate it over the next few days. He danced in his kitchen while reading obscure passages of philosophy. A few days later, while Ginsberg was browsing the shelves of the Columbia University bookstore, the people around him began to transform into wild animals. One clerk appeared to have the face of a giraffe.[34] For a spell and in a moment of lucidity, Ginsberg wasn't sure if he, in fact, was suffering the same fate as his mother, Naomi (schizophrenia is, after all, hereditary). But he didn't seek help for what could have easily been perceived as a spiraling condition of psychosis. Not only did Ginsberg bury these concerns, but he began to see delirium as central to his creative process.

▪ ▪ ▪

"There is something seductive about decadence," Ginsberg once wrote. "Perhaps it is because it is accompanied by Bohemianism, in its turn, an outgrowth of Libertinism."[35] Few in Ginsberg's circle were as eager to spiritualize decadence as the St. Louis, Missouri–born and Harvard University–educated William S. Burroughs. Burroughs was born into wealth. His grandfather had invented the Burroughs adding machine, which then spawned the Burroughs Corporation. As a child, Burroughs attended elite preparatory schools in St. Louis and New Mexico, and could afford treatment from some of the best psychoanalysts in the country such as Kurt Eissler in Chicago and Paul Federn, a student of Freud. Yet, Burroughs wasn't interested in processing his childhood; he wanted to exist in a permanent state of ecstasy. As it turned out, he got more than he could handle. He developed a lifelong addiction to heroin (later, it turned to morphine) after meeting Herbert Huncke in the mid-1940s.

The event that changed Burroughs's life was on September 6, 1951, in his Mexico City apartment. That night, he accidentally shot and killed his wife, Joan Vollmer, after a drunken game of "William Tell." After several drinks, Burroughs, suffering from heroin withdrawal, told Joan, who was high on and addicted to Benzedrine, to put a glass of gin on her head. Burroughs took out his .38-caliber pistol and fired a single shot at point-blank range. The bullet missed the glass and hit Vollmer in the forehead, leaving a small blue puncture, and a trickle of blood. Distraught, Burroughs rushed to her side, pleading for her to wake up. Eventually he took her to the hospital, where Vollmer was pronounced dead. Burroughs was arrested and imprisoned for thirteen days. It was only after bribing Mexico City officials that Burroughs was able to flee Mexico for the US. He was given a two-year suspended sentence. The event haunted him for the rest of his life: "The death of Joan brought me in contact with . . . the Ugly Spirit, and maneuvered me into a lifelong struggle, in which I had no choice except to write my way out."[36]

Surprisingly, Jean Vollmer's death didn't shake Burroughs's convictions about drugs; it only intensified his commitment to them and to writing about his drug-induced experiences. Whether methadone, heroin, or codeine (he preferred downers), Burroughs was always high when writing. It may be apocryphal, though it's been said that he never wrote anything of substance while sober.

At the time of Vollmer's death, Burroughs had completed a novel. Entitled *Junky*, it was a semi-autobiographical account of his life in the New York underground. "There is a type person occasionally seen in these neighborhoods who has connections with junk, though he is neither a user nor a seller," one line of the book reads, an illustrative example of *Junky*'s hard-boiled, ethnographic style, mixed with magical realism, "But when you see him the dowser wand twitches. Junk is close."[37] *Junky* didn't find a publisher. One editor at Doubleday said it was too graphic. Besides, the editor said, Burroughs wasn't famous enough. It could work, maybe, the editor said, if it were written by someone like Winston Churchill, not an unknown writer for whom it was a literary debut.

When *Junky* was eventually published in 1953, under the pseudonym "William Lee," alongside a reprint of Maurice Helbrant's memoir, *Narcotic Agent* (1941), it wasn't because its publisher, Ace Books, a specialist in pulp fiction titles, thought it would be hailed as a transgressive work of genius. To the contrary, it was because the book's sensational material would attract eyeballs and make its founder, A. A. Wyn, more money. To be sure, Wyn didn't discover *Junky* by chance. He was given the book by his nephew, Carl Solomon, who heard about it from Allen Ginsberg. Ginsberg had sung *Junky*'s praises to Solomon in 1950, and it was to him he would dedicate the book *Howl* five years later.

Ever the savvy literary promoter, like Walt Whitman himself, Ginsberg implored Kerouac—the only published one of his friends—to write a blurb for *Junky*. Kerouac did so under considerable protest. It turned out that the easygoing Kerouac, who valorized outsiders in his fiction, cared deeply about his personal brand. He didn't want to attach his name to any book, especially if he had any chance of one day becoming a household name. Selectively forgetting how instrumental Ginsberg had been in giving feedback on and promoting his own debut novel, Kerouac was instead annoyed that Ginsberg, whose in-progress poetry manuscript, *Empty Mirror*, had been rejected by Random House, was himself working tirelessly as an unpaid literary agent for Burroughs and for a market research company specializing in cosmetics to pay his bills.

In truth, if it weren't for the dedication of Ginsberg's marketing efforts, neither Kerouac nor the Beat Generation would have even taken off. But to underscore this fact would ruin the myth of the Beats as self-made geniuses. Perhaps it's true that Burroughs wrote his follow-up to *Junky*, *Naked Lunch* (1959), in an opium-induced haze. Yet, given its attentiveness to detail, it seems apocryphal that Burroughs had absolutely no memory of writing it. Ginsberg, for his part, claimed to have come up with the title *Naked Lunch* after he misread the phrase "naked lust" in the manuscript, while Kerouac said the title was "a frozen moment when everyone sees what is on the end of every fork."[38] As for Kerouac? Less a master of spontaneous writing, he was a master of the *myth* of spontaneity (and, by extension, authenticity). It was a well-rehearsed legend that Kerouac's best-selling book, *On the Road* (1957), was written single-spaced on one 120-foot scroll of paper in twenty-one days under the influence of Benzedrine at 454 West Twentieth Street, without any serious revision. The book is centered on his literary alter ego, Sal Paradise, and his travels with Dean Moriarty (based on Neal Cassady), and it includes characters like Old Bull Lee (Burroughs) and Carlo Marx (Ginsberg). *On the Road*, Kerouac must have feared, would be less appealing to readers if they knew that the author wrote the book while drinking coffee, not swallowing amphetamines. *On the Road* was no accident. Kerouac meticulously taped together eight strips of paper upon which he typed the manuscript to give the image of an endless scroll. Even before these eight strips existed, early drafts of the text appeared in some of his personal journals.

It's fair to say that the Beat Generation was a carefully stylized image as much as a kind of postwar literature; it's also fair to say that the Beat Generation explicitly silenced voices who didn't fit their curated image of this generation, defined as the white male hipster. Ginsberg worked overtime for his friends, but not so much for the talented women in his circle. "The social organization which is most true of itself to the artist," Ginsberg declared, without any hint of irony, "is the boy gang."[39] But what if the reading public knew that the Brooklyn-born and Swarthmore-educated Diane di Prima, whose first poetry book, *This Kind of Bird Flies Backward*

(1958), was written even earlier than *Howl*, and used street language—words like *uncool* and *pads*? Or that *This Kind of Bird Flies Backward* was unpublished precisely because it tackled the foundational questions of marriage, reproductive rights, the body, sexual assault, with infinitely more rigor than the "boy gang"?

The boy gang could never accept this fact. One evening at a New York party, di Prima was smoking marijuana with Ginsberg and Kerouac. It was 11:30 p.m., and di Prima had promised to go home before midnight, to relieve her sitter watching her child back at her apartment. Di Prima was, like the boy gang, trying to forge connections, to facilitate her art, but, as a woman, she had to confront patriarchic oppression. Jack Kerouac couldn't fathom this reality. "UNLESS YOU FORGET ABOUT YOUR BABYSITTER," he hollered, drunkenly, across the room, to di Prima, "YOU'RE NEVER GOING TO BE A WRITER."[40]

Kerouac was fast to criticize di Prima for her indebtedness to another woman, but careful to elide his own indebtedness to a woman, the Berlin-born poet ruth weiss—who fled Nazi Germany as a child and later made a name for herself through jazz poetry readings at the Cellar in San Francisco. It was with weiss with whom Kerouac wrote haiku poems at the Hotel Wentley in the mid-1950s. If you were to compare weiss's self-published chapbook, *Steps* (1958), to Kerouac's *On the Road*, for instance, you see not only a similarity in motifs—of hitchhiking, getting lost and not found, daydreaming—but a language brimming with a sense of resilience amid the danger of the male gaze lurking everywhere: "they fed me / and a deer-hunter shared his cantaloupes / before depositing me on broadway and colombus [sic]/ he had stopped before the golden gate bridge / to let me see the city on first-time entering."[41]

Another talented Beat writer largely overlooked by Kerouac and Ginsberg was Sheri Martinelli. Martinelli was a regular at the North Beach's Co-Existence Bagel Shop and was known for the makeshift literary salon she hosted in her small apartment in San Francisco's Chinatown, from which she established the little magazine *Anagogic & Paideumic Review*, sold at City Lights. It was in that publication that her "Duties of a Lady Female" appeared. The piece is an ironic, scathing, and unabashedly feminist take on how young women should learn to please their male hipster partners: "Put into your lover's mind a picture of the KIND of PERSON you feel he secretly thinks he is. . . . No high or harsh tones of voice. He is more sensitive than you, to them. . . . In your love talking put a picture in his mind of something wildly adventurous, suiting his male nature."[42]

■ ■ ■

The reason why the Beats were household names wasn't because their work was irresistible to critics. It was because they became a touchpoint for debates around free expression in a country battling the anti-intellectual Red Scare of McCarthyism.

On March 25, 1957, the San Francisco office of the federal US customs division seized 520 copies of the 3,000-copy second printing of *Howl* as it was being delivered from the Villiers Press in England, on the premise that it contained graphic language. Lawrence Ferlinghetti, owner of City Lights Books and publisher of *Howl*, brought the case to the American Civil Liberties Union. Upon receiving his phone call, the ACLU threatened the government with litigation. Recognizing that the government might be on thin legal grounds and that censorship might cause a national uproar, the San Francisco customs office released the copies.

Today, *Howl* is considered a masterpiece of high modernist verse among literary scholars, but in 1957 the book was suffering from poor sales (which was saying something, even for a poetry book). Save for a few decent reviews, it was ignored by the literary world. Divided into three parts, *Howl* is, stylistically and spiritually, an homage and update to Walt Whitman's ecstatic poetry of American identity. Whereas Whitman exalts the cast of characters and experiences with which he was familiar but which society largely denigrated—blacksmiths with hairy chests, the farmer, the lunatic, the carpenter, the runaway slave, the married and unmarried children, the excited crowd, clam-diggers—Ginsberg exalts the "angelheaded hipsters" who light cigarettes, who, only dressed in underwear, cower in rooms, in subways, who vomit, who do dope in Turkish baths.

Although Ginsberg never acknowledged the debt, *Howl* is also a literary descendant of Langston Hughes's blues-infused poetry, Jean Toomer's surrealism, and John Reed's boots-on-the-ground gonzo journalism. If Hughes and Toomer's enemies are race and class, and if Reed's enemy is poverty, then Ginsberg's is—as he puts in the second part of *Howl*—the bull-headed figure of Moloch, from the book of Leviticus, who, in

Ginsberg's words, represents the entirety of Western acquisitive individualism and middle-class conformity: "Robot apartments! Invisible suburbs! Skeleton treasuries! Blind capitals! Demonic industries! Spectral nations! Invincible madhouses! Granite cocks! Monstrous bombs!" *Howl* was a strong debut collection, no doubt. But Ferlinghetti elevated it as *the* gold standard for nonconformist art. Days after the customs office seized *Howl*, writing an op-ed in the *San Francisco Chronicle*, Ferlinghetti declared the poem the greatest piece of writing since T. S. Eliot's *Four Quartets* (1941). A questionable assertion given that Ginsberg's contemporaries included established poets like Philip Larkin, Sylvia Plath, William Carlos Williams, Robert Frost, and H.D., who were arguably more technically gifted and more innovative in their craft. Also included in this group is the Black poet Gwendolyn Brooks, who won the Pulitzer Prize for her collection *Annie Allen* in 1950.

The scene was set for the ensuing confrontation. On May 21, 1957, two plainclothes officers entered City Lights Bookstore and purchased *Howl* from the manager at the front desk, Shigeyoshi (Shig) Murao. If the government was looking to make an example of Murao, he was a terrible target for national hostility. Murao was a Seattle-born Japanese American who had been interned in a Japanese concentration camp during the Second World War and, despite this harrowing experience, had worked as a US military interpreter in postwar Japan. He was arrested and remained in jail until the ACLU paid his five-hundred-dollar bail. Ferlinghetti was also arrested and faced up to six months in prison.

The trial unfolded later that summer. At issue was whether *Howl* was in fact a work of art and, if so, whether it could skirt US obscenity laws under the First Amendment of the US Constitution. To make the case on behalf of Ferlinghetti, the ACLU culled a pair of esteemed lawyers—Lawrence Speiser and Albert Bendich. Their task was to convince the presiding judge, Clayton W. Horn, a Sunday school teacher who, in an earlier case, made national headlines for sentencing five women convicted of shoplifting to watch the film *The Ten Commandments*. The lawyers first tried to get Horn to throw out the case on the basis that, upon reading *Howl*, he would agree the material was not obscene. Horn, however, wanted the defense to make a less subjective case: its argument had to demonstrate the objective merits of publishing the book. The judge wanted to know, was *Howl* serious art?[43]

Horn may have thought he was setting a high evidentiary bar, but there were plenty of scholars willing to make the case for the defense, irrespective of whether they thought *Howl* was an instant classic. Mark Schorer, a professor of English at the University of California, was the first of nine witnesses for the defense to address the court. Schorer gave a close reading of each section and supported its inventive use of street language. During cross-examination with the government prosecutor, Schorer declared that that a poem wasn't an assemblage of distinct words, but words that, only together, in their entirety, conjured an overarching feeling, or idea. "Angelheaded hipsters," "fuck," and "balls" may be obscene in themselves but take on a different meaning when added together and when considering underground youth culture in the postwar era.[44] Another defense witness, Kenneth Rexroth, one of the poets who read alongside Ginsberg at the Six Gallery in 1955 when he debuted the poem, wasn't as smitten with *Howl* as Schorer. But when Rexroth took the stand, he understood the larger political implications of saying he did, calling *Howl* "probably the most remarkable single poem published by a young man since the second war." Schorer's colleague, University of California professor Leo Lowenthal, put *Howl* in its historical perspective—a time of war, a time of anxiety about nuclear apocalypse, and the rise of mass media. Professor Herbert Blau of San Francisco State compared it to Dadaism; and the writer Vincent McHugh put Ginsberg in the Western canon, right alongside Ezra Pound and Dante.

The witnesses for the government, however, were neither as skilled in their assessments nor as credible in their authority. A junior faculty member in the English department at the University of San Francisco (a Jesuit School) said *Howl* was a third-rate impression of Whitman, and that, even if it were Dadaistic, Dada was a heretical movement dedicated to overthrowing everything that was beautiful. Gail Potter, an adjunct at Catholic University in San Francisco, told the courtroom that the writing was so "crude," it made her feel as if she were "going through the gutter." Some in the audience might have agreed, but even they laughed out loud when Potter claimed that her authority as a literary critic came from the fact that she had, in the past, written fan fiction: Potter told Judge Horn that she was proud of rewriting Goethe's classic play *Faust*.[45]

Judge Horn was left with no choice. On October 3, 1957, he found Ferlinghetti innocent. Not only did *Howl* have artistic merit, Horn claimed, but vulgar language alone wouldn't lead to lustful thoughts—if anything, the negative reaction of the witnesses of the prosecution proved just the opposite.

Howl became City Lights' best-selling book, and Ginsberg was asked to be interviewed for *Time* magazine. Kerouac's *On the Road* was published by Viking Press on September 5, 1957. Hailed by the *New York Times* as a "major novel," the book would become an instant bestseller. The American edition of *Naked Lunch* was released by Grove Press in 1962 to intense fanfare (it was originally published in Paris through Olympia Press in 1959). Like *Howl*, it too was subject to an obscenity trial in Boston, which resulted in no conviction but, predictably, elevated the book's sales.

■ ■ ■

In 1948, the writer John Clellon Holmes asked Jack Kerouac how he would explain the increasing number of hipsters lurking around Times Square. With no real conviction or authority, Kerouac shrugged his shoulders and said he wasn't sure. He did have a hunch. Perhaps his generation of bohemians was governed by a feeling of defeat. "I guess," he replied, "you might say we're a beat generation."[46] A decade later, Holmes asked Kerouac the question again. This time it was for the February 1958 issue of *Esquire*, for a long essay entitled, "Philosophy of the Beat Generation." No longer a character in any of his published novels—neither young, nor unknown, nor on the road—Kerouac was now confident in his answer: "A generation of crazy, illuminated hipsters," he told Holmes, who are "suddenly rising and roaming America, serious, bumming and hitchhiking everywhere, ragged, beatific, beautiful in an ugly graceful new way."[47]

Everyone was so busy asking the Beats to define their generation that few bothered to ask them about their own politics. Yes, the Beats wrote unflinchingly about drugs, sex, and violence. Yes, the Beats hated conformity. But what exactly did nonconformity mean, if anything, in terms of the free market, tax policy, economic redistribution, military intervention, immigration? Then and now, young people who revere the Beats' literature interpret their work as an injunction to take up causes associated with the left. This means to resist everything from the police state to imperialism, from conspicuous consumption to mind-numbing corporate existence.

In the 1960s, antiwar activists saw themselves as the inheritors of Dean Moriarty's nonconformity in *On the Road* as they were protesting racism, capitalism, and war. A devout Roman Catholic, Jack Kerouac was furious to learn that, as he put it, he became "the great white father and intellectual forebear who spawned a deluge of alienated radicals, war protesters, dropouts, hippies and even 'beats.'"[48] Kerouac, who died in 1969 at the age of forty-seven after a long struggle with alcoholism, described *On the Road* as a "story about two Catholic buddies in search of God." Kerouac hated hippies; he also didn't like Jews or Communists either, which, for him, were indistinguishable. "The Communist is the main enemy—the Jew," he once said.[49] Kerouac's father, Leo, referred to Ginsberg as a "cockroach," and his mother prayed that her youngest son would stop seeing the "Jewish boy."

William Burroughs wasn't a reactionary like Kerouac, but no one would accuse him of being a progressive. (The characters in *Junky* and *Naked Lunch* are misanthropes, and the overarching theme is to legalize drugs, not illegalize class hierarchy.) An old-school libertarian, he wanted government off his back. (If Burroughs were alive today, one can imagine him being a supporter of the Freedom Caucus and of Elon Musk.) Burroughs complained of the "octopus of bureaucratic socialism," and wrote to Ginsberg that the "U.S. is heading in the direction of a Socialistic police state similar to England, and not too different from Russia."[50] An entrepreneur who wanted to grow the $200 stipend (around $3,000 in today's dollars) his family had sent him, Burroughs was, between 1948 and 1949, a landlord in New Orleans. If he had one, Burroughs's utopian ideal was to transform America into a state where, as he put in his description of the fictional Freelandia in *Naked Lunch*, "If a citizen wanted anything from a load of bone meal to a sexual partner some department was ready to offer effective aid. The threat implicit in this enveloping benevolence stifled the concept of rebellion."[51]

In a 1949 letter, Ginsberg criticized Burroughs for the unnecessarily low wages he was paying his migrant workers on the small farm he owned in South Texas to grow carrots, peas, and lettuce (and some marijuana and opium on the side). Writing in reply, Burroughs dismissed Ginsberg's socialism, saying that without profits there would be no work. At least, in Burroughs's mind, he was an upstanding, even if paternalistic, employer— his labor broker, Burroughs told Ginsberg, wasn't as nice. He had shot and killed two workers the night before. "We farmers in the Rio Grande Valley depend entirely on Mexican laborers who enter the country illegally with our aid and connivance," Burroughs wrote. "The 'civil liberties' of these workers are violated repeatedly."[52] Yet Burroughs's individualism also had a profound cost on those who needed him most, like his son, Billy Jr. After William Burroughs killed Billy's mother, he shipped Billy off to live with his parents, who moved to Palm Beach, Florida, where Billy was raised until the age of sixteen. In 1963, Burroughs brought Billy to Tangier, Morocco, where he was living, and introduced him to marijuana. Billy never looked back. A new liver (his first was destroyed by alcohol-induced cirrhosis) and the turmoil of being in and out of rehab for amphetamines did little to slow his inevitable decline. Billy Burroughs was dead at thirty-three in 1981.

Allen Ginsberg's art was, by far, the most political, and his politics were far to the left of Kerouac's and Burroughs's. For Ginsberg, there was no meaningful tension between individual enlightenment and revolution. "I don't see a conflict between political and meditative activity," he declared during a 1974 visit to the Hill Auditorium in Ann Arbor, Michigan, as part of the Gay Liberation Front, "because the prospect is of clarification of one's own awareness, which necessarily precedes action."[53]

Ginsberg may have been right—there may not be a conflict between political and meditative activity. But neither does that mean there's a direct link between the two. One can pursue individual enlightenment independent of their politics, or vice versa.

Was the true inheritance of the Beats the hippie or the New Left, the young libertarian, the misogynist, the feminist, the womanizer, or the antiwar activist? Was the philosophy embedded in the Beat Generation a plea for young people to drop out of collective struggle, or tune into it? Maybe the reason there's no clear answer to these questions has to do with Beat ethics. The life and art of the Beat Generation doesn't gesture toward a set of commitments, or even a worldview. If anything, it's defined by trying to put into words an anti-philosophy, an anti-worldview. When Ginsberg declared that *Howl* came from a place of "defeat," he never said worldly defeat was defeated, only that he (and his friends) had witnessed, attended to, and spoken about worldly defeat. And he, like the Beats, did this with force, without constraint. Originally and authentically.

CHAPTER 8

FLOWERS OR POWER?

O n Saturday, January 14, 1967, Timothy Leary, a social psychologist with a PhD from the University California, Berkeley, stood before a crowd. Leary was a former lecturer at Harvard University, now turned guru for the use of psychedelic drugs—specifically psilocybin and LSD. The crowd that Leary addressed ranged from twenty thousand to thirty thousand at Golden Gate Park, in San Francisco, California. This crowd of misfits (even if some professionals were among them, they preferred to blend in) came from all over the country. It was mostly white and under thirty. Some of them were teens not finished with high school. What most of them shared was that they were recent arrivals, runaways from middle-class households. They lived just outside the park in the Haight-Ashbury neighborhood. It was there where some slept on streets and others in abandoned, or barely habitable, Victorian homes. First it was a trickle of newcomers enjoying the warmth of San Francisco, then a stream following them; then it became a cascade, where everyone who knew everyone was telling them the Haight was the place to be.

The forty-seven-year-old Leary wasn't from their generation. In fact, he was the same age as their parents. What Leary embodied, however, was the spirit they desperately desired. He was cool because he gave them permission to do what parents never tell their kids: it's okay to be kids forever. As Leary stood on the podium, speaking into a microphone and clapping his hands, dressed in a white desert robe, a handmade beaded necklace, and flowers draped around his ears, he urged his children to bloom. No one had to rise upward, or go anywhere, or change anything about the world outside. They had to, in fact, stay in place. To bloom meant changing their own minds. "Tune in, turn on, drop out," Leary bellowed to widespread applause, in what had become a mantra for the new social category he represented, the hippie.

Organized by Allen Cohen, the editor of the underground newspaper *San Francisco Oracle*, the event, billed as the "Human Be-In" (a play on "human being"), wasn't intended to be fun and games. It was a serious affair. Yes, Cohen wanted to give hippies another opportunity to let their "freak flags fly" (by the looks of the Haight, however, they seemed to be doing okay in that regard). More pressing matters were at stake. The Vietnam War was escalating. On January 8, 1967, sixteen thousand US forces and fourteen thousand of the South Vietnamese Army, in "Operation Cedar Falls," sought to capture a sixty-square-mile area around the Saigon River being held by Viet Cong forces. In the next three weeks, seventy Americans were killed by Viet Cong snipers, and seven hundred Viet Cong perished. On February 21, 1967, thirty thousand American troops launched "Operation Junction City" to incapacitate Viet Cong military headquarters. On April 24, the US began its assault on North Vietnam's airfields.

The antiwar movement was always a conundrum for the hippie. As much as she hated violence and wanted us to give peace a chance, the hippie was a cynic at heart: she didn't want to get involved in anything organized or political because it was another myth perpetuated by the man. The hippies had a special power, according to Allen Ginsberg. It was "Flower Power"—a term he coined in a 1965 essay. That is to say, the hippie's public acts of nonviolent noncooperation, rooted in love, were forms of resistance.

Driven by the Marxist ideal of class struggle, the New Left thought the hippies were a joke. Ann Arbor–based, University of Michigan student Tom Hayden, of Students for a Democratic Society (SDS), and antiwar activists at the University of California, Berkeley, associated with the Free Speech Movement, led by Mario Savio, cared about real power, the kind that exists under capitalism, the kind that greases the war machine. Much to Allen Cohen's disappointment, the New Left wasn't eager to be part of the Human Be-In. Most hippies didn't care.

In their mind, their aesthetic itself was a revolutionary act. The hippie refused to cut their hair because they despised the clean-cut look of their corporate, briefcase-toting fathers. They wore tie-dye clothes, headbands, sandals, pins, and handmade jewelry because they believed in being closer to nature and living an authentic experience. Hippies listened to local rock bands like Jefferson Airplane and Grateful Dead, burned incense, shook tambourines, and rang bells. They treated the figure of the Hobbit in J. R. R. Tolkien's *Lord of the Rings* trilogy with reverence. Hippies said "groovy" and "far out," because they preferred to bask in the warm comfort of generalities; they saw such words as the way toward mystical consciousness. Taking LSD meant opting out of capitalism; crashing on a friend's couch meant avoiding the drudgery of bourgeois family life.[1]

A major reason hippies felt so approachable was that they played the role of mellow cats, free of judgment and full of tolerance. But hippies could yet be vicious against those who wanted to dance to the beat of their own drum. In February 1967, on a houseboat owned by Alan Watts on Sausalito Bay, Timothy Leary turned to Allen Ginsberg and told him point-blank what he believed: the New Left were a bunch "menopausal minds" who "cry for a leader . . . for organization."[2] From the moment Leary took psilocybin in Cuernavaca, Mexico, in 1960, he claimed to have learned more about the mind and the brain in four hours than in his fifteen years as a practicing research psychologist. "As soon as enough people" become a "little tribe wandering around," Leary continued, "it'll bring about an incredible change in the consciousness of this country, and of the Western world."[3]

Ginsberg dug what Leary was saying. He, too, had a religious experience after taking ayahuasca with a shaman in Mexico. And at the Be-In a month earlier, Ginsberg was leading a crowd in spiritual om chants (he had been slowly gravitating toward Buddhism for years now). But even Ginsberg couldn't resist calling bullshit on Leary. "But you're not dropped out of the very highly complicated legal constitutional appeals [to legalize psychoactive drugs]," he retorted, "and you haven't dropped out of planning and conducting community organization and participating in it."[4]

There was a bigger problem with Leary and the hippie ethos generally that Ginsberg ignored. It's not that the hippies never truly dropped out; it was that the process of trying to drop out became a gateway drug for dropping *into* existing hierarchies of power. The hippie may have been free from the man, but she was held hostage to life on the street. She was at the mercy of profit-seeking drug dealers, greedy hustlers, unscrupulous sex traffickers, racist Hells Angels, violent street gangs, and crooked cops.

The writer Joan Didion arrived in the Haight-Ashbury area in the spring of 1967 and got to know some of these kids, who were aimlessly walking the streets, their stomachs full of acid but hungry and homeless. What Didion described was "not a country in open revolution," but a bunch of "children who have moved around a lot, *San Jose, Chula Vista, here. They* are less in rebellion against the society than ignorant of it, able only to feed back certain of its most publicized self-doubts, *Vietnam, Saran-Wrap, diet pills, the Bomb.*"[5] The journalist and editor of *Ramparts* magazine, Warren Hinckle, was less forgiving than Didion. He noticed a bitter irony: the kids who had little to their name, and fewer prospects for living a decent life— the very ones who would stand to benefit from big government—were parroting right-wing talking points that would have stirred the pride of 1964 Republican presidential candidate, US senator from Arizona Barry Goldwater. "They talked about reducing government controls," Hinckle wrote, "the sanctity of the individual."[6]

Whatever one thought of the hippie, it was clear that he was a cultural force to be reckoned with. The Human Be-In was a dress rehearsal for what came to be known as the hippies' crowning achievement. During the 1967 "Summer of Love," tens of thousands descended upon the Bay Area. The feeling was epitomized through the event held one hundred miles south of San Francisco—the Monterey International Pop Festival, a three-day music festival that ran from June 16 to June 18, 1967. Concert-goers, many for the first time, got to hear Janis Joplin, wearing a beaded necklace, gold sweater dress, and gold heels, yelling out the blues standard "Ball and Chain." They were introduced to the Black rock guitarist Jimi Hendrix, wearing a multicolored headband, a striped, yellow ruffled shirt, and red bell-bottoms. Hendrix and his band performed "Wild Thing," which he concluded by setting his guitar on fire and throwing pieces of it to the crowd.

Performances like this had hippies convinced that they had hacked the system, that the cosmic energy they had brought into the world was spreading rapidly like wildfire. In their mind, they were at the dawn of the Age of Aquarius.

■　■　■

Their elation was premature. Four months after the Summer of Love concluded, on October 6, 1967, a small group of two hundred people in the

Haight walked behind ten pallbearers who were holding a coffin, which was filled with beads, incense, and flowers. The mock funeral was called the "Death of the Hippie." And it was organized by those affiliated with another countercultural group in the Haight. They called themselves Diggers, modeled on the Protestant sect of agrarian socialists that originated in England in 1649 and whose leader was Gerrard Winstanley. The original Diggers cultivated common land for mutual subsistence. The 1960s Diggers were neither religious nor located in the English countryside. They took up the original Diggers' commitment to mutual aid, along with mixing in a little bit of street theater and, for good measure, satirical critique.

"FORGET the war in Vietnam. Flowers are lovely," said one of the Digger broadsides.[7] "Pretty little 16-year-old middle-class chick comes to the Haight to see what it's all about and gets picked up by a 17-year-old street dealer who spends all day shooting her full of speed again and again," declared another, entitled "Uncle Tim$ Children" (in reference to Timothy Leary), "then feeds her 3,000 mikes [sic] and raffles her off temporarily unemployed body for the biggest Haight Street gang bang since the night before last."[8]

The Diggers saw themselves as the Socratic gadflies of the Haight—everything was subject to critique. Nothing was out of bounds. The local bands, Jefferson Airplane and Grateful Dead? They sold out. The widely successful Psychedelic Shop and Far Fetched Foods? Just another way for "hip merchants" to keep profits flowing. The newly formed Haight Independent Proprietors? At heart, it was concerned with evicting the young panhandlers from their storefronts—the very hippies that they glorified on the other side of the window. "Peace and love" was why, ostensibly, the co-owner of one of these shops, the Psychedelic Shop, put a sign in its window urging locals to "Take a Cop to Dinner." But even this, according to Diggers, was a naked plea for police protection.[9]

Everybody likes peace and love, but you can have both without freedom. Which is to say, freedom is a different thing altogether (here we're not talking about liberty). Freedom is about ensuring one has the resources to make reasoned choices. To do this, you can't be crippled by debilitating wants and needs. This kind of freedom is what the Diggers wanted.

Not content with debating freedom, the Diggers put their vision into practice. In October 1966, they distributed a stew to anywhere from fifty to one hundred people every day at 4 p.m. in Golden Gate Park. The stew was a combination of food donations of vegetables and fifty pounds of chicken and turkey leftovers from the San Francisco Produce Market and forty-gallon milk cans that they stole from a local dairy plant. The stew wasn't tasty, but it was free. The same could be said for the day-old stale bread Diggers served alongside it, which was donated by a Ukrainian bakery that Allen Ginsberg and his friends would frequent in the 1950s. The Diggers also had a small fleet of used vans, which were barely functional, though they could, occasionally, be used to pick up hitchhikers. Diggers held free dance classes and concerts—though the artistic quality of both was questionable. Digger staffers were homeless kids from the street who, in exchange for food and makeshift accommodations called "crash pads," would contribute their labor by cooking, organizing, scavenging, and performing.[10]

The Diggers created temporary stores—some were painted orange, others yellow—that they called the "Free Frames of Reference." Everything in the stores—the clothes, jewelry, utensils, and televisions—was as free as the roles of customer and worker were unstructured. The people who worked at a Free Frame of Reference weren't paid wages. No managers were on duty. When someone walked through the store asking for the manager, they would be told by the all-volunteer staff: "You are the manager!"

One Digger who later became a Hollywood actor, Peter Coyote, recalled how he once noticed a woman stealthily stuffing clothing in her bag. Coyote approached her, saying, "You can't steal here."

The women became indignant. "I wasn't stealing!" she screamed.

"I know," he replied, "But you thought you were stealing. You can't steal here because it's a Free Store. Read the sign, everything is free! You can have the whole fucking store if you feel like it. You can take over and tell me to get lost."[11]

After the tense exchange, Coyote and the woman spent the next hour looking over sweaters, which fit her aesthetic tastes. A week later, she returned with a tray of donuts, which she set on the table to share with others as she went to look for more clothing. Coyote's story, no doubt, is heartwarming, but the lessons it has for social transformation are far from clear. Is this an argument for anarchism? Is this a society where each does what they can according to their abilities, and takes only what they need? Perhaps. What Coyote neglected to mention in his anecdote, however, was that the goods you could find in a Free Frame of Reference were goods you could also find at the local shelter or at a clothing drive. Also, a Free Frame of Reference was a neatly contained tent that could be conveniently folded up and stowed away; it was not a government building, or a city with real infrastructure.

As much as the Diggers portrayed themselves as the moral conscience of the '60s counterculture, they were identical to hippies in the following way: they were desperate to shift their consciousness by whatever means available. What this meant was that the Diggers had no qualms with drugs. They dealt heroin and speed at high rates. At the Human Be-In, Diggers would be seen handing out free roast turkey sandwiches (which kept kids full), laced with tabs of acid (which kept them high). Hippie icons Jimi Hendrix and Janis Joplin died within weeks of each other in fall 1970; he from asphyxiation in London by barbiturates, she by a heroin overdose in Los Angeles. Many Diggers experienced similarly cruel fates. By late 1967, not even a year into their experiment, the Digger free food program fizzled out because many of the cooks were strung out (many others were also arrested for theft).

Diggers chastised the hip merchants but depended on the weekly tithes these merchants paid to fund their programs—tithes that came entirely from the merchants' retail sales. "The Diggers were not very good at institutions," said Peter Coyote in a moment of candor. "Things were based on what you felt like doing. After you'd hustled the food for a while, that got to be a drag."[12] A typical Digger "crash pad" was a Victorian house crammed with people who slept in sleeping bags. Cardboard and sheets functioned as partitions between "bedrooms." Maintaining decent hygiene, let alone getting decent sleep—amid the constant talking, guitar playing, chanting, tripping, and sex—was difficult, if not impossible, under such circumstances.

Bill Fritsch, a mustached Digger known around the Haight as the "Free Banker," would ride his Harley-Davidson motorcycle in his leather jacket while throwing nickels, dimes, and quarters in the air. Fritsch would carry a hundred dollars under his red headband in case anyone needed an interest-free loan. But this "Free Banker" was also part of the Hells Angels motorcycle gang, whose antiauthoritarianism was linked to the gospel of conservative traditionalism and white supremacy. Some Diggers ate amphetamines by the handfuls and became increasingly paranoid that they would be robbed. They started to carry guns. They put out a manifesto that said, "An Armed Man Is a Free Man."[13]

There were, no doubt, successful instances of Digger mutual aid. But, as is often the case, this mutual aid survived only because of the hidden domestic labor of women. To support the free food program, Digger women stood for hours cooking stew, arriving in the morning and leaving at night.

And yet, when Digger women would go to Free Stores to work their second and third shifts, they would see handbills plastered around that declared, "Spaces should be available for chicks to sew dresses, make pants to order, recut garments to fit."[14] Digger men basked in the public-facing glory of handing out cash to the needy; it was Digger women, however, who would have the unsexy job of keeping meticulous track of finances. Someone had to know who borrowed twenty dollars to fix a truck on a Monday, or two dollars for toothpaste and floss on a Tuesday.[15] It was also Digger women who, behind closed doors, advocated on behalf of small children; Digger kids needed new shoes, even if their Digger dads wanted new brakes for their pickup trucks. Such Digger gender hierarchy remained intact, but over time, the Diggers became more and more like their seventeenth-century ancestors and, thus, like the hippies they claimed to loathe. Diggers dropped out. They left the Bay Area and moved to rural communes. Of course, gender hierarchy traveled there too. A visitor recalled how Digger women who were part of "Free Families" in the countryside seemed as if they were "from another century. How did they know how to do all that gardening, cooking for hundreds, embroidery?"[16]

If one were to summarize who the Diggers were and what they did, you would say they were primarily a theatrical movement, and were more interested in producing spectacles of opposition rather than durable institutions that could make such opposition last. The poverty of Digger politics was evident in their response to the events surrounding September 27, 1966, when a white cop shot a sixteen-year-old Black teen named Matthew Johnson, setting off six days of rebellion in San Francisco. The uprising began in the predominantly Black neighborhood of Hunters Point and spread throughout other Black areas of the city. San Francisco mayor John Shelley deployed hundreds of police and requested that California governor Pat Brown bring in the National Guard. To leave nothing to chance, Shelley put in place a strict curfew throughout the city. Students for a Democratic Society and the Free Speech Movement encouraged supporters to defy the curfew in solidarity with Black citizens, whose lives were ignored by the power elite. The Diggers? They told their followers it didn't matter what they did—break curfew or stay indoors. What mattered is that they did what they wanted.[17] Indeed, this is the beauty and problem with freedom—you can have it, but you get to decide what you do with it.

Another event that revealed the limits of Digger politics occurred at 5:30 p.m. on Halloween night 1966. That was the time of day that the Diggers held a public performance called "Full Moon Public Celebration on Halloween." They carried a large "Frame of Reference," holding eight-foot-tall puppets, to a street intersection, and distributed seventy six-by-six-inch replicas of the frame to the audience. Next, Diggers passed out instructions for what they called the "Intersection Game," which the audience would play by blocking street traffic while performing silly walks—the "squat-jump," "finger-crawl," or "cake walk."[18] A total of six hundred people played the game. And the farce created exactly what the Diggers wanted: a chaotic scene. When San Francisco police arrived and addressed the puppeteers, informing them that they would be arrested for public disturbance, the puppeteers—through the puppets—said, "I declare myself public—I am a public. The streets are free."[19]

With this event, the Diggers registered a moral victory. After a few hours of fun, however, the crowd slowly dispersed. If anything, the "Intersection Game" did more to alienate bystanders, who were walking or driving home from work at the height of rush hour. The Diggers, in this way, were radically different from the hippies: if the hippies wanted to drop out of the limelight, the Diggers wanted to be center stage. Whether positive or negative, grabbing any kind of attention was their politics.

▪ ▪ ▪

In June 1967, several Diggers, including Peter Berg and Bill Fritsch, crashed a Students for a Democratic Society meeting in Denton, Michigan. SDS attendees were looking dapper and professional, the men wearing shirts and ties. Peter Berg, looking unpolished and disheveled, was disgusted. He yelled, "Property is the enemy—burn it, destroy it, give it away. Don't let them make a machine out of you, get out of the system, do your thing. Don't organize students, teachers, Negroes, organize your head."[20] Some SDS attendees were annoyed. Others were furious. SDS was in the business of organizing opposition, not doing soul-searching or publicity stunts. But one audience member, a thirty-one-year-old from Worcester, Massachusetts, and graduate of Brandeis University by the name of Abbie

Hoffman, liked everything Berg did. What Berg said, how he looked, and what he was all about.

Albert "Abbie" Hoffman had gotten his activist sea legs by becoming involved with the Student Nonviolent Coordinating Committee. In recent years, SNCC had taken a Black nationalist turn under the leadership of Stokely Carmichael and then H. Rap Brown, as the organization was growing disenchanted by Washington's inability to get behind anything other than modest reforms regarding Black voting rights. Hoffman decided to leave, turning his attention to antiwar protests in New York.

Before attending the SDS conference in Michigan that summer, Hoffman, whose trademark curly black hair, deep-set eyes, and infectious smile gave him a natural stage presence, had gotten a taste of street performance. In protest of a pro-war march organized by the Veterans of Foreign Wars in May 1967, Hoffman had organized a group to walk alongside the marchers with flowers, called the "Flower Brigade" (in reference to the hippie "Flower Power" slogan). The older patriots threw punches at the hippies. Thanks to Hoffman's media savvy, the reporters whom he contacted in advance were on hand to publish an account of the violent beating.

That year, Hoffman synced up with another prankster with whom he collaborated and became publicly associated: Jerry Rubin. Born in Ohio, Rubin had been a sociology PhD student at University of California, Berkeley, before dropping out. Sporting a beard, he was an unlikely mayoral candidate for the city of Berkeley when he ran in 1967, though he managed to win 22 percent of the vote. And yet, legislation wasn't Rubin's main interest; his heart was in political comedy. Subpoenaed to appear before the House Un-American Activities Committee (HUAC) on August 18, 1966, Rubin was charged with disorderly conduct after he decided to appear dressed up in the eighteenth-century colonial garb of a revolutionary American solider. On October 3, 1968, when forced to appear again at HUAC for his role in the Chicago 1968 Democratic National Convention protests, Rubin, shirtless and outfitted in a cape, dressed as a rebel guerrilla fighter (from either Cuba or North Vietnam) before being escorted out of the Cannon Building.

On October 21, 1967, after an antiwar rally organized by the National Mobilization Committee to End the War in Vietnam gathered at the Lincoln Memorial in Washington, DC, Rubin and Hoffman led a group of fifty thousand protesters, including Allen Ginsberg, to march two miles over Memorial Bridge toward the Pentagon. Consistent with the theatrics of their movement, their goal was to levitate the Pentagon, and then to exorcise it of evil spirits. Hoffman gave out witches' hats. The protesters were greeted by several thousand helmeted, stoic-looking military police and federal marshals, armed with rifles, and a rope to protect the building's perimeter. The hippies surrounded the building and sat cross-legged on the ground. The stench of marijuana saturated the air. Beards, tie-dye, and blue jeans were everywhere.

Hoffman found willing participants to kiss one another. Traditional Mayan healers sprinkled the ground with cornmeal. Organizers handed out two hundred pounds of flowers to the participants, and some thought it would be nice to put them in the barrels of the loaded guns the police were holding. As Allen Ginsberg was shouting om mantras to keep everyone grounded and calm, he thought something truly magical had materialized: "The Pentagon was symbolically levitated in people's minds in the sense that it lost its authority which had been unquestioned until then. But once that notion was circulated in the air and once the kid put his flower in the barrel of the kid looking just like himself but tense and nervous, the authority of the Pentagon psychologically was dissolved."[21] This may have been true for some. Less debatable is that after their permit expired at 7 p.m., and the temperature dropped, these hippies went home. The few hundred who camped out that night only burned their protest signs in order to stay warm. By turns, they bantered with, and criticized, soldiers and DC police, in what at the end of the day appeared to be a run-of-the-mill antiwar protest, with a little bit of flair.

The effort to levitate the Pentagon may have looked like a prank, but, at the same time, it spoke to something serious—a growing sense of desperation for the counterculture. If civil disobedience wouldn't grab the attention of America, could street performance? Not all street performance is the same, and not all hippies were happy to go to music festivals, drop acid, and smoke dope. Some were willing to be more reckless than anyone previously imagined. This would be on display in 1968. The city was Chicago. The stage was the Democratic National Convention, where Hubert Humphrey, vice president to the incumbent Lyndon B. Johnson, was seeking the Democratic Party's presidential nomination.

America in 1968 was hanging on by a thread. Earlier that summer, on June 5, 1968, the day after he won the South Dakota and California primaries, the Democratic Party's presumed frontrunner, US senator from New York Robert F. Kennedy, had been assassinated by Sirhan Sirhan at the Ambassador Hotel in Los Angeles. Sirhan committed the assassination as a protest against Kennedy's support of Israel's treatment of Palestinians. Two months before that, on April 4, 1968, the civil rights icon Martin Luther King Jr. had been assassinated by James Earl Ray at 6 p.m. at the Lorraine Hotel in Memphis, Tennessee. King was in town organizing striking sanitation workers as part of his Poor People's Campaign. After King's assassination, rebellions—based in a combination of rage and frustration—broke out in over 125 American cities.

Hoffman and Rubin, now calling themselves the Youth International Party, "Yippies" for short (though Hoffman was thirty-two and Rubin was thirty), arrived in Chicago with a specific goal: to provoke confrontation with city authorities. It was widely known that Chicago's mayor, the Democrat Richard J. Daley, was positioning himself as a law-and-order politician and was eager to meet any dissent with a swift response. Under Daley's watch, two April days of rebellion after King's assassination left eleven Chicagoans dead, hundreds injured, and over two thousand arrested.

Daley's administration seemed eager to do battle. They denied permits for the Yippies to protest at the International Amphitheatre, where the Democratic Convention itself was being held. Undeterred, Rubin, Hoffman, and the protesters camped out nearby in Lincoln Park. They danced, smoked, practiced karate, did yoga, and nominated a pig for president, which they named "Pigasus."

Meanwhile, the city of Chicago was beginning to look nightmarish, as the city's police presence increased dramatically. On August 25, the day before the first session of the Democratic Convention, the respected and usually stoic CBS news anchor Walter Cronkite turned to the television camera and confirmed what millions of Americans saw on their screens: "The Democratic Convention is about to begin in a police state. There just doesn't seem to be any other way to say it."[22]

At 11 p.m. that evening (when Mayor Daley's citywide curfew went into effect), protesters who wouldn't disperse were met with thousands of armored police. Police threw canisters of tear gas and hit protesters with clubs to punish them for their rule-breaking. Three days later, on August 28—the day on which the Democratic Party was debating whether to officially adopt a peace platform against the Vietnam War—a teen lowered an American flag at the center of Grant Park. A shouting match between activists and police turned into a scuffle, which led to the spilling of tear gas, which led to a panicked stampede out of the park. Bones were broken; flesh was bruised; splatters of blood dotted the landscape. That night, fifteen thousand protesters marched toward the Amphitheatre. They were met by a wall of National Guardsmen surrounding its perimeter.

William Burroughs, flying in from London on a writing assignment for *Esquire* magazine, was at the scene in Chicago covering these events. In a full business suit, hat, and rimmed glasses, Burroughs, on the other side of forty, could have been a father to some of the kids. At once finding it inconceivable why anyone would resort to nonviolence ("I find myself feeling out of place," he confessed, "since nonviolence isn't exactly my program"), Burroughs seemed sympathetic to what he saw: "Millions of young people all over the world are fed up with shallow unworthy authority running on a platform of bullshit."[23] Ginsberg, who marched alongside Burroughs, felt the opposite way: he didn't like the Yippies' "bloody vision of the apocalypse." A few months earlier, in a May 7, 1968, televised interview with the editor of the conservative magazine *National Review*, William F. Buckley, for his show *Firing Line*, Ginsberg asserted his hope that America would "be orderly and gentle," and that the call to "make love, not war" was what helped to create a spirit of "our unity, particularly black and white, particularly square and hippie, particularly police and student."[24] On August 28, the day that violence erupted at Grant Park, Ginsberg, dressed in a blue sports jacket, tie, and brown corduroy pants, sat cross-legged on its grass. He tried to lead the crowd in om chants and Hare Krishna devotionals. "I think everybody who watched television during the convention experienced a widening of consciousness," Ginsberg later declared, "because . . . outright police brutality was shown so clearly."[25]

By any concrete measure, however, power relations remained as fixed as ever. When the Democratic National Convention concluded on August 29, 1968, seven hundred protesters had been arrested. The antiwar plank wasn't included in the Democratic Party platform. Hoffman and Rubin, along with six more—known as the Chicago Eight—were arrested and indicted for inciting a riot at Grant Park. In November 1968, Hubert Humphrey lost the presidential election to Republican Richard Nixon. Nixon's attack on the "longhairs" and "radicals" was part of the reason he found a wide base of support in many white American households, which he called the "silent majority." Far from eroding support, Democrat Richard J. Daley's crackdown worked to his political advantage: Daley was reelected to his fifth term by an overwhelming 40 percent margin in 1971 over his Republican challenger.

▪ ▪ ▪

If the Democratic National Convention of 1968 alienated many Americans from the counterculture's antiwar cause, it had the opposite effect on some participants. Among those arrested that summer in Chicago in 1968 was a twenty-three-year-old University of Michigan student by the name of Bill Ayers. Ayers had come back home to Chicago, where he had grown up, but in the years prior, he had rebelled against his middle-class roots with involvement with SDS. (His father, Thomas G. Ayers, was first the president, then the CEO, of Commonwealth Edison, the largest electric utility in Illinois, and was onetime chairman of the Board of Trustees at Northwestern University.) Another activist, who would later become Ayers's wife, was a suburban Wisconsin-raised recent graduate of the prestigious University of Chicago Law School. Her name was Bernardine Dohrn.

Increasingly disenchanted by the conventional protest tactics of SDS and inspired by the burgeoning Black Power movement (specifically the Marxist, anti-imperialist Black Panther Party for Self-Defense, founded in 1966), Dohrn, Ayers, and nine others published a sixteen-thousand-word manifesto on June 18, 1969, in *New Left Notes*. It was called "You Don't Need a Weatherman to Know Which Way the Wind Blows." (The title was taken from "Subterranean Homesick Blues," a song by folk singer Bob Dylan, though Dylan had no involvement with the group.) The manifesto called for a revolutionary youth movement. "To survive and grow in the face of [military repression] will require more than a larger base of supporters," it declared. "It will require the invincible strength of a mass base at a high level of active participation and consciousness, and can only come from mobilizing the self-conscious creativity, will and determination of the people."[26]

Shortly after the trial of the Chicago Seven began, in late September 1969, hundreds of participants of this new vanguard—they would call themselves the Weathermen—arrived in Chicago on October 8. Their objective was to begin what they called the "Days of Rage." On the first night, a group of Weathermen swarmed Chicago's wealthy Gold Coast neighborhood. It was there, for approximately an hour, that they smashed everything in sight. A sea of glass and debris glittered on the road. On October 10, the Weathermen marched through Chicago's main business district, where they were flanked by lines of police. Some Weathermen managed to break the blockade and smash a few car windshields. The vast majority were arrested within minutes.

The Days of Rage were just the beginning of a wider violent escalation. On February 21, 1970, a Weathermen cell threw three gasoline Molotov cocktails in front of the Inwood Heights home of John M. Murtagh, a New York Supreme Court justice who was presiding over a trial of members of the Black Panther Party accused of a conspiracy to bomb public places. That same day, a Molotov cocktail was thrown at the Columbia University International Law Library, and another was placed at the ROTC headquarters of Brooklyn College on Nostrand Avenue. On June 9, 1970, ten sticks of dynamite exploded at what was then the Centre Street headquarters of the New York Police Department (NYPD). The Weathermen were responsible for dozens of bombings over the next few years. All of this was in an effort, as their manifesto *Prairie Fire* (1974) put it, "to disrupt the empire . . . to put pressure on the cracks."[27]

In a 1971 *Partisan Review* interview, Ginsberg offered a mildly sympathetic assessment of the Weathermen. He drew attention to the way their violence was centered on the destruction of private property, whereas US military violence destroyed real human lives—tens of thousands of North Vietnamese dead, and the spraying of eighteen million gallons of an infamous chemical weapon, the herbicide called Agent Orange, which led to millions of people being exposed to everything from cancer to serious birth defects: "The government is indulging in murderous violence on so vast a scale that nobody's mind can contain it. That's why it's easy to headline the Weatherman's bomb, lonely little bomb, lonely little antirobot bomb, that wasn't intended for humans, even."[28]

The Weathermen (soon to be called the Weather Underground) became widely associated with terrorism. (And for this reason, they were hunted by the FBI. Dohrn and Ayers were placed on the FBI's most-wanted list, which appeared in US post offices across the country.) And yet, as much as they talked of crushing the state, the paramilitary organization wasn't interested in ideological purity. The Weather Underground was willing to take on unrelated jobs and make questionable alliances. One of its most notable operations was to assist Timothy Leary. In 1970, Leary was in the middle of serving a ten-year term (on top of another ten-year term for a prior arrest in 1965) for smuggling marijuana from Mexico into the US. In 1970, a Weathermen cell helped Leary scale a twelve-foot chain fence at California Men's Colony West, a low-security prison in San Luis Obispo, California. Leary escaped. His blue prison robes were found in a gas station bathroom eight miles away.

Timothy Leary was less of a revolutionary socialist and more of a revolutionary *partier* at his LSD commune, called Millbrook. Located two hours north of New York City, which was on the grounds of a mansion filled with large aquariums on 2,500 acres, Millbrook was owned by Wall Street broker and fortune heir William Mellon Hitchcock. (After Millbrook was shut down by local New York authorities in 1967, Hitchcock moved to California and supplied a large percentage of LSD for the Summer of Love.) Hitchcock and Leary seemed to symbolize the profit-making and frivolity that the Weathermen believed depressed revolutionary movements. But Bernardine Dohrn described it as an "honor and pleasure" to help Leary escape. It didn't hurt that, for their service, Dohrn and the Weathermen were paid $25,000 by the Black Panthers. The Panthers themselves got the money from the Brotherhood of Eternal Love, the Laguna Beach, Southern California–based LSD-smuggling group also known as the "Hippie Mafia," which believed that widespread LSD use could cure all social ills.

It was only after Leary and his wife, Rosemary, fled the US to Algeria, where they were granted political asylum—and at a safe distance from the US—that Leary espoused a more militant tone. Arguing on behalf of Palestinian guerrillas in Lebanon, the Viet Cong in North Vietnam, and the Communists in North Korea and China, Leary called his escape a "beautiful miracle," and wrote, "To shoot a genocidal robot policeman in the defense of life is a sacred act. . . . I am armed and should be considered dangerous to anyone who threatens my life or my freedom."[29] No longer the prophet of "dropping out," Leary was now advocating the mantra "Shoot to live / Aim for life," which he declared in an open letter to Allen Ginsberg. Upon hearing of Leary's shift in philosophy—from nonviolence to violence—Ginsberg was unsettled. He would sit outdoors for one hour every day, rain or shine, meditating on Leary's mantra while reciting the om chant. What remained after Ginsberg concluded each meditation session, however, was a feeling of ambivalence. He wasn't sure what good "armed and dangerous" might accomplish. But being "unarmed and not considered dangerous" didn't seem like an adequate approach, either.[30]

▪ ▪ ▪

Allen Ginsberg's ambivalence was an exception. The shift toward direct, and violent, confrontation was becoming increasingly central to the counterculture. A case in point was the gay freedom movement. In the early morning hours of June 28, 1969, NYPD officers raided and arrested over a dozen patrons at one of the city's most popular gay bars, the Stonewall Inn, on Christopher Street in Greenwich Village (which also had a large LGBTQ population). This wasn't the first time the Stonewall had been raided that week. On average, it had been raided once a month on the basis that it served alcohol without a liquor license. Usually, the owners, the Genovese crime family, who bought the venue in 1966, were tipped off by cops. But not that summer night. As the police officers were leaving Stonewall, they ordered the crowd to disperse. What happened next, no one expected. A queer woman was being forcibly dragged from the venue into a cop car, and she yelled at the top of her lungs, "Do something!"[31] Her plea lit a fuse in the crowd, many of whom had been emboldened by participation in the antiwar, women's, labor, and Civil Rights movements. A crowd of two hundred began throwing at the cops whatever they could find lying there on the ground—spare change, broken beer bottles, and small rocks. Then, they tried to set Stonewall ablaze.

Five more days of rebellion followed Stonewall. Thousands participated. What they witnessed between June 28 and July 3 stood in stark contrast to the legal routes that mainstream gay rights organizations, like the Mattachine Society, had long advocated. "We homosexuals plead with our people to please maintain peaceful and quiet conduct on the streets of the Village—Mattachine," said a message on the boarded-up window of the Stonewall Inn. The plea was too little, too late.[32]

In the wake of Stonewall, a new movement modeled on guerrilla tactics in Algeria and Vietnam was formed. Calling itself the Gay Liberation Front (GLF), it held meetings at the Church of the Holy Apostles in Chelsea and on the second floor of a former dance studio on 69 West Fourteenth Street, off Sixth Avenue. Disruptive action, combined with a capacious vision of liberation in solidarity with the Global South, Black Power, and feminist movements, served as the GLF's motivation. "Gay Power" became its slogan. On the third night of the rebellion, Ginsberg, who would eventually join the GLF, came to the Stonewall and walked around the dance floor, where he saw a group of men moving to Motown music. Walking along the streets, he sensed a different mood in the air. "It's about time we did something to assert ourselves," he reflected to a *Village Voice* reporter. "The guys there were so beautiful. . . . They've lost that wounded look."[33]

One of the GLF's cofounders was at that time earning a graduate degree in comparative literature at New York University. Her name was Karla Jay. Born Karla Jayne Berlin in Brooklyn in 1947 to a conservative Jewish family, she attended an elite, all-girls private finishing school called the Berkeley Institute, before coming to Barnard College to study French in 1964. As a student at Barnard in 1968, Jay got involved with Columbia University's SDS chapter because she objected to the school's known affiliation with the Institute for Defense Analyses, which provided the US Army strategic assessments to be used on the battlefield in Vietnam. She was also angry that Columbia was planning to build a new gym on two acres of Morningside Heights in the predominantly Black neighborhood of Harlem, and that it was only after receiving pushback that it decided to have 15 percent of the space allotted to Harlem residents.

Columbia students, led by Mark Rudd (an SDS leader, who would also become a Weatherman), seized the university's Hamilton Hall in protest. Jay wanted to get in on the action too. She walked over to the student center, which was called Ferris Booth Hall, the site of student activism. Jay asked a scraggly white guy, "Can I help?"

"Yea, man," he said, "take some tuna sandwiches over to Fayerweather Hall. . . . Then," here he pointed to female Barnard students who were making peanut butter and jelly sandwiches behind him, "come back and join the other girls making the sandwiches."[34]

It wasn't long after this that Jay traded the misogyny of SDS for a feminist, consciousness-raising group called Redstockings, where she, in the safety of other young women, could mobilize around issues that affected her life. Redstockings was appealing to Jay precisely because it had a confrontational style. On February 13, 1969, one of its two co-founders, Ellen Willis, a daughter of an NYPD lieutenant, and others had stormed the chamber of the New York State Joint Legislative Committee on Public Health in Albany. The session had convened fourteen men and one nun to recommend legislative reforms to abortion law. Willis shouted: "Let's hear from the real experts . . . the women!"[35] Stunned, the only thing the panelists could do was beg her and fellow protesters to "act like ladies."

Another cofounder of Redstockings was Shulamith Firestone. She was a shy and academically gifted student born to an Orthodox Jewish family in Ottawa, Ontario, and raised in Kansas City and St. Louis, Missouri. On Labor Day weekend 1967, while earning a degree in painting from the School of the Art Institute of Chicago, Firestone attended the National Conference for New Politics. It was at this conference that Firestone authored a resolution giving women 50 percent of the convention votes (since they were, in fact, 50 percent of the US population). Outraged when the resolution was summarily struck down, Firestone ran to the podium. As she came up to the stage, the male chair of the meeting patted her head. "Cool down, little girl," he said, laughing. "We have more important things to do here than talk about women's problems."[36]

After Firestone left Chicago and moved to New York, she became involved with the feminist group New York Radical Women. On September 7, 1968, NYRW was part of a demonstration in Atlantic City, New Jersey, during the forty-second Miss America Pageant, in which Firestone, among a group of over four hundred, threw into a dumpster and proceeded to burn brooms, pairs of high heels, expensive makeup, women's hygiene products, and copies of *Cosmopolitan*.

If Willis's and Firestone's feminism was dismissed by SDS, then Jay's concerns as a lesbian woman were elided entirely from the mainstream women's movement. The president of the National Organization for Women (NOW) and second-wave feminist icon, Betty Friedan, warned that the "lavender menace" was a grave threat to women's rights. Friedan worried about the reputational stakes to NOW if it were perceived as, she put it, a "bunch of dykes."[37]

On May 1, 1970, during NOW's Second Congress to Unite Women, held in New York on 333 West Seventeenth Street at Intermediate School 70, a group of women were ready to put Friedan's fears to the test. Wearing "Lavender Menace" T-shirts, they flicked off the lights in the auditorium during the opening plenary of three hundred. Seventeen Menaces lined the room chanting, "Lesbianism is a women's liberation plot." Another twenty hidden among the seated audience slowly rose from their seats. Karla Jay was one of them. "Yes, yes, sisters!" she recited. "I'm tired of being in the closet because of the women's movement."[38] The next two hours of conversation turned into two days of workshops, followed by a GLF-sponsored dance at the Church of the Holy Apostles. On May 3, the Second Congress passed a resolution acknowledging lesbian concerns as feminist issues.

■   ■   ■

The story of the counterculture from the publication of *Howl* in 1956 to the formation of the Gay Liberation Front could be told as an evolution from existential frustration to collective outrage, from angsty poetry in the dark to revolution in the streets. But did the counterculture achieve what it set out to do politically? To an extent. Without the counterculture, the Vietnam War might have continued for much longer. The sexual revolution may have never happened. The personal might not have been seen as the political. The university wouldn't have been politicized. The two-party system wouldn't have been called into question.

Yet, it's also true that the riotous youthful energy inspired a backlash that sought to reverse the incremental, though real, progress that had been made since the end of the Second World War. With the election of Richard Nixon, 1968 was the year the New Right was born. Emboldened and hungry to make its imprint on the nation, the New Right, a coalition of free market evangelists, Christian conservatives, and social traditionalists, would spend the next four decades making all the groups in that coalition happy, striving to privatize and deregulate anything and everything in sight, to lower taxes, to gut any and all antidiscrimination and equal opportunity measures, to pump an unprecedented amount of money into the military, police, and prison system, to eviscerate the line between church and state, to give men total control over women's bodies.

Forget about socialist revolution. Or a wholesale overthrow of bourgeois life. By the 1970s, the aim of social movements would be to keep in place what was left of the New Deal and had just been put in place during the Great Society: Social Security, the right to join a union, equal access to the franchise for Black Americans, and basic access to contraception and abortion.

As for the countercultural figures themselves? Many left for the very institution they once fiercely attacked: academia. Ginsberg became a distinguished professor of English at Brooklyn College; Karla Jay, a professor of women's studies at Pace University; Bernardine Dohrn, a law professor at Northwestern University; Bill Ayers, a distinguished professor of education at University of Illinois at Chicago.

Abbie Hoffman fell off the grid. And then he hit rock bottom. Hoffman was arrested for cocaine possession in 1974 and was on the run for six years. He was caught in 1980 and spent several months in prison. Upon release, he was involved with the pressing issues of his time; he campaigned for the environment and criticized US anti-communist policy in South America. Tragically, after chronic pain caused by an auto accident, Hoffman, suffering from acute depression, died by suicide at the age of fifty-two in 1989 by taking a large dose of phenobarbital.

In the 1980s, Hoffman's onetime co-conspirator, Jerry Rubin, was no longer a Yippie. Now he was proud to call himself a "Yuppie"—a young urban professional. Rubin became a diehard evangelist for free-market capitalism, supporting the latest exercise fads and diet regimes. He propped up the use of personal computers and Walkman cassette players. "Perhaps you remember me from the '60s," he told an audience in 1985. "I was known and not wanted in many states." Now, his goal was to never be caught "anywhere without my American Express card," because "the people with money control this country."[39] The counterculture of the 1960s did have a second life from the 1970s onward, not in the streets but in the modern corporation. In 1971, Coca-Cola ran an ad campaign that featured men and women drinking the carbonated soft drink—men in turtlenecks and women in simple dresses—singing "I'd Like to Teach the World to Sing (in Perfect Harmony)." In 1993, the clothing company The Gap rolled out an ad campaign featuring Jack Kerouac, showing a photo of him taken in 1958 in the Village, with his hands in the pockets of slacks, along with the tagline "Kerouac wore khakis." Another series from this ad campaign is of Allen Ginsberg sitting cross-legged on the floor. His hands are clasped together and he is in a sports jacket and button-down shirt and tie: "Allen Ginsberg wore khakis." In 1994, a seventy-nine-year-old William Burroughs appeared in a Nike commercial to sell its line of Air Max sneakers, proclaiming on a recording, "The purpose of technology is not to confuse the brain but to serve the body, to make life easier, to make anything possible. It's the coming of the new technology."

To say that the counterculture sold out risks romanticizing it—to imply as if the people involved in its making were somehow pure to begin with. They weren't, no matter how critical they were, or professed to be. Moreover, to argue that capitalist co-option of the counterculture was inevitable is, well, not saying much since that's precisely what capitalism does: it aims to co-opt everything for profit. It just happens to be especially drawn to anything that aims to challenge it (rebellion is sexy, and it always sells). Finally, to tell the story of the counterculture as one of progressive decline, from the glory days to some violent unraveling, is unsatisfying. Even the counterculture's so-called heights were marked by blatant contradictions and embarrassing lows. Sexism, racism, opportunism, miscalculation, and petty feuds, were there throughout.

The '60s counterculture never developed a serious infrastructure to sustain itself not because it didn't want to, but precisely because its philosophy wouldn't allow it. The counterculture's professed antiestablishment and libertarian ethos stood in direct contradiction to its ability to transform hierarchical institutions. The way to remember the '60s, perhaps, might be as one of the last major youth rebellions that glimpsed a utopian spirit in fits and starts, with all its beautiful chaos.

CHAPTER 9

NEW ARC

I n the early Wednesday morning hours of October 18, 1961, a twenty-seven-year-old Black poet named LeRoi Jones from Newark, New Jersey, was awoken by a team of agents from the US Postal Service and the FBI. They came to arrest him because he had disseminated the ninth issue of a Beat newsletter that he and Diane di Prima edited, called *The Floating Bear*. This issue of *The Floating Bear* was sent to an imprisoned poet in Rahway, New Jersey, by the name of Harold Carrington. When the Rahway prison censor obtained it, he discovered two pieces he deemed objectionable. The first was by Jones from his novel in progress, *The System of Dante's Hell*, which gave a searing account of a young Black man's encounters with racism and sexual predation by other men. The second was William Burroughs's "Roosevelt After Inauguration," a satire in which the thirty-second president of the US, Democrat Franklin Delano Roosevelt, names a motley crew of sex workers, hustlers, criminals, and thieves to important cabinet positions.

Although the obscenity case against Jones and di Prima never went to trial, Jones demanded a grand jury hearing. At the stand in his defense, he read from the decision of US District Court judge John M. Woolsey in *United States v. One Book Called Ulysses* (1933). Woolsey had decided that Irish novelist James Joyce's classic modernist text, *Ulysses*, wasn't obscene (though it did have frank depictions of sexuality). His decision set an important precedent about how the US courts would judge sexually explicit literature. "I had read all the parts of Joyce's *Ulysses* . . . aloud to the jury and then read . . . Woolsey's decision," Jones recalled of his testimony, which described obscene literature as being arousing to "the normal person. . . . But I know none of [the grand jury] were aroused by any of these things."[1]

The jurors were convinced of Jones's position; no indictment was issued. Moreover, it seemed that Jones's confrontational style was, in fact, an effective rhetorical strategy. This style is what Jones would be known for (depending on whom one asked, either famously or infamously) to a broader American public as the voice of Black militancy. This happened when he changed his name to Amiri Baraka.

LeRoi Jones wasn't born a Black nationalist. He became one in his late twenties. The one consistent theme throughout his life was the quest for authenticity. What Jones despised above all were phonies. He was born on October 7, 1934, to Coyette LeRoy Jones, a postal supervisor, and Anna Jones, a social worker. At an early age, Baraka bristled at the petty way his religious middle-class parents pushed him to make friends with Italian American kids in the predominantly white schools he attended in his working-class neighborhood of Newark. Called racial slurs daily, Baraka made few friends, though he did leave high school knowing how to curse fluently in Italian.

Baraka first went to the state university of New Jersey, Rutgers University, but transferred after only one year to Howard University in 1952. While living in DC, Baraka enjoyed lectures at Howard by towering Black intellectuals like the poet Sterling Brown and religious studies scholar Nathan Scott. But Baraka was embittered that, at Howard, the epicenter of Black intellectual life, "they taught you to pretend to be white." One afternoon, as he was eating a cold watermelon outside a Howard campus building on a warm day, the dean of male students walked up to him. "Do you realize that you're sitting in front of the highway where white people can see?" the dean furiously asked, gritting his teeth. "Do you realize that you are compromising the Negro?"[2]

Baraka didn't like to compromise, so he dropped out of Howard University in 1954. He enlisted in the Air Force and became part of the Strategic Air Command. Baraka's hope was that, at least, the daily grind of military life would be free from the frills of social decorum. At the same time, he could pursue his intellectual interests. As the head librarian of his base, he spent his time combing through the lush sentences of the French modernist Marcel Proust and the absurd fables of Franz Kafka. "The service," he recalled, "was graduate school or maybe it was undergraduate school," because now, "so completely off, I read constantly."[3] Yet the military was no worse and no better than Baraka's middle-class upbringing or his undergraduate days at Howard. It demanded absolute conformity. For his higher-ups, high European modernism may have been tolerable. But radical European political thought? That was a bright red line. Once Baraka's superiors discovered that their head librarian was well-versed in Karl Marx and once affiliated with Communist youth groups at Howard, he was given an "undesirable discharge" in 1957.

■ ■ ■

Amiri Baraka came to Greenwich Village in 1957. A militant in search of personal expression, Baraka was an aspiring Beat poet influenced by William Carlos Williams, T. S. Eliot, and Charles Olson, not an activist inspired by Pan-Africanists like Léopold Senghor or Amílcar Cabral. His poetic verse was a cry for existential meaning, not revolution. "It's so diffuse / being alive," one poem declares. "Suddenly one is aware / that nobody really gives a damn."[4] In the Village, Baraka felt at home. He met a white Jewish woman named Hettie Cohen, and the two were married in 1958 in a New York City Buddhist temple. Soon, the couple had two daughters. And their cozy West Twentieth Street apartment was a revolving door for the avant-garde—jazz musicians like Archie Shepp and Sonny Rollins and painters like Willem de Kooning, Franz Kline, and Jackson Pollock.

Jones and Cohen were known among Village hipsters for their editorial work on the short-lived *Yugen* magazine (which had eight issues and ran between 1958 and 1962) and for their legendary spaghetti dinners accompanied by large kegs of beer—dinners which they served regularly to a hundred or more who came to their parties. Allen Ginsberg, a close friend of the couple, said the vibe back then was defined by "good feelings. A lot of mixing, black white hip classic."[5] Baraka liked Village Bohemia because it offered a flight from the "moral hypocrisy of American life— whether white or Black," he wrote in his first published essay in 1958, "the provinciality, the philistinism."[6]

Things changed in July 1960. As part of an effort by the postrevolutionary Cuban government under the leadership of Fidel Castro to cultivate sympathy from the West, Baraka traveled to Cuba with the Fair Play for Cuba Committee. To be sure, Baraka didn't come to Cuba to find

Pan-African revolution. He was there merely out of curiosity, to broaden his horizons about the world. After arriving, during one panel with a Mexican graduate student, Baraka said that "I'm a poet" and "I write, that's all, I'm not even interested in politics."[7] But Baraka left Cuba a changed man. Cuban students cared deeply in the revolution, believed in it, and were willing to overlook its flaws, warts and all. There was something appealing about such commitment, which, for Baraka, stood in contrast to "the rebels among us who have become merely people like myself who grow beards and will not participate in politics."[8]

As these words suggest, Baraka saw politics as a matter of choice, an exercise in personal responsibility. But he changed his mind after a cold winter evening on February 15, 1961. Baraka was part of a demonstration in front of the United Nations building in New York City. The group had convened to protest the US government's complicity in the assassination of Patrice Lumumba. Lumumba, the democratically elected president of the Congo, opposed the secessionist movement of Katanga Province. (The successionist movement was supported because it had rich mineral deposits and was hospitable to US interests.) He represented an anti-colonial, Third World alternative to Western empire. But he was assassinated by the secessionists in close cooperation with the US and Belgium governments. In front of the United Nations building, sixty men and women wearing armbands, dressed in black, stormed the Security Council's chamber, interrupting Chief Delegate Adlai Stevenson's speech to the assembly. The group fought with security guards and was promptly arrested by police. Baraka was marching outside the building, but he too was among the many beaten by the NYPD.

This newfound awareness of being a dissident Black activist who was a target of the state was what made Baraka unsympathetic to Martin Luther King Jr.'s absolutist philosophy of nonviolence. "We did not feel part of that movement," Baraka recalled. Since its opening salvo with Rosa Parks's refusal to sit in the back of a Jim Crow bus in Montgomery, Alabama, on December 1, 1955 (and the 381-day-long boycott that followed), the Civil Rights Movement had been picking up steam through student sit-ins in the 1960s (Greensboro, North Carolina, Hampton, Virginia, and Little Rock, Arkansas, to name a few). Then came the Freedom Rides of 1961, when a multiracial coalition of students descended on segregated bus terminals in the Deep South, in places like Alabama, Louisiana, and Mississippi.

The Civil Rights Movement may have been winning incremental political victories, but Baraka wasn't interested in results. As an artist, he was drawn to questions of representation. Representations of rebellion—rather than actual rebellion in the streets—were as important for heightening Black consciousness.

Turning away from King, Baraka tuned in to the Omaha, Nebraska–born Malcolm Little (born in 1925) known in the 1960s as Malcolm X. "King wanted to kneel in the streets and pray," Baraka recalled, while Malcolm said that "all the white racist crackers in the world could only be reached if one spoke the same [violent] language that they spoke."[9] It wasn't Malcolm's Black nationalist philosophy as much as his confrontational style that appealed to Baraka. "Malcolm X," Baraka recalled, "supported my attack," to go on a "tirade against whites," who allowed for "these torturous years the African and African American have spent as slaves and chumps for this white supremacist society."[10]

Compared to the college-educated Baraka, Malcolm had seen the horrors of white supremacy firsthand and had dedicated the final decade of his life strategizing to confront it. When Malcolm was a young boy at the age of six, his father, Earl Little, was lynched by a group of white men in Lansing, Michigan, who threw him under a streetcar. Malcolm's mother was placed in a psychiatric hospital in Kalamazoo in 1937, and the twelve-year-old Malcolm and his brothers and sisters were sent to foster homes. As a teen, Malcolm turned to the streets. He became a hustler and a pimp. After a stint in a Massachusetts petitionary for larceny between 1946 and 1952, Malcolm became an avid disciple of Elijah Muhammad and the Nation of Islam, which preached Black self-defense and self-determination.

Malcolm was ideologically committed, but not bound by the straitjacket of ideology. In 1964, as a devout Muslim, upon taking his hajj to Saudi Arabia and visiting the African continent, he discovered Third World solidarity and socialism. No longer a Black capitalist who called white people "devils," Malcolm broke with Muhammad and founded the Organization of Afro-American Unity in June 1964. His break with the Nation didn't go unnoticed and had fateful consequences. As Malcolm was delivering a lecture on February 21, 1965, in the Audubon Ballroom in Harlem, a Nation of Islam member gunned him down. The thirty-nine-year-old leader was dead. "I was stunned, shot myself. I felt stupid, ugly, useless," Baraka remarked. In response, he wrote a poem in April published in the *Negro Digest* that yearned for "Malcolm's hands raised to bless us all black and strong in his image of ourselves."[11]

Even before Malcolm X had died, Baraka had begun a Black nationalist turn. A good example is what critics consider to be Baraka's best play, the Obie Award–winning *Dutchman*, staged at the Cherry Lane Theatre in March 1964. Set in a New York City subway car, the play is an interracial melodrama that doubles as a statement on Black identity and white supremacy. Clay, a twenty-year-old Black man in a suit and tie, is solicited to embody the image of Black male hypersexuality that Lua, a red-haired thirty-year-old white woman, desires. Although there are many available seats in the subway car, Lua, innocently eating an apple and clutching her purse, sits right next to Clay and tells him to do "the nasty. Do the gritty grind, like your ol' rag-head mammy," she says. "Grind till you lose your mind. Shake it." Clay wants to be "safe with [his words]" and have no "clean, hard thoughts, urging me to new conquests." Lua presses Clay further. She calls him "Uncle-Tom Thomas Woolly Head." Eventually, Clay loses it and slaps Lua twice, threatening to murder her. He tells her that she knows nothing of Black love or Black rage. As Clay reaches over to grab his briefcase and his books to exit the subway car, Lua stabs him in the chest. The white passengers sitting nearby methodically dispose of Clay's body. Lua fixes herself up and waits for another Black man to board. He comes aboard on the next stop.[12]

In *Dutchman*, one can see Baraka's articulation of a distinct Black aesthetic, an unapologetic assault on white American racism and an incisive account of its impact on the Black psyche. And yet, as he became more direct in his critique of white supremacy, he also became less critical of his own reactionary prejudices. In a poem Baraka wrote in the mid-1960s, he refers to his ex-Jewish wife, Hettie Cohen, as a "fat jew." He writes, "Smile, jew. Dance, jew. Tell me you love me, jew. . . . I got the extermination blues, jewboys. I got the hitler syndrome figured."[13] In another of his poems, "Black Art," the speaker says, "We want . . . dagger poems in the slimy bellies of the owner-Jews."[14] Baraka would later renounce his antisemitism, acknowledging his error in a *Village Voice* essay published in 1980, "Confessions of a Former Anti-Semite," in which he said his prejudice was a product of his petit bourgeois mentality. (And yet, two decades later in 2001, he would absurdly state after the September 11 terrorist attacks upon the World Trade Center that Jewish people working in the Twin Towers somehow had advance knowledge of the plot and knowingly didn't show up to work.)

It wasn't just racism. In the mid-1960s, Baraka was embracing homophobia to boost his radical credentials. In the late 1950s, he had claimed Allen Ginsberg as one of his greatest influences, but now he mocked the '60s counterculture as "degeneracy," "a vague, integrated, plastic, homosexual rEVolUTion."[15] The head of the NAACP, Roy Wilkins, was in Baraka's eyes too moderate and, therefore, "an eternal faggot."[16] In 1966, Baraka declared that "most white men are trained to be fags."[17]

In addition to antisemitism and homophobia, misogyny was also evident in Baraka's work. In *Dutchman*, the white woman, Lua, is represented as singularly driven by uncontrolled sexual desire toward Black men, whereas Clay's violence toward her is implied as being legitimate in order to keep her in line. In another essay, Baraka doubled down on this logic, speculating upon the cleansing power of sexual violence. Deep down, "the white woman," he wrote, "understands that only in the rape sequence is she likely to get cleanly, viciously, popped."[18] Baraka failed to examine his patriarchal impulses. More troubling is that he, at times, equated Black revolution with antifeminism. He advocated for Black women to engage in making the "house we live in, the clothes we wear, the food we eat, the words we speak," and to "inspire her man."[19] Such an assertion led the Black feminist bell hooks to accuse Baraka of seeing the "black male-dominated household with its inherent antiwoman stance as if it were a positive reaction against white racist values."[20]

▪ ▪ ▪

Malcolm X's assassination represented a turning point for Amiri Baraka. He left his wife Hettie and their two daughters in the Village. He moved to Harlem, with the aim of continuing Malcolm's legacy through cultural means. "We heard and understood Malcolm," Baraka recalled, and "were trying to create an art that would be a weapon in the Black liberation movement."[21] His first order of business was to establish the Black Arts Repertory Theater/School (BARTS). It opened in May 1965, in a four-story brownstone at 109 West 130th Street. What we now call the Black Arts Movement was born.

The list of artist-intellectuals affiliated with BARTS is legendary. Central to its day-to-day operations was the poet, essayist, and playwright Larry Neal, whom Baraka met during the Lumumba demonstration on February 15, 1961, at the UN. Born in Atlanta on September 5, 1937, to a domestic servant and a railroad worker, Larry Neal (named after the poet Paul Laurence Dunbar) moved to North Philadelphia when he was six and grew up in the James Weldon Johnson Housing Project. As a child, Neal liked to hang out in Black barbershops. As a teen, he fell hard for Marxism while working at a local bookstore. After graduating from Lincoln University, Neal earned a graduate degree from the University of Pennsylvania. An eclectic intellectual, he tried to fuse his love of jazz, bebop, and his membership in a Black nationalist group known as the Revolutionary Action Movement. Art was, he said, the "aesthetic and spiritual sister of the Black Power concept."[22]

Neal was the cosmopolitan spark behind BARTS. He wore a leather cap, a tweed jacket, and purple scarves, which stood out elegantly against his thick mustache and large eyeglasses. Harold Cruse was BARTS's elder statesman. A hard-nosed, no-nonsense intellectual, Cruse wore button-down shirts, simple ties, and light sweater cardigans. Born in Petersburg, Virginia, on March 8, 1916, he grew up in Harlem and Queens, then joined the US military in 1941 during World War II. He served in, and became a sergeant of, a segregated army unit with tours in Africa and Italy. After Cruse came back to New York, he joined the Communist Party USA and worked for the *Daily Worker*. In between stints of studying at the Forty-Second Street Library, working at Macy's as a clerk, and waiting tables around Union Square, he lived in the Village and wrote Broadway musicals on the side. Baraka met Cruse in the late 1950s around MacDougal Street. (The two would also go to Cuba together in 1961.) Baraka remembered Cruse sitting at Café Figaro, cantankerously "complaining about how Broadway producers were turning down the musicals he was writing."[23] If Cruse wouldn't be recognized by the white "power elite" of Broadway (a term coined in 1956 by one of his longtime favorite sociologists, the Columbia University professor C. Wright Mills), he would become a leading figure of a new Black cultural vanguard. Cruse became a key part of *The Liberator* magazine. Not to be confused with the socialist outfit edited by Claude McKay and Michael Gold in the 1920s called *The*

Liberator, Liberator was a newsletter for the Liberation Committee for Africa, which advocated for an all-Black political party.

At BARTS, Cruse taught a class entitled, "History: The Afro-American Presence as a Culture Within a Culture." By all accounts, he was an unpretentious but dynamic teacher. To his class of twelve to fifteen working-class students (activists mostly, not scholars), Cruse would read from a collection of little note cards, which would define terms like *dialectics, pragmatism,* and *anarchism,* or he would remark on the different roles Harlem played in a mass movement, explaining the difference between what it meant to be a base in the cultural sense and a base in the political sense.[24]

Through it all, Cruse retained a flair for the dramatic from his days as a playwright. Nowhere was this on fuller display than in his 1967 classic text, *The Crisis of the Negro Intellectual.* An iconoclastic book, it expressed Cruse's ruthless criticism of virtually everything. Cruse problematized the question of Black politics rather than providing clear answers: What is the relationship between the elite and the masses? What about aesthetics and revolution? Organization and resistance? Above all else, the lasting contribution of *The Crisis of the Negro Intellectual* was its acerbic style. No great Black figure was safe. Ralph Ellison built a "dreary world" in his award-winning novel *Invisible Man* (1952); Paul Robeson wasn't a "creative artist but an interpretative one."[25] The brilliant playwright Lorraine Hansberry "did not learn much about Harlem that stuck.[26]

A political scientist in his heart of hearts, Harold Cruse interpreted Black history to make reasoned predictions about available Black political choices. Another man who taught at BARTS, Herman Poole Blount, the jazz musician better known as Sun Ra (1914–93), wanted to reinvent the future, so he treated history with irreverence. What mattered to Ra was what he saw and how he saw it.

The modern father of what is known as Afrofuturism, Sun Ra was a dreamer. Having one's head in the clouds, Ra claimed, was a good thing. In addition to performing during BARTS's opening weekend, the Birmingham, Alabama-born Ra taught a course called the "Music of the Spheres," which developed what he called an "Astro-Black mythology." An idiosyncratic figure, Ra's individual mythmaking was as vibrant as his legendary performances with his band, the Arkestra. On stage, he would wear a spacesuit and kilt, with a golden *nemes* headcloth—to remind his audience of the glory of Black history in ancient Egypt. The Arkestra's mixture of cymbals, horns, and electric keyboard in the background made it sound as though Ra were a visitor from another world. He was obsessed with escape because imprisonment was a recurrent theme in his story. He claimed to have been briefly abducted by aliens and brought to Saturn in the 1930s. Another instance of imprisonment—and one easier to verify as factual truth—was when he was briefly jailed in 1942 as a conscientious objector after refusing to be conscripted into World War II. Still, neither Ra's imagination nor his creative process were imprisoned by racism. Black pride was never something he questioned. It was always asserted. Ra's cosmic Black love knew no bounds. Whether in Chicago, New York, or Philadelphia (all places that he, at one time or another, lived), Ra's goal, as expressed through the organization he founded in 1967 with his business partner, Alton Abraham, called "Infinity Inc.," was to create work of a humanitarian nature. It would be for his community, for the earth, and for the cosmos.[27]

Despite their different intellectual orientations, Black artists were drawn to BARTS because, according to the poet Sonia Sanchez, who taught a class there called "Remedial Education and Skills," "it was like going to the community, being in the community, and beginning to talk about art that would transform a community."[28] A graduate of Hunter College with a degree in political science, the Birmingham, Alabama–born Sanchez tried to forge community wherever she was. Though she was politically aligned with Malcolm, she appreciated Martin Luther King's call for direct action—which Sanchez applied as a teacher working at the Downtown Community School and in her involvement with the New York branch of the Congress of Racial Equality (CORE).

After studying creative writing at New York University with Louise Bogan, a poet laureate to the Library of Congress who encouraged Sanchez to read her poetry aloud to give it a rich texture and visceral force, Sanchez devoted her life to making space for considering her experiences as a Black woman. In 1968, Sanchez left New York for San Francisco State College. She taught a college course titled "The Black Woman," which became the springboard for the nation's first Black studies program. Though she briefly was a member of the Nation of Islam from 1972 to 1974 (as a single mother, she said it provided her kids better schooling opportunities than the public schools), Sanchez wouldn't abandon her womanist ideals. "One dude said to me once that the solution for Sonia Sanchez was for her to have some babies," she remembered. "I wrote a long satirical poem called 'Solution for Sonia Sanchez,' which was my response."[29] When asked to review Black Panther Party minister of information Eldridge Cleaver's misogynistic *Soul on Ice* (1968), in which he infamously described raping Black women as practice for raping white women, Sanchez wouldn't hold her tongue for the sake of Black unity: "Eldridge Cleaver is not a revolutionary," she wrote, "he's a hustler. I come from New York, and I've seen quite enough hustlers in my time."[30]

As a Black nationalist outfit, BARTS excluded white people for reasons both philosophical and political. Also, because its small theater could only hold ninety people. But given its open-door policy to all Black citizens, BARTS had trouble filtering out a friendly Black FBI agent named Don Duncan. Duncan infiltrated Harold Cruse's classes and prepared detailed reports to the bureau about BARTS's inner workings. More devasting for the theater and school, however, was not FBI subversion. It was that BARTS funding came from the US federal government. BARTS was awarded $115,000 ($1 million in today's dollars) from Project Uplift (PUL), which in turn was funded by the Office of Economic Opportunity (OEO), established in 1964 as part of Democratic president Lyndon Johnson's Great Society program. PUL was administered by an organization called HARYOU-ACT, which was led by Congressman Adam Clayton Powell, and had a budget of $1.9 million. Ironically, PUL was established to stifle the very thing that BARTS aimed to facilitate: Black rebellion. The summer before BARTS was founded, in Harlem in July 1964, a white NYPD officer, Thomas Gilligan, shot and killed a fifteen-year-old Black teenager, James Powell, in broad daylight, after a dispute between Powell and the superintendent of an apartment building in the Upper East Side. After the six days of uprising ended, a hundred people were injured and hundreds of businesses were destroyed. (Gilligan was cleared of wrongdoing later that year.)

Many of New York City's elected officials thought PUL's funding of BARTS was an unqualified success. On the hot evening of August 16, 1965, as the NYPD was enjoying the BARTS mobile arts program at the Hotel Theresa along with Harlem community members, fourteen thousand National Guard troops were storming into the Black neighborhood of Watts, Los Angeles—where six days of unrest resulted in $45 million in property damages, thirty-four dead, a thousand injured, and four thousand arrested. "Only in America could one receive a Rockefeller Grant while blasting the Rockefellers, or a federal grant from HARYOU-ACT," wrote the novelist Ishmael Reed, reflecting on BARTS, "while preaching revolution."[31] Even still, after only five weeks, on September 16, 1965, the OEO pulled the plug on PUL. Leaders of PUL rejected the decision's rationale. There was no longer a threat of Black rebellion in Harlem, PUL believed, because the summer was over, as public school was now back in session.

In response, hundreds of BARTS supporters picketed the HARYOU-ACT headquarters at the Hotel Theresa. Ironically, New York city officials now became concerned that the anger they thought they had successfully pacified would ultimately explode. According to a redacted FBI report, after a Sunday morning service led by Adam Clayton Powell at the Abyssinian Baptist Church at 132 West 138th Street, a group led by a BARTS staff member, William Patterson, said it was prepared to take matters into their own hands and expose Powell. The director of Arts and Culture at HARYOU-ACT, a man by the name of Julian Euell, was so nervous about the atmosphere that he carried a gun and asked the local leader of a crime syndicate, Bumpy Johnson, for muscle to protect him.

As for BARTS? It got no additional funding. What it got instead was damaging national headlines like "White-Hating Theater Uses Federal Funds." As a result, BARTS did what the Harlem Suitcase Theatre once tried: it turned to fundraising. Langston Hughes generously donated five dollars to BARTS, but he was the exception, not the rule. Baraka didn't have a trust fund to which he could turn. "The little money I got, from royalties and readings," he recalled, "I needed to support myself."[32]

BARTS was on life support, but the death blow came on March 10, 1965. Two men, John Moore and Charles Patterson (William Patterson's brother), both affiliated with BARTS and supportive of Elijah Muhammad's Nation of Islam, shot Larry Neal, a devoted follower of Malcolm, one block away from the BARTS brownstone. On March 16, Moore and Patterson were arrested by the NYPD. As the police stormed the BARTS building, they found three guns, a pipe bomb, several knives, and a stash of marijuana. This was all the pretext they needed to monitor everyone coming in and out of BARTS. By December 1965, after months of surveillance, Baraka was exhausted. He left Harlem and went home to Newark. BARTS was finished.

▪ ▪ ▪

Black migration after the Second World War and white flight during the 1960s (in which one hundred thousand whites fled New York City to adjoining suburbs) ensured that Newark in 1970 had a Black population of 54 percent and a white population of 36 percent. Between 1950 and 1960, Newark had lost 250 manufacturers and twenty thousand jobs.[33] From 1962 to 1970, Italian American Democrat Hugh Addonizio had been the city's mayor. Like many Democratic politicians, he needed the Black vote but couldn't explicitly run on a pro-Black platform for fear of alienating his white constituency, who would accuse him of "racial preference." Consequently, Addonizio's symbolic gesture of appointing more Black leaders to city government did nothing to end the scourge of anti-Black police brutality and segregation plaguing Newark.

Things came to a head on the night of July 12, 1967. A Black cab driver named John William Smith was arrested and beaten by two white Newark police officers after he had passed their double-parked car. The next night, a peaceful protest at the Fourth Precinct police station turned tense. Someone smashed the precinct's windows with a large metal object. Looting ensued, and the police opened fire. Chaos gripped Newark.

Stores were raided—liquor, sofas, televisions, shoes, appliances were filling the streets—and people were being shot. On the night of July 14, 1967, Baraka, and his two friends, wanting to assess the magnitude of the situation, got into a van and began to slowly drive around the city. They noticed a young man on a major avenue who had been shot in the leg. The group brought him to the local hospital for treatment. On their way home, their van was stopped at an improvised checkpoint set up by Newark officers. Baraka and his two friends were accused of being snipers.

Baraka was pulled out of the van and thrown to the ground, where he was beaten with a nightstick. A shotgun was pointed at his head. He thought he was going to die. It was only because a gathering crowd from neighboring apartments began to scream at and throw objects at the officers that the beating stopped. Baraka was taken to the precinct and charged with possession of two illegal firearms. (Many years afterward, Baraka repeatedly claimed the revolvers were planted by the cops. Given the corruption and racial animosity endemic in the nearly all-white Newark police force, this is not far-fetched.) As Baraka was being treated at the hospital, a doctor, stitching up two large cuts on his face without anesthetic, tauntingly told him, "You'll never write any more poetry!"[34]

Eventually, Baraka's case went to trial, and he was charged with gun possession. The presiding judge, reading from Baraka's poem "Black People," in which the speaker says, "Take what you want . . . take their lives if need be . . . run through the streets with music, beautiful radios on the Market Street," dubiously accused Baraka of being responsible for the Newark looting that summer, even though the poem had only been published months after the Newark rebellion, in the December 1967 *Evergreen Review* issue.[35] On the second day of the trial, Baraka stormed out of court and told the judge he "would not be judged by you or one hundred white people." Baraka's peers, including Allen Ginsberg and Diane di Prima, published a letter in support of him, writing, "LeRoi Jones is not only a black man, a Newark man, a revolutionary, he is a conspicuous American artist imprisoned for his poetry during a crisis of authoritarianism in these states."[36] (Initially sentenced for three years, Baraka's conviction was overturned in a second trial.)

Having had a taste of what Black cultural power might accomplish, Amiri Baraka set his sights away from the written page and toward raising Black consciousness. On July 20, 1967, four days after the Newark rebellion concluded, Baraka had participated in the Newark Black Power Conference, where 1,300 Black activists from thirty-nine states established a platform. It ranged from "buying black," to establishing credit unions, to recalling Mayor Addonizio, to elevating Adam Clayton Powell to full seniority in Congress. One of the speakers at the conference provocatively asked the audience, "Any Negroes who want to stand up for their white masters? We're giving you a chance to die for your white master." The speaker was a bald Black man wearing African robes, flanked by two armed bodyguards. His name was Ron Karenga.[37] Baraka was instantly struck by Karenga, who "seemed to me to be the kind of next-higher stage of commitment and organization as compared to the Black Arts."[38]

Ron Karenga was born in 1941 in Maryland. He was the fourteenth child of a Baptist preacher and tenant farmer and studied Swahili and political science at UCLA. As a student, Karenga founded the US Organization, a Black nationalist group. US was centered on the seven principles of Afrocentric communitarian philosophy called Kawaida, ranging from self-determination to faith. A charismatic leader, Karenga understood the force of new symbols—dashikis, kente cloth, beads—for raising Black consciousnesses. He was also a savvy consumer of US culture. In 1966, when Karenga founded the African American holiday that came to be known as Kwanzaa, he decided it should be celebrated around the time of Christmas, because that holiday was when, he said, most Americans "would be partying."[39]

In his quest for supremacy among Black nationalist organizations, Karenga kept close tabs on his enemies. White racists and white moderates, surprisingly, were way down on this list. Most threatening to Karenga was the Black Panther Party for Self-Defense, founded in 1966 in Oakland, California, by two Black college students, Huey Newton and Bobby Seale. If Karenga was the ideological descendant of the Nation of Islam's cultural nationalism, the Panthers were the children of Malcolm X. Invoking the Second Amendment of the US Constitution, which guaranteed the right to bear arms, the Panthers walked around the streets of Oakland with their signature berets and handguns to dramatize Black self-defense (they were "policing the police"). Drawing parallels to armed leftist rebels in Algeria, Vietnam, and Cuba, and liberally quoting from the Chinese Communist leader Mao Zedong, the paramilitary organization took Malcolm X's dying call for Black liberation to mean Marxist revolution by any means necessary.

Karenga's ideological differences with the Panthers weren't nearly as strong as his contempt for them personally. He became obsessed with the young upstarts encroaching on his turf near Los Angeles. Things turned violent when members of Karenga's US shot and killed two Panthers at the UCLA campus on January 17, 1969. Worried about retaliation, Karenga went underground—and remained out of sight until 1971, when he was sentenced to four years in prison by the US government for torturing two Black women, Gail Davis and Deborah Jones, who lived in his home and whom he was accused of poisoning. (Their account was corroborated by Karenga's wife and his head of personal security).

As Karenga faded from public view, Baraka became the most visible exponent of Black cultural nationalism. Much of his day-to-day activity in Newark involved running Spirit House, a Black theater that sought to extend the legacy of BARTS. Spirit House had a dance troupe and a publishing house called Jihad Publishers, which printed the biweekly newspaper *Black New Ark*. Spirit House also had a store that sold goods from the African continent. As the leader of the Newark branch of the Kawaida-inspired Congress of Afrikan People (CAP), which had about three hundred members and lasted about ten years, Baraka was instrumental in writing position papers and organizing conferences and protests centered on Pan-Africanism and anti-colonialism.

Baraka's wife, Amina Baraka, organized a group known as the United Sisters. Born Sylvia Robinson, Amina was a Newark-born dancer, poet, and activist whom Baraka met in 1966 and with whom he had five children. Among her greatest achievements was to develop the African Free School, which educated local youth. The accredited elementary school didn't charge tuition (though parents had to contribute their labor). A typical day, which began with students pledging allegiance to the red, black, and green Pan-African flag (founded by members of Marcus Garvey's UNIA), would involve collective learning on topics such as math, writing, and African culture.

Alternative schools affiliated with Black Power flourished in this era. In 1971, Brenda Bay, a Black Panther Party (BPP) member from New York, created the Intercommunal Youth Institute, a "home school" occupying two houses that served kids ages two to twelve. The student-to-teacher ratio was ten-to-one, and each pupil got specialized attention. Once a student turned four, they would learn basic skills in math, science, and English. Older children would write poetry and letters to incarcerated people and attend trials of BPP members. Everyone learned about Black political resistance and the impact of the transatlantic slave trade upon Black life. BPP members worked to raise money and were its primary volunteers. By most accounts, the school was a success. Its enrollment jumped from twenty-eight in 1971 to fifty by 1973. The Intercommunal Youth Institute gave way to the Oakland Community School (OCS). The Washington, DC–born Ericka Huggins, who majored in education at Lincoln University and left in her junior year to join the BPP, was its director beginning in 1973. OCS had both martial arts and calisthenics to link the mind and body. Its Youth Committee provided a venue where students could critique administrators. Students performed plays about socioeconomic conditions in their neighborhood, and in 1979 a meditation room was created. When officials at the California Department of Education visited in 1977, they identified it as an exemplary elementary school. Despite the success of such liberation schools, there was a clear dilemma: as with most organizations linked to Black Power, OCS was surveilled and infiltrated by the FBI throughout its life. After nine years, it closed its doors, in 1982.[40]

■ ■ ■

Around this time, Amiri Baraka came to believe that, to maintain relevance, the Black Power movement would need to seize the state from within—which is to say, win elections. Toward this end, an arm of Spirit House, a collection of Black men who initially called themselves United Brothers and then Committee for United Newark (CFUN), sponsored a Black political convention in Newark supporting a slate of reformist candidates for the Newark mayoral election of that year. When Newark went to the polls on November 4, 1968, all the CFUN's candidates lost. To make matters even worse, the white supremacist Anthony Imperiale, who had chaired Alabama governor George Wallace's presidential campaign in New Jersey, was elected to Newark City Council.[41]

The loss was a bitter pill to swallow, but Baraka learned a valuable lesson. To win an election, he needed to be pragmatic. In 1969, he expanded CFUN's anti-racist platform to include the concerns of Puerto Ricans (who accounted for a sizable 9 percent of the Newark population). And this time, CFUN would nominate an established political player, and an uncontroversial one at that—a Black engineer named Kenneth Gibson, who in the 1966 mayoral race had already won sixteen thousand votes, placing him third on the ballot.

Kenneth Gibson was neither a militant nor a nationalist. A moderate man who ran on an anticorruption platform, his first order of business was to hire a professional white campaign manager, and his second was to distance himself from Baraka, who now would have to rally Black support for Gibson on his own. "I do not speak of the middle class, the lower class, the poor or the hungry," Gibson would say in his campaign speeches, "I speak of an entire community."[42] On June 16, 1970, Newark rewarded Kenneth Gibson. He defeated the incumbent, Hugh Addonizio, by a vote of 55,097 to 43,086.[43]

Newark had its first Black mayor. But much to Baraka's chagrin, Gibson's tenure closely aligned with who he was as a person: a man who never wanted to ruffle feathers and was less a visionary than an anodyne bureaucrat. Rather than push any ambitious agenda, he shrugged his shoulders and played up Newark's dependence on federal funding (which it didn't have). He reminded the electorate of Newark's notorious distinction as the nation's leader in crime, infant mortality, and impoverished housing stock. In a cruel twist, when Gibson ran for reelection in 1974, he painted himself as the only leader who could keep Baraka and the Black nationalist CFUN in check. To this end, in a visible display of defiance that won him bipartisan support across the city, Gibson boycotted the 1974 Black and Puerto Rican Political Convention. He was rewarded for his efforts: in a five-person run-off on May 13, Gibson cleared the 50 percent margin and was reelected by more than ten thousand votes over his main challenger, Anthony Imperiale.

Overall, Gibson's mayoral tenure was an unqualified disappointment for Baraka. The closest Baraka came to a crowning political achievement during Gibson's mayoralty was in March 1972. That month, Baraka had secured a forty-eight-year mortgage of $6.4 million from Gibson's administration to build low- and moderate-income housing with state and federal funds in a predominantly Italian American ward of Newark. The development was called "Kawaida Towers." Now an astute political player, Baraka hired an Italian American construction company to excavate the site and framed the project as a revenue-generating venture for the city.

This had little effect on assuaging the white ethnic backlash that commenced immediately. Anthony Imperiale, the white nationalist who was now a New Jersey state senator, led demonstrations in November 1972, which resulted in Newark police officers beating Kawaida Towers supporters. These outlaw officers' dereliction of duty was so blatant, and the appetite for oversight was so low, that Newark's police chief, John Redden, resigned his post rather than try to discipline them. Gibson expressed lukewarm support for the Kawaida Towers, but the ongoing protests exacted a political cost. Eventually, with the help of Newark City Council, Gibson was given political cover to abandon the project. In a 6–3 decision, the council reversed its initial decision to approve a necessary tax abatement on the land where the Kawaida Towers would be built. The towers were never built. Their foundation was buried in 1976.

As the dream of the Kawaida Towers turned to dust, so too did Baraka's Black nationalism. Jaded by Kenneth Gibson's centrism and Ron Karenga's fraudulence as a leader, Baraka turned to socialism in the mid-1970s. In 1975, Baraka, now quoting Amílcar Cabral and Kwame Nkrumah, renamed CAP as the Revolutionary Communist League. Baraka was no longer an "Imamu"; now he was "chairman." Baraka's hero was V. I. Lenin, anti-capitalism his raison d'être. The abolition of private property was the only solution for Black colonization. "We changed our views from cultural nationalists," Baraka argued, "because we have always viewed ourselves as revolutionaries, black people struggling for national liberation."[44] In plays like *The Motion of History* (1975), *What Was the Relationship of the Lone Ranger to the Means of Production?* (1978), and a poetry collection called *Hard Facts* (1975), class struggle had replaced racial conflict. Much of everything else had remained: Baraka's militant language (without the sexism and homophobia, this time), the in-your-face directness, the defiance.

▪ ▪ ▪

Over the next three decades, up until the day he died on January 9, 2014, at the age of seventy-nine, Baraka incited fierce responses. To his supporters, he was, like Malcolm once was to him, a "shining Black prince." To his detractors, Baraka was an anti-American radical. Or, he was an authoritarian, anti-feminist antisemite. Although Baraka was never able to seize political power in Newark during his life, it was his legacy as a protest figure that helped propel his son, the forty-four-year-old Democrat Ras Baraka, to be elected as the fortieth mayor of Newark in May 2014. Winning 54 percent of the vote, Ras Baraka succeeded Cory Booker, who recently had been elected as US senator from New Jersey. A community organizer, teacher, and principal, Ras was able to rise through the political ranks in a city now 50 percent Black and only 25 percent white. Running on a progressive platform, he promised to take Newark back from the corporate interests, political bosses, and privatization campaigns that had defined the tenure of his predecessors. "Today," he declared at his victory party, "we told them that the people of Newark are not for sale."[45] Ras wasn't a centrist like Kenneth Gibson, but he also was not a socialist like his late father. Throughout his campaign and during his tenure in office, he took a moderate position on charter schools (they were acceptable as long as they didn't lead to the closing of public schools) and promised to work with everyone, even Wall Street investors whose goal was to revitalize Newark's downtown. Revolutionary art, as Amiri Baraka came to understand, is one thing. Electoral politics is another. The first demands expanding the limits of the possible; the latter is an exercise of the possible.

And yet, if it weren't for Amiri Baraka, the sense of the possible might never have been expanded in the first place. "We want live words of the hip world live flesh," Baraka once wrote.[46] One wonders whether the contemporary debate around Black politics—whether to defund the police, to abolish prisons, to have reparations for slavery, to imagine socioeconomic redistribution under capitalism—might be in a far different place if Baraka's words never hit in the way that they did.

CHAPTER 10

SILENCE WILL NOT PROTECT YOU

I n the fall of 1977, a Black lesbian poet was considering whether to go to the upcoming December meeting of the Modern Language Association (MLA), the flagship professional organization of scholars across the world devoted to the study of language and literature. The MLA's Commission on the Status of Women in the Profession and its Gay Caucus had asked her to deliver a speech at the meeting, to be held in Chicago. The panel where she would speak was "The Transformation of Silence into Language and Action." Audre Lorde didn't want to attend the conference because she had other things on her mind: she was at war with her body. On November 11, 1977, not long after she had received the invitation, she got word from her gynecologist that the lump she felt on her right breast might be cancerous. Over the next few days, as she was preparing for the biopsy, she struggled to find sleep in her Staten Island apartment.

What exactly would Lorde, the former head librarian at the Town School Library and now forty-three-year-old part-time English instructor at the City University of New York (at Lehman College and John Jay College since 1970), tell her partner, Frances Clayton? Lorde had been living with Clayton, a white woman with blond hair and blue eyes, for years. She had met the former professor of psychology at Brown University in 1968, at Tugaloo College in Mississippi, when Lorde was a visiting writer in residence. Beyond the emotional distress that the news would cause Clayton, what would it mean for Lorde, as a Black woman who prided herself on resilience, to rely on the support and care of a white partner?

More so than anything else, Lorde was worried about her two teenage children, Beth and Jonathan, who lived with her and Clayton. Lorde had them with her ex-husband, a white lawyer named Edwin Rollins whom she met in 1959 as a student at Columbia University pursuing a graduate degree in library science. (Rollins was also gay.) Lorde, a well-regarded poet, also wondered what cancer might mean for her public image, as both her work and her life were becoming a symbol for young Black lesbian feminists who wanted to think through their relationship to one another, themselves, and the mainstream feminist movement. "It feels like I've been in training for this for years—for the final testing of the manner in which I say I choose to live my live," she wrote in her journal.[1] Eventually, the emergency surgery to remove the tumor in her breast was completed. As it turned out, the tumor was benign.

After weeks of ambivalence, Lorde decided to give her lecture at the Chicago MLA that winter. As she walked up to the conference stage to address a packed audience on December 28, survival was on her mind. "I wish to survive," she wrote in a journal, "and that has always meant war."[2] Lorde was thinking about survival broadly. Not just how one survives cancer, or any kind of illness, but how one survives when their social experience in the world, one defined by multiple identities (race, gender, sexuality, class), is being marginalized. If, as Lorde said, going to war was the response, this was not a war defined by patriarchal standards—of ruthless competition, amoral ambition, or violent combat—it was a war against the traditional idea of freedom, the idea that all of us are sovereign subjects capable of acting as we wish. Ironically, going to war for Lorde meant accepting the indisputable fact of vulnerability—the inescapabilty of sickness, the fact that we all experience loss, are sometimes in pain, that we all feel sorrow. But vulnerability for Lorde also meant being dependent upon others, which is to say, to love and be loved. To accept a condition of vulnerability did not erase the fact that power and difference mattered—that Lorde, and other Black lesbian mothers like her, were more socially vulnerable than others in the white, male, and heterosexual society they inhabited.

Though Lorde felt vulnerable, she wasn't powerless. In fact, she believed it was her vulnerability, and the collective vulnerability of those like her, that could inspire the necessary solidarity to survive. Reflecting on how she survived her cancer scare, and all of the racist, homophobic, and sexist scares throughout her life, Lorde named the multiracial group of women who stood in solidarity with her—"Black and white, old and young, lesbian, bisexual, and heterosexual," and who, like her, were in a "war against the tyrannies of silence."[3] If silence, as Lorde explained, was the enemy, then language was the ally. To lovingly name a marginalized experience in words was an act of rebellion. "My silences had not protected me," she told the attendees, in what became a philosophical maxim for those who are still moved by her work. "Your silence will not protect you. But for every real word spoken, for every attempt I ever made to speak those truths for which I am still seeking, I had made contact with other women while we examined the words to fit a world in which we all believed, bridging our differences."[4]

Silence isn't a safe haven. It's a temporary escape. A better way to protect oneself is to speak, and to texture the world with meaning. Naming one's identity and experience makes one temporarily vulnerable. But, over time, the naming becomes the glue that holds all those who are vulnerable together. It keeps them in solidarity over their vulnerability. This is, in short, Audre Lorde's philosophy. And it is the philosophy of the lesbian Black feminist counterculture she inspired in the 1970s.

■ ■ ■

In 1976, at a Modern Language Association convention in New York, Black lesbian feminist Barbara Smith, a thirty-one-year-old professor of English at Emerson College in Massachusetts, asked the question that Audre Lorde, who was in the audience, had been asking for a decade: "Is it possible . . . to be a Black lesbian writer and live to tell about it?"[5] Smith's question came from experience. "I actually imagined that I would never be politically active again," she recalled, "because nationalism and patriarchal attitudes within Black organizing was *so* strong—we're talking early '70s now."[6] Many men in the Black Power movement would see Black women only as homemakers, and some even would be unapologetically homophobic. (To his credit, Huey Newton of the Black Panthers, unlike Amiri Baraka, was an exception. By the late 1960s, he embraced both the women's and gay liberation movements, saying that "we should try to unite with them in a revolutionary fashion. We must gain security in ourselves and therefore have respect and feelings for all oppressed people.")[7]

Lorde was impressed with the new generation of radical Black women, like Smith, who were inspired by her work, but with whom she couldn't always identify. Lorde was a first-generation child of immigrants from the Caribbean island of Grenada who came to Harlem a decade before Audre was born on February 18, 1934. Lorde's mother, Linda, and her father, Byron, were disciplinarians and devoted Roman Catholics. They withheld praise for Lorde and her two older sisters, Phyllis and Helen. In addition, they occasionally beat their children, insisted on strict rule-following in their traditional home, and set an unrealistic standard of academic success for their three daughters. Lorde's mother disparaged single mothers and interracial relationships. Her father forbade his wife and children to eat black-eyed peas and rice for fear it would mark them as poor. And Lorde's mother was contemptuous of dark-skinned neighbors.[8] Lorde was disproportionately affected by her parents' behavior—she was clumsy, prone to tantrums, and skeptical of authority (she was an A student in all her academic subjects but received low marks for her classroom behavior). A shy and withdrawn child, who knew Harlem more from looking out the window than playing in its playgrounds, Lorde at an early age began to wear glasses because she was declared legally blind (she was nearsighted).

Even when Audre Lorde began to assert her identity as a young woman, she did so in fits and starts. She was involved with what was then known as the "gay girl" scene in Greenwich Village in the late 1950s. Lorde was introduced to it by one of her closest friends from Hunter High School, Diane di Prima, for whom Lorde served as the midwife for the home birth of di Prima's second child. At this time, Lorde wasn't an out lesbian. Even though she knew she was attracted to women, she still married her husband, Edwin Rollins, who himself was gay and with whom she had an open relationship.

Twelve years younger than Lorde, Barbara Smith came from a different generation. She was more assertive than Lorde about politicizing race, gender, and sexuality. Smith's identity was the wellspring for her political activism. Born in Cleveland, Ohio, in 1946, Smith fondly remembered the tenderness of her grandmother, mother, and aunt—the extended family of women who raised her and her twin sister, Beverly, and whose support provided her the confidence to assert her views. Educated at Mount Holyoke College, a private women's liberal arts school in Massachusetts, Smith was involved in antiwar protests, including at the 1968 Democratic National Convention in Chicago. She went on to receive a graduate degree in literature from the University of Pittsburgh.

In 1974, Smith, along with a small group of Black lesbian socialist feminists living in and around Boston, would hold consciousness-raising meetups. (No more than ten to fifteen would attend any given event.) The group called itself the Combahee River Collective. CRC was named after an 1863 Union Army raid led by the antislavery activist Harriet Tubman, which freed 750 enslaved people near the Combahee River in South Carolina. The CRC wasn't the first radical Black feminist organization of its time, as it was preceded by the Third World Women's Alliance (originally affiliated with SNCC, it became independent in 1969 after it became dominated by white women). Around the same time that the Alliance came into being, there was the National Black Feminist Organization, active from 1973 to 1975, which included a who's who of Black women leaders: Shirley Chisholm, Alice Walker, Flo Kennedy, and Eleanor Holmes Norton.

The CRC was lesbian, socialist, and feminist. Its 1977 mission statement would revolutionize feminism and anti-racism, and thus would be credited as among the first arguments for theorizing intersectional domination. Including as its signatories Barbara Smith as well as her twin sister, Beverly Smith, and the Chicago-raised organizer Demita Frazier, the statement declared: "The most general statement of our politics at the present time would be that we are actively committed to struggling against racial, sexual, heterosexual, and class oppression, and see as our particular task the development of integrated analysis and practice based upon the fact that the major systems of oppression are interlocking."[9] The CRC represented a new brand of radical Black feminism. Its theory was, in part, inspired by Audre Lorde's work, and helped explain her life and articulate her political interests. "Audre was important to me in that way," said Smith, after the two became close and Lorde started attending some of the seven Combahee retreats held in private homes in the Northeast from 1977 to 1980. "Being able to look over to and up to someone who had been here more years than I, who shared the same kind of vision in politics."[10]

The CRC was active in South Boston in the 1970s, which was at the center of white backlash politics. Many white Boston residents were ready to riot rather than allow the courts, following the 1954 *Brown v. Board of Education* decision, to authorize the busing of Black children into their predominantly white public schools. A Pulitzer Prize–winning photograph, *The Soiling of Old Glory*, by Stanley Forman, captured the white

rage. Two individuals, Theodore Landsmark and Joseph Rakes, are featured in the photo's foreground. A Yale-educated Black lawyer, Landsmark,
who wasn't involved with the desegregation efforts but had successfully
fought for more Black contractors in the white-dominated Boston construction industry, was on his way to Boston City Hall on April 5, 1976.
He was approached by a white teenager, Joseph Rakes, who was angry
about court-ordered desegregation. The photo was taken just as Rakes
grabbed an American flag, still firmly attached to a flagpole, and began
to swing both the flag and the pole at Landsmark.

In addition to raising attention about this incident, the CRC was involved with the End Sterilization Abuse campaign and helped set up a
shelter for women of domestic violence called Transition House. Also,
despite not having a religious orientation, the CRC worked closely with
women's Black Baptist groups in local churches. It defended a Black physician in Boston, Kenneth Edelin, who was arrested for manslaughter for
performing a legal abortion. And the CRC supported Ella Ellison, a Black
woman from Boston accused of murder merely because she had been seen
in the area where it occurred.

▪ ▪ ▪

Audre Lorde had long been politically active. She was at the Lincoln
Memorial in Washington, DC, during the August 28, 1963, March on
Washington for Jobs and Freedom, though she left with then husband
Edwin Rollins just before King delivered his seven-minute "I Have a
Dream" speech. (They heard it on the drive back to New York.) As a
graduate student at Columbia, Lorde was involved with the local National
Committee for a Sane Nuclear Policy (SANE) chapter. Later, as a librarian
at the Mount Vernon Library, at the risk of being fired, she refused to par-
ticipate in required air-raid drills. (Despite her refusal, she still was able
to keep her job and also got an early taste of civil disobedience.)

But the major source of Lorde's political activism was her words—
through the act of bearing witness to what she saw and what it meant,
from her vantage point. On September 15, 1963, at the height of the Civil
Rights Movement and Ku Klux Klan hostility toward it, white terrorists
bombed the Sixteenth Street Baptist Church in Birmingham, killing four
Black girls. This wasn't the first or the last of dozens of such attacks in the
Alabama city colloquially known as "Bombingham." Lorde was stunned

that her white husband, who had two biracial children, was unmoved by the horrific slayings. Rollins was a hawkish patriot who supported the Vietnam War and believed in the doctrine of personal responsibility. Lorde, however, was horrified and wrote an elegy to the four Black girls. "Suffer the Children," published in the January 1964 issue of the *Negro Digest*, concludes, "Those who loved them remember their child's laughter."[11] After a ten-year-old Black boy, Clifford Grover, was shot from behind by NYPD officer Thomas Shea in South Jamaica, Queens, in the early morning hours of April 28, 1973, Lorde, who learned of Shea's acquittal on the radio as she was driving, pulled her car over and wrote a poem entitled "Power." In it, the speaker suggests that learning the connection between poetry and rhetoric is a matter of survival.[12] Three years later, Lorde was depressed to learn of a similar incident. In 1976, a fifteen-year-old Black boy named Randy Evans (a few years older than Lorde's son Jonathan) was killed by Robert Torsney, a white NYPD officer. Torsney had claimed to have accidentally discharged his firearm during an epileptic attack.

Although Lorde was acutely aware of anti-Black racism, she never simplified the meaning of Black identity. In 1974, after Lorde and Frances Clayton took her two children on a five-week tour of Africa with visits to Togo, Ghana, and the People's Republic of Benin, Lorde was able to feel spiritually attached to the continent without romanticizing it. She observed a woman cloth dealer in an outdoor market in Accra negotiate more shrewdly than the male merchants. Men and women danced at the Cultural Center in Kumasi in highly sexualized ways, but in ways that defied Lorde's expectations. The dancers were not young children but senior citizens.[13] Upon returning to New York, she changed her appearance without essentializing what it meant. She had her hair braided and started wearing a dashiki shirt and *gele* beads and jewelry. This wasn't to reconnect to a mythologized authentic African heritage, as Black cultural nationalists did before her, but to make her "own new religion."[14]

As a faculty member at John Jay College of Criminal Justice, Lorde had been critical of the university administration's controversial proposal of fusing Black studies and Puerto Rican studies. The two histories were interrelated, Lorde understood, but irreducible to one another. Black studies, like Puerto Rican studies, required its own academic department. In 1968, when Lorde encountered militant race-conscious Black students at Tougaloo College in her creative writing workshop, she said Blackness was "not an easy question to be resolved."[15] After all, at the time, Lorde was married to a white man and counted Diane di Prima among her closest friends. (It was di Prima's old desk, nestled in a corner of Lorde's apartment, that became the place where Lorde started her practice of writing every Sunday for three hours.)

Lorde had a broad understanding of interracial solidarity because she understood that retrograde attitudes didn't just exist among the dominant group. Asked to speak at Harvard University on the legacy of Malcolm X in February 1982, Lorde reimagined Malcolm's last years of life—when he welcomed white allies, defended gender equality, broke with the Nation of Islam, warmed to Martin Luther King, and became a Pan-Africanist—as a reflection of the self-criticism she believed was necessary for Black freedom. "As Black people, if there is one thing we can learn from the 60s, it is how infinitely complex any move for liberation must be. For we must move against not only those forces which dehumanize us from the outside, but also against those oppressive values which we have been forced to take into ourselves. . . . We can examine the dangers of an incomplete vision. Not to condemn that vision but to alter it, construct templates for possible futures, and focus our rage for change upon our enemies rather than upon each other."[16]

When it came to the questions of sexuality, Lorde understood that homophobia wasn't a problem only among white people. In 1964, Langston Hughes sought out two poems from Lorde in an anthology he was editing called *New Negro Poets, U.S.A.* He asked her to change the last section of one of the pieces, titled "Pirouette." "In the section (which is written in the first person) after a detailed depiction of intimacy between two lovers, the speaker says, 'I am come home.'"[17] Hughes, not wanting to remind readers of his own associations with *Fire!!* and the Black queer underground of the 1920s, asked Lorde to change the final line to "I cannot return."[18] Lorde, still a rising poet who needed to get her name out, agreed.

Something similar unfolded six years later. Lorde, now more established, was readying to publish her third collection, *From a Land Where Other People Live*, in 1973. The publisher was Broadside Press, whose founder was Dudley Randall, a Black writer and librarian at the University of Detroit Mercy, and one of the central figures of the Black Arts Movement. Randall telephoned Lorde from his Detroit home and, without directly explaining why, pointedly asked Lorde to omit "Love Poem," which features a description of how "honey flowed / from the split cup / impaled on a lance of tongues / on the tips of her breasts on her navel / and my breath / howling into her entrances / through lungs of pain."[19] After asking Lorde to clarify the gender of the poetic speaker (a woman), which she did, Randall threatened to withhold publication. Lorde agreed to omit the poem.

And yet, when "Love Poem" appeared in the February 1974 issue of *Ms.* magazine, Audre Lorde became the most famous representative of Black lesbianism. When she first read "Love Poem" to a packed house of women at a woman-owned bookstore and coffeeshop on West Seventy-Second Street on the Upper West Side in 1973, one poet in attendance was deeply moved. Her name was Adrienne Rich.

Rich had known Lorde since 1968, when they met as colleagues at the City College of New York. She came from a different world than Lorde. Born in Baltimore in 1929, her mother was a concert pianist and her father was a professor of pathology at Johns Hopkins University. Just after her twenty-fourth birthday, Rich married Alfred H. Conrad, an economics graduate student at Harvard whom she met as an undergraduate at Radcliffe, and with whom she would have three children. Her first collection of poetry, *A Change of World* (1951), was chosen by W. H. Auden for the prestigious Yale Younger Poets Award when she was only twenty-two. Lorde's reading of "Love Poem" struck a chord with Rich because it reminded her of how she, too, had broken her silence: to become a feminist, to leave her husband in 1970 (he committed suicide shortly thereafter), to have a short-lived affair with her psychiatrist, Lilly Engler (which inspired her collection *Twenty-One Love Poems*, published in 1976), to be part of the antiwar movement, and to fundraise for the Black Panthers. "A real, authentic genuine, human woman," was how Rich described Lorde, when they first had lunch in 1971.[20]

■ ■ ■

Lorde's *From a Land Where Other People Live* was nominated for the National Book Award for Poetry in 1974. Given the status of American publishing houses—little had changed since the Harlem Renaissance, when Black artists depended on a predominantly white publishing industry—Lorde didn't expect to win. When the two cowinners were announced that year—the prize went to Adrienne Rich and Allen Ginsberg—Lorde joined Rich on the stage at the April 18, 1974, ceremony. The two women announced they were standing together "in refusing the terms of patriarchal competition and declaring that we will share this prize among us, to be used as best we can for women."[21]

It was a planned protest. Lorde, Rich, and another Black writer, Alice Walker (whose *Revolutionary Petunias and Other Poems* was also nominated that year), had agreed to decline the award if any of them had won individually. Publicly, Lorde stood by the decision. But privately, she had mixed feelings. At the time, it was virtually a foregone conclusion that, of the three, Rich was the most likely to win the award. (That year, the three white judges for poetry were David Kalstone, a professor at Rutgers University; Jean Valentine, a close friend of Rich's who lived on the Upper West Side and whose earlier book Rich had praised; and Philip Levine, an acquaintance who taught at Fresno State and wrote about his working-class origins in Detroit.) On the one hand, in agreeing to decline the prize, it appeared that Adrienne Rich had embodied the Black queer feminist ethic of mutual aid that Lorde embraced: "You know," Alice Walker recalled, Rich "was a great poet, but it would go to her also because she was a white person. And to her immense credit, she had no desire to be honored as we would be dishonored."[22] But this didn't mean that Lorde accepted Rich's gesture uncritically. A friend of Lorde's, a woman by the name of Robin Morgan, recalled a phone conversation in which Lorde confessed that if she had won, she would have liked to keep the $1,000 prize. The prestige and the money would have improved her career prospects. But Lorde had no interest in getting into a private (or public) dispute with the more famous Rich.[23]

The question of what counts as good literature is significant—the answer can decide which books get read and whose stories get told. On some level, who gets to publish isn't a matter of life and death, but sometimes it can be. The stories we read can be crucial in determining which lives are treated with moral concern. Barbara Smith, for her part, loved books and, in 1978, wrote a seminal essay, "Toward a Black Feminist Criticism," in which she argued for an expansion of the literary canon to include Black feminism. But Smith thought this project was part of a larger political struggle, as she demonstrated in her response to a spate of killings of women in 1979. She observed in horror when, between January 28 and May 30, 1979, twelve Black women and one white woman were murdered in succession within a two-mile radius in Boston, between Roxbury, Dorchester, and the South End. The *Boston Globe* paid little attention in the first few weeks, giving it short shrift—only a handful of paragraphs in the back pages.[24] Smith attended an April 1, 1979, march of 1,500 people, which, on its way to the Harriet Tubman House in Boston's South End, paused at the apartment of Daryl Ann Hargett (the fifth victim) and the Stride Rite Factory on Lenox Street (where the bodies of the first two victims were found).[25] Shortly afterward, Smith, a longtime Roxbury resident, and other CRC members wrote, published, and disseminated ten thousand copies of a pamphlet titled *Six Black Women: Why Did They Die?*

On July 6, 1979, at the Cambridge Women's Center outside Boston, Barbara Smith and Demita Frazier convened the Fifth Black Feminist Retreat to discuss strategies to confront this horrific violence. At the retreat, Lorde lent her voice with a poem, "Need: A Choral for Black Women's Voices," which ended with a quote attributed to Barbara Deming: "We cannot live without our lives."[26] Following the example of Black artists before her, Lorde amplified issues she cared about, even if it wasn't professionally advantageous to her personally. When Lorde arrived at the conference, she agreed to do two poetry readings as fundraising events for organizations working to craft a response to the Roxbury murders. At the Sanders Theatre at Harvard University, after she and Rich did a reading, a Black journalist came to interview her, but Lorde told the journalist to instead interview younger Black writers in attendance, who were both more representative of the current state of Black feminism and who could benefit more from the exposure.

A major theme of Audre Lorde's political philosophy was that critique could forge more intimate connections among people. Nowhere was this clearer than in her well-publicized exchange with Mary Daly, a close friend of Adrienne Rich and a prominent white lesbian feminist. A lapsed Roman Catholic who fled from the Church but not from theology, Daly was a professor at Boston College when she wrote a manifesto called *Gyn/Ecology* (1978). The text called upon all women to embrace what Daly saw as a pre-patriarchal feminine energy in classic Jewish and Christian cultures. Lorde was aligned with Daly's goal of women's liberation. Her problem was with Daly's universalism. Were there really no African goddesses and only European ones, Lorde wondered? Was it true that all women were inherently feminine? "So the question arises in my mind, Mary, do you ever really read the work of Black women?" Lorde wrote Daly in a letter dated May 6, 1979. "Did you ever read my words, or did you merely finger through them for quotations which you thought might valuably support an already conceived idea concerning some old and distorted connection between us? This is not a rhetorical question."[27] Lorde waited four months for Daly's reply. She heard nothing.

Things came to a head September 27–29, 1979. Lorde had been invited to be a discussant at a New York University academic conference honoring the work of French existential feminist Simone de Beauvoir, held on the thirty-year anniversary of the publication of *The Second Sex* (1949). Lorde, knowing Daly would also be attending, hoped to have an honest discussion about their disagreements. Daly, reserved in person and uninterested in confrontation, requested that the two meet in a private space. After a brief chat, Lorde, who had been accustomed to Daly's defiant prose, was struck by her mixture of earnestness and fearfulness—how much Daly genuinely cared about women's liberation, but also how scared she was tackling the messy questions that all movements generate.

At the conference, Lorde was astounded to learn that the content of the academic papers she was asked to comment upon had so thoroughly internalized Daly's position. Rather than do what she was asked—give positive feedback—Lorde publicly criticized them for the way they ignored the implications of race and sexuality in the context of feminism. Addressing the Saturday afternoon panel entitled "The Personal and Political," Lorde uttered the words that would long be associated with her: "The master's tools will never dismantle the master's house."[28] Among the 120 conference goers, only three, including Lorde, were Black women (Camille Bristow and Bonnie Johnson were the others). She continued:

> And yet, I stand here as a Black lesbian feminist, having been invited to comment within the only panel at this conference where the input of Black feminists and lesbians is represented. What this says about the vision of this conference is sad, in a country where racism, sexism, and homophobia are inseparable. To read this program is to assume that lesbian and Black women have nothing to say about existentialism, the erotic, women's culture and silence, developing feminist theory, or heterosexuality and power. And what does it mean in personal and political terms when even the two Black women who did present here

were literally found at the last hour? What does it mean when the tools of a racist patriarchy are used to examine the fruits of that same patriarchy? It means that only the most narrow parameters of change are possible and allowable.[29]

One of the conference organizers, the psychoanalyst and NYU professor Jessica Benjamin, was angered by Lorde's statement. Benjamin thought Lorde willfully misrepresented her good faith-effort to invite prominent Black feminists—the likes of Mary Helen Washington, Robin Morgan, and Michele Wallace, all of whom politely declined. Lorde was surely surprised by Benjamin's response. Benjamin's work—popularized in her 1988 book, *The Bonds of Love: Psychoanalysis, Feminism, and the Problem of Domination*—showed how social domination structures our lives and threatens commitments to equality. In light of that reputation, it was curious that Benjamin, as a white woman, couldn't understand—or at least be empathetic toward the fact that—as Lorde told Adrienne Rich, "to be a Black woman dealing emotionally on any but the most prescribed and defended levels with white women I do not know intimately . . . means for me to be vulnerable to racial incidents of varying degrees."[30]

Regarding Benjamin's defensiveness, Lorde said that "I had hoped for, but not expected, anything different."[31] Lorde's realism made sense, given her account of vulnerability. All of us are vulnerable to contradiction—what matters is that we acknowledge it, rather than hide from it.

The master's tools are comforting—for they are familiar and can be used as bludgeons to solve complex relationships.

At various points in her life, Lorde herself would be vulnerable to the master's tools as well. As a point of pride, she claimed to have personally related to all women "in one of two ways, either as lover or as a mother." This meant that an egalitarian form of friendship, especially with those she was attracted to but who weren't attracted to her, was difficult. After inviting Lorde to Boston for a poetry reading, and graciously offering to pay for her lodging fee at a local hotel, Barbara Smith thought nothing of the fact that Lorde insisted upon staying at Smith's Roxbury apartment. It was only when Lorde arrived did it became apparent to Smith that, as Lorde's biographer, Alexis De Veaux, writes, "Lorde meant to use the opportunity as an occasion to seduce her."[32] Smith wasn't interested in Lorde sexually. And she said so. Lorde, for her part, didn't do what the patriarchy suggests—to punish Smith. To the contrary, after Smith, taking to heart Lorde's own ethic, pushed back, the two "hammered out a friendship" by establishing clear boundaries.[33] By 1980, Lorde, Barbara Smith, and Smith's lover, Cherríe Moraga, had founded Kitchen Table: Women of Color Press, the first major press run by women of color.[34]

■ ■ ■

In mid-August 1983, the twenty-year anniversary of the March on Washington, the Washington, DC–based National Coalition of Black Gays (NCBG) demanded that the organizers of the event—an alliance of civil rights, peace, labor, and women's rights groups called the New Coalition of Conscience—include an LGBTQ speaker. Audre Lorde was their choice. Walter Fauntroy—a Black Democrat, DC delegate to the House of Representatives, and onetime pastor of the New Bethel Baptist Church—thought bestowing Lorde with such an honor would be a mistake. It would, Fauntroy felt, give the impression of aligning the civil rights march with gay rights.[35] Of course, this was precisely the point. Angered by Fauntroy's position, seven NCBG activists came to his office on Capitol Hill, but he refused to meet with them. After they wouldn't leave, they were arrested and jailed by Capitol security. Finally, at the risk of making the situation escalate further, the New Coalition of Conscience, including Martin Luther King's widow, Coretta Scott King, agreed to allow Lorde to speak (though they wouldn't go so far as to support a gay rights bill). On August 27, 1983, as Lorde took the stage, she went further than any of them expected. She connected the gay rights struggle to freedom struggles across the world—from the Caribbean and South America to South Africa—saying, "Today the civil rights movement has pledged its support for gay rights legislation."[36]

Worrying that her words would fall on deaf ears, Audre Lorde left the 1983 March on Washington dejected. But in hindsight, she had it wrong. It wasn't this or that speech in Washington, or any of Lorde's anthologized essays or her poems, that made the biggest political impact—it was all of it. Lorde's life and art were an example of an alternative ethic that inspired young activists across the world—those affiliated with women's, gender, and sexuality studies programs, Africana studies departments, and English, sociology, history, and humanities courses in the 1980s and 1990s. Alice Walker was the first scholar to teach a course entirely devoted to

Black women's writers at Wellesley College in 1977, but the list of towering Black feminist critic-intellectuals inspired by Lorde is long and impressive: Mary Helen Washington, Barbara Christian, Gloria Wade-Gayle, Michele Wallace, bell hooks, Beverly Guy-Sheftall, Joy James, Angela Davis, Ruth Wilson Gilmore, and Patricia Hill Collins.

No one, certainly not Lorde, could have predicted that her willingness to go to war against silence in the 1970s would one day change American culture. It started on July 23, 2013, in a Facebook social media post written by a thirty-two-year-old queer Black feminist, Alicia Garza. Garza took to Facebook after she was distraught to hear of the acquittal of George Zimmerman, the Sanford, Florida, man who shot and killed a seventeen-year-old Black boy, Trayvon Martin. Trayvon, it was known, was unarmed, walking around a gated community with nothing but a phone, a hoodie, and a bag of Skittles. The Trayvon killing struck Garza viscerally. Her brother Joey, who worked for her Jewish stepfather's antique store in Marin County, California, where Garza was raised, could have been Trayvon Martin. "I continue to be surprised at how little Black lives matter," she wrote. "And I will continue that. stop giving up on black life. Black people. I love you. I love us. Our lives matter."[37]

Garza's friend, a thirty-year-old queer Black woman, turned Garza's post into a hashtag on Twitter: #BlackLivesMatter. It went viral, and a new movement was soon born.[38] The new movement was called Black Lives Matter (BLM), and it explicitly aimed to confront anti-Black racism, which was symbolized by the high-profile killings of Black people (especially by police officers: in 2014, Michael Brown in Ferguson and Eric Garner in New York, and in 2020, Breonna Taylor in Louisville and George Floyd in Minneapolis). BLM was, by far, the most significant anti-racist struggle since the Civil Rights Movement of the 1960s. But BLM also offered a different analysis of power. It was intersectional and Black feminist. In other words, it was the spiritual child of Audre Lorde. The description of the network reads, "We affirm the lives of Black queer and trans folks, disabled folks, undocumented folks, folks with records, women, and all Black lives along the gender spectrum. Our network centers those who have been marginalized within Black liberation movements."[39]

As an undergraduate student at the University of California, San Diego, Garza learned from "Audre Lorde, bell hooks, Cherríe Moraga, and Patricia Hill Collins" that "difference was a source of strength and power."[40]

In her 2020 memoir, she wrote, "The best way to care for ourselves is the manner that Audre Lorde described: to connect with each other in ways that propel all of us toward care—for ourselves and one another."[41] Another co-founder of BLM, Patrisse Cullors, went further than Garza in her embrace of Lorde. Though she grew up in a religious family of Jehovah's Witnesses in Los Angeles, not even the Bible provided her with the "feeling of connection and spirit I feel when reading Audre Lorde, whose books I carry with me everywhere."[42]

The Black Lives Matter movement is now in its second decade. Since its inception, it has claimed multiple political victories—from pushing cities across the country to redirect funding from police to social services, to limiting "no-knock warrants," to strengthening consent decrees for police departments. Black Lives Matter would never have been possible without Audre Lorde.

CHAPTER 11

THE MESSAGE

At 1520 Sedgwick Avenue in the South Bronx on August 11, 1973, a back-to-school house party was being held by a teenager named Cindy Campbell. Campbell was looking for extra cash to buy new clothes for the upcoming school year. The house party was held in the recreation room of her apartment building, which she rented for twenty-five dollars that night. There were bottles of Olde English and soda strewn across the room, and a wide array of snacks. Though no one could have known it yet, the most important thing about that night was that Cindy's eighteen-year-old brother, Clive Campbell, a rising DJ who had been doing house parties for three years and was known around the neighborhood, took the stage.

To publicize the party, Cindy Campbell created fliers using index cards that she distributed around the neighborhood. The fliers said the party would begin at 9 p.m. and end at 4 a.m. There was an entrance fee of twenty-five cents for women and fifty cents for men. Around a hundred people came. By all accounts, it was a good time.

Clive Campbell, known by the stage name as Kool Herc, was familiar with his father's favorite tracks, popularized through groups like Bob Marley and the Wailers in his hometown of Kingston, Jamaica. DJ Herc, who spent his childhood in Kingston before the Campbell family emigrated to New York in 1967, had seen firsthand how roots music could be turned into a critique of empire and racism. And that night, he did something unexpected. It wasn't that he played the records of the funk master James Brown and the R&B guitarist Dennis Coffey but that he played only portions of the songs, never the full tracks. Herc played several records at once, their sounds overlaying one another. His goal was revolutionary: to catch the drum break precisely, to splice it up, to move the rhythm, to remake time and punctuate the beat. The stopping and starting, the sampling of the best parts and the biggest highs, were meant to ensure that the flow never stopped. Herc's sonic improvisation recalled the spirit of ragtime; the cut-ups of the Beats; the defiance of the Black Arts Movement. A new Black renaissance began that night. With a new beat. It was called hip-hop.

It's not surprising that hip-hop, which today is a multibillion-dollar industry that influences everything from fashion to sports to film to literature, originated at a makeshift party in the Bronx run by Black youth. The South Bronx was ground zero for the new face of post–civil rights America.

From 1890 through the Second World War, the South Bronx neighborhood had been a beacon of hope for second-generation Jews from Eastern Europe, who were drawn to affordable apartments, tree-lined boulevards, and a subway system accessible to Manhattan. But then many of these white ethnic communities were able to secure loans and move to the racially segregated suburbs because of racist federal housing policies. As a result, by the 1960s, the South Bronx was two-thirds Black and Puerto Rican; many of the 267,000 people who lived there were working-class. To make matters worse for these newcomers, jobs were hard to find. In 1959, the Bronx had two thousand manufacturers. By 1974, that number had dropped to 1,350. Over the course of those fifteen years, a total of six hundred thousand jobs disappeared.[1] The average annual income per person plummeted in the South Bronx to $2,430, which was 40 percent of the national average.

As poverty increased, so too did desperation. According to federal law, welfare recipients who wanted to move could only have their moving expenses paid if they had been burned out of the buildings in which they rented. Given this perverse incentive structure, arson became a problem. To fan the flames even more, South Bronx landlords found it more profitable to collect insurance money from arson rather than to undertake costly repairs for their tenants, many of whom lived in rent-controlled units. Some landlords could make up to $150,000 per burned-down building. Between the 1960s and 1970s, forty-three thousand apartment units were lost to thirty thousand fires in the South Bronx. That number amounted to 16 percent of the neighborhood's entire housing stock.[2]

South Bronx citizens wanted decent housing and respectable jobs but got neither. What they got, they didn't want: it was called urban renewal.

Urban renewal was championed by a city planner named Robert Moses—one of the most powerful unelected officials in the history of New York, if not in US history. Over the course of his career, Moses spearheaded initiatives for massive public works, from parks to dozens of highways, about 627 miles in total. One of Moses's most controversial and ambitious projects was in the South Bronx: the Cross Bronx Expressway. The construction of the seven-mile roadway began in 1948. It required contractors to raze entire portions of the South Bronx. After the project was finally completed fifteen years later in 1963, sixty thousand citizens had been displaced. (As a result of their sacrifice, some of the poorest were offered a paltry sum of $200 for relocation assistance.)

To make way for a particular one-mile stretch of the Cross Bronx Expressway in the East Tremont neighborhood, the megalomaniacal Moses, who saw himself as both a genius and a white savior, never bothered to consult its residents. "New York has too many critics," Moses once quipped, "we ought to get rid of some of them."[3] Fifty-four structures, between sixty and seventy feet high, were demolished for the sake of Moses's vision. The expressway was a breath of fresh air for commuters flocking to Manhattan for work from the northern suburbs. It was an unmitigated nightmare for the 1,500 families who used to live below what was now the overpass. Vacant lots, debris, and abandoned buildings intensified East Tremont's hopelessness. Muggings, burglaries, car break-ins, and petty theft skyrocketed. Heroin use shot up.

South Bronx youth in particular were struggling to persist amid the rubble of postindustrial America—40 percent of Black youth and 30 percent of Puerto Rican youth lived below the poverty line, compared with 15 percent of all individuals in the city. Consequently, street gangs began to proliferate like wildfire. In the early 1960s, there was a brief decline in gang activity from 248 active gangs in New York to 130 in 1965, but by the late '60s, the trend had rapidly reversed, with roughly twenty thousand people affiliated with street gangs. They had names like the Savage Nomads, Savage Skulls, Black Spades, and Javelins.[4] On some level, street gangs provided a sense of security to youth that wasn't afforded by the NYPD, who treated the areas with benign neglect. And it gave youth a sense of structure and belonging. Loyalty mixed with machine guns, grenades, and shotguns, however, is a deadly cocktail. Shootouts dotted the Bronx, for reasons big and small—over contested turf and over shifting allegiances, petty arguments, and poorly timed words or glances. Accidentally bumping into someone or stepping on their shoe could start a weeks-long war.[5]

New York street gangs fed on such chaos and unpredictability to sustain allegiance to their profit-making enterprise (which consisted mostly of drugs, guns, and stolen goods). Early hip-hop counterculture, which became an antidote to gang membership, sought to repurpose youth energy for nonviolent and creative ends.

■   ■   ■

One of the earliest examples of hip-hop counterculture was through dance. First it was called "going off," or "burning," then it became known as "breaking," a blend of acrobatics and ballet. It was set to music, and convened through "battles," or "wars," as they were sometimes called. Breaking substituted actual violence in the streets with performance. Breakers reimagined the thing that gangs and the NYPD wanted to discipline: the body. In 1981, *New York Post* photographer Martha Cooper went to West 175th Street to cover what she thought was a riot in a subway. Cooper, though, found no blood on the platform or smashed glass underneath her feet. It was just teenage kids affiliated with the High Times Crew, talking to cops, doing different moves—the "head spin," "shoulder swipe," flips, hand spins, and "the baby."[6] This was a riot, yes—but a cultural one against dispossession.

Breaking became known around New York through "b-boys" like the Rock Steady Crew at the Common Ground in Soho (not to be confused with the b'hoys of Whitman's generation). And break battles began to appear around the country, in festivals, and outside of vaunted cultural institutions like Lincoln Center, the center of classical music. The natural habitat of breaking, however, was playgrounds, sidewalks, school cafeterias, and house parties. Most breakers were between the ages of eight and sixteen. Crews had names like the Dynamic Breakers, Breakmasters, Magnificent Force. Many of those involved were boys and young men, though young women were also there from the start. Kimmy, Yellow Banana, MC Sha-Rock, and Mother Earth were staples of Kool Herc's early parties. The Zulu Queens and Shaka Queens, inspired by the dance routines of the Jackson 5, would develop synchronized movements, replete with stunning solo dances.

Breakers weren't just dancers; they were performers, with movements that had clear messages and were meant to evoke particular responses.

At a Kool Herc party at 1159 Second Avenue, site of the Church Center, one could see the "Herculoids" doing what came to be known as "comedy breaking." Their moves—melting to the floor and other pantomimes—mirrored the legendary American silent actor Charlie Chaplin. Taunting and boasting were common in no small part because they were encouraged by the crowd. One classic move of a breaker during battle would be to drop to the floor, hide their face, and come up with it covered in shaving cream, which they would slowly shave off as they moved to the beat.[7] Another would be to come out of a sitting freeze pose eating a sandwich they had kept hidden.[8] Breakers broke rules and had a good time, but there was a cardinal ethic by which they approached their art: never steal moves from rival crews, and be as nimble and smooth as possible on the dance floor—only one's hands and feet could touch the floor, nothing else.

In 1977, one breaker crew called the "Zulu Nation" sought to develop its own social philosophy. The Zulu Nation was known to travel around the South Bronx and challenge other crews to breakdance battles; their trademarks were called "ass spins," "spider walks," and "electric boogies."[9] But the founder of the organization from which the dance crew emerged, a DJ by the name of Afrika Bambaataa (Lance Taylor), had bigger ambitions. Born on April 17, 1957, to immigrants from Jamaica and Barbados, Bambaataa was raised by his working-class mother on the ground floor of one of the fifteen-story towers of the Bronx River Projects. Through the guidance of an uncle who was a Black Muslim named Bambaataa Bunchinji, Bambaataa became steeped in the cultural memory of 1960s Black Power. The Nation of Islam and the Black Panther Party were especially fascinating to him, though Bambaataa was equally intrigued about the hippies. "Flower Power," Bambaataa recalled, "gave of lot of hope to this area to do something for itself."[10]

At the age of thirteen, Bambaataa, like many in his generation, was captured by the streets; he became involved with the Black Spades in the southeast Bronx, and quickly rose to the rank of gang warlord. His job was to increase membership and expand turf. But gang life wasn't for Bambaataa—it was soul-sucking and anxiety-inducing. At the age of sixteen, he started the Bronx River Organization, a local youth crew focused on debating music rather than starting beefs. In 1975, after Bambaataa won an essay contest sponsored by the New York Housing Authority and traveled to Nigeria, where, for the first time, he saw the reality of Black life without the daily travails of white supremacy, he returned with a new philosophy of Black uplift. His first order of business was to change the name of his organization to the "Universal Zulu Nation." (The name came from the 1964 film *Zulu*, which depicts a twelve-hour battle between a hundred British soldiers and four thousand Zulu warriors in South Africa.) A few months later, Bambaataa's cousin "Soulski" was killed by NYPD officers, who claimed that he had resisted arrest and been brandishing weapons in his car. A fateful choice lay ahead for the Zulu Nation. Would they seek vengeance, or stay silent? They choose neither option. Rather than target cops in retaliation, they decided they would facilitate lines of communication between warring gangs in their neighborhood. Music became the avenue through which to do this; the setting was the house party. To advertise for a party at the Bronx Community Center, Zulu Nation lieutenants distributed flyers to the Savage Skulls and Savage Nomads.[11] As they danced, drank, and ate snacks, they could make connections—they could see each other as human beings who had desires and aspirations. Truces were made, beefs were squashed. Bitter conflict remained, but now there was a venue for change.

Bambaataa formalized his hip-hop philosophy in what he called the "Seven Infinity Lessons," which was a blend of Ron Karenga's Kawaida cultural nationalism and Elijah Muhammad's Nation of Islam reinterpretation of biblical history. Bambaataa cared more about raising Black consciousness than inspiring durable political change. Lesson 4 of the Seven Infinity Lessons, for example, declared that "our way of life is knowledge, wisdom and understanding of everything, freedom, justice, and equality." But nowhere in the lessons was there any mention of issues regarding fair housing, socioeconomic redistribution, or equal employment.[12]

Within a few years, as hip-hop moved from the house party to the mainstream, its message of social critique moved from the margin to the center. The first well-known political hip-hop track, called "The Message," was released in a 1982 album of the same name, by Grandmaster Flash and the Furious Five (Keef Cowboy, Melle Mel, Kidd Creole, Scorpio, and Rahiem). The bandleader, Grandmaster Flash (born Joseph Saddler Jr. in 1958), was as a child fascinated by the revolutionary power of sound. His father, a former boxer and drummer who worked at the Penn Central Railroad, was physically abusive toward his mother and his four sisters where they lived at Fox and 163rd Streets. It was music that provided

Grandmaster Flash an escape from domestic turmoil, that gave him a sense of inner peace. "I remember listening to Nat sing 'The Christmas Song' over and over again. No violence. No drama. No yelling."[13]

On May 25, 1974, when Flash was a student at Samuel Gompers Vocational and Technical High School in the Bronx, he heard DJ Herc play at the Cedar Park Recreation Center. Flash was floored at the crowd's response. "There must have been a thousand people getting down to his music," he remembered. "Folks from four to forty, sweating and bouncing, breakin' and popping, doing the pancake and getting buck wild."[14] Reunited with his mother, a newly converted Jehovah's Witness (she had been institutionalized at Pilgrim Psychiatric Center, while Flash and his siblings grew up in foster homes, from 1966 to 1971), Flash began a lifelong obsession with electronics. If the Bronx was going to be treated as refuse by New York's political elite, Flash would take the refuse of found sound—discarded stereos from abandoned cars, old turntables from his high school—to make a new sound pulsating with life, bobbing with rhythm.

"The Message" was a downbeat funk anthem set to Flash's beats. Its refrain, written by lyricist Melle Mel, was: "Don't push me cause I'm close to the edge, I'm trying not to lose my head." Melle Mel was offering a defiant response to the urban decay around him, what he called "a jungle out there"—the rats in the front room, roaches in the back room, all the kids smoking reefer, number book takers, pimps, and drug pushers.[15] Hip-hop had shifted from bridge-building in the community to the broader act of bearing witness to what community was, and the fact that America decides which communities matter and which ought to be left behind. As Melle Mel's words echoed on the radio, it was as if Allen Ginsberg's *Howl* were getting an update for the 1980s. "The Message" was Melle Mel's cry for the best minds of his generation, who had been left to wither away.

Released in 1981, the "The Message" was a message to Republican president Ronald Reagan's America, a nation in which tax cutting and privatization were being coupled with racist images of Black delinquency. (It was Reagan, in a 1976 speech, who popularized the idea of the "Welfare Queen," the mythical criminal mother from Chicago who didn't work but lived off government handouts. She had fraudulent Social Security cards, eight kids, and multiple Cadillacs.)

"The Message" was also a message to centrist Democrats who believed they could win elections by presenting themselves as "more Republican" than some Republicans. One elected figure who seemed to fit this bill was New York's Democratic mayor, Edward "Ed" Koch. First elected in 1978 in the wake of a decade-long fiscal crisis, Koch promised to make tough choices when he came to power. Republican president Gerald Ford in 1975 had famously vowed to veto any federal bailout, even though New York City's cash needs were $477 million but it only had $34 million in its coffers. Bankruptcy was averted through a mixture of state financial oversight, austerity, and the use of bonds to meet the city's borrowing needs. Yet the specter of default still loomed large. To curry the favor of the economic elites looking to bring back private-sector jobs to the city, Koch went on the offensive, sponsoring pro-business development projects that benefited realtors. New developments at Waterside and Battery Park were built, as was an industrial park in the South Bronx. By 1982, 8.5 million square feet were available for corporations to do business in New York.[16]

New Yorkers of color, however, had to pay a steep price for Koch's and New York's newfound commitment to fiscal responsibility. Black workers held city jobs at a higher rate than other workers, yet these jobs were cut significantly—from 332,298 in 1975 to 245,618 in 1978. After New York State assumed responsibility of the funding for the City University of New York (CUNY) public college system, a step that included eliminating the free tuition program in 1976–77, enrollment plummeted from a high of 253,000 in 1975 (70 percent of CUNY students were nonwhite) to 180,000. To add insult to injury, in 1980, despite fierce demonstrations, Ed Koch closed Sydenham Hospital in Harlem, which, when it opened in 1892, was the first hospital to allow Black doctors to bring in their own patients.[17]

The message of "The Message" is that crime, poverty, and desperation are all of a piece. All three are unnatural and come about through a mixture of social forces. When we are talking about these social ills, we aren't talking about deficient personal responsibility. What we're talking about are political and economic choices, made by elites, that determine what options are available to the majority. From the perspective of Grandmaster Flash and the Furious Five, New York had willfully misinterpreted youth life. Yes, the youth were angry. They were depressed, and prone to acting out. But it was because of the lack of a social safety net, not because they were inherently criminals.

Koch and his top lieutenants disagreed with the implicit argument of "The Message." They were influenced by a new theory of crime, which held that the only thing impoverished youth needed more of was tough discipline. It was known as "Broken Windows" policing, and it was espoused by two conservative professors, George Kelling and James Q. Wilson of Harvard University. Their piece of the same name arrived in a 1982 issue of *The Atlantic*, declaring that the way to address crime was by focusing on lower-level offenders and minor forms of criminality—whether vandalism, homelessness, sex work, or petty theft. The Broken Windows theory overturned a long-standing consensus in criminology, which emphasized social stratification and opportunity deficiency as the root causes of crime. According to the theory, however, criminals were rational actors who made conscious choices about whether or not to commit crime. Subsequently, criminals only responded to deterrence strategies. Once the community got the message that any infraction—even one as small as a "broken window"—would be treated as a serious offense with harsh punishment, offenders would think twice before committing crime.[18]

A prime example of what needed to be policed, according to Kelling and Wilson, was graffiti. "One understands the significance of such otherwise harmless displays as subway graffiti," they warned. "As [sociologist] Nathan Glazer has written, the proliferation of graffiti, even when not obscene, confronts the subway rider with the inescapable knowledge that the environment he must endure for an hour or more a day is uncontrolled."[19]

▪   ▪   ▪

Graffiti in New York came to national consciousness in the early 1970s when the artist who combined his shortened Greek name, "Dimitraki," with his building number in Washington Heights, started writing TAKI 183 on subway station walls and other places. His tag spawned a *New York Times* story in which TAKI 183 was quoted as saying: "You don't do it for the girls, they don't seem to care. You do it for yourself. You don't go after it to be elected President."[20]

Without question, given its visibility, graffiti was a useful way for street gangs to mark their turf. But more than anything else, it was a way for individuals to make a name for themselves in public. Names like RICAN 619 and JULIO 204 began to proliferate. (Before he started DJing, Afrika Bambaataa had three tag names: BAMBAATAA, BAM 117, and BOM 117.) Where you got a "hit," how difficult it was, and how many you had—all of this was a sign of the graffiti artist's prowess. Like hip-hop and break dancing, graffiti became an alternative to gang life for teenage kids. Rather than break into cars, they tagged walls at night.[21]

Many graffiti artists couldn't afford to take extracurricular art classes, so they found outdoor canvases upon which to experiment and refine their craft: apartment buildings, corporate high rises, grocery stores, and public parks. The New York City subway system became an especially popular target because it was a hub for getting eyes, a traveling art exhibit of sorts. Subway car exteriors were like mobile murals. They went from neighborhood to neighborhood. Subway station platforms, on the other hand, were permanent. So they would provide free advertising for one's brand. The West 168th Street station in the Bronx was a popular venue because the A, B, and 1 trains all stopped there. "Subways are corporate America's way of getting its people to work," declared one graffiti advocate. "And the trains were clones themselves, they were all supposed to be silver blue, a form of imperialism and control, and we took that and changed it."[22] Dealers of high art began to take notice. Anticipating the art form's economic potential, CUNY sociology student Hugo Martinez started the first graffiti association, United Graffiti Artists, in 1972.[23] The first graffiti art show took place at the Razor Gallery in Soho in 1973.

New York City officials weren't art critics and couldn't care less if graffiti tags were sold in private art galleries. As far as public art went, however, they weren't thrilled. The city's first anti-graffiti campaign was launched in 1972. By November 1973, the MTA had its entire 6,800-car fleet repainted. Far from a deterrent, however, the fresh coat of paint was treated by taggers as an empty canvas, a fresh start. By 1976, the problem had become so bad that artists had to cross out other tags to make their own. During the 1970s, depending on who you asked, graffiti was either an eyesore, an act of youthful rebellion, or petty vandalism. Yet, the wars over graffiti changed forever in the early morning hours of September 15, 1983. After that night, one had to take sides. Graffiti became the center of a debate on Broken Windows policing, racism, and the counterculture.

▪ ▪ ▪

At 2:50 a.m., a six-foot, 135-pound Black graffiti artist, model, and art student studying at the Pratt Institute in Brooklyn by the name of Michael Stewart walked toward the Fourteenth Street and First Avenue subway station in the East Village. The twenty-five-year-old Stewart had just left a night of partying at the Pyramid Club. He needed to catch the L train home to Fort Greene in Brooklyn, where he was living with his mother and father, a retired MTA maintenance worker. Not thinking twice about it, Stewart took out a marker and scribbled his tag, ROS, on the subway platform. An MTA transit cop took notice and walked up to him. Stewart was frightened. He, like many Black New Yorkers, was aware of the high-profile examples of Black men being treated with excessive force by law enforcement in New York. In 1976, an unarmed fifteen-year-old, Randolph Evans, was shot to death by a police officer. In 1978, Arthur Miller was beaten to death by sixteen policemen in Crown Heights after he joined a scuffle between the cops and his brother, Samuel, who was about to be arrested for driving with a suspended license.

Michael Stewart didn't want to be the next casualty of police violence. So he tried to run away. A transit police officer, along with four officers, pursued him. Once they caught Stewart, they beat him with their nightsticks and landed punches all over his thin frame. Thirty minutes later, he arrived on a stretcher at the nearby emergency room at Bellevue Hospital. He was handcuffed to the stretcher, and his face was swollen beyond recognition. By then, Stewart was already unconscious. He was put on life support. Thirteen days later, Michael Stewart died.

The case against the police officers who killed Michael Stewart went to trial in July 1985. Forty-eight people spoke on behalf of the prosecution, including twenty-three students who witnessed the encounter from their dorm room at the Parsons School of Design. The defense for the assaulting officers didn't call up a single witness. And yet, on November 24, 1985, an all-white jury found reasonable doubt and acquitted the six white police officers. "The outcome of this case will cause many people distress," Mayor Ed Koch said somberly. Not wanting to alienate the NYPD and its supporters, many of whom cheered upon hearing the verdict in the courtroom, Koch added, "It was very difficult to criticize a jury."[24]

Upon hearing of Stewart's death, an artist by the name of Jean-Michel Basquiat was beside himself. By 1983, Basquiat was already the toast of the art world. He was its radiant child, a boy genius. Basquiat would be flown to Italy and Zurich. He was mentored by pop art icon Andy Warhol. He had briefly dated the aspiring singer named Madonna. He would mingle with the likes of Allen Ginsberg at the Mudd Club, a Tribeca hub for the post-punk scene. But after news broke of Stewart's death, Basquiat was shaken to his core. He turned to his lover, a white woman by the name of Suzanne Mallouk (who happened to be Stewart's ex-girlfriend), and said: "It could have been me, it could have been me."[25]

Basquiat was right. The Boerum Hill–raised Basquiat, the son of a Black Haitian father and Puerto Rican mother, born on December 22, 1960, was only two years younger than Stewart. Both were Black graffiti artists from Brooklyn. Both wore their hair in dreads and hung out in the same circles. It was only six years before Stewart's death that the seventeen-year-old Basquiat was an anonymous artist. He had run away from home and was living around Washington Square Park, where he couch-surfed with friends. Known all over lower Manhattan for tagging under SAMO ("Same Old Shit") in the late 1970s on the D line, Basquiat said the tag meant nothing, even though everyone was looking for a deeper meaning. "They're doing exactly what we thought they'd do," he once remarked. "We tried to make it sound profound and they think it actually is!"[26]

Like hip-hop DJs before him, Basquiat's art was improvised. It was made from collages of what he saw and of found materials that he scavenged, such as slabs of wood and old canvases on the street, which he dragged up the stairs of his makeshift studio on East Twelfth Street. Basquiat's paintings, which have been called neo-expressionist, blend the high and the low. Unnamed artists are represented as stick figures. They are placed alongside jazz greats like Charlie Parker. Words like "teeth" and "corpus" are splattered in scribbles next to silhouettes of snakes. The phrase "Veni vidi vici" (which means "I came, I saw, I conquered" in Latin) sits alongside a donkey head. Dollar signs are placed alongside dinosaurs; skeletons have boxing gloves.

Basquiat first made an impression on the wider art world after a June 1980 show in a shuttered massage parlor on Seventh Avenue. It became known as the "The Times Square Show." Those who saw Basquiat's second-floor mural of black, white, and red strokes that evoked mountains and valleys thought they had seen the Black version of a Willem de Kooning, Cy Twombly, and Robert Rauschenberg all mixed in one. Basquiat didn't sell anything at that show, but the *Village Voice* anointed it the "first radical art show of the 1980s."[27] A well-connected gallery owner, Annina Nosei, agreed with the paper's assessment. She approached Basquiat with an offer to represent him in her Prince Street Gallery, where he would live, rent-free, in its basement and produce a collection of paintings that would be featured in his first one-man show in October 1981. By his second show, a Basquiat would cost $2,500. Every single one of his pieces was sold. By 1987, a Basquiat would sell for, on average, ten times that amount. He was the subject of countless magazine profiles. One of the most well-known was a 1985 *New York Times Magazine* cover story called "New Art, New Money: The Making of an American Artist."

Tragically, the fame came too fast, and seemed to be all-consuming. Basquiat turned to harder drugs and, with more money and pressure than he ever had before, began to use more frequently than ever before. At the age of twenty-seven, in 1988, Basquiat died of a heroin overdose.

Basquiat's short life sparked a heated debate: Was he an amateur or a master? A sellout or a rebel? A cautionary tale for making a quick killing in art, or a Black artist exploited by a predominantly white art establishment? Basquiat epitomized cool—he wore tattered Giorgio Armani suits, black Wayfarer shades, and was as comfortable walking around barefoot as he was wearing a bowtie. Beneath this veneer was a hip-hop kid whose art couldn't avoid the politics of the 1980s world he inhabited. This was a world of free markets, racial violence, and fast money. Undoubtedly, Basquiat's rise was made possible through this world. By lowering the marginal tax rate from 50 percent to 28 percent in 1986, Ronald Reagan's Republican administration gave the 1 percent of the American elite who could afford to invest in Basquiat's art much more disposable income to do so. And by owning a Basquiat, these elites could now call themselves culturally tolerant, or even anti-racist, perhaps to insulate themselves from critiques of their enormous wealth.

But Basquiat's paintings had a different message. Like the great Dadaists and surrealists before him, Basquiat's work takes on the excesses of commodification under capitalism just as it denounces racism with a vengeance. Consider his *Defacement—The Death of Michael Stewart*, painted days after Stewart's death. A vague silhouette, standing motionless in the center of the frame, is being beaten by two police officers. The teeth of the police are gnashing, their brown nightclubs are raised, their skin is a ghoulish purple. Above the head of the silhouette is the word "¿DEFACEMENT©?"—the copyright symbol aims to draw attention to the way Black dehumanization and anti-Black racial violence are trademarks in and of American society, as American as anything else.

"He truly created a lifetime of works in ten years," a close friend of Basquiat wrote in a *Vogue* obituary. "Greedily, we wonder what else he might have created, what masterpieces we have been cheated out of by his death, but the fact is that he has created enough work to intrigue generations to come."[28] The author of the piece, who had known Basquiat since 1978 and in whose studio apartment Basquiat painted *Defacement*, was named Keith Haring.

Born in Reading, Pennsylvania, on May 4, 1958, and raised in the nearby town of Kutztown, Haring wasn't what the average citizen thought of when they thought of a street artist. He was white, rail-thin, had curly hair, and a receding hairline. He was also openly gay, wore thick glasses, button-up shirts, and tight leather jackets. Haring loved Walt Disney cartoons. At the age of thirteen, he became involved with the left-wing Jesus Movement, which had a populist attitude toward relief for the poor. Haring was a self-described "Dead Head," following the legendary '60s band the Grateful Dead on tour in 1977. He would never forget how the band gave out thousands of stickers and posters to followers like him.

When Haring moved to New York in 1977, it was to study art and the art of advertising at the School of Visual Arts. Seeking to blend these two interests, Haring's first intervention in street art came when he began to alter street ads. His second was to paste collages of these ads on streetlamps. Rather than turntables, Haring's tools were magazines and black ink. He would remix the sensational headlines from the *New York Post*, a cheap tabloid widely available in newspaper kiosks across the city, to say things like: "REAGAN SLAIN BY HERO COP, REAGAN: READY TO KILL."

Influenced by the theory of the "cut up" described in William S. Burroughs's book *The Electronic Revolution* (1971), Haring eventually shifted from reassembling existing print media to making his own trademark figures. After visiting multiple NYC subway stations and noticing that black matte paper-covered panels previously devoted to ads that had already expired, Haring decided to use white chalk to create an original cast of characters. There was the Barking Dog and Radiant Baby, Red Dog, and The Globe, among others. Haring's figures looked like they could have been taken from comic illustrations or children's books. Between 1980 and 1985, Haring drew approximately five thousand of these chalk drawings in various NYC subway stations. On the surface, the elegant lines and warm, playful shapes mobilized themes associated with innocence. Haring intentionally avoided risqué material like drugs and sex so as not to provoke the authorities. But upon closer inspection, Haring's figures could also address political issues. His Radiant Baby, a kneeling infant that gives off rays of light, could be interpreted as a frustrated child, or a warning of impending nuclear catastrophe.

A major distinction between Haring and Basquiat is that Haring was white. And unlike artists of color, Haring could freely profit off his whiteness. He worked during the day, and mostly unbothered. Though he was arrested or ticketed dozens of times, Haring met NYPD officers who were fans of his work and whom he bantered with. (The comparison with Michael Stewart, who was killed for writing three letters in marker on a subway wall, is chilling.)

Haring's big breakthrough came after his one-man show at the Tony Shafrazi Gallery in Soho in 1982. Between 1984 and 1986, Haring gave eighty interviews and was featured in *Rolling Stone* and the *Village Voice*, as well as on ABC and NBC—CBS even did a special on him. Haring parlayed his international fame into a commercial establishment: his store, the Pop Shop, was opened on Lafayette Street in Manhattan on April 19, 1986. It had a glass-front window and a rectangular awning. Its walls were sprayed with graffiti, and its shelves were filled with T-shirts, pins, magnets, calendars, postcards, earrings, coloring books, skateboards, and inflatable plastic babies. Hip-hop was blasting in the background.

Haring designed most of the trinkets that he sold at the store, and had them manufactured in the US, but the "Made in America" tag didn't disarm critics who insisted Haring's venture was either a bad joke or evidence of bad business acumen. "Is this spiritually, intellectually, morally, forceful stuff?" complained the critic Mark Stevens. "Does it have imaginative depth? Is it in some ways significantly grappling with important issues? . . . While fun, NO, it's fast food, it's a good time, its boogying on a Saturday night."[29] "Mr. Haring used to offer his art free on subway walls," grumbled the *New York Times*. "Now he sells it for five-figure sums. Mr. Haring also used to give away his pins, jigsaw puzzles, and comic books, which are now for sale at the shop."[30] The Pop Shop epitomized the contradiction of the counterculture: its style was transgressive and its spirit oppositional, but everything was for sale to the highest bidder.

And yet, the Pop Shop was much like Basquiat's paintings: it overshadowed how Haring's art had become a symbol of political resistance across the globe. In 1982, Haring designed a poster for the Rally for Nuclear Disarmament in Central Park, which drew almost one million protesters. In the poster, the Radiant Baby is surrounded by a mushroom cloud; below it is an anonymous figure with an X on their face and their arms upraised. In 1985, in support of the global anti-Apartheid movement, Haring designed a "Free South Africa" poster and distributed twenty thousand copies of it for free. The poster consists of two panels: In the first, the neck of a large black silhouette is lassoed by a small white figure. In the second, the black silhouette is stepping on the small white figure. After Michael Stewart died in 1983, Haring wrote in his journal: "They know they killed him. They will never forget his screams, his face, his blood. They must live with that forever."[31] In 1985, Haring visually represented that harrowing mental image in *Michael Stewart—USA for Africa*. In the piece, Stewart is being suffocated by a baton and crushed by the feet of law enforcement. The river of blood below his feet (a river from which multicolored arms are reaching upward) transforms into a sharp razor that splits the earth in half. In the late 1980s, Haring became involved with the activist organization ACT UP (AIDS Coalition to Unleash Power). ACT UP used direct action to bring attention to the AIDS epidemic, which had claimed almost a hundred thousand lives by the end of the decade. Haring's poster, "Ignorance = Fear, and Silence = Death," became one of its rallying cries.

Arguably, Haring's most iconic work was the 1986 *Crack Is Wack* mural, which still exists on a handball court wall in East Harlem. Sprawling against an all-red backdrop, the phrase "Crack Is Wack" hangs above bodies and limbs in motion, trampling one another for what appears to be a fix. (The image was so poignant that it was adopted by the New York Board of Education for its antidrug education campaign's newsletter.)

Haring, like Basquiat, died young. After being diagnosed with AIDS in 1988, he died from complications associated with the disease in 1990. He was only thirty-one. Basquiat's *Defacement (The Death of Michael Stewart)* hung above Haring's bed in his North Houston studio apartment.

■ ■ ■

As the 1980s were coming to a close, hip-hop culture was becoming mainstream. And more political than before. No music group exemplified this as much as Public Enemy. Chuck D and William "Flavor Flav" Drayton formed the collective as students at Adelphi University in Long Island in 1984, where both were raised. The two soon brought in fellow Long Islanders, Bill Stephney, James Boxley ("Hank Shocklee"), Richard "Professor Griff" Griffin, and Harry Allen. A track like "Timebomb" from Public Enemy's first record, *Yo! Bum Rush the Show* (1987), revealed how Grandmaster Flash and the Furious Five's "The Message" was being taken in a confrontational direction. No longer simply denouncing neoliberal devastation or calling out American disinvestment in Black youth, in this track, Chuck D takes up the mantle of a guerrilla warrior clashing against state violence: "I'm a MC protector, U.S. Defector / South African government wrecker. Panther power, you can feel it in my arm / Look out y'all 'cause I'm a timebomb."[32]

Public Enemy wanted their lyrics to scandalize. This was the group's appeal. And what appeal it had. Their second record, *It Takes a Nation of Millions to Hold Us Back*, was released on June 28, 1988, by a label called Def Jam, founded by Rick Rubin, a talented music producer, and Russell Simmons, who wanted to bring rap to suburban white kids. Within the first year, *It Takes a Nation* had sold a million records. It stayed on the Billboard 200 list for forty-seven weeks.

Calling themselves the "Black Panthers of Rap," Public Enemy revived the Black Arts Movement of the 1960s. Public Enemy was nationalist, strident, and defiant. Chuck D, its bandleader, was influenced by his mother's Pan-Africanism and Louis Farrakhan. In 1980, the first election in which Chuck D voted for president, he cast his vote for Gus Hall and Angela Davis on the Communist Party ticket.[33] Bill Stephney worked with multiple civil rights organizations, and Professor Griff would quote Malcolm X, Nelson Mandela, and Mao Zedong. Public Enemy's political theory was, without question, contradictory. Communism mixed with capitalism, nonviolence with violence, nationalism with internationalism. It was one thing for Public Enemy to position themselves as the cultural vanguard, but it was another thing entirely to see them as theorists of Black liberation. "I don't know what I was," Chuck D later admitted. "I definitely wasn't a capitalist. And I definitely wasn't American."[34] Public Enemy's clear political identity was a minor problem compared to a more pernicious issue: Public Enemy's masculinist, homophobic, and militarist language. "When Flavor Flav . . . threatens to scatter suckers' brains from here to

White Plains," wrote the music critic John Leland, in a tongue-in-cheek assessment of Public Enemy's style, "that's when I'm hooked."[35]

Public Enemy's lack of a clear political position would take a darker turn when Professor Griff went on a racist rant. Citing Nation of Islam leader Louis Farrakhan's antisemitic screed, *The Secret Relationship Between Blacks and Jews*, Griff asked conservative Black reporter David Mills of the *Washington Times*, "Is it a coincidence that the Jews run the jewelry business, and it's named jew-elry? The majority of the wickedness that goes on across the globe? Yes. Jews. Yes."[36] Chuck D, incensed by Griff's own rant, scrambled to contain the fallout. "We are not anti-Jewish. We are not anti-anyone," Chuck D said at a June 21, 1989, news conference. "We are pro-Black, pro–Black culture, pro–human race. . . . Our policy is not to offend anyone, it's to offend the system that works against us 24 hours a day, 365 days a year."[37] After concluding the written statement, Chuck D announced Griff was no longer part of the band. A week later their label, Def Jam, said it would take an indefinite pause promoting *It Takes a Nation of Millions to Hold Us Back*. Public Enemy went on hiatus, and then it disbanded.

On July 21, 1989, a month after this debacle, a new film opened in theaters. It was written and directed by a thirty-two-year-old Black filmmaker. It was his third feature film. The director had asked Public Enemy to compose a track called "Fight the Power." And it was blasted in the film's opening title sequence, during which its female lead, Rosie Perez, danced with boxing gloves. The film was titled *Do the Right Thing*, and its director was Shelton Jackson "Spike" Lee.

Born in Atlanta on March 20, 1957, Spike Lee had been steeped in Black Power from an early age. His mother was a schoolteacher and graduate of Spelman College, and his father was a prominent session musician. After a brief sojourn in Chicago, the Lees moved to Cobble Hill, Brooklyn, where they were the neighborhood's first Black family among white ethnic Italians and Irish, and then settled in Fort Greene. Lee graduated from Morehouse College in Atlanta (his grandfather was classmates with Martin Luther King Jr.) in 1977. He was one of the first Black graduate students at NYU's film program, where he earned an MFA in production.

Do the Right Thing is set on an excruciatingly hot summer day in the predominantly Black neighborhood of Bedford-Stuyvesant in Brooklyn. At the center of the drama is Sal's Famous Pizzeria, owned by an Italian

American family from the white ethnic enclave of Bensonhurst. It is there that Mookie, a Black pizza deliveryman (played by Spike Lee), tries to earn a paycheck while managing the responsibilities of being a brother, being a father to his toddler, and being present for his romantic partner. As Mookie is making his delivery rounds, coming in and out of the store, Sal's becomes the site of an unexpected protest. The business relies on Black customers, and Sal himself delights in feeding the neighborhood. But Sal's Wall of Fame is filled with portraits of Sal's own ethnic group— Italian Americans like Al Pacino and Liza Minnelli. There are no Black portraits on Sal's Wall of Fame, as a character by the name of Buggin Out observes. Already frustrated by the gentrification of the neighborhood (earlier in the film, a white hipster wearing a Larry Bird Boston Celtics jersey steps on Buggin Out's brand new Nike shoes as he walks up to his brownstone), Buggin Out demands a Black boycott of Sal's. To add heft to his claim, Buggin enlists a fixture of the neighborhood, a hip-hop kid by the name of Radio Raheem, who throughout the film has carried around a boombox playing Public Enemy's "Fight the Power" on repeat, and he also brings it into Sal's. The song's lyrics pronounce, "Cause I'm Black and I'm proud, I'm ready, I'm hyped plus I'm amped, most of my heroes don't appear on no stamps / Sample a look back you look and find nothing but rednecks for 400 years if you check."[38]

Raheem and Buggin enter the pizza shop. Sal, trying to keep his cool but visibly irritated, asks Raheem to lower the volume. Raheem refuses, which leads Sal, in a fit of rage, to smash Raheem's boombox with a baseball bat. The pizzeria is eerily silent for a moment, but then fists are thrown, and a full-out brawl breaks out. The NYPD, which we've seen riding around the neighborhood, arrives to bring law and order. But rather than turning their ire toward Sal and his sons, Vito and Pino, two white police officers restrain Raheem by placing him in a chokehold. Raheem, like the growing crowd around him, pleads with the cops to let him go, to loosen their grip. He's suffocating and poses no threat. But they continue until they squeeze out his last breath. Raheem drops to the ground, lifeless.

Upon witnessing this senseless act of police violence, Mookie, who had been ambivalent about whether to support the boycott or keep his job at Sal's, is distraught. The crowd is seeking vengeance, and they turn their gaze on Sal and his sons, ready to exact revenge. Sal tells them they should do what they "gotta do." At that moment, Mookie makes his choice. He throws a trash can through the storefront window, and the community burns Sal's Pizzeria down. The neighborhood is in tatters. Bed-Stuy looks like a war zone. But Sal and his kids are spared violence. Does Mookie do the right thing? The next morning, he shows up to the destroyed pizzeria and demands his final payment. Sal angrily crumples and throws the cash at Mookie. Mookie, shrugging off Sal's anger and distress, reminds him that insurance will cover the costs of arson.

As the movie concludes, the local DJ tells us that the New York mayor will set up a blue-ribbon commission to identify the cause of the prior night's disturbance. The scene then cuts to a dark screen featuring quotes from Martin Luther King's Nobel Lecture, given on December 11, 1964, and Malcolm X's "Communication and Reality" speech, which he delivered on December 12, 1964. These quotes are followed by a photograph of the only time the two leaders met. In the end credits, we see that *Do the Right Thing* is dedicated to the Black families of victims of racial violence in the prior decade. Five of the victims were killed by white police officers: Arthur Miller, Yvonne Smallwood, Edmund Perry, Eleanor Bumpurs, and Michael Stewart. And then there was Michael Griffith, a twenty-three-year-old Black man who in 1986, in the white suburb of Howard Beach, Queens, found himself outside a pizza parlor just past midnight after his car broke down. Griffith was beaten by a racist white mob, shouting racial slurs, armed with tire irons and baseball bats. Fearing for his life, Griffith desperately ran onto the Belt Parkway freeway, where he was struck and killed by a moving car.

After its world premiere at the Cannes Film Festival, where it was nominated for but lost the Palme d'Or to Steven Soderbergh's *Sex, Lies, and Videotape, Do the Right Thing* was met with a mixed response. Critics applauded Lee's inventive visual style, the fast-paced dialogue, and the inspired performances, but the political message of the film was condemned in major publications. A *Time* critic said, "Not since the Black Panthers cowed Manhattan's glitterati 20 years ago has there been such a virulent outbreak of radical chic—or so many political-disease detectives ready to stanch the epidemic. . . . A few fear that *Do the Right Thing* could trigger the kind of riot it dramatizes and perhaps condones."[39] *New Yorker* critic David Denby wrote, "If Spike Lee is a commercial opportunist, he's also playing with dynamite on the urban playground. The response could get away from him."[40] Denby worried that the fictionalized riot at the end of *Do the Right Thing* might provoke a real riot, though, in truth, he conveniently overlooked how the film was a direct response to the white riot that had been ongoing throughout New York's streets in the 1980s. This is what also made *Do the Right Thing* squarely part of the hip-hop counterculture—it at once bared witness to and resisted the dehumanization that the political elite had turned a blind eye to. (A decade later critics changed their tune. By 1999, *Do the Right Thing* was hailed as an American classic, selected by the National Film Preservation Board and Library of Congress to the National Film Registry.)

It was precisely the controversy surrounding *Do the Right Thing* that led to renewed public interest in Public Enemy—the music video for "Fight the Power" was played nonstop on channels like MTV and BET, and eventually jumped to number one on the Hot Rap Singles chart. Less than two months after calling it quits, on August 9, 1989, Public Enemy had reunited. They were moving forward with their third studio album, *Fear of a Black Planet.*

The summer of 1989, when *Do the Right Thing* was released, was a turning point in New York city politics. Mayor Ed Koch was running for his third mayoral term. Spike Lee was aware of this. "We knew that when the film came out, it would be right before the Democratic primary for mayor," explained Lee. "Every time we could nail Koch, we would."[41] It's impossible to know what impact the film had on the 1989 election, but Ed Koch lost the hotly contested Democratic primary against his African American challenger, David Dinkins. Later that fall, Dinkins won the general election by the narrowest of margins: forty-seven thousand votes out of almost two million cast. Dinkins's challenger was a tough-on-crime associate attorney general under Ronald Reagan by the name of Rudy Giuliani.

As soon as Dinkins entered office, he recognized there was little appetite among many white New Yorkers for racial justice. In fact, to broaden his support among this electoral consistency and follow in the footsteps of Koch's legacy as a no-nonsense Democrat, Dinkins introduced a $1.8 billion anti-crime package. In addition, he hired two thousand new police officers. After that, Dinkins and his police commissioner, Ray Kelly, recruited the coauthor of the "Broken Windows" article, George Kelling, to study the problem of "squeegee men." "Squeegee men" were itinerant window washers in the city who approached cars at stop signs during red lights and asked for money in return for scrubbing car windshields clean. Squeegee men were more a media-created problem, however, than a real one. According to city data, there were only a few hundred full-time squeegee men throughout the entire city. But Kelling convinced Dinkins that targeting them would lower crime rates.[42] Consequently, NYPD officers began to patrol the streets and were ready to arrest any lawbreaker, for any infraction, no matter how minor.

Dinkins got the ball rolling for over-policing in the 1990s, but it was Rudolph Giuliani, who defeated Dinkins in 1992, that put Broken Windows policing into full force. "The streets are overwhelmed with drug dealers," Giuliani said. "We can't allow people to walk the streets and be threatened. Those people need to be removed from the streets."[43] During his two terms in office (1994–2001), the NYPD budget increased by 57 percent. The number of uniformed officers jumped from twenty-eight thousand to thirty-six thousand.[44] From 1993 to 1995, misdemeanor arrests increased by 40 percent. Between 1995 and 2000, this number grew by another 23 percent. Police summonses increased by an astonishing 263 percent between 1993 and 2000.

In 1994, the NYPD, under the leadership of its new police commissioner William Bratton, released a new "zero tolerance" policy called the "Police Strategy No. 5: Reclaiming the Public Spaces of New York." The policy focused on minor infractions like reckless biking or loud music. Between 1994 to 1996, there were eight thousand complaints of police misconduct (compared with six thousand the three years prior). New York spent $70 million to settle these cases.

By the time Giuliani left office in 2001, he would take credit for lowering the city's crime rate. The truth was much more complicated. The crime rate plummeted not because of an increase in police, but because of shifting social trends across the country. Crime rates fell during the 1990s because the crack epidemic receded, the cocaine trade slowed down, a better economy took shape, and an aging population led to less youth making poor choices. Indeed, New York City ranked just fifth nationwide in terms of crime rate decline—behind San Diego, Washington, DC, St. Louis, and Houston. But unlike New York, which had the highest ratio of police to civilians, a city like San Diego took a different tack: it employed community-based tactics, and secured even better results, with the city's crime rate dropping 15 percent between 1993 and 1996.[45]

As police departments in major American cities were becoming more brazen in their tactics, Americans could no longer avoid the reality of police brutality against Black citizens. Nothing symbolized this more than what took place in Los Angeles on March 3, 1991. That night, a Black motorist by the name of Rodney King was kicked, clubbed, and tased by Los Angeles police officers. The encounter was captured on video by a bystander from his apartment building. As a result of the beating, Rodney King's leg was broken, his face was cut, and parts of his body burned. King required a wheelchair to move around.

A year later, on April 29, 1992, the four white officers who brutalized King were acquitted of using excessive force. Reformers prayed for peace, but realists knew the worst was about to unfold. Black Los Angeles erupted in flames, creating the largest urban uprising since the late 1960s. Los Angeles mayor Tom Bradley called a state of emergency, and California Governor Pete Wilson ordered two thousand National Guard troops into the city. When all was said and done, there were fifty riot-related deaths. Ten people were shot to death by police officers. Two thousand citizens were injured, and six thousand more were arrested. Thirty-six percent of those arrested were African American, and 51 percent were Latinx. One thousand buildings were destroyed in LA and $1 billion in property was lost.[46]

■   ■   ■

Enraged by the rise of law-and-order politics, hip-hop culture took a more aggressive tact against anti-Black state violence. By the early 1990s, a new genre emerged. It was called gangsta rap. Its lyrics were provocative and unflinching. They were explicit and sensational. Among the most well-known groups was N.W.A (Niggaz Wit Attitudes). Although its bandleader, Ice Cube, introduced himself as a "crazy mothafucka," N.W.A's song "Fuck Tha Police" was what caused a firestorm. Radio DJs playing the top hits wouldn't touch this track; Focus on the Family, the Colorado Springs–based fundamentalist Protestant organization founded by James Dobson, denounced it. Cops refused to provide security at N.W.A shows in Toledo, Ohio, and Milwaukee, Wisconsin. Even the assistant FBI director under George H. W. Bush, Milt Ahlerich, got in on the action, warning the group's record label, Priority Records, that "recordings such as the one from N.W.A. are both discouraging and degrading to these brave, dedicated officers."[47]

A similar dynamic took place after the band Body Count, fronted by rapper Ice-T, released the song "Cop Killer" (1993). "Cop Killer" was influenced by "Psycho Killer" (1977), the commercially successful radio hit by the New Wave band Talking Heads. The lyrics of "Psycho Killer" are from the perspective of a serial killer. The song, performed by David Byrne and three other white art students he met in college at the Rhode Island School of Design, was understood as what it was: a farce with a catchy beat. There were two differences, however, between "Psycho Killer" and "Cop Killer." One, "Psycho Killer" was an experiment in stream of consciousness, while "Cop Killer" had a clear message of protest—Rodney King is named in the song's lyrics, and the chorus tells the listener, "Cop Killer, fuck police brutality." Two, "Cop Killer" was performed by Ice-T, a Black man, wearing a baseball cap and a gold chain.

Former Republican president George H. W. Bush (1988–92) told reporters that Ice-T's song was "sick." The governor of New York, Democrat Mario Cuomo, chimed in as well, saying it was "ugly, destructive and disgusting." Not wanting to waste a plum political opportunity, former Republican vice president Dan Quayle denounced the track as the logical result of liberal tolerance. As Quayle put it, it was another example of the Hollywood "cultural elite's" disregard for traditional family values. The NRA (National Rifle Association) called for a boycott of Time Warner, the parent company of Sire Records, the label through which "Cop Killer" was released. The Fraternal Order of Police agreed with the NRA's call.[48] At the request of California attorney general Dan Lungren, record stores across California pulled the album from its shelves. The Philadelphia city pension fund voted to divest itself from millions of dollars of Time Warner stock.[49]

Gangsta rap was social satire with a consciousness-raising message. Its lyrics warned of dysregulated Black youth storming lily-white suburbs, of Black rage run amok, of excessive drug use, sexual exploits, violence, misogyny, and nihilism. These images played on white racist fantasies of Black people. Gangsta rap seemed to be saying something like, *If white Americans want terrifying images of Blackness, this is what we'll give them.* Gangsta rap was thus a 1990s update of Amiri Baraka's Black nationalist poetry and of Bigger Thomas, the antihero of Richard Wright's *Native Son.* This is one reason why Ronald Hampton, the director of the DC-based National Black Police Association, which had a membership of thirty-five thousand, refused to condemn "Cop Killer." "This song is not a call for murder," Hampton told reporters. "It's a rap of protest. Ice-T isn't just making this stuff up. He's expressing his concerns about police misconduct. He's responding to a very real issue that affects many Americans, especially blacks and Latinos: police brutality."[50]

Gangsta rap, above all else, was the fantasy of a few hip-hoppers who wanted to make it big—a far cry from how most Black youth lived or what they thought. Yet, this fantasy had mass appeal to white audiences, who consumed the genre with unmatched enthusiasm. N.W.A's *Straight Outta Compton* album sold two million copies, and Body Count's self-titled album, featuring "Cop Killer," sold twenty thousand copies the week after the controversy hit national media.[51]

Given gangsta rap's incredible popularity among white people, it became apparent that the genre was here to stay. For this reason, some activists wanted to make the genre more consistent with the hip-hop spirit of liberation. Just as Grandmaster Flash and the Furious Five's "The Message" made DJ Herc's funky beats to bear on the social problems of racial neoliberalism in the 1980s, Public Enemy's "Fight the Power" had taken inspiration from the "The Message" and applied it to the problem of white supremacy in politics, culture, and society. This, at least, was the hope of the seasoned activist and Black feminist and former Black Panther Angela Davis, whom Chuck D had once voted for when she ran as vice president of the US. During a conversation with Ice Cube at Cube's Street Knowledge business offices in Los Angeles, Davis, inspired by Audre Lorde's theory of intersectionality as much as by the witness borne by Billie Holiday's blues lyrics, asked Cube to address gangsta rap's misogyny and male-centered vision: "What about the women? You keep talking about Black men," Davis told Cube. "I'd like to hear you say Black men and Black women. . . . When we talk about progress in the community, we have to talk about the sisters as well as the brothers."[52] It's not clear whether Cube was philosophically skeptical, personally defensive, or uninterested in reforming the genre's masculine focus for fear of losing listeners and thus lowering record sales. Cube responded, "But the Black woman can't look up to the Black man until we get up."[53]

Black women hip-hoppers like Salt-N-Pepa, Lauryn Hill, Missy Elliott, Queen Latifah, Foxy Brown, and Lil' Kim demonstrated why Cube's response made no sense. By rapping about gender and challenging patriarchal ideas about women's sexuality and decorum, these women were reclaiming their own stories and, in so doing, announcing that hip-hop couldn't be restricted artistically. Precisely by proclaiming their perspective as Black women, women rappers made their listeners rethink both Blackness and masculinity. "More than any other generation before us, we need a feminism committed to 'keeping it real,'" wrote Joan Morgan, who coined the termed *hip-hop feminist* in her 1999 book *When Chickenheads Come Home to Roost*. "We need a voice like our music—one that samples and layers many voices, injects its sensibilities into the old and flips it into something new, provocative, and powerful. And one whose occasional hypocrisy, contradictions, and trifeness guarantee us at least a few trips to the terror-dome, forcing us to finally confront what we'd all rather hide from."[54]

▪ ▪ ▪

In 1991, a new hip-hop industry magazine called *The Source*, only three years old, had a decent, if modest, circulation of about forty thousand. By the end of the 1990s, its circulation was five hundred thousand. By that point, *The Source* was bringing in $30 million in revenue every year, outselling *Rolling Stone* magazine, which, for years, had been the standard-bearer for music news and culture.[55] The average reader of *The Source* was part of the demographic every industry wanted to reach: twenty-one-year-old males (half of its subscribers were Black, and a quarter were white).[56] Another magazine, *Vibe*, hit the scene in 1992. Inside the cover was advertising for a who's who of global companies—GAP, Swatch, and Nintendo. The first issue of *Vibe* printed two hundred thousand copies. Reebok and Nike, once on the cultural fringes, were now mainstream footwear brands. Urban marketing and advertising agencies like Mingo Group emerged. Every year, hip-hop record sales generated $400 million.[57] Hip-hop was no longer a counterculture; it was the culture.

Today, hip-hop captures the largest share of the music market (30 percent). It comes in many genres. Trap. Drill. Crunk. Hardcore. There's the Black feminism of Cardi B and Megan Thee Stallion, and the progressive rap of Kendrick Lamar. Jay-Z was once a kid named Shawn Carter who grew up in the Marcy public housing projects in Bedford-Stuyvesant, Brooklyn, in the 1970s. Over the past two decades, he has won dozens of Grammy Awards and sold over a hundred million records. A business mogul and founder of the entertainment agency Roc Nation, Jay-Z is worth over $1 billion.

In a 2021 advertising campaign for the jewelry company Tiffany, titled "About Love," Jay-Z sits back in a wooden chair in a Black tuxedo looking at his wife, Beyoncé (a global superstar in her own right), who is wearing a black dress and a diamond-studded necklace. Jay-Z's pose is a recreation of Jean-Michel Basquiat's February 10, 1985, *New York Times Magazine* cover image for the story "New Art, New Money" by Cathleen McGuigan. In the Tiffany ad, behind Jay-Z and Beyoncé is a 1982 painting by Basquiat, *Equals Pi*. If McGuigan's Basquiat story was meant to question the implications of capitalism's profiting off hip-hop culture, the Tiffany ad is meant to put hip-hop culture in the service of promoting a luxury that is unattainable to the masses.

Jay-Z is a fan of Basquiat. In 2013, he bought the artist's 1982 *Mecca* at Sotheby's auction for $4.2 million.[58] Whatever Jay-Z thinks of Basquiat's artistry, one thing is clear: owning a Basquiat is a prudent financial investment. In May 2016, one of Basquiat's paintings from his "Head" series sold for an astounding $57 million. The next year, a Basquiat *Untitled* piece from 1982 sold for a staggering $110.5 million. This purchase price remains one of the highest figures ever for a painting.[59]

Hip-hop culture has gone pop beyond anyone's wildest dreams. Yet one can't help but remember its hardscrabble roots on Sedgwick Avenue in 1973 in the South Bronx. While hip-hop is now at the forefront of capitalist culture, fifty years ago it was on its margins, if not in direct opposition to its exploits. Hip-hop was a space for b-boys, DJs, graffiti artists, music-heads, and clubbers who wanted to imagine a world beyond the grim one they inherited, a world filled with freedom and possibility.

CONCLUSION

On May 25, 2020, a forty-six-year-old Black man walked out of a Cup Foods store on Chicago Avenue and East Thirty-Eighth Street, in Minneapolis, Minnesota. He had given the store clerk twenty dollars and then got into his parked car. The clerk, believing that the twenty-dollar bill was a counterfeit, called the local police. When the police arrived, they pulled the man out of the car and handcuffed him face down on the ground. One white Minneapolis police officer by the name of Derek Chauvin, who had already been the subject of over a dozen complaints and had been involved in three fatal police shootings, put his knee on the man's neck. And held it there.

The man's name was George Perry Floyd. He was six foot seven, and in the early 1990s had been a star tight end for the Jack Yates High School football team in Houston, where from the age of two he had been raised. (He was arguably an even more talented basketball player and had accepted a scholarship to play for South Florida State College, where he played for several years before returning home to Houston.) Floyd, known to classmates as the "Big Friendly," begged Derek Chauvin to stop. He couldn't breathe. Floyd had come a long way by 2020—between 1997 and 2004, he had several stints in jail for drug possession and aggravated robbery. Between 2009 and 2013, he was incarcerated. After he was paroled, however, Floyd became a staple of his community in Houston. One of his main tasks was to help a local pastor, Patrick Ngwolo, assist residents of Cuney Homes, a five-hundred-unit apartment complex south of downtown Houston known as "The Bricks." Floyd delivered groceries to the elderly and played pickup basketball with local youth. In 2014, he moved to Minneapolis, where he worked as a security guard at the Salvation Army's

Harbor Light Center, the city's largest homeless shelter, before working as a truck driver and bouncer at the Conga Club. "He would regularly walk a couple of female co-workers out at night and make sure they got to their cars safely and securely," said someone who worked with him at the shelter. "Just a big strong guy, but with a very tender side."[1]

Derek Chauvin saw none of that when he restrained George Floyd. As Chauvin pressed his knee onto Floyd's neck, Floyd called for his mother and gasped, "I can't breathe," over and over again. He begged, but Chauvin pressed on for nine minutes and twenty-nine seconds.

George Floyd was part of the hip-hop generation. Known as "Big Floyd" around Houston, he would rap alongside Robert Earl Davis Jr., known as DJ Screw, and was part of the Screwed Up Click. Floyd's time in prison and his iterant work life were products of a post-1970s era when mass incarceration became the solution to deindustrialization across the nation, a period where prisons were being built at a higher rate than good-paying jobs were becoming available.

Floyd's murder was not the only high-profile killing of an unarmed Black citizen that year. On February 23, 2020, Ahmaud Arbery, a twenty-five-year-old jogger in Brunswick, Georgia, was gunned down by two white men in broad daylight. On March 13, 2020, a twenty-six-year-old medical technician, Breonna Taylor, was shot to death in her apartment in Louisville, Kentucky, as law enforcement officers stormed into her home while executing a no-knock warrant.

George Floyd's murder was caught on camera. The video went viral. Several months into the global COVID-19 pandemic, it became a catalyst for the largest social justice protests since the 1960s. Millions took to the streets. They chanted, "Black lives matter!" The phrase "Say their names" became a rallying cry for remembering the Black men and women killed by law enforcement over the previous decade. The list is long, but the most well known, in addition to Floyd, Arbery, and Taylor, are Michael Brown, Eric Garner, Philando Castile, Alton Sterling, Michelle Cusseaux, India Kager, and Korryn Gaines. As these 2020 protests began to unfold, it became clear that young people would create their own counterculture in response, one suitable for this moment. This counterculture's central idea would be racial justice.

■　■　■

A twenty-seven-year-old Black woman, Johnniqua Charles, sought to reenter a strip club in Dillon, South Carolina, where she had left her purse. On her way back, Charles was apprehended by a security guard, Julius Locklear, who handcuffed her. "You About to Lose Yo Job," Charles raps to Locklear, as she dances. The amateur music video of Charles went viral, and became a protest song that summer, showing up in Black Lives Matter marches across the globe.

On June 8, 2020, six blocks of Seattle, Washington, came to be known as the Capitol Hill Autonomous Zone (also known as the Capitol Hill Organized Protest, or CHOP). At two intersections of Cal Anderson Park, CHOP had a community garden, free food, hand sanitizer, and an area of couches called the "Decolonization Conversation Café." At CHOP, there were teach-ins and speeches at night.[2] A "Black Lives Matter" mural lined several streets. CHOP activists demanded a 50 percent cut to police funding and an increase in restorative justice efforts. CHOP was a police-free zone.

Inspired by CHOP's example, ten days later, in Portland, Oregon, on the night of June 18, 2020, the Patrick Kimmons Autonomous Zone, named after a twenty-seven-year-old Black man shot by Portland police in September 2018, was created. According to one participant, it was "pretty magical."[3] That magic dissipated five hours later, when at 5:30 a.m. the following morning police took it apart. Four days later, on June 22, in Washington, DC, just north of Lafayette Square, activists set up a Black House Autonomous Zone, to stand in contrast to the White House, then occupied by Republican Donald Trump.

After the Black House Autonomous Zone was demolished the following morning, Donald Trump took to Twitter to warn protesters that they would be met with "serious force" if they deigned to rebuild it. Trump had a similar response to the Seattle CHOP, when he threatened to "take back" the zone through force and expunge it of its so-called anarchist influence.

The right-wing firestorm against these autonomous zones in summer 2020 was fierce. 2020 was an election year, and as public opinion seemed to be shifting against them, Republican leaders saw a unique opportunity to paint Democrats as soft on crime, and to call themselves the party of law and order.

Yet the counterculture kept going. CHOP was the inspiration for a Philadelphia crowd of one hundred, composed of nurses and patients, who set up their own autonomous zone on June 27, 2020. Health workers occupied the entrance of the shuttered Hahnemann Hospital. Banners that declared "Care Not Cops" were hanging next to a makeshift health-care tent, where health-care workers—who had toiled long hours with little compensation during the harrowing first months of the COVID-19 pandemic—treated patients in the community for free. It was dismantled by police the next day.

In late June 2020, an encampment of one hundred people in New York's City Hall Park called "Occupy City Hall," emerged. Activists demanded the NYPD budget be cut by $1 billion. They set up tents with medicine, food, and water stations. On July 22, on the order of Democratic mayor Bill de Blasio, police in riot gear cleared the area. "We do always respect the right to protest, but we have to think about health and safety first, and the health and safety issues were growing," de Blasio stated. "So it was time to take action."[4] Seattle's CHOP had a similar fate. On the morning of July 1, 2020, Seattle Democratic mayor Jenny Durkan issued an executive order allowing police to clear the area. Law enforcement swarmed CHOP, took down the barricades, and arrested thirty people.

The 2020 protests, marked by youth practicing mutual aid, direct action, and democratic reciprocity, were yet another example of how the American counterculture can always crop up during unexpected moments. For a brief moment, it seemed like their message was bearing political fruit. In June 2020, nine of thirteen Minneapolis City Council members pledged to dismantle the police. Milwaukee, New York, and Portland followed suit. Austin, Texas, cut $20 million from its policing budget, San Francisco pledged that over the course of five years it would shift $120 million away from police and toward health-care programs and workforce training.[5]

These political shifts were short-lived. After Democrat Joe Biden was elected in November 2020 on the promise of restoring national unity and civility, he began to position himself as a pro–law enforcement president. A year later, when the question of police reform was put on the ballot to Minneapolis voters, 56 percent rejected the proposal. By 2022, New York City's police budget increased slightly. New York wasn't an outlier. From 2021 to 2022, a survey of 109 budgets in major cities revealed that 91 of them had increased police budgets by an average of 2 percent.[6]

■　■　■

Historical comparisons are essential, but the parallels between the present and the past might be more complicated than cynics would admit.

Yes, the anarchist movement of the early twentieth century was used as the pretext for FBI director J. Edgar Hoover's nativist anti-immigrant campaigns, but it was also anarchism that inspired bohemian intellectuals to take a central role in the peace movement during the First World War. Similarly, Black communists of the 1930s became an easy target for red-baiting McCarthyites in the 1950s during the Red Scare, but they were also central in raising awareness about issues of imperialism that inspired a generation of radical intellectuals in the 1960s. Certainly, one can argue that the hippie movement's Summer of Love of 1967 and the Democratic National Convention protests of 1968 inadvertently helped elect Richard Nixon in 1968, but they also helped end the Vietnam War. The Black Arts Movement was at the center of the US's assault on radical Black organizations in the early 1970s, but it also produced the vocabulary that informed Black feminism, which, in turn, inspired the Black Lives Matter protests of 2020.

The countercultural experiments we saw in 2020 are still barely in the rearview mirror. It's hard to tell what kind of reforms they might yet catalyze, what art they will create, what visions they will inspire. With history as our guide, the only thing that we can be sure of is that new counter-cultures will arise. Maybe not tomorrow, or the day after. But eventually. This is because dissent will always percolate, opposition will forever exist, and future generations will be unsatisfied with the world as it exists. They will resist. Their resistance will lead to demands for change, which will morph into unruly experiments in feeling, thought, and action. These people, many of them young—though some of them not so young—will join movements that demand individual freedom. They will connect this aspiration of individual freedom to collective liberation.

The countercultures that are created will be what they've always been: messy, perplexing, frustrating, sparkling, and enlivening. They will never be boring. They will feel fresh. They will arise from unexpected encounters, without premeditation. They will sell out and be reborn. They will be the subject of scathing criticism from the inside and outside. They will police themselves and will be policed by society.

The counterculture will imagine utopian worlds and betray those visions. The quest for revolutionary freedom will be at its core. The counterculture will leave a lasting imprint on the world. It will change our meaning of political possibility.

ACKNOWLEDGMENTS

This book would have been impossible without the support of many friends, family, and colleagues. I would like to thank my colleagues and students at the University of Detroit Mercy and Rutgers University. Special thanks also go to my dear friends Nick Rombes and Alix Olson. The folks at Beacon Press have been a joy to work with—Susan Lumenello, Emily Powers, and Marcy Barnes. I cannot ask for a more insightful and brilliant editor, Rachael Marks. I am forever grateful and honored for your support. Finally, I dedicate this book to my partner, Alison Powell, and my children, Sam and Anita. I cannot begin to express my gratitude for having you in my life.

NOTES

INTRODUCTION

1. Isaiah Berlin, *Two Concepts of Liberty* (Oxford: Oxford University Press, 1966).

2. Theodore Roszak, *The Making of a Counter Culture: Reflections on the Technocratic Society and Its Youthful Opposition* (1969; repr., Berkeley: University of California Press, 1995).

3. Harold D. Lasswell, *Politics: Who Gets What, When, How* (New York: Whittlesey, 1936).

CHAPTER 1: I CONTAIN MULTITUDES

1. David S. Reynolds, *Walt Whitman's America: A Cultural Biography* (New York, Knopf: 1995), 300.

2. Reynolds, *Walt Whitman's America*, 357.

3. George J. Lankevich, *New York City: A Short History* (New York: New York University Press, 2002), 75.

4. Justin Kaplan, *Walt Whitman: A Life* (New York: Harper, 2003), 108.

5. Cited in Michael Fitzgibbon Holt, *The Fate of Their Country: Politicians, Slavery Extension, and the Coming Civil War* (New York: Hill and Wang, 2004), 141.

6. Cited in Alin Fumurescu, *Compromise and the American Founding: The Quest for the People's Two Bodies* (New York: Cambridge University Press, 2019), 211.

7. Walt Whitman, *Leaves of Grass* (New York: Modern Library of America, 1954), 29.

8. Reynolds, *Walt Whitman's America*, 341.

9. Reynolds, *Walt Whitman's America*, 228.

10. Robert Owen, *A New View of Society* (New York: Everyman's Library, 1927), 37.

11. Chris Jennings, *Paradise Now: The Story of American Utopianism* (New York: Random House, 2016), 124.

12. Cited in Lawrence Foster, "Free Love and Feminism: John Humphrey Noyes and the Oneida Community," *Journal of the Early Republic* 1, no. 2 (Summer 1981): 170.

13. Kaplan, *Walt Whitman*, 58.

14. Kaplan, *Walt Whitman*, 57.

15. Reynolds, *Walt Whitman's America*, 104.

16. Reynolds, *Walt Whitman's America*, 106.

17. Kaplan, *Walt Whitman,* 101.

18. Kaplan, *Walt Whitman,* 101.

19. Ralph Waldo Emerson, "Self-Reliance," in *Self-Reliance and Other Essays* (New York: Dover, 2019), 21.

20. Alan M. Levine and Daniel S. Malachuk, *A Political Companion to Ralph Waldo Emerson* (Lexington: University Press of Kentucky, 2011), 5.

21. Ralph Waldo Emerson, "Politics," in *Emerson: Political Writings,* ed. Kenneth Sacks (New York: Cambridge University Press, 2008), 117.

22. Henry David Thoreau, *Walden* (New York: Oxford University Press, 1999), 8.

23. Jennings, *Paradise Now,* 194.

24. Jennings, *Paradise Now,* 198.

25. Jennings, *Paradise Now,* 200.

26. Jennings, *Paradise Now,* 195.

27. Joanna Levin, *Bohemia in America, 1858–1920* (Palo Alto, CA: Stanford University Press, 2009), 16.

28. Levin, *Bohemia in America,* 16.

29. Levin, *Bohemia in America,* 38.

30. Levin, *Bohemia in America,* 29.

31. Levin, *Bohemia in America,* 33.

32. Reynolds, *Walt Whitman's America,* 377.

33. Reynolds, *Walt Whitman's America,* 405.

34. Kaplan, *Walt Whitman,* 133.

35. See Amanda Gailey, "Walt Whitman and the King of Bohemia," in *Whitman Among the Bohemians,* ed. Joanna Levin and Edward Whitley (Iowa City: University of Iowa Press, 2014), 30.

36. Reynolds, *Walt Whitman's America,* 443.

37. Reynolds, *Walt Whitman's America,* 454.

38. Reynolds, *Walt Whitman's America,* 454–55.

39. Jennings, *Paradise Now,* 126.

40. Reynolds, *Walt Whitman's America,* 456.

41. Reynolds, *Walt Whitman's America,* 464.

42. Cited in Ivy G. Wilson, "Slavery and Abolition," in *Walt Whitman in Context,* ed. Joanna Levin and Edward Whitley (New York: Cambridge University Press, 2018), 297.

43. Reynolds, *Walt Whitman's America,* 466.

44. Reynolds, *Walt Whitman's America,* 466.

45. Reynolds, *Walt Whitman's America,* 470–71.

46. Reynolds, *Walt Whitman's America,* 469.

47. Kaplan, *Walt Whitman,* 12.

48. Reynolds, *Walt Whitman's America,* 496.

49. Reynolds, *Walt Whitman's America,* 516.

50. Reynolds, *Walt Whitman's America,* 535.

51. "Sylvester Baxter to Walt Whitman," Walt Whitman Archive, July 13, 1888, https://whitmanarchive.org/biography/correspondence/tei/loc.07103.html.

52. Michael Robertson, *The Last Utopians: Four Late Nineteenth-Century Visionaries and Their Legacy* (Princeton, NJ: Princeton University Press, 2018), 39.

53. Robertson, *The Last Utopians,* 33.

54. Rebecca Zurier, Elise K. Kenney, and Earl Davis, *Art for the Masses: A Radical Magazine and Its Graphics, 1911–1917* (Philadelphia, Temple University Press, 1989), 69–70.

55. Cited in Ralph Edward McCoy, *Banned in Boston: The Development of Literary Censorship in Massachusetts* (Champaign: University of Illinois Press, 1954), 107.

56. Steve J. Shone, *American Anarchism* (New York: Brill, 2013), 18.

CHAPTER 2: REBEL MISFITS

1. Emma Goldman, *Living My Life* (New York: Penguin, 2006), 3.

2. Goldman, *Living My Life*, 17.

3. Goldman, *Living My Life*, 17.

4. George J. Lankevich, *New York City: A Short History* (New York: New York University Press, 1998), 122.

5. Lankevich, *New York City*, 122.

6. Lankevich, *New York City*, 128.

7. Lankevich, *New York City*, 129.

8. Goldman, *Living My Life*, 5.

9. Goldman, *Living My Life*, 5.

10. Karen Avrich, *Sasha and Emma: The Anarchist Odyssey of Alexander Berkman and Emma Goldman* (Cambridge, MA: Belknap Press of Harvard University Press, 2012), 18.

11. Goldman, *Living My Life*, 20.

12. Eric Hobsbawm, *The Age of Empire, 1875–1914* (New York: Pantheon, 1987), 179.

13. Lankevich, *New York City*, 126.

14. Lankevich, *New York City*, 126.

15. Kenyon Zimmer, *Immigrants Against the State: Yiddish and Italian Anarchism in America* (Chicago: University of Illinois Press, 2015).

16. Emma Goldman, *Anarchism: What It Really Stands For* (New York: Mother Earth, 1910).

17. See Candace Falk, *Love, Anarchy, and Emma Goldman: A Biography* (New Brunswick, NJ: Rutgers University Press, 2019), 27–31.

18. Avrich, *Sasha and Emma*, 38.

19. Falk, *Love, Anarchy, and Emma Goldman*, 89.

20. Goldman, *Living My Life*.

21. Goldman, *Living My Life*, 37.

22. Avrich, *Sasha and Emma*, 79.

23. Avrich, *Sasha and Emma*, 67.

24. Avrich, *Sasha and Emma*, 77.

25. Avrich, *Sasha and Emma*, 79.

26. See Voltairine de Cleyre, *Selected Works*, https://theanarchistlibrary.org/library/voltairine-de-cleyre-selected-works-of-voltairine-de-cleyre.

27. Paul Avrich, *An American Anarchist: The Life of Voltairine de Cleyre* (Oakland: AK Press, 2018).

28. Avrich, *An American Anarchist*.

29. Avrich, *An American Anarchist*.

30. Avrich, *An American Anarchist*.

31. Goldman, *Living My Life*, 193.

32. "Early Chicago, 1833-1871," Office of the Illinois Secretary of State, https://www.ilsos.gov/departments/archives/teaching_packages/early_chicago/doc23.html.

33. Jacqueline Jones, *Goddess of Anarchy: The Life and Times of Lucy Parsons, American Radical* (New York: Basic Books, 2017).

34. Jones, *Goddess of Anarchy*.

35. Jones, *Goddess of Anarchy*.

36. Jones, *Goddess of Anarchy*.

37. Jones, *Goddess of Anarchy*.

38. Falk, *Love, Anarchy, and Emma Goldman*, 101-2.

39. Falk, *Love, Anarchy, and Emma Goldman*, 101-2.

40. Falk, *Love, Anarchy, and Emma Goldman*, 113.

41. Falk, *Love, Anarchy, and Emma Goldman*, 108.

42. Falk, *Love, Anarchy, and Emma Goldman*, 142.

43. Falk, *Love, Anarchy, and Emma Goldman*, 142.

44. Eric Hobsbawm, *The Age of Empire, 1875-1914* (New York: Vintage, 1987), 30.

45. Hobsbawm, *The Age of Empire*, 205.

46. David Kennedy, *Birth Control in America: The Career of Margaret Sanger* (New Haven, CT: Yale University Press, 1971), 12.

47. Paul Avrich, *The Modern School Movement: Anarchism and Education in the United States* (Princeton, NJ: Princeton University Press, 1980), 80.

48. Avrich, *The Modern School Movement*, 74.

49. Rebecca Zurier, Elise K. Kenney, and Earl Davis, *Art for the Masses: A Radical Magazine and Its Graphics, 1911-1917* (Philadelphia: Temple University Press, 1988), 67.

50. Emma Goldman, *Anarchism: What It Really Stands For* (New York: Mother Earth, 1910).

51. Avrich, *The Modern School*, 88.

52. Avrich, *The Modern School*, 85.

53. Avrich, *The Modern School*, 102.

54. Avrich, *Sasha and Emma*, 229.

55. Kenneth Z. Chutchian, *John Reed: Radical Journalist, 1887-1920* (Jefferson, NC: McFarland, 2019), 85.

56. Avrich, *Sasha and Emma*, 235.

57. Avrich, *Sasha and Emma*, 225-35.

CHAPTER 3: PATRONS OF THE REVOLUTION

1. See Joanna Levin, *Bohemia in America, 1858-1920* (Palo Alto, CA: Stanford University Press, 2009), 339-95.

2. Rebecca Zurier, Elise K. Kenney, and Earl Davis, *Art for the Masses: A Radical Magazine and Its Graphics, 1911-1917* (Philadelphia: Temple University Press, 1988), 79.

3. Zurier, Kenney, and Davis, *Art for the Masses*, 82.

4. Zurier, Kenney, and Davis, *Art for the Masses*, 77.

5. Zurier, Kenney, and Davis, *Art for the Masses*, 83.

6. Zurier, Kenney, and Davis, *Art for the Masses*, 84.

7. Zurier, Kenney, and Davis, *Art for the Masses*, 77.

8. Christoph Irmscher, *Max Eastman: A Life* (New Haven, CT: Yale University Press, 2017), 209.

9. Irmscher, *Max Eastman*, 105.

10. Jay Sherry, "Beatrice Hinkle and the Early History of Jungian Psychology in New York," *Behavioral Science* 3, no. 3 (September 2013): 492–500.

11. Zurier, Kenney, and Davis, *Art for the Masses,* 79.

12. Robert Rosenstone, "Mabel Dodge: Evenings in New York," in *The Genius in the Drawing Room: The Salon in Europe and America from the 18th to the 20th Century,* ed. Peter Quennell (London: Weidenfeld and Nicolson, 1980), 131–51.

13. Rosenstone, "Mabel Dodge."

14. Rosenstone, "Mabel Dodge."

15. Gerald MacFarland, *Inside Greenwich Village: A New York City Neighborhood, 1898–1918* (Amherst: University of Massachusetts Press, 2001), 125.

16. Lauren Kroiz, *Creative Composites: Modernism, Race, and the Stieglitz Circle* (Berkeley: University of California Press, 2012), 25.

17. Kroiz, *Creative Composites: Modernism, Race, and the Stieglitz Circle*, 25.

18. Linda M. Grasso, *Equal Under the Sky: Georgia O'Keeffe and Twentieth-Century Feminism* (Albuquerque: University of New Mexico Press, 2019), 51.

19. Kroiz, *Creative Composites*, 36.

20. Kroiz, *Creative Composites*, 54.

21. Edith Evans Asbury, "Georgia O'Keeffe Dead at 98; Shaper of Modern Art in US," *New York Times*, March 7, 1986.

22. Grasso, *Equal Under the Sky*, 4.

23. Zurier, Kenney, and Davis, *Art for the Masses*, 67.

24. Zurier, Kenney, and Davis, *Art for the Masses*, 71.

25. Leslie Fishbein, "The Paterson Pageant (1913): The Birth of Docudrama as a Weapon in the Class Struggle," *New York History* 72, no. 2 (April 1991): 197–233.

26. David M. Kennedy, *Birth Control in America: The Career of Margaret Sanger* (New Haven, CT: Yale University Press, 1970).

27. Kennedy, *Birth Control in America*.

28. Eric Hobsbawm, *The Age of Empire, 1875–1914* (New York: Vintage, 1987), 192–219.

29. Cheryl Black, *The Women of Provincetown, 1915–1922* (Tuscaloosa: University of Alabama Press, 2002).

30. Black, *The Women of Provincetown*.

31. Black, *The Women of Provincetown*.

32. Black, *The Women of Provincetown*.

33. Black, *The Women of Provincetown*.

34. Patricia A. Carter, "From Single to Married: Feminist Teachers' Response to Family/Work Conflict in Early Twentieth-Century New York City," *History of Education Quarterly* 56 (2016): 36–60.

35. Carter, "From Single to Married," 3.

36. Carter, "From Single to Married," 4.

37. Gerald W. McFarland, *Inside Greenwich Village: A New York City Neighborhood, 1898–1918* (Amherst: University of Massachusetts Press, 2001), 200.

38. Margaret Sanger, *An Autobiography* (New York: Norton, 1938), 109.

39. Sanger, *An Autobiography*, 91.

40. Sanger, *An Autobiography*, 92.

41. Kennedy, *Birth Control in America*, 34.

42. Kennedy, *Birth Control in America*, 35.

43. Kennedy, *Birth Control in America*, 44.

44. Kennedy, *Birth Control in America*, 116.

45. Kennedy, *Birth Control in America*.

46. Kennedy, *Birth Control in America*.

47. Michael Robertson, *The Last Utopians: Four Late Nineteenth-Century Visionaries and Their Legacy* (Princeton, NJ: Princeton University Press, 2018), 101.

48. Robertson, *The Last Utopians*, 101.

49. Zurier, Kenney, and Davis, *Art for the Masses*, 74.

50. Zurier, Kenney, and Davis, *Art for the Masses*, 26.

51. Zurier, Kenney, and Davis, *Art for the Masses*, 74.

52. Richard Bernstein, "The Philosopher and the Millionaire," in *A New Literary History of America*, ed. Greil Marcus and Werner Sollors (Cambridge, MA: Harvard University Press, 2009), 540–45.

53. Bernstein, "The Philosopher and the Millionaire," 207, 209.

54. Zurier, Kenney, and Davis, *Art for the Masses*, 35.

55. Zurier, Kenney, and Davis, *Art for the Masses*, 32.

56. Zurier, Kenney, and Davis, *Art for the Masses*, 33

57. Zurier, Kenney, and Davis, *Art for the Masses*, 33.

58. Zurier, Kenney, and Davis, *Art for the Masses*, 35.

59. Irmscher, *Max Eastman*, 125.

60. Irmscher, *Max Eastman*, 128.

61. V. I. Lenin, introduction to John Reed, *Ten Days That Shook the World* (New York: Boni and Liveright, 1922).

62. John Reed, *Ten Days That Shook the World* (New York: Boni and Liveright, 1919), vii.

63. Falk, *Love, Anarchy, and Emma Goldman*, 232.

64. Emma Goldman, preface to *My Disillusionment in Russia* (New York: Doubleday, 1923), https://theanarchistlibrary.org/library/emma-goldman-my-disillusionment-in-russia.

CHAPTER 4: BELOVED COMMUNITIES

1. Paula Marie Seniors, *Beyond Lift Every Voice and Sing: The Culture of Uplift, Identity, and Politics in Black Musical Theater* (Columbus: Ohio State University Press, 2017), 23.

2. Mike Wallace, *Greater Gotham: A History of New York City from 1898 to 1919* (New York: Oxford University Press, 2017), 817.

3. Wallace, *Greater Gotham*, 816.

4. See Reynolds J. Scott-Childress, "Paul Laurence Dunbar, New Yorker," *New York History* 92, no. 3 (2011): 167–208.

5. James Weldon Johnson, *Black Manhattan* (Charlottesville: University of Virginia, 1968), 119.

6. James Weldon Johnson, *The Autobiography of an Ex-Colored Man* (New York: Dover Books, 1995), 45.

7. Johnson, *The Autobiography of an Ex-Colored Man*, 60.

8. See David Gilbert, *The Product of Our Souls: Ragtime, Race, and the Birth of the Manhattan Musical Marketplace* (Chapel Hill: University of North Carolina Press, 2015), 41.

9. Paul Laurence Dunbar, *The Sport of the Gods* (New York: Dodd, Mead, 1902), 82.

10. "Star Spangled Banner," Library of Congress, https://www.loc.gov/item/ihas .200000017.

11. Seniors, *Beyond Lift Every Voice and Sing*, 15.

12. Seniors, *Beyond Lift Every Voice and Sing*, 16.

13. Seniors, *Beyond Lift Every Voice and Sing*, 35.

14. Gilbert, *The Product of Our Souls*, 106.

15. Seniors, *Beyond Lift Every Voice and Sing*, 40.

16. Seniors, *Beyond Lift Every Voice and Sing*, 126.

17. Frances E. W. Harper, *Iola Leroy, or Shadows Uplifted* (Philadelphia: Garrigues Brothers, 1892), 279.

18. Harper, *Iola Leroy*, 279.

19. Utz McKnight, *Frances E. W. Harper: A Call to Conscience* (London: Polity Press, 2020), 18.

20. Hazel Carby, introduction to Pauline Hopkins, *The Magazine Novels of Pauline Hopkins* (New York: Oxford University, 1988), xxxii.

21. Pauline Hopkins, *Of One Blood. Or, the Hidden Self*, in *The Magazine Novels*, 568.

22. Sutton E. Griggs, *Imperium in Imperio* (New York: Modern Library, 2004), 144.

23. Griggs, *Imperium in Imperio*, 149.

24. Edward A. Johnson, *Light Ahead for the Negro* (New York: The Grafton Press, 1904), 80.

25. W. E. B. Du Bois, "The Comet," in *Darkwater: Voices from Within the Veil* (New York: Dover, 1999), 157.

CHAPTER 5: LOST AND FOUND

1. James Weldon Johnson, *Black Manhattan* (Charlottesville: University of Virginia, 1968), 145.

2. David Levering Lewis, *When Harlem Was in Vogue* (New York: Penguin, 1981), 21.

3. Stephen Robertson, "Constrained but Not Confined: Patterns of Everyday Life and the Limits of Segregation in 1920 Harlem," in *The Ghetto in Global History*, ed. Wendy Z. Goldman and Joe William Trotter (New York: Routledge, 2017), 223–38.

4. Gilbert Osofsky, "A Decade of Urban Tragedy: How Harlem Became a Slum," *New York History* 46, no. 4 (October 1965): 339.

5. Osofsky, "A Decade of Urban Tragedy," 345.

6. Osofsky, "A Decade of Urban Tragedy," 344.

7. Langston Hughes, *The Big Sea: An Autobiography* (New York: Farrar, Straus and Giroux, 1993), 39.

8. Cited in Arnold Rampersad, *The Life of Langston Hughes*, vol. 1, *1902–1941, I: Too, Sing America* (New York: Oxford University Press, 1986), 53.

9. Hughes, *The Big Sea*, 41.

10. Rampersad, *The Life of Langston Hughes*, 46.

11. Rampersad, *The Life of Langston Hughes*, 46.

12. Rampersad, *The Life of Langston Hughes*, 19.

13. Rampersad, *The Life of Langston Hughes*, 19.

14. Rampersad, *The Life of Langston Hughes*, 69.

15. Carl Van Vechten, "Introducing Langston Hughes to the Reader," in Langston Hughes, *The Weary Blues* (New York: Alfred A. Knopf, 1926), xii.

16. Hughes, *Weary Blues*, 24.

17. Hughes, "Epilogue," *Weary Blues*, 109.

18. Langston Hughes, "Songs Called the Blues," *Phylon* 2, no. 2 (1941): 143–45.

19. Rampersad, *The Life of Langston Hughes*, 123.

20. "Columbia Matrix 81226. Jailhouse Blues/Bessie Smith," *Discography of American Historical Recordings*, UC Santa Barbara Library, February 9, 2024.

21. "Columbia Matrix W146895. Poor Man's Blues/Bessie Smith," *Discography of American Historical Recordings*, UC Santa Barbara Library, February 9, 2024.

22. Hughes, *The Big Sea*, 242.

23. Charles Larson, *Invisible Darkness: Jean Toomer and Nella Larsen* (Des Moines: University of Iowa Press, 1993) 170.

24. Larson, *Invisible Darkness*, 170.

25. Larson, *Invisible Darkness*, 171.

26. Barbara Foley, *Jean Toomer: Race, Repression, and Revolution* (Champaign-Urbana: University of Illinois Press, 2014), 20.

27. Foley, *Jean Toomer*, 21.

28. Foley, *Jean Toomer*, 26.

29. Equal Justice Initiative, *Lynching in America*, 3rd ed. (Montgomery, AL: EJI, 2017), 39, https://eji.org/wp-content/uploads/2005/11/lynching-in-america-3d-ed-110121.pdf.

30. Jean Toomer, *Cane* (New York: Boni and Liveright, 1923), 99.

31. Larson, *Invisible Darkness*, 22.

32. Larson, *Invisible Darkness*, 36.

33. Cited in Ismail Muhammad, "How Jean Toomer Rejected the Black-White Binary," *Paris Review*, January 14, 2019, https://www.theparisreview.org/blog/2019/01/14/how-jean-toomer-rejected-the-black-white-binary.

34. Larson, *Invisible Darkness*, 44.

35. Hughes, *The Big Sea*, 243.

36. Larson, *Invisible Darkness*, 42.

37. Wayne F. Cooper, *Claude McKay: A Rebel Sojourner in the Harlem Renaissance* (New York: Schocken Books, 1990), 160.

38. Joy Gleason Carew, *Blacks, Reds, and Russians: Sojourners in Search of the Soviet Promise* (New Brunswick, NJ: Rutgers University Press, 2010), 16.

39. Claude McKay, *A Long Way from Home* (New Brunswick, NJ: Rutgers University Press, 2007), 29.

40. Rampersad, *The Life of Langston Hughes*, 30.

41. McKay, *A Long Way from Home*, 30.

42. Claude McKay, *Harlem Shadows* (New York: Harcourt, Brace, 1922), 53.

43. Cooper, *Claude McKay*, 161.

44. See Andrew Gene Jarrett, *Representing the Race: A New Political History of African American Literature* (New York: New York University Press, 2011), 108.

45. Cooper, *Claude McKay*, 179.

46. Cited in Steven S. Lee, *Ethnic Avant-Garde: Minority Cultures and World Revolution* (New York: Columbia University Press, 2015), 19.

47. Cooper, *Claude McKay*, 179–82.

CHAPTER 6: FRUITS OF SPLENDOR

1. Cooper, *Claude McKay*, 225.

2. Alain Locke, *The New Negro Aesthetic: Selected Writings* (New York: Penguin, 2022), 13.

3. David Levering Lewis, "Dr. Johnson's Friends: Civil Rights by Copyright During Harlem's Mid-Twenties," *Massachusetts Review* 20, no. 3 (1979): 501–19.

4. Quoted in Barbara Foley, *Spectres of 1919: Class and Nation in the Making of the New Negro* (Champaign-Urbana: University of Illinois Press, 2008), 34.

5. Rampersad, *The Life of Langston Hughes*, 160.

6. Cooper, *Claude McKay*, 244.

7. Cooper, *Claude McKay*, 244.

8. Eric H. Newman, "Ephemeral Utopias: Queer Cruising, Literary Form, and Diasporic Imagination in Claude McKay's 'Home to Harlem' and 'Banjo,'" *Callaloo* 38, no. 1 (2015): 167–85.

9. Gary Edward Holcomb, *Claude McKay, Code Name Sasha: Queer Black Marxism and the Harlem Renaissance* (Gainesville: University Press of Florida, 2007), 96.

10. George Chauncey, *Gay New York: Gender, Urban Culture, and the Making of the Gay Male World, 1890–1940* (New York: Basic Books, 2008), 244.

11. Chauncey, *Gay New York*, 249.

12. Chauncey, *Gay New York*, 258.

13. Jeffrey B. Ferguson, *The Sage of Sugar Hill: George S. Schuyler and the Harlem Renaissance* (New Haven, CT: Yale University Press, 2005), 76.

14. Hughes, *The Big Sea*, 273.

15. Hughes, *The Big Sea*, 243.

16. Hughes, *The Big Sea*, 248.

17. Hughes, *The Big Sea*, 254.

18. Bruce Nugent, *Gay Rebel of the Harlem Renaissance: Selections from the Work of Richard Bruce Nugent* (Durham, NC: Duke University Press, 2002), 21.

19. Rampersad, *The Life of Langston Hughes*, 70.

20. Farah Jasmine Griffin, "On Time, in Time, Through Time: Aaron Douglas, *Fire!!* and the Writers of the Harlem Renaissance," *American Studies* 49, nos. 1/2 (Spring/Summer 2008): 45–53.

21. Nugent, *Gay Rebel of the Harlem Renaissance*, 81.

22. Langston Hughes, "The Negro Artist and the Racial Mountain," *The Nation*, June 23, 1926.

23. Valerie Boyd, *Wrapped in Rainbows: The Life of Zora Neale Hurston* (New York: Scribner, 2003), 99.

24. Boyd, *Wrapped in Rainbows*, 30.

25. Boyd, *Wrapped in Rainbows*, 38.

26. Boyd, *Wrapped in Rainbows*, 53.

27. Boyd, *Wrapped in Rainbows*, 81.

28. Boyd, *Wrapped in Rainbows*, 94.

29. Zora Neale Hurston, "How It Feels to Be Colored Me," in *The Norton Anthology of American Literature: 1914–1945*, ed. Henry Louis Gates Jr. and Valerie Smith (New York: W. W. Norton, 2014).

30. Cited in Hughes, *The Big Sea*, 240.

31. Zora Neale Hurston, *I Love Myself When I Am Laughing . . . and Then Again When I Am Looking Mean and Impressive* (New York: Feminist Press, 2010).

32. Hurston, "How It Feels to Be Colored Me."

33. Hurston, "How It Feels to Be Colored Me."

34. Hurston, "How It Feels to Be Colored Me."

35. Hurston, "How It Feels to Be Colored Me."

36. Zora Neale Hurston, "Crazy for This Democracy," in *Zora Neale Hurston: Folklore, Memoirs and Other Writings* (New York: Library of America, 1995), 957.

37. See Ernest Julius Mitchell II, "Zora's Politics: A Brief Introduction," *Journal of Transnational American Studies* 5, no. 1 (2013), http://dx.doi.org/10.5070/T851019732, retrieved from https://escholarship.org/uc/item/38356082.

38. See Mitchell, "Zora's Politics."

39. See Mitchell, "Zora's Politics."

40. Larson, *Invisible Darkness*, 66.

41. Larson, *Invisible Darkness*, 87.

42. Nella Larsen, *Passing* (New York: Dover, 2004), 3.

43. Nella Larsen, *Quicksand* (New York: Penguin, 2002), 49.

44. George Schuyler, *Black No More* (New York: Dover, 2012), 53.

45. Schuyler, *Black No More*, 63.

46. Eleonore van Notten, *Wallace Thurman's Harlem Renaissance* (London: Brill, 1994), 287.

47. Larson, *Invisible Darkness*, 144.

48. Cooper, *Claude McKay*, 351.

49. Rampersad, *The Life of Langston Hughes*, 216.

50. Rampersad, *The Life of Langston Hughes*, 293.

51. Rampersad, *The Life of Langston Hughes*, 293.

52. Gerald Horne, *Paul Robeson: The Artist as Revolutionary* (London: Pluto Press, 2016), 42.

53. Emma Goldman, *Living My Life* (New York: Dover, 1970), 980.

54. Horne, *Paul Robeson*, 3.

55. Horne, *Paul Robeson*, 65–66.

56. Cited in Lindsey Swindall, *Paul Robeson: A Life of Activism and Art* (Landham, MD: Rowman and Littlefield, 2013), 83.

57. Langston Hughes, *The Collected Works of Langston Hughes: Essays on Art, Race, Politics, and World Affairs* (Columbia: University of Missouri Press, 2001), 180.

58. Langston Hughes, *The Collected Works of Langston Hughes*, vol. 5, ed. Leslie Catherine Sanders with Nancy Johnson (Columbia: University of Missouri Press, 2003), 538–70.

59. Hughes, *The Collected Works of Langston Hughes*, vol. 5, 568.

60. Sharon L. Jones, *Rereading the Harlem Renaissance: Race, Class, and Gender in the Fiction of Jessie Fauset, Zora Neale Hurston, and Dorothy West* (New York: Bloomsbury, 2002), 122.

61. Cherene Sherrard-Johnson, *Dorothy West's Paradise: A Biography of Class and Color* (New Brunswick: Rutgers University Press, 2012), 109.

62. Richard Wright, *American Hunger* (New York: Harper and Row, 1977), 115.

63. See Hazel Rowley, *Richard Wright: The Life and Times* (New York: Henry Holt, 2002), 111.

64. Rampersad, *The Life of Langston Hughes*, 383.

65. Rowley, *Richard Wright*, 192.

66. Rowley, *Richard Wright*, 311.

67. James Baldwin, "Many Thousands Gone," in *The Price of the Ticket: Collected Nonfiction: 1948–1985* (Boston: Beacon Press, 2021), 83.

68. Michael Denning, *The Cultural Front: The Laboring of American Culture in the Twentieth Century* (New York: Verso, 1998), 325.

69. Denning, *The Cultural Front*, 327.

70. Angela Y. Davis, *Blues Legacies and Black Feminism: Gertrude "Ma" Rainey, Bessie Smith, and Billie Holiday* (New York: Pantheon Books, 1998), 211.

71. Davis, *Blues Legacies and Black Feminism*, 163.

72. Allen Ginsberg, "Billie Holiday Centennial," The Allen Ginsberg Project, https://allenginsberg.org/2015/04/tuesday-april-7-billie-holiday-centennial.

73. Allen Ginsberg, *Deliberate Prose: Selected Essays, 1952–1995*, ed. Bill Morgan (New York: HarperCollins, 2000), 97.

CHAPTER 7: PROPHETS OF THE LIVING AND THE DEAD

1. Michael Schumacher, *Dharma Lion: A Biography of Allen Ginsberg* (Minneapolis: University of Minnesota Press, 2016), 214.

2. Schumacher, *Dharma Lion*, 216.

3. Schumacher, *Dharma Lion*, 1–47.

4. Lionel Trilling, *The Liberal Imagination: Essays on Literature and Society* (New York: Viking Press, 1950), xi.

5. Allen Ginsberg, *The Letters of Allen Ginsberg* (New York: Hachette Books, 2008), 1.

6. Schumacher, *Dharma Lion*, 15.

7. Schumacher, *Dharma Lion*, 43.

8. Ted Morgan, *Literary Outlaw: The Life and Times of William S. Burroughs* (New York: Norton, 1988), 111.

9. Morgan, *Literary Outlaw*, 96.

10. Schumacher, *Dharma Lion*, 92.

11. Schumacher, *Dharma Lion*, 54.

12. Schumacher, *Dharma Lion*, 44.

13. Schumacher, *Dharma Lion*, 45.

14. Schumacher, *Dharma Lion*, 45.

15. Morgan, *Literary Outlaw*, 117.

16. Morgan, *Literary Outlaw*, 117.

17. James Polchin, "The Queer Crime That Launched the Beats," *Paris Review*, June 27, 2019, https://www.theparisreview.org/blog/2019/06/27/the-queer-crime -that-launched-the-beats.

18. Schumacher, *Dharma Lion*, 55.

19. Schumacher, *Dharma Lion*, 47.

20. Schumacher, *Dharma Lion*, 46.

21. Morgan, *Literary Outlaw*, 118.

22. Morgan, *Literary Outlaw*, 118.

23. Morgan, *Literary Outlaw*, 38.

24. Morgan, *Literary Outlaw*, 114.

25. Polchin, "The Queer Crime That Launched the Beats."

26. Schumacher, *Dharma Lion*, 112.

27. Schumacher, *Dharma Lion*, 112.

28. Schumacher, *Dharma Lion*, 118–22.

29. Schumacher, *Dharma Lion*, 125.

30. Jack Kerouac, *The Town and the City* (New York: HarperCollins, 1970).

31. Neal Cassady, *The Joan Anderson Letter: The Holy Grail of the Beat Genera-tion* (London: Black Spring Press, 2021).

32. David L. Ulin, "The Beats' Holy Grail: The Letter That Inspired *On the Road*," *Literary Hub*, October 5, 2018, https://lithub.com/the-beats-holy-grail-the-letter.

33. Allen Ginsberg, *Howl* (New York: HarperCollins, 1996), 4.

34. Schumacher, *Dharma Lion*, 97.

35. Schumacher, *Dharma Lion*, 65.

36. Morgan, *Literary Outlaw*, 213.

37. William S. Burroughs, *Junky* (New York: Grove, 2012), 110.

38. Paul Varner, *Historical Dictionary of the Beat Movement* (Lanham, MD: Scarecrow Press, 2012), 209.

39. Allen Ginsberg, *Journals: Early Fifties, Early Sixties* (New York: Grove Press, 1977), 80.

40. Diane di Prima, *Recollections of My Life as a Woman: The New York Years* (New York: Viking, 2001), 202.

41. Steven Belletto, *The Beats: A Literary History* (New York: Cambridge Uni-versity Press, 2020), 248.

42. Belletto, *The Beats*, 295.

43. Schumacher, *Dharma Lion*, 258–64.

44. Schumacher, *Dharma Lion*, 261.

45. Schumacher, *Dharma Lion*, 262.

46. James Campbell, *This Is the Beat Generation: New York–San Francisco–Paris* (Berkeley: University of California Press, 2001), 79.

47. Ann Charters and Samuel Charters, *John Clellon Holmes, Jack Kerouac, and the Beat Generation* (Jackson: University Press of Mississippi, 2010), 410.

48. Jack Kerouac, *The Portable Jack Kerouac* (New York: Penguin, 1995), 573.

49. Christopher Orlet, "Why Kerouac's Anti-Semitism Matters," *Hedgehog Re-view*, January 13, 2022, https://hedgehogreview.com/web-features/thr/posts/why -kerouacs-anti-semitism-matters.

50. William S. Burroughs, *The Letters of William S. Burroughs*, vol. 1, *1945–1959* (New York: Penguin, 1993), 57.

51. Jesse Walker, "The Sultan of Sewers," *Reason*, July 2014, https://reason.com/2014/06/04/the-sultan-of-sewers.

52. Burroughs, *The Letters of William S. Burroughs*, vol. 1, 25.

53. Allen Ginsberg, "I Don't See a Conflict Between Political and Meditative Activity," *Ann Arbor Sun*, May 17, 1974, online at https://aadl.org/node/196945.

CHAPTER 8: FLOWERS OR POWER?

1. John Anthony Moretta, *The Hippies: A 1960s History* (Jefferson, NC: MacFarland, 2017).

2. Robert Greenfield, *Timothy Leary: A Biography* (New York: Harcourt, 2006), 303.

3. Alan Watts, Gary Snyder, Timothy Leary, and Allen Ginsberg, "The Houseboat Summit: Changes," *San Francisco Oracle* 1, no. 7 (February 1967): 150–65.

4. Watts, Snyder, Leary, and Ginsberg, "The Houseboat Summit," 150–65.

5. Joan Didion, *Slouching Towards Bethlehem*, in *We Tell Ourselves Stories in Order to Live* (New York: Knopf, 2006), 93.

6. Robert C. Cottrell, *Sex, Drugs, and Rock 'n' Roll: The Rise of 1960s Counterculture* (Landham, MD: Rowman and Littlefield, 2015), 203.

7. Bradford D. Martin, *The Theater Is in the Street: Politics and Performance in Sixties America* (Amherst: University of Massachusetts Press, 2004), 92.

8. Greenfield, *Timothy Leary*, 315.

9. Martin, *The Theater Is in the Street*, 96.

10. Martin, *The Theater Is in the Street*, 86–124.

11. Gerard J. DeGroot, *The Sixties Unplugged: A Kaleidoscopic History of a Disorderly Decade* (Cambridge, MA: Harvard University Press, 2009), 256.

12. Martin, *The Theater Is in the Street*, 17.

13. Charles Perry, *The Haight-Ashbury: A History* (New York: Random House, 1984), 197.

14. Martin, *The Theater Is in the Street*, 107.

15. Martin, *The Theater Is in the Street*, 109.

16. Martin, *The Theater Is in the Street*, 110.

17. Martin, *The Theater Is in the Street*, 91–92.

18. Karen M. Staller, *Runaways: How the Sixties Counterculture Shaped Today's Practices* (New York: Columbia University Press, 2006), 79.

19. Michael William Doyle, "Staging the Revolution: Guerrilla Theater as a Countercultural Practice," in *Imagine Nation: The American Counterculture of the 1960s and '70s*, ed. Peter Braunstein and Michael William Doyle (New York: Routledge, 2002), 84.

20. Craig J. Peariso, *Radical Theatrics: Put-Ons, Politics, and Sixties* (Tacoma: University of Washington Press, 2015), 43.

21. Peter Manseau, "Fifty Years Ago, a Rag-Tag Group of Acid-Dropping Activists Tried to 'Levitate' the Pentagon," *Smithsonian*, October 20, 2017, https://www.smithsonianmag.com/smithsonian-institution/how-rag-tag-group-acid-dropping-activists-tried-levitate-pentagon-180965338.

22. David Farber, *Chicago '68* (Chicago: University of Chicago Press, 1994), 203.

23. William S. Burroughs, "The Coming of the Purple Better One," *Esquire*, November 1968, 89–91.

24. Allen Ginsberg, "The Avant-Garde," *Firing Line with William F. Buckley*, WOR-TV, May 7, 1968.

25. Cottrell, *Sex, Drugs, and Rock 'n' Roll*, 276.

26. Harold Jacobs, ed., *Weatherman* (New York: Ramparts, 1970), 87.

27. Ron Jacobs, *The Way the Wind Blew: A History of the Weather Underground* (New York: Verso, 1997), 157.

28. Arthur M. Eckstein, *Bad Moon Rising: How the Weather Underground Beat the FBI and Lost the Revolution* (New Haven, CT: Yale University Press, 2016), 246.

29. Cottrell, *Sex, Drugs, and Rock 'n' Roll*, 297.

30. Peter Conners, *The White Hand Society: The Psychedelic Partnership of Timothy Leary and Allen Ginsberg* (San Francisco: City Lights, 2010), 233.

31. David Carter, *Stonewall: The Riots That Sparked the Gay Revolution* (New York: St. Martin's Press, 2004), 151.

32. Carter, *Stonewall*, 196.

33. Carter, *Stonewall*, 198.

34. Karla Jay, *Tales of the Lavender Menace: A Memoir of Liberation* (New York: Basic Books, 1999), 13.

35. Nona Willis Aronowitz, "The First Time Women Shouted Their Abortions," *New York Times*, March 23, 2019, https://www.nytimes.com/2019/03/23/opinion /sunday/abortion-speakout-anniversary.html.

36. Joyce Antler, "Shulamith Firestone, 1945–2012: In Memoriam," Jewish Women's Archive, August 31, 2012, https://jwa.org/blog/shulamith-firestone-1945 -2012-in-memoriam.

37. Jay, *Tales of the Lavender Menace*, 137.

38. "Lavender Menace Action at Second Congress to United Women," NYC LGBT Historic Sites Project, https://www.nyclgbtsites.org/site/lavender-menace -action-at-second-congress-to-unite-women.

39. Morning Call Staff Report, "From Chicago 7 to Fortune 500 Jerry Rubin Embraces Capitalism as the Way to a New World," *Morning Call*, May 2, 1985, updated October 2, 2021, https://www.mcall.com/news/mc-xpm-1985-05-02 -2473929-story.html.

CHAPTER 9: NEW ARC

1. Amiri Baraka, *The Autobiography of LeRoi Jones* (Chicago: Chicago Review Press, 2012), 251.

2. Theodore R. Hudson, *From LeRoi Jones to Amiri Baraka: The Literary Works* (Durham, NC: Duke University Press, 1973), 10.

3. Baraka, *The Autobiography of Leroi Jones*, 163.

4. Amiri Baraka, *Selected Poetry of Amiri Baraka/LeRoi Jones* (New York: Morrow, 1979), 10.

5. Jerry Gafio Watts, *Amiri Baraka: The Politics and Art of a Black Intellectual* (New York: New York University Press, 2001), 45.

6. Watts, *Amiri Baraka*, 35.

7. Watts, *Amiri Baraka*, 53.

8. Watts, *Amiri Baraka*, 53.

9. Baraka, *The Autobiography of LeRoi Jones*, 274.

10. Baraka, *The Autobiography of LeRoi Jones*, 285.

11. LeRoi Jones, "A Poem for Black Hands," *Black Word/Negro Digest* (September 1965): 58.

12. Amiri Baraka, *Dutchman and The Slave: Two Plays* (New York: Harper, 1971), 1–38.

13. Watts, *Amiri Baraka*, 148.

14. Watts, *Amiri Baraka*, 151.

15. Watts, *Amiri Baraka*, 253.

16. Watts, *Amiri Baraka*, 233.

17. Watts, *Amiri Baraka*, 332.

18. Watts, *Amiri Baraka*, 332.

19. Watts, *Amiri Baraka*, 339.

20. Watts, *Amiri Baraka*, 339.

21. Watts, *Amiri Baraka*, 311.

22. Nilgun Anadolu-Okur, *Contemporary African American Theater Afrocentricity in the Works of Larry Neal, Amiri Baraka, and Charles Fuller* (New York: Routledge, 2013), 27.

23. Jerry Gafio Watts, introduction to *Harold Cruse's* The Crisis of the Negro Intellectual *Reconsidered*, ed. Jerry Gafio Watts (New York: Routledge, 2004), 21.

24. Van Gosse, "More Than Just a Politician: Notes on the Life and Times of Harold Cruse," in Watts, *Harold Cruse's* The Crisis of the Negro Intellectual *Reconsidered*, 36.

25. Harold Cruse, *The Crisis of the Negro Intellectual: A Historical Analysis of the Failure of Black Leadership* (New York: New York Review of Books, 2005), 289.

26. Cruse, *The Crisis of the Negro Intellectual*, 275.

27. See Alex Zamalin, *Black Utopia: The History of an Idea from Black Nationalism to Afrofuturism* (New York: Columbia University Press, 2019), chapter 6.

28. La Donna Forsgren, *In Search of Warrior Mothers: Women Dramatists of the Black Arts Movement* (Evanston, IL: Northwestern University Press, 2018), 73.

29. Forsgren, *In Search of Warrior Mothers*, 76.

30. Forsgren, *In Search of Warrior Mothers*, 77.

31. Joshua Kotin, "Funding the Black Arts Repertory Theatre/School," *American Literary History* 34, no. 4 (Winter 2022): 1370.

32. Kotin, "Funding the Black Arts Repertory Theatre/School," 1374.

33. Watts, *Amiri Baraka*, 353.

34. Watts, *Amiri Baraka*, 299.

35. Watts, *Amiri Baraka*, 300.

36. Watts, *Amiri Baraka*, 301.

37. Watts, *Amiri Baraka*, 306.

38. Watts, *Amiri Baraka*, 316.

39. Watts, *Amiri Baraka*, 315.

40. Ericka Huggins and Angela D. LeBlanc-Ernest, "Revolutionary Women, Revolutionary Education: The Black Panther Party's Oakland Community School," in *Want to Start a Revolution? Radical Women in the Black Freedom Struggle*, ed. Dayo Green, Jeanne Theoharis, and Komozi Woodard (New York: New York University Press, 2009), 161–84.

41. Watts, *Amiri Baraka*, 359.

42. Watts, *Amiri Baraka*, 364.

43. Watts, *Amiri Baraka*, 362.

44. Watts, *Amiri Baraka*, 431.

45. Dale Russakoff, "Ras Baraka's Newark Victory," *New Yorker*, May 14, 2014, https://www.newyorker.com/news/news-desk/ras-barakas-newark-victory.

46. Amiri Baraka, "Black Art," in *The LeRoi Jones/Amiri Baraka Reader*, ed. William J. Harris (New York: Thunder's Mouth Press, 1991), 219–20.

CHAPTER 10: SILENCE WILL NOT PROTECT YOU

1. Alexis De Veaux, *Warrior Poet: A Biography of Audre Lorde* (New York: Norton, 2004), 189.

2. De Veaux, *Warrior Poet*, 190.

3. Audre Lorde, "The Transformation of Silence into Language and Action," in *Sister Outsider: Essays and Speeches* (New York: Cross Pressing, 2007), 41.

4. Lorde, "The Transformation of Silence into Language and Action," 41.

5. De Veaux, *Warrior Poet*, 187.

6. De Veaux, *Warrior Poet*, 187.

7. Huey Newton, *The Huey P. Newton Reader*, ed. David Hilliard and Donald Weise (New York: Seven Stories Press, 2011), 157.

8. De Veaux, *Warrior Poet*, 21.

9. Combahee River Collective, *The Combahee River Collective Statement* (New York: Kitchen Table Press, 1986), 9.

10. Wini Breines, *The Trouble Between Us: An Uneasy History of White and Black Women in the Feminist Movement* (New York: Oxford University Press, 2006), 125.

11. De Veaux, *Warrior Poet*, 82.

12. De Veaux, *Warrior Poet*, 160.

13. De Veaux, *Warrior Poet*, 146–47.

14. De Veaux, *Warrior Poet*, 152.

15. De Veaux, *Warrior Poet*, 86.

16. Audre Lorde, "Learning from the 60s," in *Sister Outsider*, 135.

17. De Veaux, *Warrior Poet*, 85.

18. De Veaux, *Warrior Poet*, 85.

19. De Veaux, *Warrior Poet*, 129–31.

20. Hilary Holladay, *The Power of Adrienne Rich: A Biography* (New York: Knopf, 2020), 222.

21. Holladay, *The Power of Adrienne Rich*, 133.

22. Holladay, *The Power of Adrienne Rich*, 133.

23. Holladay, *The Power of Adrienne Rich*, 134.

24. Duchess Harris, "From the Kennedy Commission to the Combahee Collective: Black Feminist Organizing, 1960–1980," in *Sisters in the Struggle: African American Women in the Civil Rights–Black Power Movement*, ed. Bettye Collier-Thomas and V. P. Franklin (New York: New York University Press, 2001), 298.

25. Harris, "From the Kennedy Commission to the Combahee Collective," 299.

26. De Veaux, *Warrior Poet*, 244.

27. De Veaux, *Warrior Poet*, 244.

28. Audre Lorde, "The Master's Tools Will Never Dismantle the Master's House," in *Sister Outsider*, 100–103.

29. Lorde, "The Master's Tools Will Never Dismantle the Master's House," 100.

30. De Veaux, *Warrior Poet*, 251.

31. De Veaux, *Warrior Poet*, 251.

32. De Veaux, *Warrior Poet*, 241.

33. De Veaux, *Warrior Poet*, 242.

34. De Veaux, *Warrior Poet*, 277.

35. De Veaux, *Warrior Poet*, 325–26.

36. De Veaux, *Warrior Poet*, 327.

37. Jelani Cobb, "The Matter of Black Lives," *New Yorker*, March 6, 2016, https://www.newyorker.com/magazine/2016/03/14/where-is-black-lives-matter-headed.

38. Cobb, "The Matter of Black Lives."

39. "About," Black Lives Matter, https://blacklivesmatter.com/about.

40. Alicia Garza, *The Purpose of Power: How We Come Together When We Fall Apart* (New York: Random House, 2021), 50.

41. Garza, *The Purpose of Power*, 288.

42. Patrisse Khan-Cullors and Asha Bandele, *When They Call You a Terrorist: A Black Lives Matter Memoir* (New York: St. Martin's Press, 2018), 72.

CHAPTER 11: THE MESSAGE

1. Joe Austin, *Taking the Train: How Graffiti Art Became an Urban Crisis in New York City* (New York: Columbia University Press, 2001), 23.

2. Austin, *Taking the Train*, 23.

3. "The City and the World" (episode), *New York: A Documentary Film*, dir. Ric Burns, PBS, October 1, 2001.

4. Austin, *Taking the Train*, 36.

5. Joseph C. Ewoodzie Jr., *Break Beats in the Bronx: Rediscovering Hip-Hop's Early Years* (Chapel Hill: University of North Carolina Press, 2017), 53.

6. Sally Banes, "Breaking," in *That's the Joint! The Hip-Hop Studies Reader*, ed. Murray Forman and Mark Anthony Neal (New York: Routledge, 2004), 14.

7. Michael Holman, "Breaking: The History," in Forman and Neal, *That's the Joint!*, 36.

8. Holman, "Breaking," 36.

9. Holman, "Breaking," 36.

10. Ewoodzie, *Break Beats in the Bronx*, 52.

11. Jeff Chang, *Can't Stop Won't Stop: A History of the Hip-Hop Generation* (New York: Picador, 2005), 104.

12. Chang, *Can't Stop Won't Stop*, 106.

13. Ewoodzie, *Break Beats in the Bronx*, 60.

14. Ewoodzie, *Break Beats in the Bronx*, 63.

15. Grandmaster Flash and the Furious Five, "The Message," *The Message*, Sugar Hill Records, 1982.

16. Lankevich, *New York City*, 277–78.

17. Lankevich, *New York City*, 278.

18. James Q. Wilson and George L. Kelling, "Broken Windows," *Atlantic Monthly* 249 (March 1982): 29–38.

19. Wilson and Kelling, "Broken Windows."

20. Ronald A. Reis, *The New York City Subway System* (New York: Chelsea, 2009), 98.

21. Chang, *Can't Stop Won't Stop*, 32.

22. Chang, *Can't Stop Won't Stop*, 122.

23. Chang, *Can't Stop Won't Stop*, 118.

24. Isabel Wilkerson, "Jury Acquits All Transit Officers in the Death of Michael Stewart," *New York Times*, November 25, 1985.

25. Eric Fretz, *Jean-Michel Basquiat: A Biography* (Santa Barbara: ABL-CLIO, 2010), 113.

26. Philip Faflick, "Jean-Michel Basquiat and the Birth of SAMO," *Village Voice*, March 20, 2019, https://www.villagevoice.com/jean-michel-basquiat-and-the-birth-of-samo.

27. Fretz, *Jean-Michel Basquiat*, 57.

28. Keith Haring, "Remembering Basquiat," *Vogue*, November 1988, 230–34.

29. Amy Raffel, *Art and Merchandise in Keith Haring's Pop Shop* (New York: Routledge, 2020), 110.

30. Raffel, *Art and Merchandise in Keith Haring's Pop Shop*, 111.

31. Matt Barker, "The Brutal Death That Politicised New York's Art World," BBC, July 15, 2019, https://www.bbc.com/culture/article/20190710-the-brutal-death-that-politicised-new-yorks-art-world.

32. Public Enemy, "Timebomb," in *Yo! Bum Rush the Show*, Def Jam Records, 1987.

33. Chang, *Can't Stop Won't Stop*, 253.

34. Chang, *Can't Stop Won't Stop*, 254.

35. Chang, *Can't Stop Won't Stop*, 255.

36. Chang, *Can't Stop Won't Stop*, 285.

37. Chang, *Can't Stop Won't Stop*, 290–91.

38. Public Enemy, "Fight the Power," in *Do the Right Thing: Original Motion Picture Soundtrack*, Motown, 1989.

39. David Sterritt, *Spike Lee's America* (New York: Polity, 2013), 45.

40. Chang, *Can't Stop Won't Stop*, 278.

41. Sterritt, *Spike Lee's America*, 62.

42. Jess Bird, "The Scourge of the '90s: Squeegee Men and Broken Windows Policing," Gotham Center for New York History, February 4, 2021, https://www.gothamcenter.org/blog/the-scourge-of-the-90s-squeegee-men-and-broken-windows-policing.

43. Catherine S. Manigold, "Giuliani, on Stump, Hits Hard at Crime and How to Fight It," *New York Times*, October 13, 1993.

44. Themis Chronopoulos, "Broken Windows Policing and the Orderly City: New York Since the Late Twentieth Century," Gotham Center for New York History, October 19, 2017, https://www.gothamcenter.org/blog/broken-windows-policing-and-the-orderly-city-new-york-since-the-late-twentieth-century.

45. Bernard E. Harcourt, "The Broken Windows Myth," University of Chicago Law School, September 11, 2001, https://www.law.uchicago.edu/news/broken-windows-myth.

46. Anjuli Sastry Krbechek and Karen Grigsby Bates, "When LA Erupted in Anger: A Look Back at the Rodney King Riots," NPR, April 26, 2017, https://www.npr.org/2017/04/26/524744989/when-la-erupted-in-anger-a-look-back-at-the-rodney-king-riots.

47. Chang, *Can't Stop Won't Stop*, 325.

48. Chang, *Can't Stop Won't Stop*, 397.

49. Alan Light, "The Rolling Stone Interview: Ice-T," *Rolling Stone*, August 20, 1992, https://www.rollingstone.com/feature/ice-t-1992-cover-cop-killer-interview -247663.

50. Chuck Philips, "'Cop Killer' Controversy Spurs Ice-T Album Sales," *Los Angeles Times*, June 18, 1992, https://www.latimes.com/archives/la-xpm-1992-06 -18-ca-913-story.html.

51. Philips, "'Cop Killer' Controversy Spurs Ice-T Album Sales."

52. Chang, *Can't Stop Won't Stop*, 336.

53. Chang, *Can't Stop Won't Stop*, 336.

54. Joan Morgan, "Hip-Hop Feminist," in Forman and Neal, *That's the Joint!*, 281.

55. Chang, *Can't Stop Won't Stop*, 415.

56. Chang, *Can't Stop Won't Stop*, 424.

57. Chang, *Can't Stop Won't Stop*, 419.

58. Angelica Villa, "Beyonce and Jay-Z Pose with Long Unseen Basquiat in Tiffany Campaign," *ARTnews*, August 23, 2021, https://www.artnews.com/art-news/ news/beyonce-jay-z-tiffany-basquiat-1234602125.

59. Nate Freeman, "Record-Breaking $110.5 M. Basquiat Shocks Attendees at Sotheby's $319.2 M. Postwar and Contemporary Evening Sale," *ARTnews*, May 18, 2017, https://www.artnews.com/art-news/market/record-breaking-110-5-m -basquiat-shocks-attendees-at-sothebys-319-2-m-postwar-and-contemporary -evening-sale-8374.

CONCLUSION

1. Associated Press, "A Long Look at the Complicated Life of George Floyd," *Chicago Tribune*, June 11, 2020, https://www.chicagotribune.com/2020/06/11/a -long-look-at-the-complicated-life-of-george-floyd.

2. Hallie Golden, "Seattle's Activist-Occupied Zone Is Just the Latest in a Long History of Movements and Protests," *The Guardian*, June 21, 2020, https://www .theguardian.com/us-news/2020/jun/21/seattle-activist-occupied-zone-chop-long -history-movements-protests.

3. Ashitha Nagesh, "This Police-Free Protest Zone Was Dismantled—But Was It the End?" BBC, July 11, 2020, https://www.bbc.com/news/world-us-canada -53218448.

4. Jennifer Peltz, "Police in Riot Gear Clear New York City's 'Occupy City Hall' Camp," *PBS NewsHour*, July 22, 2020, https://www.pbs.org/newshour/nation/police -in-riot-gear-clear-nycs-occupy-city-hall-camp.

5. Sam Levin, "These US Cities Defunded Police: 'We're Transferring Money to the Community,'" *The Guardian*, March 11, 2021, https://www.theguardian.com /us-news/2021/mar/07/us-cities-defund-police-transferring-money-community.

6. Grace Manthey, Frank Esposito, and Amanda Hernandez, "Despite 'Defund- ing' Claims, Police Funding Has Increased in Many US Cities," ABC News, October 16, 2022, https://abcnews.go.com/US/defunding-claims-police-funding-increased -us-cities/story?id=91511971.

INDEX

abolitionism, 11, 17, 19, 20–21
ACT UP (AIDS Coalition to Unleash
Power), 239
advertising, 3, 119, 186–87, 249–50
African Blood Brotherhood, 108
Afrofuturism, 196
American Colonization Society, 26
American Federation of Labor (AFL), 39
anarchism, 5, 30–31, 35–55, 255; and acci-
dental bombing of tenement, 53; an-
archist journals, 30, 48–49; Alexander
Berkman and (*see* Berkman, Alexander
"Sasha"); Voltairine "Voltai" de Cleyre
and, 42–44; Ferrer School, 49–53; and
freedom of the individual, 30; Emma
Goldman and (*see* Goldman, Emma);
Hippolyte Havel and, 73; Haymarket
Martyrs, 45; legacy of, 76, 255; Johann
Most and, 40–41; origins of anarchism
in the US, 35, 36, 38–39; and transcendentalists, 17; Benjamin R. Tucker and,
30–31; and US immigration laws, 45;
views on capitalism, 31, 39; views on
government, 39; and violence, 42–45,
52–53; Walt Whitman and, 30. *See also*
bohemians
antisemitism, 8, 33, 37, 42, 109, 149, 193–94
antiwar activism: antiwar protests at
Democratic National Convention
(1968), 178–79, 211, 255; Alexander
Berkman and, 70; conscientious objectors, 49, 70, 197; Max Eastman and,
71–74; Allen Ginsberg and, 175–76, 178;
and Vietnam War, 163–64, 167, 175–79,
211, 255; and World War I, 70–74
art and artists, 8; abstract art/surreal-
ism, 48–49, 57, 60, 104; Jean-Michel

Basquiat, 234–37; bohemians and,
57–61; *The Chinese Restaurant* (Weber),
60; *Crack Is Wack* (Haring), 239;
*Defacement—The Death of Michael
Stewart* (Basquiat), 236, 239; Freud
and, 56; graffiti culture, 232–39; Keith
Haring, 237–39; *Michael Stewart—USA
for Africa* (Haring), 239; *Negro Spiritual* (Salemme sculpture), 132; *Nude
Descending a Staircase* (Duchamp),
57; Georgia O'Keeffe, 61, 105, 128; and
politics, 57, 70–71, 73; *Rush Hour, New
York* (Weber), 60–61; Max Weber,
60–61; Marguerite Zorach, 65. *See also*
photography
Ayers, Bill, 179, 180, 186

Baldwin, James, 139
Bambaataa, Afrika (Lance Taylor),
228–29, 232
Baraka, Amiri (LeRoi Jones), 1, 8, 188–207,
247; Air Force and, 189–90; and
antisemitism, 193–94; Amina Baraka
and, 203; and Black Arts Repertory
Theater/School, 194–99; and Black
nationalism, 192–207; and censorship,
188–89; and Civil Rights Movement,
191–92; Hettie Cohen and, 190, 193, 194;
and communism, 190; Harold Cruse
and, 195; and demonstration at UN
(February 1961), 191; *Dutchman*, 193;
family background and early life, 189;
Allen Ginsberg and, 190, 194, 201; in
Greenwich Village, 190; gun possession trial, 200–201; and homophobia,
194; at Howard University, 189; Ron
Karenga and, 201–2; Malcolm X and,

Liberator, 106; and *The Masses*, 70–74; Claude McKay and, 107; and Men's League for Women's Suffrage, 72; as pragmatist, 71–72; and psychoanalysis, 72; and socialism, 72

economic inequality, 10, 93, 130; and anarchist views on capitalism, 39; and organized labor, 39; and origins of anarchism in the US, 38–39; poverty and hip-hop culture, 225–26, 231; and real estate market, 93, 225; and settlement house movement, 36; and transcendentalism, 17

education: African Free School, 203; anarchist Ferrer Schools, 49–53; and Black Arts Repertory Theater/School, 194–99; Black Power-associated schools, 203–4; and desegregation, 212–13; Intercommunal Youth Institute, 203; New York public schools, 51; Oakland Community School, 203–4; origins of Black studies programs, 197; and settlement house movement, 36

The Electric Revolution (Burroughs), 237

Ellison, Ralph, 196

Emerson, Ralph Waldo, 12, 15–18, 20, 31

Enlightenment, 2, 3, 13–14, 17

eugenics, 69–70

Fagan, Eleanor. *See* Holiday, Billie

Fauset, Jessie Redmon, 96, 113, 114

FBI, 180, 188, 198, 199, 204, 255

"Female Apartment" (women's cooperative apartment), 66–67

feminism: Black feminist novelist Pauline Elizabeth Hopkins, 86–87; Black feminists inspired by Audre Lorde, 221–23; Black lesbian feminism, 208–23 (*see also* Lorde, Audre; Smith, Barbara); Black revolution equated with antifeminism by Amiri Baraka, 194; Combahee River Collective (CRC), 212–13; Mary Daly and, 218–19; Shulamith Firestone and, 184; Betty Friedan and, 184; and hip-hop, 248–49; Karla Jay and, 183; and lesbianism, 184–85, 208, 223; literature and Black feminism, 216–18; National Black Feminist Organization, 212; National Organization for Women

(NOW), 184–85; "New Woman" movement, 64–69; New York Radical Women (NYRW), 184; Georgia O'Keeffe and, 61; Redstockings, 183–84; relation between Black Arts Movement and Black feminism, 255; Margaret Sanger and, 63–65; Third World Women's Alliance, 212; Ellen Willis and, 183–84

Ferlinghetti, Lawrence, 145, 160–62

Ferrer School, 49–53, 64

Fire!! (magazine), 118–20

Fourier, Charles, 17, 19

Frank, Waldo, 104, 105, 106

freedom, 2–3; and anarchism, 30; and anarchist education, 51–52; and the cabaret, 115; Diggers and, 170, 174; gay freedom movement, 182, 221 (*see also* Black lesbian feminism; Gay Liberation Front; homosexuality; queer counterculture); Emma Goldman and, 51; Frances Harper and Black freedom, 86; Audre Lorde and, 209, 215; positive and negative freedom, 2; and ragtime, 82; revolutionary freedom, 2–3, 7, 8, 255; and wealthy patrons of bohemians, 57; and *The Weary Blues* (Hughes), 98; and women, 64, 66

"Free Frames of Reference" (free stores in San Francisco), 171–72, 174

Free Inquirer (newspaper), 14

free love, 13, 17, 23, 47–48

Free Speech Movement, 167

Freud, Sigmund, 55–56, 72

Frick, Henry Clay, 41–42

Friedan, Betty, 184

Fugitive Slave Act, 11, 25

gangs, 19, 226–27, 229, 232

gangsta rap, 246–48

garment industry, 39, 50–51

Garrison, William Lloyd, 11, 31

Garvey, Marcus, 92, 127

Gay Liberation Front, 165, 182–83, 185

Gilman, Charlotte Perkins, 69–70

Ginsberg, Allen, 1, 144–65, 168, 171, 234; and ad campaigns, 186; adolescence, 147; and antiwar activism, 175–76, 178; Amiri Baraka and, 190, 194, 201; William S. Burroughs and, 158,

Zora Neale Hurston and, 120, 128; "I, Too," 98; and John Reed Club (Carmel, California), 131; Alain Locke and, 117; Claude McKay and, 114; *Mule Bone* (Hurston and Hughes), 128; "The Negro Speaks of Rivers," 96; Bruce Nugent and, 116–17; and politics, 130–32, 134; Paul Robeson and, 133; George Schuyler and, 126; "Scottsboro," 131; and Scottsboro trial, 130–31; and sexuality, 117; Bessie Smith and, 99, 116; in the Soviet Union, 131–32, 136; and Spanish Civil War, 134; statement on Black liberation in *The Nation*, 119; Jean Toomer and, 100, 106; *The Weary Blues*, 97–98; Richard Wright and, 137, 138
"Human Be-In" (San Francisco, 1967), 166–67, 169, 172
Huncke, Herbert, 152–53, 156
Hurston, Zora Neale, 98, 120–24; at Barnard College, 122; *Color Struck*, 118, 120; employment and odd jobs, 121; family background and early life, 120–21; "How It Feels to Be Colored Me," 122–23; *Mule Bone* (Hurston and Hughes), 128; personal characteristics, 122; and politics, 123–24; *Their Eyes Were Watching God*, 122

immigration, 33, 35, 58–59, 69, 70, 92
individualism, 1, 12, 16, 43, 98, 123, 161, 165
Industrial Workers of the World (IWW), 62, 64

Jackson, Andrew, 23, 25, 26
James, C. L. R., 133
Jay, Karla, 183, 185
jazz, 139–142
Jews: and anarchism, 36–37; and anti-immigrant hostility in the US, 35, 70; antisemitism, 8, 33, 37, 42, 109, 149, 193–94; and garment industry in NYC, 39; immigration of Russian Jews in the late 1800s, 33; Jack Kerouac's views on, 164; pogroms in Russia following Alexander II's assassination, 33, 37; radicalism associated with Jewish and Italian immigrants, 70
Jim Crow, 77, 92

"Joan Anderson" letter (Cassady), 154–55
Johnson, Edward A., 88–89, 91
Johnson, James Weldon, 136
Johnson brothers (James Weldon and J. Rosamond Johnson), 77–85; arrival in NYC in 1901, 77–80; *The Autobiography of an Ex-Colored Man* (James Weldon Johnson), 77–78, 81; family background and early life, 78; "Lift Every Voice and Sing," 83; and musical theater, 83–85; partnership with Bob Cole, 83–85; *The Red Moon* (Cole and Johnson brothers), 85; *The Shoo-Fly Regiment* (Cole and Johnson brothers), 84–85
Jones, LeRoi, 188–89. *See also* Baraka, Amiri
Jordan, June, 24–25
Junky (Burroughs), 157–58

Kammerer, David, 149–52
Karenga, Ron, 201–2, 205, 229
Kawaida, 201, 203, 229
Kerouac, Jack, 5; and ad campaigns, 186; Neal Cassady's "Joan Anderson" letter and, 154–55; at Columbia University, 147–48; death of, 164; Diane di Prima and, 159; family background, 147–48, 152; Allen Ginsberg and, 147–49, 154; hypermasculine persona, 151; and *Junky* (Burroughs), 157–58; and Kammerer killing, 150, 151; *On the Road*, 158, 159, 163–64; and origin of "Beat Generation" term, 163; "Philosophy of the Beat Generation," 163; and politics, 163–64; and sexuality, 148–49, 151; *The Town and the City*, 154
King, Martin Luther, Jr., 177, 191, 197, 213
Kool Herc, 224, 227–28, 230
Kronstadt rebellion (Russia), 75–76

labor, 75–76; economic inequality and organized labor, 39; garment industry, 39, 50–51; Homestead Strike of 1892, 41, 42, 52, 75–76; Ludlow Massacre, 52; Paterson Strike Pageant, 62–64; and Taft-Hartley Act, 123; and Triangle Shirtwaist Factory fire, 50–51; working conditions in New York City in the late 1800s, 39